Genghis Khan

and the
Quest for God

Genghis Khan

and the

Quest for God

How the World's Greatest Conqueror
Gave Us Religious Freedom

JACK WEATHERFORD

VIKING

VIKING
An imprint of Penguin Random House LLC
375 Hudson Street
New York, New York 10014
penguin.com

Copyright © 2016 by Jack Weatherford
Penguin supports copyright. Copyright fuels creativity, encourages
diverse voices, promotes free speech, and creates a vibrant culture.
Thank you for buying an authorized edition of this book and for
complying with copyright laws by not reproducing, scanning, or
distributing any part of it in any form without permission.
You are supporting writers and allowing Penguin to continue
to publish books for every reader.

Map illustrations by Jeffrey L. Ward

ISBN: 9780735221154 (hardcover)
ISBN: 9780735221161 (ebook)

Printed in the United States of America
1   3   5   7   9   10   8   6   4   2

Set in Sabon LT Pro
Designed by Amy Hill

Dedicated to the *Toriin Sulde*,
the guiding spirit of the Mongol nation,

and to all people who
struggle for spiritual freedom.

CONTENTS

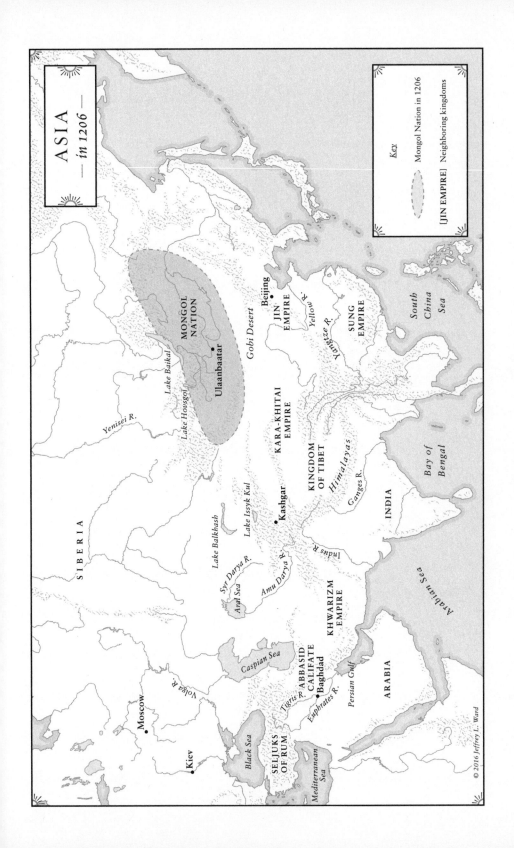

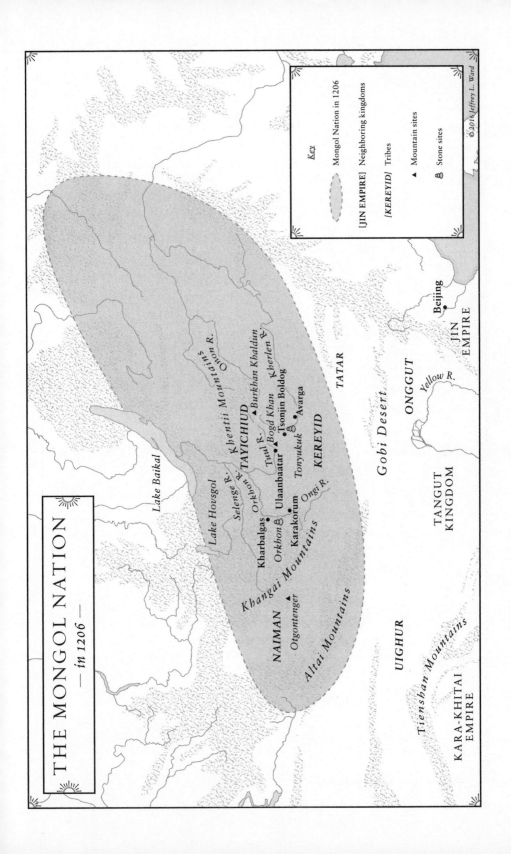

THE MONGOL NATION
— in 1206 —

Key

Mongol Nation in 1206
[JIN EMPIRE] Neighboring kingdoms
[KEREYID] Tribes
▲ Mountain sites
⚭ Stone sites

Lake Baikal

Lake Hovsgol

Selenge R.
Khentii Mountains
Onon R.
▲ Burkhan Khaldun
TAYICHIUD
Tuul R.
Orkhon
Bogd Khan
⚭
Tsonjin Boldog
Kherlen R.
Avarga
⚭
Tonyukuk
KEREYID

Kharbalgas
Orkhon ⚭
Karakorum
Ulaanbaatar
Ongi R.

Khangai Mountains

NAIMAN
Otgontenger ▲

Altai Mountains

Gobi Desert

TATAR

ONGGUT
Yellow R.

Beijing
JIN
EMPIRE

TANGUT
KINGDOM

UIGHUR

Tienshan Mountains

KARA-KHITAI
EMPIRE

©2016 Jeffrey L. Ward

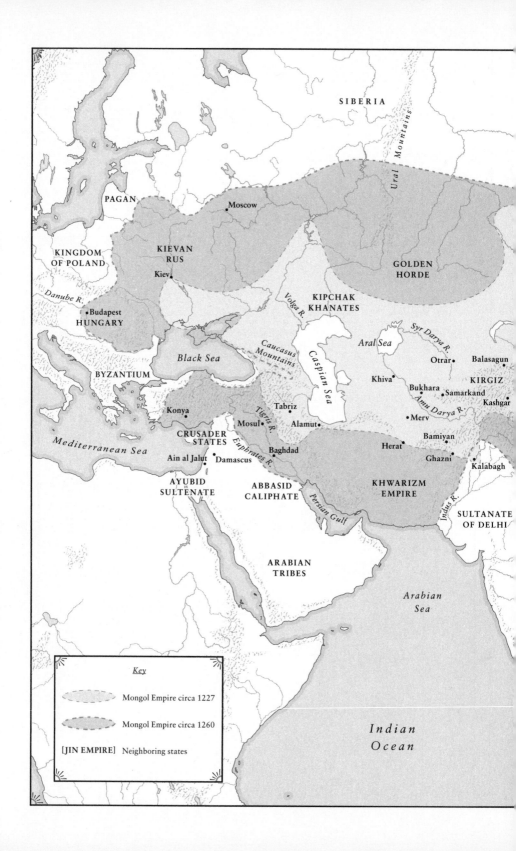

SIBERIA

Ural Mountains

PAGAN

KINGDOM
OF POLAND

•Moscow

KIEVAN
RUS

Kiev•

GOLDEN
HORDE

Danube R.

•Budapest
HUNGARY

KIPCHAK
KHANATES

Volga R.

Aral Sea

Syr Darya R.

Caucasus
Mountains

Black Sea

BYZANTIUM

Caspian Sea

Khiva•

Otrar•

Balasagun•

KIRGIZ

Bukhara•

Samarkand•

Kashgar•

Konya•

Tabriz•

Mosul•

Tigris R.

Alamut•

Amu Darya R.

•Merv

CRUSADER
STATES

Mediterranean Sea

Euphrates R.

Baghdad•

Bamiyan•

Herat•

Ghazni•

Kalabagh•

Ain al Jalut•

•Damascus

AYUBID
SULTANATE

ABBASID
CALIPHATE

KHWARIZM
EMPIRE

Persian Gulf

Indus R.

SULTANATE
OF DELHI

ARABIAN
TRIBES

Arabian
Sea

Indian
Ocean

Key

Mongol Empire circa 1227

Mongol Empire circa 1260

[JIN EMPIRE] Neighboring states

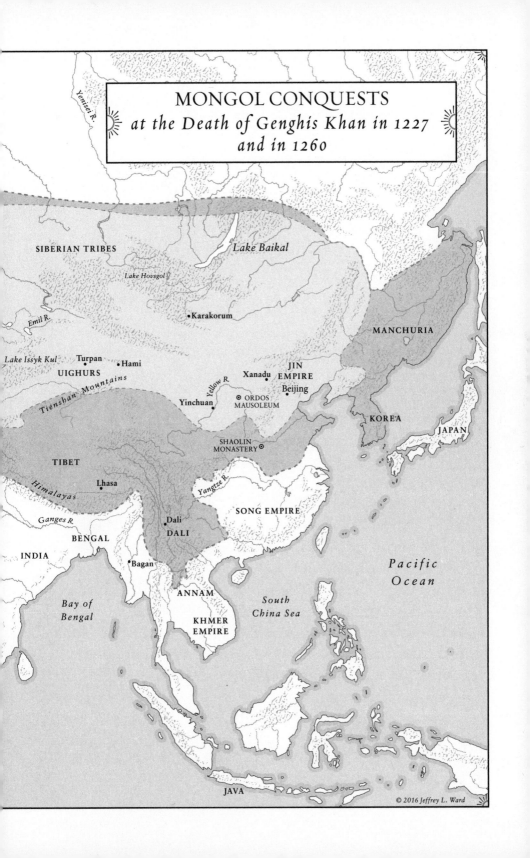

MONGOL CONQUESTS
at the Death of Genghis Khan in 1227 and in 1260

Yenisei R.

SIBERIAN TRIBES

Lake Baikal

Lake Hovsgol

•Karakorum

Emil R.

MANCHURIA

Lake Issyk Kul •Turpan •Hami

UIGHURS

•Xanadu JIN EMPIRE

Yellow R. •Beijing

Tienshan Mountains

•Yinchuan ⊙ ORDOS MAUSOLEUM

KOREA

JAPAN

SHAOLIN MONASTERY ⊙

TIBET

•Lhasa

Himalayas

Yangtze R.

Ganges R.

•Dali SONG EMPIRE

BENGAL DALI

INDIA

•Bagan

Bay of Bengal

ANNAM

South China Sea

Pacific Ocean

KHMER EMPIRE

JAVA

© 2016 Jeffrey L. Ward

Genghis Khan, Thomas Jefferson, and God

On an early summer night in 1787, the British historian Edward Gibbon sat in his garden house in Lausanne, where he had retreated to finish writing the last of six massive volumes on the Roman Empire, covering 170 emperors spread over 25 dynasties and 1,500 years, encompassing Europe, Africa, and Asia from the assassination of Julius Caesar on March 15 of the year 44 BC until the fall of Constantine XI to the Turks on May 29, 1453. Gibbon knew more about empires and emperors than any other scholar then or now.

Toward the end of this fifteen-year project, he showed as much interest in the future as in the past as his attention turned from the Mediterranean empires across the Atlantic Ocean to the newly formed American nation destined to become the imperial heir to Rome. Fascinated by the frequently grotesque relationship between power and religion, Gibbon closely followed the heated American debate regarding the place of religion in society, in public life, and in politics. He had been a student at Oxford, where some of these young American rebels had studied. He recognized how radical their ideals were, and how difficult it would be to give them form. Philosophers sometimes mused over the ideal of religious freedom, but no one knew how to create a society that embodied it or to implement laws to enforce religious tolerance. The Americans, led by Thomas Jefferson, were opting to offer citizens total religious freedom and a complete separation of church from state.

Gibbon had acquired his insights into the complicated relationship between power and religion through his education in continental Europe and his service as a member of Parliament. He explored the world's religions both intellectually and spiritually, having at various points been a Catholic, a Protestant, and a Deist. In his monumental history of the Roman Empire and the foundations of Europe, he carefully charted the ebb and flow of religious currents and persecutions, and he found little to admire. After a lifetime of study, he concluded that one ruler stood above all others in matters of politics and God: Genghis Khan.

Earlier in his career, while writing the initial volumes of his history, Gibbon had shared the prejudices of his time about the Huns, Turks, and Mongols. He was repelled by their savagery and expressed a mild disdain for their leaders, including Attila the Hun and Genghis Khan, whom he called "Zingis Khan." But as he grew older and matured as a scholar, he increasingly saw more to admire in the so-called barbarians than in the civilized rulers of Europe. He wrote that the Roman emperors had been filled with "passions without virtues," and he denounced their lack of political and spiritual leadership.[1] He reflected on the wanton cruelty of the Romans, who first persecuted Christians, then became Christian themselves and persecuted all others.

From his assiduous study of Western history, Gibbon came to believe that Europe offered no sound model for the establishment of religious freedom. "But it is the religion of Zingis that best deserves our wonder and applause," he boldly asserted in the last volume on the Romans. Gibbon explained that in the Mongol camps different religions lived "in freedom and concord."[2] As long as they would abide by *Ikh Yasa*, the Great Law, Genghis Khan respected the rights of "the prophets and pontiffs of the most hostile sects." By contrast, European history had often been shaped by religious fanatics "who defended nonsense by cruelty" and "might have been confounded by the example of a Barbarian, who anticipated the lessons of philosophy, and established by his laws a system of pure theism and perfect toleration."

Few European scholars were given a chance to evaluate Gibbon's comments, as his entire work was banned across much of the continent. The Catholic Church inscribed his name and book titles on the *Index Librorum Prohibitorum*, the Vatican's list of banned books, thereby making the reading or printing of his books a sin and in many countries a crime. His ideas were too radical, and his books remained on this list of forbidden books until the church finally abolished it in 1966.

In his discussion of Genghis Khan's career, Gibbon inserted a small but provocative footnote, linking Genghis Khan to European philosophical ideas of tolerance and, surprisingly, to the religious freedom in the newly emerging United States. "A singular conformity may be found between the religious laws of Zingis Khan and Mr. Locke," Gibbon wrote, and he cited specifically John Locke's utopian vision in the Fundamental Constitutions of Carolina, which Locke had written in 1669 for his employer, Lord Anthony Ashley Cooper, to govern the newly acquired North American lands south of the Virginia colony.

I first read Gibbon's remarkable claim while writing *Genghis Khan and the Making of the Modern World*, a book on the Mongol Empire. The small footnote in Gibbon's work was but one of the approximately eight thousand footnotes spread throughout his one-and-a-half-million-word history, but it was the one idea that seized my attention. Gibbon was the only historian to link Genghis Khan to my homeland in South Carolina. I found the claim exciting, yet incredible. As much as I wanted to believe Gibbon, the idea seemed too farfetched even for me, an admirer of Genghis Khan and lover of all things Mongol. What possible connection could there be between the founding of the Mongol Empire in 1206 and that of the United States of America almost six hundred years later? I could find no other scholar who took the idea seriously. Nevertheless, I could not let go of this tenuous thread of connection. For my peace of mind, I decided to search for the evidence to support or refute Gibbon's remark. Did the treasured Western law of religious freedom, embodied in the Constitution of the United States, originate in Asia? Was it a legacy not just of Enlightenment philosophers but also of an illiterate medieval warrior?

I did not realize at the time that the search to answer that question would take me more than twelve years. Writing this one book, inspired by one small footnote in Gibbon's work, would take me almost as long as it took him to complete the six volumes of *The History of the Decline and Fall of the Roman Empire.*

Gibbon recognized that the desire for religious freedom had a strong basis in European thought and society, but the philosophers, idealists, religious dissenters, and politicians disagreed on how to make that into law. Did people first have to believe in God to deserve such freedom? Should there be a national religion controlled by the state? Was religious freedom an individual right or one that should be extended only to established churches? Could an individual refuse to belong to any religion and still be a citizen? Most attempts to shape a law of tolerance at the time focused on a handful of different types of Christian churches. They addressed believers as a community and did not really consider the freedom of an individual to belong or not belong to any religious group.

Following Gibbon, I spent the first few years plowing through the writings of the English philosopher John Locke and his patron Lord Anthony Ashley Cooper, and scoured the Fundamental Constitutions of Carolina, an original handwritten copy of which was kept by the Charleston Library Society, only a few minutes' walk from my home.[3] This idealistic model for society in the Carolina colony offered some civil rights for members of minority sects, but it placed many new limitations on them as well and upheld the Church of England as the official and only true religion. The plan granted limited religious toleration to churches rather than true freedom to individuals, and restricted even that to those sects that supported the government. Despite some general similarities to the overall principle of tolerance of Genghis Khan, I found nothing specific to indicate inspiration—no similarity in wording or reasoning, not even a thin thread with which I could make a link.

Reluctantly, I abandoned the idea that Locke had found inspiration in the laws of Genghis Khan or that my home of South Carolina had been shaped by such ideas. Yet the larger question remained open. Did the Founding Fathers of the United States somehow have access to knowledge about Genghis Khan's Great Law, and if so, had they copied it? I switched focus from Locke to the American Founding Fathers themselves. I was quickly encouraged by the discovery that Martha Washington had given her husband a novelized biography of Genghis Khan entitled *Zingis: A Tartarian History* by Anne de La Roche-Guilhem, originally published in French in 1691 and translated into English the following year.[4] George Washington kept the book in the library at Mount Vernon, where it remains.

I thought I had struck gold, but it turned out to be fool's gold. Frustratingly, although this book has been in Washington's library for more than three hundred years, I could find no evidence that anyone had actually read it. George Washington never mentioned the book, nor could I find in his papers or correspondence any reference to Genghis Khan. I felt so close to the answer, but lacking evidence I feared that I was chasing a myth.

Several years later, my optimism heightened again when I stumbled across evidence that American merchants from Charleston to Boston had imported and sold books on the Mongol leader. In addition to the novel in George Washington's library, the most popular book in the American colonies in the eighteenth century was *The History of Genghizcan the Great, First Emperor of the Ancient*

Moguls and Tartars, an authoritative and lengthy biography published by the French scholar François Pétis de la Croix in 1710. Benjamin Franklin, a connoisseur of French culture, did much to popularize
the book, printing advertisements in his newspaper and selling it by
mail order from the post office in Philadelphia for delivery throughout
the American colonies.

Who bought these books on Genghis Khan in the 1770s? Who
was interested in him, and what happened to those books? Once
again, I plunged into Franklin's voluminous papers and publications
looking for elusive evidence of a direct connection between Genghis
Khan's edicts on religious toleration and the decision of the Founding
Fathers to give all citizens of their new nation freedom of belief. The
Americans, like Genghis Khan, were attempting to invent a new nation unlike any that preceded it. Eighteenth-century American scholars, without an intellectual history of their own, were eager to find
models of government and justice from beyond the stagnant pool of
Western thought. In the search for something better, they read widely
and were particularly intrigued by Asian leaders. But although Franklin seemed to have an opinion about every topic in the world, I could
not find anything aside from tantalizing hints at a connection to the
Mongols.

A crucial clue came when I discovered that among the founders of
the United States, the one who purchased the most copies of Pétis de la
Croix's biography was Thomas Jefferson, author of the Declaration of
Independence. Jefferson bought copies of the biography in the original
French language for himself and offered them as gifts for others. He
inscribed the copy he presented to his granddaughter, Cornelia Jeffer-
son Randolph, as a seventeenth birthday gift, urging that she study it.[5]
One of his copies of the biography of Genghis Khan entered the United
States Library of Congress, and another was placed in the library of
the University of Virginia; Jefferson was the founder of both. As late
as May 26, 1795, in a letter to Parisian bookseller Jean François
Froullé, Jefferson was ordering still another copy of the Genghis Khan

biography and requesting that the book "be packed in a good trunk, covered with leather, or rather with sealskin."[6]

I cautiously examined a photocopy of one of the Genghis Khan biographies owned by Jefferson. The book emphasized Genghis Khan's religious tolerance and reproduced a text of the Mongolian Law of Religious Freedom, which Pétis de la Croix had stressed was the first law of Genghis Khan. As presented in this biography, the Mongol law was a general law offering freedom, in very simple words, for everyone of every faith. In 1777, one year after drafting the Declaration of Independence, Thomas Jefferson translated its lofty words into specific legislation when he composed America's first law of religious freedom for his native state of Virginia. He had embraced the idea of religious freedom before reading about Genghis Khan, but what he found in the biography was a specific way to translate the desire for religious freedom into law. Religious freedom was an individual right, not a prerogative of the church.

Mongol law forbade anyone "to disturb or molest any person on account of religion."[7] Similarly, Jefferson's law prescribed "that no man shall . . . suffer on account of his religious opinions or belief." Genghis Khan's law insisted "that everyone should be left at liberty to profess that which pleased him best." Jefferson's law echoed this in the statement "that all men shall be free to profess . . . their opinions in matters of religion." The First Law of Genghis Khan and the Virginia statute were both similar in spirit to, but different in wording from, the First Amendment to the United States Constitution, which reads: "Congress shall make no law respecting an establishment of religion, or prohibiting the free exercise thereof."

The Mongol Empire encompassed people from a greater diversity of faiths than that of any other empire in prior history. Never had one man ruled over followers of so many religions without belonging to one of them: Muslims, Buddhists, Taoists, Confucians, Zoroastrians, Manichaeans,

Hindus, Jews, Christians, and animists of different types. Each of the major religions was divided into myriad competing, and often viciously warring, sects. Genghis Khan's greatest struggle in life was not to conquer so many tribes, cities, and nations—that had come fairly easily to him—but to make them live together in a cohesive society under one government.

In 1997 I began research on the *Secret History of the Mongols*, attempting to locate all the episodes in the manuscript and to evaluate the text based on an analysis of the places where the events unfolded within Mongolia and across China and Central Asia. The first year, I thought that I would complete the work in a single summer, then in two summers, in order to trace the conquests from Karakorum to the Balkans. But now, after nearly two decades, the work continues, by foot, camel, horse, or four-wheel drive. I began alone, but gradually the project expanded to include a team of dedicated Mongolian scholars as well as nomadic herders who contributed their unique knowledge of the area to the project. Over time the scope expanded from only the events of Genghis Khan's life into areas such as northern Burma, conquered by the Mongols after Genghis Khan, and the remains of the Khmer Empire, which was never conquered by the Mongols but developed a working relationship with the Great Khans. The latter phase of the research goes well beyond the *Secret History*, but still it remains my guide.

The horror of the Mongol conquests is well-documented in books and films, but Genghis Khan's role as a religious lawmaker remains largely unexplored. Late in life he drew religious leaders from far and wide to his camp in his struggle to create a lasting peace among competing religions whose belligerent animosities plagued humanity. What began as a personal struggle to find his own spiritual core gradually became a quest to understand the role of religion in society. The more he considered the laws and attributes of the different warring sects, the more he came to believe that no empire could be stable so long as men were allowed to kill or be killed for their faith.

The influence of Genghis Khan in the modern world was far wider and deeper than I had previously imagined, and this realization spurred me to write this second book. From the beginning of my research I recognized, but did not truly understand, the importance of Genghis Khan's spirituality and his unusual approach to religion. The transmission of ideas and beliefs is much harder to trace than the spread of technological innovations such as the printing press, gunpowder, or the compass. Only now, after nearly two decades spent researching the life of Genghis Khan and the Mongol Empire, do I feel ready to tentatively offer my findings.

I wrote this book largely at the behest of Walker Pearce, my wife of forty-four years, who felt that my earlier work ignored the rich and unique spiritual life of Genghis Khan and the Mongols. She named the book. Although I read the manuscript to her as I wrote it, and she had a clearer vision than I did of what it would become, she did not live to see the book completed. I was greatly encouraged and guided in finishing the book by my editor Joy de Menil, and I benefited from additional editorial assistance from Stephanie Hunt in Charleston.

The ideas of Genghis Khan were revolutionary in the thirteenth century, when he lived, and in the eighteenth century, when the founders of America rediscovered him, and they remain so today. He faced many of the same problems we face in a global society where religious pluralism often results in polarity and conflict. How should one balance freedom of belief with the actions of fanatics? What happens when such fanatics break free of civic control to become masters of the society? How can followers of one religion be prevented from attacking those of another? How can competing religions, each claiming to be the only true one, be compelled to live harmoniously in society? What are the limits of religion? Genghis Khan's quest to answer these questions remains as urgent today as it was eight hundred years ago.

The Anger of the Gods

The evening hours in a military camp belong to the revelry of the young soldiers, but the final dark hours before the sun rises belong to the old veterans, who silently stir the ashes of memory and await the light of day. This is the hour when restless spirits wander the Earth and haunt men with past regrets and future fears. At sixty, Genghis Khan had many memories to savor, and ample ones to regret.

In 1222, entering the final years of his life, he was still out on campaign. He had spent as long as he could remember fighting. Under his guidance, one son was now fighting across northern Iran, two others led campaigns in the Khwarizm Empire of Uzbekistan, and another was with him in the mountain valleys of Afghanistan. His generals were sweeping up the Caucasus Mountains on their way to attack the soft underbelly of European Russia. The list of cities and countries he had conquered, and those he had annihilated, was far too long to remember.

"According to trustworthy persons," wrote the Persian chronicler Juzjani, he was "a man of tall stature, of vigorous build, robust in body, the hair on his face scanty and with cats' eyes, possessed of great energy, discernment, genius, and understanding." To his enemies he appeared "awe-striking, a butcher, just, resolute, an overthrower of enemies, intrepid, sanguinary, and cruel."[1] The appearance of Genghis Khan and his Mongol warriors inspired instant fear. "They had a hellish and frightening appearance," wrote the Armenian chronicler Kirakos of Gandzak. "They had no beards, although some of them had a few hairs above their lips or on their chins," wrote Chao Hung, the Chinese envoy. "They had narrow and quick-seeing eyes, high, shrill voices; they were hardy and long-lived."[2] The envoy expressed surprise that instead of wearing his hair like an emperor, the Great Khan had the same distinctive hairstyle as his soldiers—shaved on top, with bangs on the forehead, to protect the soul, and two braids reaching down to the shoulders—strange but practical for controlling lice.[3] In old age his sparse but long beard had turned gray.

Measured against the lives of other men, Genghis Khan had achieved much. Although born into a minor lineage in a remote part of the Mongolian steppe, he had slowly conquered one more powerful enemy after another. He was not the son of a khan or the heir to a powerful family. Far from it: he and his mother had been cast out by his tribe and left to die. He was forty-five years old when he acquired full control of the nomadic steppe tribes of nearly a million people. Only then did he set off to fight beyond the Mongolian Plateau that had confined his early life. After conquering adjacent Siberia, northern and western China, and the Kara Khitai Empire of the Tien Shan Mountains, he moved against the shah of Khwarizm, who ruled most of Central Asia from the Caspian Sea to Afghanistan. His army continued on to invade Iraq, Armenia, Georgia, and southern Russia.

With about 100,000 men he defeated armies ten times the size of his and subjugated hundreds of millions of people. Genghis Khan "conquered lands which had never even been heard of before," wrote Injannasi, one of his proud descendants. His empire "reached the far corners of the world, where foot had never been set before." He "conquered the four directions and eight quarters beyond the ocean and included so many strange nations."[4] He conquered more lands and peoples than all the emperors in the entire history of the Roman Empire. He buried his enemies in the dust of his fast Mongol horses.

He combined the genius of a hunter stalking his prey with the agility of the herder deftly guiding goats, sheep, cows, horses, yaks, and camels across vast distances while protecting them from predators and natural calamity. His army moved across the land with such speed and skill that observers repeatedly compared it to a wind storm, flood, or other fierce force of nature. Cities fell before him as effortlessly as his horses trampled weeds or flowers. He routed enemy armies and relocated thousands of people as seamlessly as moving his herds to a new pasture. He decreed life or death for defeated enemies as swiftly as deciding which animals to slaughter at the start of winter.

It is difficult to grasp the breadth and scope of the Mongol invasions. In a period of approximately seventy-five years, Genghis Khan and his immediate descendants fought armies on the territory of some forty modern countries. From the time Genghis Khan launched his first invasion in 1209 until the death of his grandson Khubilai Khan near the end of the century, the Mongols successfully invaded what are today Russia, China, Korea, Kazakhstan, Tajikistan, Uzbekistan, Kyrgyzstan, Turkmenistan, Afghanistan, Pakistan, Iran, Iraq, Syria, Armenia, Georgia, Azerbaijan, Turkey, Bulgaria, Bosnia, Serbia, Croatia, Romania, Belarus, Ukraine, Czech Republic, Slovenia, Moldova, Lithuania, Hungary, Greece (Thrace), northern Albania, Poland, Burma, and a few smaller nations such as Tibet and Kashmir that are now part of larger ones. They also received tribute from the kingdoms of what are now Vietnam, Thailand, and Cambodia. Their battles stretched over five thousand miles from Budapest to modern Seoul, and almost the same distance from Hanoi to Budapest.

The scope of their conquests is probably best marked by what the Mongols tried but failed to conquer. They suffered a small defeat on the outskirts of Vienna, but the army was stopped in the west by the Mamluk of Egypt, in the east by the army of Japan, and in the south by a Javanese kingdom in modern Indonesia. No other army managed to fight simultaneous wars so far apart until the United States went to war against Germany and Japan in World War II.

Genghis Khan erupted into history in a century when gods flourished on Earth, when religion ruled the world. Sounds of the muezzin's call to prayer, tolling church bells, chanting monks, and singing pilgrims filled the air across cities and villages from Japan in the Pacific to Ireland in the Atlantic. Ostentatious displays of religious piety dominated art, literature, architecture, and philosophy, whether at the Sung capital in China, the palace of the caliph in Baghdad, the papal throne in Rome, the court of the Byzantine emperor in Constantinople, the Al-Azhar University in Cairo, the fortress of the sultan in Delhi, or the mosques of Seville and Granada in Spain. In that Golden Age of Religion, tall, thin towers rose up as pagodas in eastern and southern Asia, minarets across the Muslim world, and cathedral spires in Europe. They lifted up the thoughts of humanity toward the heavens, and they stood as victory columns proclaiming the dominance and seeming permanence of the new power of religion.

Religion triumphed over secular life. Priests, lamas, monks, and mullahs controlled the calendar, set borders between rivals, and collected taxes. They operated judicial courts, staffed prisons, built universities, opened hospitals, and managed wineries, banks, brothels, and torture chambers. Lavishly spending the voluntary and forced donations from poor and rich believers, they produced a historic high point for sacred art, literature, music, and architecture. Through the words of Allah in calligraphy, the sculpted image of Buddha on mountains and in temples, and paintings depicting scenes from the life of Jesus, art had become the servant of religious indoctrination.

Arrogantly ignoring the Will of Heaven while claiming to be its representative on Earth, the many masters of organized religion violated the spirit of their own scriptures and focused on what they most enjoyed: collecting wealth, punishing violators of their arbitrary dietary and sexual laws, constructing massive buildings, staging fancy dress rituals, and enthusiastically fighting one another over whether there should be punctuation in the scriptures and what color the ink should be. In the presence of weak emperors, senile kings, and an aristocracy engaged by hunting or poetry, religion grew more powerful.

In Europe the pope claimed supreme power and suppressed kings and heretics with ever-vigilant vigor. In the Muslim world, the tottering Abbasid caliph ruled from Baghdad as both secular emperor and the sacred successor to Muhammad while lesser mullahs enforced the word of God in towns and villages across the land. The assassins of Alamut, a cult of particularly vicious Shiite fanatics in the mountains of Iran, plagued Muslims, Christians, and pagans alike, emerging regularly to kill any ruler who dared to criticize them or refused to pay their extortionary demands for tribute.

The prevalence of religion had generated neither peace nor prosperity. As each sect consolidated power within its home area, it struggled against rival faiths each asserting sole ownership of the word of God on Earth. Followers of a trio of militant movements—Christianity, Buddhism, and the growing new faith of Islam—fought bitterly against one another in an effort to dominate the world. Some sects of Buddhist monks cultivated martial arts while Christians and Muslims organized large sacred militias dedicated to spreading the word of their God and creating the kingdom of God on Earth. Rival religions controlled history and claimed authority over the future. Each one offered an array of techniques and rituals guaranteed to produce eternal peace, claiming exclusive control of the path to spiritual salvation.

Rather than creating a spiritual utopia of art, compassion, and beauty, religion had saturated the world with resentment and hate. History's earlier wars had been fought mostly for the simple human emotions of lust and greed, but the rise of the world religions had encouraged the hatred and killing of innocent people for no greater reason than that they worshipped God in another way. Religiously motivated or justified warfare posed the greatest threat to world peace and social stability. Wars in the name of competing gods now surpassed avarice, envy, and ethnicity as a source of violence, and these gods proved insatiable. As soon as one conflict subsided, people of faith easily invented another excuse to make war against nonbelievers, pagans, and heretics, or whatever they called people of other religions. In the name of a peaceful and compassionate God, the religiously devout found it easy to torture, rob, beat, blind, rape, burn, drown, starve, dismember, or enslave anyone. From infanticide to genocide, no punishment was too great or too evil when directed against someone perceived as a danger to the true religion. Such killing was not a sin; it became a sacred duty, a sacrament that promised the killer eternal rewards.

Suddenly, amid the spiritual chaos and cruelty of the thirteenth century, a fierce army mounted on shaggy horses descended from the icy northern horizon and charged into the temples, mosques, monasteries, forts, palaces, and cathedrals of the world. Never had an army moved so fast across continents. With every man mounted on a horse and no foot soldiers or baggage train to slow them, the Mongols could ride for days, changing mounts as they went, and, when needed, sleeping and eating in the saddle without pausing to make camp or build a fire. The Mongol horde descended on warring nations, proclaiming itself the punishment of God and claiming to have been sent to break the power of ruling monarchs, harness them to the service of humankind, and restore the Will of Heaven and the Order of God.

Heaven had sent many messengers to Earth: Confucius, Buddha, Jesus, Moses, Zoroaster, Mani, Muhammad, and many lesser prophets. Scriptures in Persian, Sanskrit, Chinese, Arabic, Hebrew, Greek, Aramaic, and other now lost languages were received with an initial burst of enthusiasm and then quickly succumbed to abuse and neglect. Genghis Khan did not deliver fresh scriptures from heaven or establish a new church. He believed that heaven had already sent enough scriptures, and all people basically knew right from wrong. Instead, he set about to discipline wayward nations and guide existing religions to fulfill their mission of helping humanity in obedience to the Order of God. Persuasion, flattery, and bribery were not enough to convince the established religious authorities and the rulers who held power in their name. He would bring them back by force, with the crack of the whip, and herd them back onto the moral path.   ❧

Genghis Khan valued the moral truths he found in all of the religions he encountered. It was the men who claimed and often abused their religious authority whom he mistrusted. He held the wrongdoers accountable for their deeds, executed some and banned others. To the general populace he promised freedom and financial support if they would fulfill their duties to society and to heaven.

Genghis Khan's army was initially composed exclusively of Mongols, but it quickly became a truly international conglomerate. Armenian, Georgian, Kipchak, and Ossetian units descended from the Caucasus Mountains. Turks from dozens of different ethnic tribes joined from Central Asia. Chinese engineers assembled horrific war machines with which to batter the city walls and to rechannel whole rivers while their doctors bandaged the wounded. Slavs were brought from Russia, miners from Saxony, and even one English noble defected to join the global army. An Arab writer described the army as filling the sky like a swarm of locusts.[5] After his death, Genghis Khan's sons and grandsons continued their wars targeting corrupt religious and political institutions. In 1257, after crushing the Cult of Assassins, demolishing their heavily fortified mountain hideout in Syria, and sending their leader to Mongolia for execution, the Mongols rode toward Baghdad to deal with the caliph.

The conquest of Baghdad in 1258 ended the long and already tarnished Golden Age of the Arabs, but the Mongol horsemen did not stop. They continued to expand their empire throughout the rest of the century. They destroyed the cultural center of the Orthodox Slavic world with the destruction of Kiev and its great cathedral. They swallowed Tibet without a struggle and defeated the skilled fighting monks of Korea. On the battlefields of Hungary and Poland, they permanently broke the power of the Christian military orders of religious knights who had sworn to give their fortune and life to the church. The Mongols invited them to fulfill their promise and killed their leader, Duke Henry the Pious of Silesia. The remaining prisoners were sent off to the mines of Siberia and the mountains of Kazakhstan.

The Mongols swept up to Damascus, accepted the submission of the Christian Crusader Bohemond VI, who was the prince of Antioch and count of Tripoli, and pushed west as far as the Palestinian lands of Gaza on the edge of Egypt. In the years after, they took southern China and reached into Southeast Asia, easily conquering the Bai kingdom of Dali, where the kings customarily abdicated their earthly powers to become Buddhist monks. They also took Pagan in Burma, where the kings lavished riches on massive pagodas instead of building defenses.[6]

The Mongols targeted religious centers both because they protected rival authorities and because they contained great piles of treasure. They looted the temples and religious monuments, seized objects of gold and silver to be cut up or melted down for new uses, took everything of value and destroyed much of what remained. From the cathedral of Kiev to the mosques of Baghdad, the Mongols treated religious buildings no differently from opulent palaces or daily markets. They put the great stores of religious wealth back into commercial circulation. This wealth became the first global economic stimulus as they revitalized the Silk Route, opened an international network of hostels and banks for merchants to travel freely, suppressed bandits and pirates, built bridges, cleared harbors, lowered taxes, and tried to introduce a global paper currency system. Thousands of merchants, including Marco Polo and his father and uncle, soon trod the Mongols' routes from Europe to Asia and back home again. By breaking the grip of fanatical religions, they opened an era of unprecedented global prosperity.

"By Virtue of God," proclaimed Genghis Khan's grandson Guyuk, "from the rising of the sun to its setting, all realms have been granted to us. Without the Order of God, how could anyone do anything?"[7] Mongke Khan, another grandson of Genghis Khan and successor to his cousin Guyuk, told King Louis IX of France, "This is the order of Eternal God: In heaven there is none but one eternal God, over the Earth let there not be but one lord and master Genghis Khan." The Mongols believed that God spoke through those to whom he gave power, and that he had entrusted Genghis Khan with the task of ensuring "happiness and peace from sunrise to sunset."[8]

To his enemies and their descendants through the centuries, Genghis Khan has remained the enemy of God. After his death the outside world remembered only the conquests and destruction without the achievements. His mighty armies have been depicted in books, plays, songs, and films, but their victories have usually been portrayed as needless and mindless destruction with rivers of blood, bonfires of books, sacks of ears, and pyramids of heads. If Genghis Khan had any role at all to play in history, it was only as a punishment inflicted by heaven. He was the Whip of God.

In contrast to this foreign perception, the Mongols have always seen Genghis Khan as their spiritual guide and religious teacher, comparable to Buddha, Jesus, or Muhammad. Mongke Khan referred to him not only as the founder of the Mongol nation but as "Genghis Khan, sweet and venerable son of God."[9] God's commandment was simple: every nation must obey the Mongols. Only through submission, explained the Mongol queen Oghul Ghaimish in a letter to Louis IX, will there be peace on Earth for "those who walk on all fours" and for "those who walk on two legs."[10]

Much of what we know about Genghis Khan's early life comes from a document known as *The Secret History of the Mongols*, written two years after his death. Someone, probably the chief Mongol judge Shigi-Khutukhu, gathered all the information that he could find about the man who had created their nation. Genghis Khan's words held a certain power because he had conquered the world, and so it was thought that the person who controlled his words might harness that magic. The resulting text was a closely guarded treasure of mythic power. It was soon locked away. The manuscript belonged to the royal family, but they guarded it jealously, often even from one another, allowing copies to be made only when necessary, such as to accompany one of them on the conquest of a new land. The document was written in a code that few people understood, and in time it was lost, only to be rediscovered in the nineteenth century and finally decoded in the twentieth.

Possession of a copy of the *Secret History* became a source of power as the manuscript was thought to channel the spirit of Genghis Khan, inspiring fear among its owner's rivals and foreign enemies. The owner could pull out a saying or story as needed to support whatever strategy he might wish to pursue at the moment, and only distant members of the family lucky enough to own one of the few other copies could challenge it. Telling the difference between a true saying and one composed at the spur of the moment became increasingly difficult. The few circulating copies may never have been identical, and over time they were deliberately altered further, as inconvenient sections were lost and new pages added as the contingencies of politics demanded.

These various versions formed the basis for overlapping texts which eventually became known by a number of different titles including *Sheng-wu ch'in-cheng lu* (*Description of the Personal Campaigns of the Holy Warrior*) in China, and *The Secret History of the Mongols* in Mongolia. (In the Ilkhanate of Persia it was referred to as the *Altan Debter*, a golden book or registry.) In general, the words, wisdom, laws, and teaching of Genghis Khan became known collectively by variations on the Mongol word *yasa*, meaning edict, order, or law, as in *Ikh Yasa, Yasa-nama, yasa-yi-buzurg, as-Si-yasa, yasaq, zasag,* and *jasaq*.

After Genghis Khan left Mongolia and began his conquests, he became the focus of much attention, and thus we have early chronicles about him in Chinese, Latin, Persian, Arabic, Armenian, and Georgian, offering the contrasting views of Muslims, Christians, Confucians, Buddhists, Taoists, and Jews. Rarely in prior history had one person been the focus of so much attention from such markedly different cultural perspectives.

After conquering his enemies, looting their cities, and taking control of their markets, Genghis Khan considered how well their actions

matched their stated beliefs. Religious authorities accustomed to issuing verdicts of guilt or innocence and dispensing judgments of life
or death now found themselves and their faith on trial by a nonbe-
liever. "You have committed great sins," Genghis Khan shouted at
the newly conquered leaders of Bukhara. "The great ones among you
have committed these sins," he explained. "If you ask me what proof
I have for these words, I say it is because I am the punishment of God.
If you had not committed great sins, God would not have sent a punishment like me upon you."[11]

He paused for the interpreters to translate what he had said, and
then he told the people about his "intimate communication" with
God "and the authority he had by Inspiration received from him to
govern all the Kingdoms of the Earth."[12] Just as he held the defeated
leaders accountable for misguiding their society, he held religious
leaders responsible for their actions and the behavior of their followers. He showed little interest in judging the accuracy of scriptures,
the authenticity of prophets, or what anyone claimed to believe. He
judged them simply by their deeds.

Genghis Khan seemed unaware of or uninterested in how he compared with other conquerors. He treated his triumphant superiority
as a burdensome duty more than an honor. He was fulfilling the role
placed on him by fate; he was following his duty to his people. Lingering in the pleasant climate of Afghanistan, his attention strayed
from the details of battles which he now easily won by force of habit,
almost without thinking. He enjoyed the higher altitude and crisper
climate of the mountain valleys and fertile plains of Afghanistan, and
his attention turned away from the past and present to focus on the
future. What would happen when he was gone? What was to become
of his family? His Mongol people? His great empire?

Genghis Khan freely admitted that he had few outstanding qualities, but he had an ability to find and to inspire the best talent around
him. He had never been as strong a warrior as his brother Khasar, as
good a strategist as his general Subodei, as decisive as his wife Borte, or
as steadfast as his mother Hoelun. Yet he recognized their outstanding

traits and incorporated them into himself. His closest advisers were his fellow Mongols, particularly his wives and generals, but as he moved beyond the Mongolian steppe and into the sedentary lands of the south, he quickly applied the same technique of seeking out those with skills. After conquering each city, he ordered a complete census of its people and resources, including their skills. Thus, he incorporated engineers, clerks, and physicians from China, and accountants, auditors, and metalsmiths from the Muslim countries.

In his old age in Afghanistan, clearly aware that the end of life was approaching, he wanted to talk with learned men and hear ideas from the most educated minds of civilization. He summoned the best Muslim and Chinese scholars to meet with him. He beckoned mullahs from his newly conquered territory and Taoist priests all the way from their tranquil monasteries in China to the still-smoldering cities of Afghanistan to hear about their religion and ask what advice they had to offer.

Genghis Khan initially viewed the religious institutions of the sedentary civilizations with deep skepticism. He suspected that the great religions with their temples, wealth, and pageantry might be frauds. Yet, he wanted to hear what the leaders of these strange institutions had to say. The chronicler Bar Hebraeus, a prolific thirteenth-century scholar, wrote that Genghis Khan had summoned "the lords of wisdom" to read from their sacred books in the various languages and to discuss their religion and debate with one another in his presence.[13] Monks, priests, astrologers, magicians, prophets, alchemists, soothsayers, sages, fortune tellers, and charlatans traveled for months from across the widest rivers, over the tallest mountains, and beyond distant borders to search out his nomadic camp.

One at a time, he talked with these self-proclaimed men of God, listened to their teachings, questioned their practices, examined their achievements, and tested their morals. He scrutinized each religion known in his empire—Christianity, Taoism, Buddhism, Islam, Manichaeism, Confucianism, and smaller branches from the world tree of faith. He campaigned by day, and the sages met with him during the evening hours to discuss Taoist and Muslim theology, life's meaning, fate, the relationship of heaven to Earth, and the roles of war, violence, peace, and law in human affairs. Genghis Khan was a warrior pursuing a lifelong battle for power and dominance, but he was also a man struggling for spiritual understanding. The bloody battlefields of Afghanistan served as a backdrop for one of history's strangest set of philosophical debates, whose effects reverberate in seen and unseen ways throughout the world today.

The quest began many years earlier on Mongolia's most sacred mountain, Burkhan Khaldun.

PART I

Becoming Temujin

More than three thousand two hundred and fifty years after Buddha entered Nirvana, many evil kings were born and caused suffering to all living things. In order to suppress them, Buddha gave the order and Genghis Khan was born.

~*Lubsang-Danzin,* The Golden Chronicle, *circa 1651*

1

The Teeth That Eat Men

The boy who would become Genghis Khan was born in a small encampment at the head of the Onon River in the fall of 1162, in the busy season of the year between the processing of dairy products from summer and the slaughtering of meat for winter. This was a time for gathering cedar nuts, wild onions, forest mushrooms, medicinal seeds, and wilted flowers to flavor winter soup and tea. It was the season when the herders could drink a constant supply of fermented mare's milk and enjoy the final wild strawberries and raspberries with sheep or goat yogurt. It was, in short, the best time of year.

The acknowledged facts surrounding his birth are few and inauspicious. Only a short time before he was born, his mother, Hoelun, had been stolen from her husband by his father, the Mongol warrior Yesugei, who already had another wife and son. Despite the considerable effort Yesugei had expended to capture and claim his new bride, he almost immediately rode off again to raid the Tatars, a richer tribe of nomads living on the steppe with close ties to China. While her new husband was away, Hoelun gave birth to a son, who reportedly entered life clutching a small blood clot in his right fist. Later, the presence of this blood clot was interpreted to mean the boy was destined to conquer, something viewed positively by the Mongols but seen as a sign of his inherently barbaric nature by his enemies.

We know the childhood history of Genghis Khan from a series of Mongolian manuscripts derived from the one document, *The Secret History of the Mongols*, written immediately after his death.[1] It contains a genealogy and myths about the origin of his family and combines the collected memories of eyewitnesses and participants in the key events of his life, often recalling the exact words of conversations. The *Secret History* presents information in a straightforward manner, with little embellishment. Later works added decorative flourishes to the story.

Because any story worth telling is worth improving, the simple facts about the birth came to be embroidered with the passage of time. In some versions the blood clot became a sacred stone, a jade seal, or a precious gem. According to the Buddhist *Pearl Rosary*, Genghis Khan was born with "beautiful signs" and "with a shining red jewel in his hand. On the same day a rainbow appeared in the sky."[2]

When Yesugei returned from his campaign against the Tatars, he named his new son Temujin, after one of the warriors he had killed. The name meant Iron Man. Yesugei had built a reputation as a warrior willing to take chances, and he expected as much of his son. Although he was descended from a lineage of tribal khans, he himself had not been chosen as a khan. He owned some animals, but the *Secret History* portrays him as a hunter and warrior more than a herder.

The little that is recorded about Temujin's relationship with his father is disturbing. In a society of nomadic warriors, fathers were frequently away when their children were born, but Yesugei's absence may not have been entirely accidental. The problem seems to have stemmed from a question of paternity. Who was Temujin's actual father? According to one eighteenth-century Mongolian manuscript, Hoelun was pregnant when she was kidnapped, thus making her first husband, Chiledu of the Merkid, his biological father.[3] Later manuscripts, especially those written by Buddhists, gave no father's name or endowed him with supernatural origins, presenting him as the reincarnation of a Buddhist deity, but few in his clan thought of him so highly.

Mongol society valued social paternity over biological ties. If a man accepted a child as his own, he would be taken as such by the tribe. Several times in Yesugei's ancestry, the biological line of paternity had clearly been broken, but the child had nevertheless become a full member of the lineage and clan. Yet Yesugei had chosen to reject Temujin or to show a consistent indifference toward him.

Normally, at the birth of a Mongol child the father presented the first gift, usually a felt figure made from the wool of his sheep, but Temujin's father was far away fighting. Another mysterious man happened to be present, a simple hunter of seemingly no importance called Jarchigudai. Though he was certainly not Temujin's father, he played a fatherly role in the boy's childhood.

Jarchigudai belonged to a small band of Uriyankhai, forest people living around the sacred mountain Burkhan Khaldun. The Uriyankhai hunted wolves, foxes, sables, ibex, deer, and forest antelopes, and unlike the herding nomads, who constructed circular felt *gers*, they lived in small conical tents of wood and bark. There were many bands of Uriyankhai, and although none herded steppe animals, some herded reindeer, which they milked and on which they rode through the forest while hunting. When the snow was too deep for the reindeer, Jarchigudai's people strapped on wooden planks and propelled themselves forward with two poles. They could also attach bones to the bottom of their boots and skate across rivers and lakes. People who saw them soaring down the mountainsides or skimming across the ice sometimes thought they were flying. These uncanny skills inspired awe but also fear and suspicion among the steppe nomads, who attributed unseen magical powers to the Uriyankhai.

Mongols traditionally called a wise elder at the time of birth to foretell the child's future. According to the *Blue Chronicle*, Old

Jarchigudai, who would make an appearance at many important moments in Temujin's life, was such a man, a Reader of Signs.[4] He is said
to have been the first to recognize the boy's importance and to interpret the meaning of the blood clot. Too poor to own a horse, he had
walked over the mountain to see the child. As a hunter he had neither
sheep nor wool from which to fashion a gift of felt, so he brought the
most valuable offering he had—a thick black sable fur that could be
used as a blanket.

After Temujin's birth, his mother had three more sons, Khasar,
Khachiun, and Temuge, and finally one daughter, Temulun. Sochigel,
Yesugei's first wife, also produced another son, Belgutei, who was a
few years younger than his brother Begter. By 1170 Yesugei's household consisted of two women with a total of seven children under the
age of ten. Because of the size of the family, each woman almost
certainly had her own *ger*, but the two women lived close together.
At this point, all dates are approximate, as the Mongols had no calendar. They gauged life by the moon and by how many times the
forest or grass had turned green. Each year in the short summer new
vegetation appeared, and thus another annual cycle had passed. Few
people had the need or desire to measure time in spans longer than a
few years. They calculated the age of infants in *oi*—they would be
three, four, or five forests old—but after a few years or the birth of
the next child, the family lost count so the term was not used for
older children or adults.

The Armenian chronicler Hethum, who was generally favorable
toward the Mongols, wrote in his 1307 work *The Flower of Histories
of the East* that they lived "like brute beasts, possessing neither writing nor religion. They tended flocks of animals and moved from place
to place searching for fodder for their herds. They were unskilled in
arms, scorned by, and tributary to, everyone."[5]

While the men were frequently absent hunting, herding, or raiding, the wives made clothes and the walls of their homes from wool,
fleece, fur, and leather. Felt was their most sophisticated material,

which they made by beating layers of wool together into a thick and rough but warm and water-resistant cloth used to line their boots and homes. Occasionally, the men returned from a raid with woven cloth from China, but the Mongols did not weave.

Lacking metal for pots, they cooked by heating stones in a dung fire and dropping them into a bowl or leather pouch filled with water and meat, or they cooked an animal in its own skin using the same method. Nothing was wasted. Before serving the meat, they passed the warm stones around so that every bit of animal fat that clung to them might be absorbed by their hands or rubbed onto their bodies as protection against the bitter dry air. Because the cold weather made bathing nearly impossible, Mongol men removed most of their body hair to protect themselves from lice, leaving only their facial hair and long wisps coming from the parts of the scalp not covered by a hat.

ॐ

Throughout his life, Temujin maintained a close, albeit sometimes contentious, relationship with his mother, who generally favored her second son, Khasar, and her youngest son, Temuge. Temujin's troubled status within the family was evident on several occasions. At one point when he was still very young, his father moved the family on to a new camp, leaving Temujin in the old abandoned camp. It is hard to determine whether this was by accident or design, but fortunately the young boy was found by Targutai Khan of the Tayichiud, who took him in. He described Temujin even then as having "fire in his eyes and light in his face." Although Mongolian documents do not reveal how long Temujin lived with the Tayichiud, it was long enough for Targutai to take some credit for having raised him. As he later explained, "It seemed as though he could learn; so I taught him as though training a two- or three-year-old colt."[6]

Eventually Temujin returned to his family, but not for long. Around 1170, when he was eight years old (or in his ninth year, by

Mongol reckoning), his father decided to take him to live with his mother's clan, the Olkhunuud, supposedly in search of a wife. Normally a boy lived with his future wife's family for a few years and offered a type of service to them, giving them a chance to train and test him before allowing their daughter to leave with him, but eight years old was young for such an arrangement.

The story is filled with gaps. Normally the eldest son, Begter, would have been the first to be sent off. And why would Yesugei go to the clan of a woman whom he had kidnapped? Was he trying to make amends by giving them the boy? Or did he bring him because he believed that the son was not his? Was he trying to defuse some type of tension with other family members? Did Hoelun want him sent to her family for safekeeping?

In any event, Yesugei and Temujin never reached the pastures of his mother's relatives. Several days after leaving home, they stopped for the night at the *ger* of a stranger named Dei-Sechen whose daughter, Borte, was one year older than Temujin. The *Secret History* describes both Borte and Temujin as "having fire in their eyes and light in their face." Dei-Sechen offered to take Temujin as his intended son-in-law, and after spending only one night with the family, Yesugei impulsively gave his son to his host. The two men agreed to a marriage between the two children, and Yesugei left the boy and a horse with Dei-Sechen.

The casual manner in which the two men agreed to this marriage within a few hours of having met gives no indication of how important it would be, not only for the two of them but for world history. Although the intended bride and groom were mere children with no voice in the arrangement, they eventually became not only husband and wife, but the most powerful couple on Earth. Their descendants would rule vast empires, and their genes would find their way into royal families and aristocratic elites from China to Europe.

As he was leaving Temujin behind in Dei-Sechen's *ger*, Yesugei said something puzzling. "I leave my son as your son-in-law, but he is frightened by dogs," he said. "Don't let him be frightened by dogs."[7] What did this mean? There was never any other evidence in the *Secret History* that Temujin was afraid of dogs or much of anything. Because they were in close proximity to Yesugei's mortal enemies, the Tatars, he may have been referring to them. Another possibility is that he was referring to Temujin's brother Khasar, whose name meant Wild Dog. Whatever the reason, the comment seems odd because Yesugei's lineage claimed descent from a golden light beam that had turned into a dog, and much later in life Temujin constantly referred to his closest companions as dogs.

Temujin seemed to be in no immediate peril, but Yesugei was about to undertake a totally unnecessary risk. Having killed several notable Tatars in battle, including the warrior for whom his son was named, he nonetheless chose to travel through extremely hostile Tatar territory. Despite the obvious danger, when he encountered a camp and saw that it was in the midst of a feast, he decided he would join the drinking. Thirst triumphed over reason. Assuming, or hoping, that he could remain anonymous, he joined the festivity. The feasting Tatars recognized him at once. As shedding blood at a celebration would have brought terrible luck to all the participants, according to the *Secret History*, instead of disrupting the festivities, they gave him a slow-acting poison. Gradually, over the next three days, as he continued home on his horse he became increasingly ill. Upon arrival back at his family compound, Yesugei died. Monglik, a trusted friend of the family, went in search of Temujin and brought him home. He had lived with Borte and her family for barely more than a week, but the experience would remain seared in his memory.

In the wake of his father's death, Temujin learned one of the most important lessons of his young life: never trust your relatives. Normally, at the death of a married man, one of his brothers or another close male relative would marry his widow and take responsibility for their children. But Temujin's uncles refused this customary obligation. They would not marry Yesugei's two widows or take in their seven children. The women were unwanted and the children simply too young and numerous to feed or to be of benefit to anyone.

After Yesugei's death, the clan tolerated his widows and their brood through the first winter, but as spring approached, they exhausted the preserved dairy products and meats of the previous year. The forest animals in the surrounding area had been hunted or scared away. Hunger and wolves stalked the meager band. A single blizzard, a late cold snap, or an unusually heavy frost could thrust the community into disaster. Raiding enemies for food became nearly impossible for the weakened, emaciated horses and their poorly nourished warriors. It was at this time of year that the feeble perished and family members turned against one another. The weakest were sacrificed so that the strongest might survive.

A few months after Yesugei's death, the clan exiled his two widows and their young children, who were a burden to them, and sent them to the steppe to die. Hoelun was a captive bride, stolen from her first husband; she was not a proper wife whose marriage had been arranged between two lineages, and thus the clan felt they owed her nothing. They passed the same judgment on Yesugei's other wife, Sochigel, who may also have been a kidnapped bride. The announcement of the decision to abandon the destitute family came at the annual spring ceremony, when meat was burned in offering to the ancestors. The old women who controlled the clan rituals publicly and viciously excluded the two new widows and their children from participating. When Hoelun insisted on attending anyway, the women rebuked her. "You are one for whom the law does not require us to call you and give you food," one snarled.[8] "You are one for whom custom does not require us to call you and give you food," echoed the other.

The ancestral ceremony concluded with plans to lead the surviving animals in search of desperately needed pasture. In the presence of the entire assembled lineage, the senior women pronounced a virtual death sentence on Yesugei's widows and their children. Exclusion from the ceremony had been a mere prelude to their final condemnation. "Leave these mothers and children in the camp," they ordered their fellow clan members, "and move on without taking them along!"[9]

To be abandoned on the steppe is the worst fate for a nomad. As explained in the seventeenth-century manuscript the *Golden Chronicle*, "If one separates from one's own kith and kin, one will become food for men around. If one separates from one's relations, one will become food for orphans. If the many people perish, one will become food for isolated men. One may find all moving things; one will not find kith and kin. One may find tribes and people; one will not find one's related families."[10]

The clan headed away, searching for the warm mouth of summer and leaving the unwanted family to its doom. To ensure that they would not survive to pester them in the future, the departing relatives stole the family's animals and possessions before deserting them. Only one old man among the whole tribe objected to the unjust betrayal of the women and children. Upon denouncing his fellow clan members, he was stabbed and left to die with the abandoned widows and their brood. What was done was done! "The deep water has dried," pronounced the *Secret History*, "the bright stone has shattered."[11]

The Mongolian plateau is a high, dry, cold landscape that becomes steadily drier and warmer as one moves from north to south. Three ecological belts run from east to west. The south is a dry rocky desert steppe known as *govi* or Gobi, the central band consists of green steppes known as *tal* or *kheer*, and the north consists of a mountainous forest zone known as *khangai*. Temujin's clan lived at the intersection of the steppe belt and the mountainous *khangai*, where the world of nomadic herders rubbed up against that of the forest hunters. They could venture out onto the steppe to herd their animals in the summer and retreat to the shelter of the mountains in the winter.

Life on the steppe is harsh even in the best of years. Scorching heat during the brief summer is followed by an interminably long winter. Dust storms, blizzards, and the threat of drought or flood constantly plague the land. Despite the hardships, Hoelun struggled defiantly to save her children. Rather than face certain death on the open steppe, she fled with them into the forests. Sochigel and her two sons either accompanied Hoelun or joined them soon thereafter. They headed to the highest and most sacred mountain in the territory. Because mountains are so venerated by the Mongols, naming them was viewed as taboo, so the Mongols used various circumlocutions or substitute names. The mountain to which Hoelun retreated is called *Khentii Khan*, King of the Khentii region, or, more commonly, *Burkhan Khaldun*, the Mountain of God. This was the mountain from which Jarchigudai had come to bring the sable fur to the infant Temujin.

To the nomad accustomed to the bright light of the steppe, where a horse and rider tower above all else and can be seen for miles around, the looming shadows of the forest must have inspired an awesome but eerie feeling. As described in the *Secret History*, it was a place of "swallowing quagmires . . . in woods made so impenetrable that a gutted snake could not creep in."[12] Yet the verdant patches of land on the mountainside contained fields of delicate edelweiss, waving feather grass, asters, lilacs, forget-me-nots, majestic veronica, and beautiful fireweed. In the summer, the fields swarmed with bees, black and orange butterflies, and spiders frantically spinning silk webs between flowers. Fat flies clustered as soon as the wind subsided, and the crisp, clear call of the cuckoo echoed from the cliffs.

The beauty and bounty of that first short summer and fall quickly gave way to the relentless cold of winter, when the streams and small rivers froze and animals disappeared into the earth. The green needles of the larch trees turned yellow and covered the ground with a golden carpet that was soon blanketed with snow. The bitter wind whipped around the edge of the cliffs with such force that it could peel the skin from an exposed face or cause toes to break off. Wolves howled through long nights that were so cold the moonlight itself seemed to have frozen.

Hoelun faced the dangers and made this land of shadow and mystery a refuge for her children. In the forest, she foraged vigorously to find anything they might eat. She dug roots from the ground with a black stick and made her sons search for rodents, small birds, fish, and other unclean foods that no herder would normally consider worthy of cooking. Fishing and hunting birds were talents of the Uriyankhai, the mountain people from whom the outcast boys soon learned these skills. The refugees hid in the small openings along the cliffs and built barricades to prevent men from entering the forest on horseback from capturing them.

Through Hoelun's insistent striving and resourcefulness, Temujin and his siblings survived. She taught them what she could, but as a young woman from another tribe on a distant steppe, she did not know the specific traditions of her late husband's land or the sacred spirits and stories of this strange place. For the steppe tribes, their land was their religion. They honored the mountains, rivers, passes, sacred stones, and trees. Exile from the tribe and from their homeland had meant exile from their spiritual community as well. Without father, grandmother, aunts, uncles, or elders of his lineage, having been rejected by his closest relatives as unfit to live, Temujin would have to find his own personal connection to the spiritual world.

As best she could, Hoelun instructed her children in the *Ancient Sayings*, a mixture of proverbs, myths, riddles, and poems. These held seeds of wisdom but no foundation for a united dogma or doctrine. The sayings were not prescriptive or instructional so much as they were stimulating of thought. They provided guidelines toward solutions and could be easily adapted to new situations, thus forming a living and flexible body of knowledge. Few Mongols were literate. They passed stories from mother to daughter and father to son, but mostly they believed in learning by example, by following the behavior of others rather than putting all their faith in words alone.

The abandoned family's direst need was for food, warmth, and safety. Survival was the first order of business; idle curiosity, even the thirst for revenge, would have to wait for many years. An ostracized and condemned child who had done no wrong, Temujin buried his emotions deep inside, but the anger at the injustice of his situation gnawed constantly at his heart. "The teeth in the mouth eat meat," offers one of the old Mongol sayings, but "the teeth in the mind eat men."[13]

The teeth of Temujin's mind grew sharper with each new indignity, each unwarranted insult, and each new winter.

Unexpectedly one day, while Hoelun and her family camped on the Burgi Escarpment, the old hunter Jarchigudai emerged again from the forest.[14] Strapped to his back was his drum, the traditional bridge by which spiritually powerful men and women communicated with the spirit world.[15] From then on Temujin's moral and spiritual education was informally shaped by three people: his mother Hoelun, an old woman who had joined them and had "ears like a weasel and eyes like an ermine,"[16] and the hunter of the mountain, Old Jarchigudai.

On Burkhan Khaldun, the old man taught Temujin the basics of spiritual life. It is not clear whether Jarchigudai was his name from birth or one bestowed respectfully later. The name signifies both a guide and messenger as well as moral principles.[17] In name and in deed, Jarchigudai was Temujin's spiritual guide, pointing the way toward the correct life.

He taught him that the Universal Mother existed in the great void, an abyss with no time or space, no person or spirit, no light or form, neither up nor down, no good or evil. She was the primal love searching for something on which to bestow her passionate affection, and for this she needed a child. From her infinite soul she created the sky, and because there was no light in the sky she took out her beating heart and made it into the sun to light the heaven. With the sky as her mate, she conceived a child in her golden womb, but because the world lacked a place for a child to be born, she made her body into the earth. To give the earth life, her breasts became the springs from which nurturing rivers flowed. As a good mother, she gave her body that her children might have life, grow, and flourish.[18] She was every mother who gave her body to her children that they might survive.

The mountain had protected Temujin when the men of his clan and tribe would not, and from his mother and the old hunter he had learned to revere the mountain as the center of the world, the place where life begins. The three dimensions of the cosmos meet at the mountaintop. Above is the ocean of light known as *Tenger,* or heaven, and below is the ocean of water, *Dalai.* Where the male sky and the female sea join is the earth, which floats in the ocean of light and the ocean of water. It is on the mountaintop that Mother Earth meets Father Sky. Here the sunrays melt the ice and the water trickles down among the rocks and earth. As recorded on a stone near the Orkhon River more than a thousand years ago, "When the blue sky above and the reddish-brown earth were created, between the two, human beings were created."[19]

The forested region of the mountain, the *khangai,* was the bountiful mother of life, but in the mountain heights above the tree line, where the large boulders and stony cliffs jutted upward out of the eternal snow and ice, the land was seemingly without life. This male element provided the hard bones of the earth. Together the female forest and the male rocks formed the origin of all being. They formed a universe consisting of three souls: male, female, and immortal. So each creature received an immortal and imperishable spirit as well as two mortal ones. According to Mongol belief, humans, like other animals, enter life with the male spirit in their bones, the female spirit in their flesh and blood, and the eternal soul in their mind and heart.

Winter on the mountain was a time for hunting and killing, and yet it was the most sacred season of the year. Snow, like milk, was thought to possess a spiritual purity that cleansed the soul as well as the body. Hunters rubbed their exposed flesh vigorously with fresh snow until the snow melted and their skin turned bright red, to prepare their bodies for the cold that always followed the snow, and purify them of their recent misdeeds. Though generally associated with the first big snowfall of the winter and performed primarily by men, the ritual could be enacted as often as the body or spirit might need restoration.

More experienced hunters such as Jarchigudai encouraged young men to push their bodies to the limits of physical endurance in other ways as well. Every day was a competition against whatever hazard presented itself—cold, heat, hunger, thirst, loneliness, or pain. When the day offered no new challenges, the Mongols invented them. They routinely held hot stones in their hands and rubbed them on their bodies or sat by the hottest fires trying to show no signs of pain. Each challenge was an opportunity for conquest, a personal conquest over oneself.

Rashid al-Din, a Persian chronicler who converted from Judaism to Islam but faithfully served the Mongols, wrote that in Genghis Khan's homeland between the Onon and Kherlen rivers, the shaman used to "sit naked in the middle of a frozen river, and from the heat of his body the ice would melt and steam would rise from the water."[20] Others reported that the holy men walked naked in the winter snow.[21] Central Asian mythology frequently connects nudity with spiritual powers, as the spirits were rarely clothed beings.[22]

The Mongols did not worship anthropomorphized deities. They recognized no god in human form with arms or legs, a head or face, or any deity that spoke to them in words. They simply acknowledged a supreme, divine power over the universe, an ineffable sacred presence without form or word that saturated the world. They did not believe in a god who descended to Earth to perform magical tricks, speak with burning tongues of fire, or copulate with human beings. They did not ascribe the human emotions of jealousy and anger to beings in the sky. Similarly, they saw no need for a god to speak to them or give them laws. They believed that each person contained a part of the divine essence of the universe, and from this divinity, each soul possessed a basic morality beyond anything that could be contained in human words or inscribed into law.

From the mountaintop, one can see the sky and judge its mood by the weather, but the earth displays its moods through the trees of the forest.[23] In the Mongolian language, the forest, in addition to measuring the years of a child's life, literally holds the collected wisdom of the Earth, as the word for "forest," *oi*, also means "mind" and "memory." When Mother Earth was happy with her human children, the trees prospered and fruits, nuts, or pinecones grew abundantly; their fragrance filled the air. When humans misbehaved, the trees no longer thrived, fruits withered, and their vibrant colors faded. The nomads who worshipped the highest mountain in the area honored the largest tree in the same way with offerings, prayers, and rituals to solemnize special.occasions.

Persian chronicler Juvaini, who lived among the Mongols, wrote, "they approached the trees and made such obeisance as dutiful children make to their parents; they also showed respect and honor to the ground in which the trees grew."[24] The tree turns water into fire by absorbing the rain and transforming it into wood that burns. In a similar way, the tree produces incense that, when burned, transforms prayers into smoke and lifts them up to the sky. Earth, fire, and water—the female elements of life—unite in the tree.

The *Secret History* vividly describes the turmoil prevailing on the steppe during the period of Temujin's childhood and youth: "the stars rolled in the sky," one passage reads. "People fought without rest, and the earth rolled."[25] The Mongols lived in chaos churning without purpose or benefit, in a world where evil persisted without cause and without end: "People fought without wishing to; they betrayed and killed without wishing it." Temujin grew up outside organized religion and beyond the reach of his tribe and ancestors, and for the rest of his life he remained deeply suspicious of both.

Amid the "whirling waters" and "blazing fire" of Temujin's young life, Burkhan Khaldun became his refuge.[26] Exile from the tribe went from a punishment to a unique opportunity for the physical, mental, and spiritual training that forever set him apart from the lesser men of the world. Like prior generations of nomadic children, he learned to use the mountain as a teacher, the rocks and trees as his scripture. The loosening of a strap on his horse, a falling rock, or an oddly placed tree could hold a message that the mountain was sending him from heaven. He gradually came to read these messages and to understand. Several times on the mountain, Temujin slipped in the saddle, and so he learned the value of constant balance. The greatest effort of strength or will could be quickly dashed by the slightest imbalance in the saddle. Horsemen must constantly adjust the packs that they strap to their camels, onto yaks, on their carts, and on their backs. Learning to arrange each item properly in its container, bind it, and balance it becomes one of the necessities of survival.

In the harsh and frequently unforgiving school of nature, Temujin acquired the skills to navigate, to find the way. On the open steppe a rider can find his way easily, because there is little to hide it. Dangers can be seen hours before they arrive. The sun by day and the North Star by night help the nomad to determine the location and thereby find the path to safety; but in the mountains, the way is rarely open or clear. Danger can lurk anywhere. Temujin learned to find his way by reading the patterns of the trees and the tracks of animals, and determining by their droppings which ones had passed and how long ago.

The young boy's survival depended on learning to distinguish the echo of his horse's hooves from the sound of other approaching beasts. It was on the mountain that his "intelligence came bursting forth; his mind began opening."[27] As powerful as the mountain was, it would not compel him to do what he did not want to do. It could only point the way. At a young age he had to choose for himself, and he frequently made the wrong choice. The Mongols believed that it takes seven mistakes to make one lesson, and Temujin had as much to fear from his own mistakes as from any other steppe warrior.

The ravines and rocky outcroppings of Burkhan Khaldun offered shelter, but they also offered a place where he could whisper his fears and his greatest hopes, wishes, and desires. In time, the intimacy between the young boy and the mountain substituted for what he was missing from his male kinsmen, who had rejected him and left him to die. The mountain became his confidant and guide. He rarely trusted or confided in people and seldom seemed as much at home or as happy as he was on his beloved Burkhan Khaldun. The important principles in his life, and the important relationships, originated there on its slopes, in its forests, under its shadow.

Temujin credited his survival to the blessings and protection of the mountain, and he vowed to honor and pray to it for the remainder of his life. He climbed to the summit, "hung his belt around his neck, put his hat over his hand, beat his breast with his fist, and nine times kneeling down towards Mother Sun, he offered a libation and a prayer," the *Secret History* recorded. In the world order, his life had no more importance than that of a louse or a grasshopper, and yet, undeserving and hapless as he was, the mountain had saved and nourished him. "Every morning I will sacrifice to Burkhan Khaldun, and every day I will pray to it," he vowed. "The children of my children must remember this."[28]

2

The Golden Whip of Heaven

The *Secret History* rarely presents the events or thoughts of family members preceding a major conflict; the words simply explode into unforeseen and inexplicable violence. When Temujin was in his early teens he came into conflict with his half brother Begter, Sochigel's elder son, who was probably only two or three years older than he. The only provocation seemed to be that Begter had snatched a small fish from the hook of Temujin's fishing line, demonstrating that he was the older, stronger brother and, in the absence of their father, he planned to take charge of the household.

When Temujin complained to his mother, she sided with Begter rather than Temujin. "You have no friend but your shadow," she admonished her son, "no whip but your horse's tail." Tribal tradition dictated that if a woman's late husband's brothers refused to marry her, then a son by another wife should do so even if he was much younger. Begter may have been in the process of claiming Hoelun, and this could account for her siding with her stepson against her own son. Whatever the source of the tension, his mother's scolding only darkened Temujin's mood and stoked the hatred in his heart.

At some point Temujin decided that he would rid himself of

Begter. Once he had made up his mind, it did not take him long to execute his plan. He and his younger brother Khasar stalked Begter as if they were hunting a wild wolf or deer. When they found him sitting on a small hill, they approached him from opposite sides. Begter, who was unarmed, offered no resistance. He repeated the words that Hoelun had spoken, first taunting Temujin for having no friend but his shadow, and no whip but his horse's tail. Then he pleaded with his brothers, saying that they should fight together against their common enemies and not each other.

Temujin and Khasar each shot arrows and thus killed Begter together. He was the first victim in the rise of Genghis Khan.

When she realized what had happened, Hoelun became enraged. She screamed insults at her son, calling him a tiger, a leopard, a dragon-snake, a wolf, and a dog. "You have destroyed!" she screamed. But despite her anguish and tears, Begter was gone. Temujin remained unmoved, and his younger siblings soon recognized the fate that might await them if they crossed him. Only Khasar, who had participated in the killing, was never afraid of Temujin. Despite the murder, Begter's full brother Belgutei remained eternally loyal and eventually survived all other members of the family.

During the prior crises in his life—his abandonment, the death of his father, the long struggle to scratch out a living on the desolate mountain—Temujin had been a child forced to react and unable to alter the situation. He had been too young to resist the adult forces around him. Begter's killing was a turning point. For the first time he had taken fate into his own hands. It was a dramatic demonstration of his toughness and courage, but it came at a cost. It drew the attention of new enemies who recognized that a young man who could kill his own brother might pose a future threat to them as well. The leader of the Tayichiud who had once saved Temujin's life now felt threatened by him. He said dismissively, referring to Temujin and Khasar, "the chicks are growing wings, the lambs are shedding their fleece, the snotty ones have grown up." He ordered his men to capture Temujin.[1]

Temujin fled from the Tayichiud raiders and took refuge in the forest. Tired and hungry after several days, he thought it would be safe to emerge, imagining that his attackers would have tired of looking for him by now. As he sought to exit the narrow gulley where he had been hiding, he found that a large white rock had fallen into it and barred the way. He tried to move it, but the bushes and trees resisted him. He recognized that these were a divine sign not to leave, but he remained determined to defy his destiny. After nine days without food he knew that his fate would be to die on the mountain an unknown boy unless he was willing to fight the band of well-fed and well-armed men waiting on the other side. "How shall I die without a name?" he asked himself. "I shall go out."[2]

Armed with nothing more than the small knife he used to sharpen his arrows, he began slowly cutting through the branches that barred his way until he finally fashioned an opening large enough to escape. There, waiting for him on the other side of the thicket, were the Tayichiud warriors, who "captured him and took him away," tying him in a cangue like an ox under a yoke.[3] Enslaved by his captors, humiliated and at constant risk of death, Temujin endured the worst without losing sight of his single goal: to survive, escape, and make a name for himself.

His chance to escape came a long but unspecified time later, when his captors were drunk in celebration. The cangue to which his head and arms were securely tied was a formidable obstacle designed to prevent any possibility of escape. He turned the obstacle into a weapon, attacking one of his captors with the heavy wooden frame, knocking him out, and then fleeing. Still attached to the cangue, he jumped into a cold river and hid while his captors searched for him. Late at night, with help from a family that had befriended him, he managed to free himself from the cangue, flee from his enemies, and make it back to his family and the safety of Burkhan Khaldun.

ꑭ

As a child, Temujin had seen his mother struggle daily to keep her children alive. From her he had learned that despite the toughest difficulty and most painful tragedy, fate was never wicked or malevolent.

It was not a punishment. Fate presented obstacles, but they could be overcome by a strong will. Despite having been kidnapped, widowed, and then abandoned, Hoelun had been determined to prevail and to save her children. This determination had strengthened her courage, her cunning, and ultimately her wisdom. Hoelun had learned from each setback, and Temujin had learned from her.

The Mongols believed that the destiny of each creature was ordained by the sky above. If God did not want humans to strive, he would not have given them the ability to dream as they did. Like other children, Temujin was captive to a destiny that determined when and where he was born, who his parents were, if he was to be rich or poor, and whether he would be short or tall. Fate determined the weather and many other factors over which he exercised no control, but his spirit determined what he could do with these circumstances.

The Mongols said that Mother Earth and Father Sky granted each person a *Khiimori*, a Windhorse, the spirit of inspiration. Sometimes it galloped along the road ordained by destiny, but sometimes it offered a new challenge and pointed in an unexpected direction. To catch a Windhorse a youth had to chase it barefooted across the frozen earth and endure whatever discomfort nature presented. Although each person had a Windhorse, none but the bravest ever caught it and learned to ride and tame it. While akin to the ancient Greek notion of *charisma* and the Roman *genius*, the Windhorse is not wholly external to the person. The power of the spirit grows with repeated good behavior, and it can wither and atrophy for those who act in a manner that is lazy, inappropriate, wicked, or contrary to tradition and good sense.

The Universal Mother was said to have left an umbilical cord of golden light inside the mind of every child, stretching up to the North Star, to which the universe was tied. The cord of light was a golden tether, like the long rope used to prevent cows from wandering while giving them plenty of room to graze. It provided each individual with a direct and personal connection to the sky, giving everyone the means to climb constantly higher in life. As the child grew into a young adult, he retained the power of choice, the unseen golden tie that eternally connects his mind and soul to the Universal Mother.

From a young age Temujin believed he could choose his destiny. He learned that a person could summon the power to overcome even the worst fate. One could accept the drought or search for water. One could succumb to the wolf or confront it. One could cower before enemies or seek to conquer them.[4] To those who accepted defeat, more defeat would come, for that was what they deserved and the sky grew indifferent to them. To those rare individuals who remained determined to win, more victories would come and with them greater love and reward from the sky. God intended humans to think and not to obey blindly. Much later this way of thinking was reflected on one of the arrow messages the Mongol warriors fired into Baghdad: "If God wanted his will carried out, he would strip the sensible of their senses."[5]

When riding a horse, steppe nomads used a small riding crop or whip to make their mounts run. It usually consisted of a short wooden handle with a piece of braided rawhide attached to one end, and a leather loop around the other so that it could hang around the wrist of the rider, leaving his hands unencumbered. This whip could be used only behind the rider, on the rump of the horse, and never in front, as striking a horse on the face or neck was a crime punishable by death. Just as the rider of an ordinary horse needed such a whip, the rider of a Windhorse needed a special whip with which to drive away evil spirits and misfortune. The whip was used for speed, but it also symbolized political power and spiritual charisma. A person without a whip was thought to have no direction in life, but with a whip, he could go anywhere and achieve anything.

Temujin knew he needed to find his own whip. His mother's taunts only deepened his resolve. Without a whip, how could he manage to ride his Windhorse?

According to a Mongol proverb, "knowledge learned while growing up becomes like the morning sun."[6] The physical and spiritual training Temujin had acquired in the forests around Burkhan Khaldun was deep, but his mountain refuge had not provided him with a broad knowledge of the world. After nine years in the isolated protection of Burkhan Khaldun, the desire for companionship and urge to confront his destiny drew him out of his secure world. By the age of seventeen, he was ready to leave the mountain and pursue his future, but he never forgot his promise to his beloved Burkhan Khaldun. Over the years, he repeatedly returned to the mountain to contemplate his path and find the solace needed to make difficult decisions and to dream beyond what any steppe boy had ever dreamed.

His first act was to seek out Borte, the girl to whom he had been engaged when he was eight and she was nine, shortly before his father's murder. Since the moment he first saw her, she was the girl with "light in her face and fire in her eyes." It did not take him long to find her, and he was pleased to find that she had not yet taken another husband. The *Secret History* tells us that her parents were happy to see him, but they must have been surprised to discover that this strange young man had not forgotten his commitment to marry her so many years ago. He was not a part of her family, but he joined them for a while and through them, he experienced the family rituals that he had been denied by his clan. Borte would eventually bring Temujin into a larger cultural and spiritual world beyond his mountain refuge.

Accompanied by her mother, Borte came to live with Temujin and his family. He remained among the poorest of the poor, and it must have been difficult for her to accept a husband with no riches, allies, or apparent likelihood of success. For a girl accustomed to the large herds and abundance of steppe life, the semiforested area where Temujin lived must have seemed stark. It had limited grazing grounds, and the family depended primarily on hunting wild animals that were not always plentiful. Life must have been a little lonely for her when it came time for her mother to return home and leave her amid this outcast family of strangers. But Borte proved as loyal to Temujin as he was to her. Their love became one of the binding forces of his life.

Love, or its illusion, has the ability to wipe away years of deprivation and suffering. It can make the heart forget. Through the romantic fog of memory, Temujin and Borte were later remembered by their descendants as beautiful and heroic lovers. Borte was described as bright as the morning rays with phoenix eyes, a nose like polished jade, and lips resembling coral buttons. She was like a goddess of the nine heavens, the mother of a nation.[7] Temujin had a jadelike face resembling the full moon, with dragon eyes, a nose like a holy mountain, and lips like turquoise. His ears were big, his chest broad, and he smelled like jasmine. From ten paces away, anyone could see that he would rule a dynasty.

A fairy tale could end with the heroes having braved incredible dangers and suffering only to survive and find true love in each other's arms. However, no such future awaited our heroes. For Temujin and Borte, finding each other and falling in love was only the beginning of their adventure.

Word spread on the steppe that a beautiful girl had joined the small family of outcasts living in the shadow of Burkhan Khaldun. Despite Temujin's reputation for ruthlessness, his bride stood out as a tempting prize in a society where men were eager to fight over anything, especially control of women. Hoelun's first husband had belonged to the Merkid, and when some of his relatives heard about Borte, they decided to seize her in revenge for Hoelun's kidnapping.

A few months after Borte's arrival, a Merkid raiding party swooped down on the isolated camp. Hoelun rushed to the horses and ordered all of her children, including Temujin, to mount them and flee. Knowing what the Merkid warriors were after, she left behind Sochigel and Borte, and the old woman who had been helping the family shear sheep. Hoelun was above all a mother, and her sole goal was to save her children even if she had to sacrifice her son's wife. Temujin followed her without thinking of the consequences. At seventeen, he was as much a boy as a man. He had not yet mastered control of his own fate. In his own words, he later admitted, "I was greatly frightened."[8] At a younger age, he had been defiant and determined enough to kill his own brother. When he was angry, he had disgusted his mother by killing Begter, but when he was frightened, he instinctively obeyed his mother's decision to abandon Borte without recognizing the pain of losing her.

The family raced toward Burkhan Khaldun, while Borte and the old woman tried to flee in an oxcart in the opposite direction. Sochigel did not run away; she simply waited. The soldiers seized Sochigel first, flung her over a horse with both feet dangling in the air, and then set off after the other two, who were dashing through the woods, as the axle on their oxcart had broken. It did not take the soldiers long to find them. The capture of the three women diverted the raiding party's attention long enough for Mother Hoelun to escape with the horses and her children to the mountains.

The Merkid had failed to capture Hoelun or any of her six children, but they were pleased with their bounty and took the three women back to their camp as trophies. They had taken revenge for Yesugei's stealing of Hoelun from Chiledu, and in Borte they had acquired a prize equal to what they had lost. Borte was given to Chilger, Chiledu's younger brother.

Temujin realized that the time had come for him to learn to master his emotions, because just as he had killed his brother in anger, now he had deserted his wife in fear. If fear and anger dominated over him, he would forever be a slave to forces beyond his control, but if he could master his emotions and focus his energy, everything would be within his grasp.

However strong, brave, and determined he may have been, Temujin knew that he was no match for a large group of armed men. With no earthly ally and seemingly without hope of retrieving his wife, Temujin turned to prayer. He climbed to the top of Burkhan Khaldun, where he stood to face Mother Sun. He removed his hat, took off his belt, and hung it around his neck in a sign of total submission. With his fist clenched, he beat on his breast and knelt nine times to the Sun. Then he prayed.

At this point Temujin made the first adult decision of his life. He vowed to find his bride. He refused to accept that someone had deprived him of the woman he loved, and he swore to rescue Borte or to die trying. Better to lose his life as a warrior fighting than surrender to a cruel fate.

Until this time, he had relied on the help of one or two people, such as his brother Khasar or Old Man Jarchigudai, but to raid the Merkid and rescue his bride he needed many more allies. Two major tribal groups dominated the steppe: the Kereyid to the west and the Tatars to the east. At various times, the tribes had been united, but the Kereyid had broken away from the Tatars and the two were now sworn enemies.

Since the Tatars had killed his father and been mortal enemies to his clan, Temujin's only acceptable choice was to renew his family's commitment to Torghil Ong Khan, the leader of the Kereyid, and beg for help. Although it was an easy choice, it carried profound consequences. The Tatars and Kereyid followed similar ways of life with one major cultural distinction: the Tatars and other eastern tribes looked to China as the appropriate model for civilization, and the Kereyid looked west, wrote with an alphabet of Semitic origin, and had embraced Christianity as their official religion. When Temujin made his choice and cast his lot with the Kereyid, he probably did not know and certainly did not care about this distinction, but in time, it would become a major factor in his life and that of the nation he would create.

Not long after Borte's abduction, Temujin, Khasar, and their faithful half brother, Belgutei, set off from Burkhan Khaldun, riding past Bogd Khan Mountain to the camp of Ong Khan on the Black Forest of the Tuul River, a little south of the modern Mongolian capital Ulaanbaatar. When he reached Ong Khan's camp, Temujin begged him "to rescue my wife and return her to me."[9] Although Ong Khan and his people lived in *gers* and moved in a nomadic lifestyle, a cultural chasm separated the simple life of Hoelun's camp from that of the great khan, whose large *gers* were lined with fur and whose wives dressed in silk. They drank the same fermented mare's milk, but Ong Khan's people drank from bowls of silver and rode horses with stirrups of iron. Instead of the simple prayers to Father Sky and

Mother Earth, ornately dressed Christian priests chanted "*Abui Ba-bui*," the mysterious opening words of the Lord's Prayer, from their holy books.[10]

Temujin's father had once been of great help to Ong Khan in one of the many internecine struggles within the Kereyid royal family, and he had played a key role in several of the Kereyid campaigns against the Tatars. Realizing the potential value of securing Yesugei's son as a follower, Ong Khan eagerly agreed to help. "We will crush all the Merkid," he promised. "We will return your wife. We will bring her back to you!"[11]

The visit to Ong Khan's court inspired Temujin and gave him a new confidence. Almost as soon as he summoned the courage to fight, fate suddenly bestowed upon him an unexpected blessing: he found a whip. He was riding back from the old khan's camp through a narrow pass on the northern side of the Bogd Khan Mountain when he reached a fertile steppe that gently opens on the southern side of the Tuul. Nearly five centuries earlier, this area had formed the far eastern border of the Turkic tribes and marked the spot where they rubbed up against the Tatars and the powerful Chinese civilization to the south. Soon after passing Bogd Khan Mountain, Temujin would have seen a series of increasingly large stones planted in a ceremonial roadway, culminating in two monuments inscribed in Turkic around the year 716.

Oral tradition maintains that it is here, at the political and spiritual birthplace of the great Turkish Empire, that Temujin found a whip lying on the ground on a small hill known as Tsonjin Boldog. For a Mongol, finding a lost animal or object comes with the strict obligation to locate its owner. This would particularly have applied to something as personal and symbolically important as a whip. According to the thirteenth-century Persian historian Juzjani, Genghis Khan's law specifically stated that for Mongols, "it was impossible for any person to take up a fallen whip from the group except he were the owner of it."[12] Nevertheless, Temujin picked up the whip and decided it belonged to him. It was his destiny.

This was the moment when Temujin took control of his life. The whip would serve throughout his life as a constant image, not only in the Mongol chronicles but in foreign ones as well. As Juvaini wrote, Temujin "prospered and the stars of his fortune were in the ascent," and he struck the breath from his enemies "with the whip of calamity and the sword of annihilation."[13]

Ong Khan agreed to set out from his camp, but he ordered Temujin to recruit another warrior, Jamuka, to join the attack from the east. Jamuka was a distant cousin, and the two had been childhood friends. Jamuka's family had camped near Temujin's on the Onon River, and the two boys had frequently played together on the frozen river. Twice they took the oath of eternal friendship, or *anda*, and became sworn brothers. The first time they sealed the vow by exchanging knucklebones that young boys used to play games and foretell the future. Then, at puberty, when they were becoming hunters, they crossed paths again and remade their vows with an exchange of arrowheads that Jamuka had made from horn and Temujin had made from wood. Now they would come together for the third time in life.

With his newfound confidence, Temujin's tone changed. When he first approached Ong Khan, he had hesitantly pleaded with the khan to rescue Borte for him, but now he spoke with new confidence and heightened determination. "We are sworn brothers; we are kinsmen of the same liver," he reminded Jamuka. "But the Merkid have made my bed empty. How can we avenge this injury?"

"It pains my heart and makes my liver hurt to know that your bed has become empty," Jamuka replied, and he vowed to ride with his warriors to help in the rescue. "We will rescue Borte!"

The Merkid lived beyond the confluence of the Orkhon and Selenge rivers, but because it was not yet winter, when the Mongols most commonly raided, the rivers were not yet frozen. Jamuka offered to make rafts to cross the river and enter Merkid territory. "We will utterly destroy these people. We will kill even their women and children until nothing remains of them." As he prepared his warriors, he sent another message to Temujin. "I have sprinkled milk on my horse-hair banner; I have beaten the loud drum. I have pulled my arrow on the bowstring. Let us fight to the death."

Having heard of Borte's kidnapping and of the preparation for the raid to rescue her, Jarchigudai came looking for Temujin. The old man brought his son Jelme, who was about the same age as Temujin, to serve as his first follower. "Now let Jelme put on your saddle, open your door," said Jarchigudai according to the *Secret History*, and he "handed him over to Temujin."[14] Just as Jarchigudai had been the first person to bring a gift to Temujin after his birth, he now became the first to bring a warrior to serve him in his coming conquests. Soon followers came from many clans, and later two of Jelme's clan cousins, his "younger brothers" Subodei and Chaurkhan, joined them as well. Although Temujin's own relatives betrayed him, these men never did. They had a tie much stronger than bone, blood, and flesh. They were united spiritually through Old Jarchigudai and Burkhan Khaldun. Subodei eventually became the conqueror of Russia and much of Eastern Europe. He was the greatest of the Mongol strategists and possibly the greatest military general in history.

Temujin, his brothers, and Jelme converged with the raiding party sent by Jamuka and the warriors of Ong Khan. As they crossed the river, however, some Merkid men fishing and trapping sables spotted them and raced to warn their fellow clansmen. With no time to break camp or recruit assistance, the panicked people bolted in different directions in the middle of the night.

Borte had by then become pregnant, but when the raiding party arrived, they found she had been abandoned to her own resources while her new husband, Chilger, fled in fear. Perhaps he suspected that whoever was coming would want to steal Borte. He lamented at having taken her as his wife. In the words of the *Secret History*, he was nothing more than a vulture wanting to eat swans and cranes when he should have been eating rats and mice. If he stayed with Borte, now his life would be "worth nothing more than sheep dung," and if caught he might lose his head.

As the raiders swept through camp, Borte recognized Temujin and fled to him. "In the moonlight, he looked at Borte, and they fell into each other's arms."[15]

Temujin rescued Borte and the old woman; only Sochigel remained missing. Her son Belgutei raced through the nearly deserted camp searching for her. He heard that she was living in another camp, but when he approached her *ger* she fled from him "in a ragged sheepskin coat."[16] She wished to stay with her new husband in her new life and did not want to return to the camp of a man who had killed her elder son. She dashed off into a dense forest while her son shot whistling arrows at any man he could see, screaming, "Bring me my mother!" No one obeyed, and Sochigel disappeared among the trees. Belgutei never saw his mother again.

Temujin had tasted real war for the first time. He was no longer fleeing from attackers as he had so often in his life. Now he was the aggressor. He relished his coming of age as a warrior. Happy not only to have Borte back by his side, but also to find himself with a new father in Ong Khan and a new brother in Jamuka, he celebrated the victory. "Called by Mighty Heaven, carried through by Mother Earth, we emptied the breasts of the Merkid," he boasted. "We tore their livers to pieces. We emptied their beds. And we exterminated their relatives. Thus we destroyed the Merkid."[17] Despite the youthful boasting of this novice warrior, most of the Merkid had fled successfully and survived to fight him again in the years ahead.

3

Wisdom of the Steppe

On Burkhan Khaldun, one wise person such as Old Jarchigu-dai could know everything there was to be known, but hidden in the tall standing grass of the steppe were traces of men who had built empires that stretched beyond the realms of Temujin's imagination. They had left accounts of their successes and failures and advice to future inhabitants carved on the stones across the steppe. Temujin could not read the stone inscriptions, but he was mesmerized by them and knew he would need to learn from their valuable lessons.

The nomadic herders and hunters who had passed over the land in earlier centuries had various names: Kirgiz, Tatars, Naiman, Merkid, Uighurs, and Xianbei, but the most important and famous were the Huns, who created the first steppe empire in Mongolia under their leader Modun in 209 BC.[1] According to legend, the Huns shared a close mythical connection to the wolf. The title of their ruler, *shanyu*, who was also a spiritual leader, may have originated from the word for wolf.

As nomads requiring grass and water and roaming from place to place, the Huns constantly searched for the right relationship with

the ever-changing spirits of the landscape. According to Chinese accounts, the Huns, whom the Chinese called Xiongnu, gathered three
times a year to offer sacrifices to heaven, Earth, and their ancestors.[2]
The tribal gatherings provided occasions for ancestral ceremonies of
the type from which Temujin and his family had been ostracized soon
after the murder of his father. The largest gathering of the year occurred in the fall, when the animals were fattest and healthiest after
a summer of grazing. The *shanyu* carefully controlled the rituals, as
this was also the time when taxes were collected.[3] Based upon the
number of animals owned by a herder and the weather the preceding
summer, the *shanyu* assessed and collected tribute.

The activities that Temujin saw at the court of Ong Khan resembled those of the Huns more than a thousand years earlier. At the
Hun gatherings, the *shanyu* heard appeals, issued judgments, settled
feuds, and performed the practical tasks of administration. The acquisition and distribution of goods were the most important part of
the political and religious office of the leader, and the two roles were
closely entwined. The sacrifice of animals, invocations to the gods,
wafting incense, great pots of boiled or charred meat, abundant skins
of fermented mare's milk, and mass rituals involving thousands of
people created a powerful spiritual and sensory drama of importance
around tax collection and to smooth administration of government.

In the early years of the Hun Empire clear signs of a state cult had
already appeared. The Chinese chronicler Sima Qian, who lived at
the same time as Modun, wrote that the Huns worshipped "Heaven
and Earth and the gods and spirits." Every day "at dawn the *shanyu*
leaves his camp and makes obeisance to the sun as it rises, and in the
evening he makes a similar obeisance to the moon."[4] They often buried their dead with images of the sun and quarter moon. From the
beginning of the Hun Empire, their religion glorified the ruler. In a
letter to the Chinese court, the *shanyu* claimed, like the Chinese emperor, to have been chosen by heaven.

During decades of generous rainfall, the luxuriant grasses of the steppe permitted the Huns' herds to flourish, and with increased milk and meat production, their children grew more numerous and stronger. As their grazing needs surpassed the available pastureland and as these children matured, the older ones left with some of their family's animals to seek new pastures farther away. Successful herders constantly required more land, and this need created a persistent push outward from the Khangai Mountain valleys and steppe, off the Mongolian Plateau and into farms and villages from China to Europe. Along the way, the Huns occasionally raided the sedentary villagers and, when they had to, traded their prized animals.

Precursors to the Turks and Mongols, the Huns stretched across the continent, reaching India to the south and France to the west. From China to Rome, scholars, soldiers, and bureaucratic clerks began to record their passing, always couched in derogatory comments about these mysterious and fierce people. As the Huns pushed into distant parts of Europe and Asia, they broke into distinct tribes that gradually lost contact with their home base in Mongolia and became small, independently roaming kingdoms.

The Huns left no written record, so our understanding of their history is based on the contemporary accounts of their enemies, supplemented by modern archaeology. The challenge of recording unbiased information about these tribes was demonstrated by the fate of a Chinese court historian in the year 99 BC. The Huns had just routed the Chinese army, but the historian pleaded with the outraged Chinese emperor for mercy for his defeated commanding general. This recommendation so outraged the emperor that he had the historian castrated.[5] Facing such dangers, scholars tended to be careful as to what they wrote about the barbarian tribes.

By the time of Attila, the most infamous of all the Huns, in the fifth century, the tribe had reached the western edge of the Eurasian steppes in the land where they had established their own kingdom and to which they gave their name, Hungary. By this point, Huns controlled much of eastern Europe and campaigned throughout

Europe, from the Balkans to the Rhine. From their new base on the plains, close to the centers of European civilization, the Huns raced wherever they detected the alluring scent of wealth and weakness, and in the fifth century, the decaying Roman Empire reeked of this irresistible smell.

In the fourth century, Roman warrior and historian Ammianus Marcellinus described the Huns as people from the "Frozen Ocean . . . a race savage beyond all parallel." What he wrote of the Alan, a steppe tribe related to modern Ossetians, also seemed true of the Huns, with whom they shared a herding lifestyle and political affiliation: "Nor is there any temple or shrine seen in their country," he declared with amazement, "nor even any cabin thatched with straw."[6]

Attila, though he was not the most important or successful leader of the Huns, became the most famous as chroniclers expressed both terror and fascination at his attacks on Rome and cities across Europe. He became the prototype of raiding barbarians everywhere. By his time, the Western Huns had been far from Mongolia for generations, and along the way they had absorbed religious and cultural traditions from many of the peoples they conquered and encountered. They augmented their core beliefs, borrowing a worship of the sword from the Scythians, and absorbing Christian elements into their ideology.

Greek observers and Chinese envoys reported that the Huns practiced scapulimancy, divining the future by reading the cracks and fissures in the charred shoulder blades of sheep, a practice still followed by the Mongols at the time of Temujin. The Huns also consulted seers like Jarchigudai, who read omens and predicted the future, as well as shamans, who were referred to as priests in Greek. Little of the Hun language has survived to indicate precisely what these shamans were called, but the occurrence of the term *kam*, which is Turkic for *shaman*, in personal names suggests that the term originated with them.[7] The similarity and interchangeability of the words *khan* and *kam* for king and shaman in steppe history is a reflection of the near inseparability of religious and political power at that time. Powerful military leaders were considered spiritually gifted and powerful. Only a strongly spiritual individual would win in battle. Such strong leaders were usually men, but often on the steppe women possessed the same mixture of spiritual, military, and political power.[8]

Latin chroniclers described Attila the Hun as the *Flagellum Dei*, the Whip of God, sent to punish and scourge humanity. This description would later be applied to many steppe conquerors, including Genghis Khan and Tamerlane.

The steppe nomads did not think of themselves as land conquerors, because land, in their world, seemed nearly infinite. They conquered water, a much scarcer resource. They sought to control rivers and lakes and often called one another by the body of water near where they lived. Attila was the first of the Hun rulers to claim not just the Danube River but all the waters of the Earth. He considered himself ruler of everything within the great sea that surrounded the land. His name, *Attila*, meant something like Father of the Sea, derived from the same root as Turkish *talay* or Mongolian *dalai* for sea.[9] Roman chroniclers translated his name into Latin as *Rex Omnium Regum*, King of Kings,[10] and described him as "the lord of Huns, and of the tribes of nearly all Scythia . . . the sole ruler in the world." Attila named his son and successor *Tengis*, meaning "ocean" in Turkic and Mongolian.[11]

While the Huns left a vivid mark on world civilization, they could sustain little direct connection to their original homeland in Mongolia. Following their successful expansion, they were unable to maintain a united world empire, as a series of steppe confederations replaced one another through the millennium. After Attila died in 453, the Hun empire in Europe quickly dissolved. By this time the land they controlled in Mongolia had fractured into competing states, and gradually the Huns faded away, absorbed into many different tribes, nations, and empires. The Huns inaugurated the first imperial era on the steppe, and they lived on in myth and memory long after their eclipse.

༖

Sometime before the eighth century, a new lineage of Turkish khans began to unite the tribes around them from the center of the Khangai Mountains, the original heartland of the Hun nation. They built the first steppe city, their capital Kharbalgas, meaning Black City, near the Orkhon River.[12] Almost in reaction to the wandering ways of the Huns, the Turkish khans embraced an ideology of fierce isolation in their homeland, which they called Otukan (*Ötükän*).

The Turks became the first steppe people to record their history and ideas in wonderful detail. When Temujin left his sanctuary of Burkhan Khaldun, he found the steppe covered with Turkish inscriptions. Instead of lugging heavy books, scrolls, or tablets around with them from one camp to another, steppe nomads carved their messages on stones, thousands of which remain today scattered across the steppe, on the sides of cliffs, scratched into boulders, and carved into mountaintops.[13]

For centuries, preliterate hunters and herders had left their marks by laboriously carving images onto stones. We find illustrations of deer with elaborate antlers elegantly springing toward the sky, shamans beating drums and dancing in a trance, camels and horses pulling carts. Nearly life-size statues of people from earlier epochs graced the sacred landscapes of the steppe, buffeted by the elements, but respected by the tribes who fought in their wake.

Then, at about the sixth century, the old images gave way to written messages carved on stones in Chinese characters, Sogdian and Sanskrit script, or Turkic runes. For more than five hundred years before Temujin was born, these earlier nomads had been recording their ideas. The steppe nourished an ancient and hardy civilization that spoke in many languages with a loud and clear voice.

Many of the informal inscriptions boasted of a great hunt or offered a single phrase praising a beautiful horse, beloved person, or simply "O, my home," and "O, my land." Others commemorated the life and history of the area, and larger ones honored important leaders. The steppe people communicated with heaven through rocks and by carving inscriptions on the sides of mountains. The inscriptions had to be open to the light and sky and not hidden inside a building or buried in the pages of a book, as though they were shameful or secret.

The oldest official state-sponsored memorial appeared in the sixth century in Sanskrit, the sacred language of India, and Sogdian, a trade language related to Persian but written with a Semitic alphabet. This bilingual stone column was mounted on the back of a Chinese turtle-dragon figure, symbolizing the power and authority of the state. Moved from its original location and taken to the mountain town of Tsetserleg, the stone still stands serenely and majestically in the courtyard of a jewel-like Buddhist monastery that fortuitously escaped the socialist plague of destruction that eradicated many religious structures in Mongolia during the twentieth century. The stone was saved by the fact that it had been carried into a museum and turned into history, preserving a message that had survived fourteen centuries. The combination of Chinese, Indian, Persian, Turkic, and Semitic elements demonstrated the cultural complexity and pluralism flourishing on the steppe more than five centuries before Temujin's birth.

These first inscriptions were called "stones of law," *nom sang*, derived from the Greek word *nomos*, meaning law, and the Persian *sang*, for stone. The Mongols eventually adopted this phrase to mean "library," a meaning it still holds in the Mongolian language today.[14] The engraved words affirmed the sanctity of the khan, who sponsored the stones and attested to the blessing of history and the spirit world's approval of his rule. Without such support, the earth, sky, wind, or rain would have thrown down the monument, broken it, and buried it. The engraved words did not just represent the dictates of the state; they were "the great stone of law."[15]

Most of these stones appeared in the two centuries between 552 and 742, when a series of Turkic empires controlled large stretches of surrounding territory with their competing clans assuming and losing power in a sequence of short-lived dynasties. For a thousand years up until then, information about the steppe nomads came from their enemies. Beginning with the Turks, the steppe nomads recorded words about themselves.

Although the earliest stones erected by the Turkish khans were written in the Sogdian language, the Turks quickly began recording messages in their own language to convey the full complexity of Turkish life, culture, and thought. They wrote in Turkic runes, a simple alphabet of thirty-eight letters well suited to carving in stone or wood, in use on the Asian steppe centuries before the Vikings began writing with similar runes. The Turkic runes consisted of distinct letters, each of which looked very much like a horse brand, similar to ones that continued to be used in Mongolia until the modern era. The people called themselves the Sky Turks (Kök Türk), which they wrote in runes but in the Semitic fashion from right to left—ᚻᚤᚱᚼ ᚤᚿᚻ.

Temujin had found his whip near the Tonyukuk stone, whose text included the first written use of the name *Turk* by the steppe tribes. Tonyukuk, a general, offered a final record of his life and advice to future generations of nomads and their leaders, speaking directly through the stones: "*I, Tonyukuk,*" the inscription began with proud authority. The writing clearly identified the intended reader of the inscription: "You, my younger siblings and the children of my sisters and all my relatives," or "You, my Turkish people."

An inscription in stone, like all attempts to write history, should be approached with skepticism. Its author is eager to impose a particular point of view and to provide an account of events for contemporary and future generations. Inscriptions, whether political, religious, or personal, are made as a form of propaganda. Their creation is often accompanied by the destruction of rival messages carved in stone or wood. Inscriptions are intended to restrict the truth and confine knowledge to a single, highly staged image. They are often land deeds or other claims to property or glory, assertions of dubious rights, or boasting to God and humankind of the sponsor's meritorious deeds.

Yet despite the dubious credibility of what is presented as fact, such inscriptions reveal how people thought and what they valued. In choosing to exaggerate military deeds, acts of compassion, and declarations of love or of sexual conquest, the text reveals what the rulers valued most. What was omitted is always as important as what was included. Historical lies are still cultural truths. They tell us what the people wanted us to believe and what they feared, what they respected and what they despised or desired. The stones clearly exposed the ideals of the era.

Tonyukuk stressed the urgent necessity of tribal unity if his people were to prevail against the enemies perpetually surrounding them. "To bend a thing is easy while it is slender; to tear asunder what is still tender is an easy thing," he wrote. "But if the slender thing becomes thick, it requires a feat of strength to end it, and if the tender thing coarsens, a feat of strength is required in order to tear it asunder." By uniting, the tribes could become thick and more difficult to "tear asunder."

Of all the Turkic stones scattered across Mongolia, the two largest are close together on the Orkhon River, near Karakorum, where the Mongols eventually built their imperial capital. One stone from the year 731, during the Second Turkic Empire or Khanate, honors the life of the general Kultegin, and the other from 734 honors the life of his brother Bilge Khan. Together they had defeated the Tang dynasty's Emperor Xuan Zong in 721, an incredible achievement for a steppe tribe fighting against the largest military state in Asia.

These monuments were not mere historic markers; they consisted of large stone slabs more than twelve feet high, with carvings on four sides, planted within sight of one another at a distance of about half a mile. "Hear my words from the beginning to the end, my younger brothers, and my sons, and my folks and relatives, hear these words of mine well," commanded Bilge Khan, the emperor of the Turks. "A Land better than the Otukan Mountains does not exist!"[16] It is the center of the world, and who controls it has power over all. "The place from which the tribes can be controlled is the Otukan Mountains." The point is repeated for emphasis. "If you stay at the Otukan, and send caravans from there, you will have no trouble."

From the whole of humanity, the Sky had chosen the Turks to live in this ideal place where beautiful rivers watered the land and luxuriant steppes nourished the animals. The inscriptions explained that the First Turkic Empire had violated its destiny when the tribe chose to settle near the Chinese cities of the Tang dynasty, where the sweet foods and words seduced and enervated the nation. The Sky punished them by destroying their empire. Now with this second empire, the Turks once again had the opportunity to flourish in this place, the center of the world. The inscriptions affirmed that law extended beyond the customs of a particular tribe or the commands of an individual khan. Certain moral principles persisted no matter who ruled. The legal and religious ideology of the Turks was simple, direct, and carved into stone.

The stones evidenced belief in a powerful divine law that superceded any individual. As soon as people were created, "over the human beings, a supreme law was created," pronounces Bilge Khan's edict.[17] This law is known as *Toro* (*Törö*). The Turks identified themselves as the people of the law. The Mongols adopted the same concept and used a similar word: *tor* (*töre*). Despite regional difference in custom and language, all recognized a set of ultimate principles guiding life. To be civilized was to follow these moral principles, which are natural, divine laws, not man-made ones. *Toro* is close to the word for birth in Mongolian, suggesting that these principles are there from the moment the Universal Mother created life and at the moment of each person's birth into this world. They are part of the inner light born within each child that can be seen shining from an infant's eyes.

Juvaini, who lived among the Mongols near the Turkic stones for a year, examined them and attested to their importance to the Mongols. He described one occasion when new stones were found. "During the reign of the Great Khan [Ogodei], these stones were raised up, and a well was discovered, and in the well a great stone tablet with an inscription engraved upon it. The order was given that everyone should present himself in order to decipher the meaning."[18] That particular stone had been engraved in Chinese and could not be translated until they brought someone from China to do so.

Although some steppe tribes adopted elements of Christianity, Buddhism, and Zoroastrianism, the Sky Turks sternly rejected foreign religions along with other external influences.[19] Instead, the Turks developed their own national religion or state cult derived from their ancient animism, without priests or scriptures. They depended on shamans and soothsayers to communicate with their ancestors, to control the weather, predict the future, and commune with heaven. Unlike priests in other religions, shamans had no scriptures, and in a sense each shaman was a different religion, assembling a mélange of stories, rituals, clothes, and sacred objects in a highly idiosyncratic manner; the more unusual their spectacles, the more awe they inspired. What united them was their ritual of beating the drum, dancing, chanting, and going into trance. Theirs was a religion of action and motion, not merely of being or believing.

The messages on the official Turkish stones were more political than spiritual, encouraging the nomads to "follow the water and the grass" and to avoid the customs of the settled nations.[20] The Turkic stones offer a clear picture of the steppe as the center of the four sides of the world with the sun rising and setting to the east and west, the forest in the north, and the great Tang Empire to the south. The stones reveal important information about the people of lands far beyond their own, not only other Turks and the Chinese, but also

Tibetans, Avars, Kirgiz, Sogdians, and the people of distant Byzantium, which they called Rum.

The writers of the stones understood the temptation of foreign goods and foreign religious ideas, and they proclaimed this mortal danger to the steppe nomads. The messages repeatedly warned of straying away from the steppe and its way of life. The people should stay on the steppe, obey their khans, and worship the sky and earth.

Bilge Khan articulated a clear political and moral message beyond praising his Ashina clan and boasting of his power. He saw that the Turkic dynasty before him had been seduced by civilized life in China and, like the Huns who headed for Europe, they never returned.[21] And so he warned his fellow nomads to avoid sedentary civilizations. He warned them in clear terms of the demise of his Turk predecessors who went to live in China: "Your blood ran like a river, and your bones piled up like a mountain; your sons worthy of becoming lords became slaves, and your daughters, worthy of becoming ladies, became servants." The same sentiment was recorded later by another Turk who warned against contact with other civilizations. "When the sword rusts the warrior suffers, when a Turk assumes the morals of a Persian he begins to stink."[22]

Despite the vehement denunciation of all things foreign, the stone texts show clearly that the Turks had already absorbed many ideas from foreigners, particularly the Chinese and Sogdians. The early Turkic engravings displayed a sophisticated cosmography. Father Tengri ruled the heavens, Mother Umay ruled the earth, and the khan ruled the people. The primary spiritual force of the Turkic state was the Sky. Tengri was not a supreme God so much as a vast reservoir of spiritual energy that inspired and guided men by granting them power and fortune or denying them. The sky was an ocean of light and functioned like a giant spirit of the universe, animating humans by granting them a soul and a destiny. In the same manner that the Sky provided the destiny of animals and people, it granted tribes, clans, and nations their individual destinies.

According to some accounts, Tengri was a broader concept of the divine and not confined merely to the sky. The Islamic scholar Mahmud al-Kashgari, writing about the beliefs of the Turks (whom he called Infidels) around the year 1075, offered this view: "The Infidels—May God destroy them!—call the sky *Tengri*; also anything that is imposing in their eyes they call *Tengri*, such as a great mountain or tree, and they bow down to such things."[23]

The Turkic Tengri was the same heaven worshipped by Temujin as Tenger.[24] As a somewhat removed sacred presence in the universe, Tenger rarely intervened in daily affairs. It designated someone on Earth to manage the mundane affairs of the people, and this was the khan. People could discern the thoughts and words of the divine through the actions of their ruler. Tenger spoke to people only when it was necessary to reinforce the power of their designated khan. To explain why the Turks had suffered from such ill fortune in an earlier era, the inscription on Tonyukuk's memorial offered that heaven must have said: "I had given you a khan; but you abandoned your khan."[25] The text makes it clear that no person actually heard these words; Tonyukuk deduced this meaning based on the punishments the people had endured. It was the Will of Heaven, not the Voice of God.

The inscriptions carved into stones and dotted across the steppe display a fierce fatalism by a people resigned to a preordained destiny who felt no need to place a supernatural explanation on whatever happened. At death, one's mortal remains of bone and flesh rotted and the immortal part of the soul simply flew away or rose up to the sky. One may be tempted to think that the soul departed the body and went to heaven, but no such destination was stated. If the Turks of that time believed in an afterlife or in reincarnation, they did not reveal it through their written messages.

Life is simply life, and death is death. When Kultegin died in 731, his elder brother Bilge Khan recorded his grief. "I mourned. My eyes, which have always seen, became as if they were blind, and my mind which has always been conscious became as if it were unconscious." He voiced a simple message that became a persistent theme in steppe spiritual philosophy in the coming centuries: "Human beings have all been created in order to die." In facing such pain, the Turks had to look to their own disciplined minds for guidance. "When tears came from the eyes, I mourned holding them back, and when wails came from the heart, I mourned turning them back. I mourned deeply."[26] Despite Bilge Khan's demonstrable pain, there is no sense that heaven should or could have intervened in the life of a single person, not even a person as high ranking and important as the khan's brother. Precisely the same fatalism permeated the life and deeds of Temujin. Action was always more important than mourning or complaining.

History shows that nations often enjoy the richest luxuries and raise the most imposing monuments to themselves immediately before they fall. Rather than marking the height of Turkic imperial power on the steppe, the impressive Turkic monuments chronicled the end of their great empire, when rulers proclaimed their greatness through their words more than through their accomplishments. The boasts carved on the stones endured, but the empire of the ruling Ashina dynasty perished. Their former subjects, the Uighurs, rose up, overthrew them, and declared a new empire in the year 742 with the justification that the sacred land Otukan had withdrawn its blessing and abolished the charisma of its khan from the prior dynasty and bestowed it on the Uighurs. Over the coming centuries, descendants of these early Turkic tribes would found far greater empires in India and modern-day Turkey, but their heyday in Mongolia had ended.

Temujin could not read the inscriptions on the Turkish monuments, but in time he acquired followers who could. The important lessons of the Turkic rulers passed into the oral history and the lore of the steppe. Temujin was able to absorb many of these lessons and, just as important, to learn from their failures. These earlier Turkish rulers had been much more successful in creating an empire and in dealing with outside nations than the khans he had known, so he paid close attention to their messages. And yet he showed no compulsion to obey their instructions or commands.

Though interesting and important, the advice outlined on the stones was not to his mind part of the immutable law of the heavens. It offered temporary solutions to the problems of a particular situation. Temujin decided that he could pick and choose which piece of advice to accept and which to ignore. He agreed with the stones' spiritual teachings about Earth and the Will of Heaven and their injunctions about unity and the corrupting influence of cities, but he rejected their isolationism and antiforeign sentiment. In time, he came to believe that the steppe tribes could not have a good life without products and goods from distant places. He founded his empire on military strength and victory in battle, but to secure and expand it, he decided to encourage and facilitate trade.

The stones on the steppe and the experiences of the earlier Huns and Turks showed him two contrasting paths. Temujin searched for a new path between the total dispersion of the Huns across Eurasia and the stubborn but unrealistic isolation of the early Turks. He wanted to remain Mongol while conquering the world.

4

Conflicting Selves

Each person contains within them a multitude of selves, and within these various incarnations conflict and contradiction are inevitable. A certain part of one's character seems to be set at birth, but gradually, with the experience of life, new aspects emerge and compete for dominance. Such a struggle marks the beginning of an independent personality, as we choose the person we wish to become. The constellation of conflicting selves changes over time, with different selves struggling to the fore while older ones fade away or stubbornly cling to their former importance. In the midst of these converging and competing claims one can sometimes hear the voices of one's past, the phrases, stories, myths, and songs that the child learns and that remain in the adult as artifacts of an abandoned past.

Part of Temujin remained the bitter boy abandoned by the world, but over time, he also became the spiritual child of Burkhan Khaldun, the passionate and loyal friend of Jamuka, the aroused husband of Borte, the vengeful warrior who would not rest until he punished those who had tormented him or stolen from him. He had the pride of the self-made man of the steppe, but he recognized that others resented him as nothing more than a barbaric outcast hunting rats to survive. He became a resolute commander on the field and yet a hesitant and sometimes fearful head of family inside the *ger*.

His life unfolded as the struggle of these characters within him. How did a crying boy allegedly afraid of dogs become the indomitable conqueror of the world? Will the youthful, loyal lover of a girl of his age keep in check the rising conqueror with access to many women? Will loyalty to childhood friends dominate family needs? For Temujin, as for most of us, the rivalry within was often more significant than the outward strife.

ঌ

After the rescue of Borte around 1179, Temujin was not yet twenty years old but he was becoming his own man. In addition to having found the romantic love of his life in Borte, he appeared to have found in Jamuka an eternal ally. With the determined optimism of a youthful friendship, the two men undertook for the third time the *anda* ceremony of bond brothers. This time they were not boys trading knucklebones or adolescents exchanging arrowheads: they were men making a solid vow. Each tied a gold sash around the other's waist, and they exchanged horses. They swore to lead a single life and never abandon each other.[1] By performing the ceremony in front of their followers, they showed that their union was both political and personal. Jamuka later claimed that he had been conquered by Temujin's charisma.[2] The words of the *Secret History* are simple and unadorned: "When Temujin and Jamuka loved each other, they loved each other."[3]

The two young men feasted, drank, and slept together as sworn brothers under one blanket. Away from Burkhan Khaldun, Temujin became a herder as well as a hunter, and the two sworn brothers rode together at the front of their united band. For the first time in his life, Temujin had a boon companion. He was no longer struggling alone. At last he could create the family that fate had denied him. In addition to taking on Jamuka as his brother, Temujin acknowledged Ong Khan as his father. The Mongols refer to such an elective relationship as a "dry father" or a "son born with clothes"—in contrast to a natural son, who is born naked.

Temujin was simultaneously creating two new families. Sometime soon after the *anda* ceremony, probably in the winter of 1179–80, Borte gave birth to her first child, a son. Temujin named him Jochi, meaning *guest*. The name could have been given because Temujin and Borte were then living with Jamuka as a guest, but the choice was admittedly odd, and fed conflicting accounts of whether Temujin or Borte's kidnapper was the biological father. Although he was always one of his father's favorites, the controversy eventually prevented Jochi from being included in the line of succession. Remembering his own childhood, Temujin publicly and stubbornly embraced Jochi as his son. But families are sometimes easier to form than to sustain.

Within a year of Jochi's birth, the great love between Jamuka and Temujin began to grow cold. Borte described Jamuka as emotionally fickle and said, "he has grown tired of us."[4] Jamuka either grew bored of Temujin, or he sensed the beginnings of a rivalry. One day, after riding together in front of a long line of oxcarts and herd animals, Jamuka told Temujin to camp apart from him. He was treating Temujin like a younger brother or subordinate, rather than as his *anda*.

Bewildered and humiliated by this fall in status, Temujin consulted with his mother and wife. Borte, who seemed never to have liked Jamuka and resented his influence over her husband, strongly favored leaving Jamuka and striking out for a new grazing area far away. She recommended that they not pitch tents where Jamuka suggested but instead that the family keep moving all through the night to get as far from him as they could. Temujin agreed. In a dramatic move, he fled with his household and livestock through the whole night, accompanied by a few who chose on the spot to follow him, and later joined by some who deserted Jamuka to find Temujin.

With this break, eternal friends had become permanent rivals.

Over the next eight years, the rivalry between Jamuka and Temujin festered. Both were vassals of Ong Khan, but rather than controlling the animosity between his two subordinates, Ong Khan provoked it, favoring one and then the other, sometimes goading them against each other. Ong Khan needed both men to help him fight his many battles inside as well as outside his tribe. Jamuka and Temujin both remained loyal to Ong Khan, calling him father and defending him repeatedly when he might otherwise have lost power, but they competed against each other.

While Temujin and his warriors were away fighting on behalf of Ong Khan, his base camp had grown into a small nomadic town, moving with the seasons and the flow of events. In the winter of 1183, Borte gave birth to another son, Chagatai, and three years later, in the early winter of 1186, she had a third son, Ogodei, a sickly infant whom she nursed diligently until he became healthy and strong. Possibly because of his childhood illness, Ogodei would always be her favorite; indeed, he was destined to become the favorite of all the sons and ultimately his father's successor. By the time Borte gave birth to her third son, she was just over twenty-five, and Temujin about twenty-four. By modern standards, they were still quite young, but in a time when the majority of people would not reach age forty, they were a middle-aged couple with three growing children.

Temujin's small and frequently changing band of followers included an eclectic mix of individuals who had joined him willingly and some who had been taken as captives. They were a true amalgam of herders and hunters from many clans and tribes—Uriyankhai, Tatar, Tayichiud, Jalayir, Barulas, Olkhunuud, and Khongirad. They constituted a multiethnic cross-section of the steppe, and represented a mixture of spiritual and religious practices. Although heavily influenced by many of the major religions of surrounding civilizations, they combined their beliefs and practices with animist beliefs in whatever way they deemed appropriate. None of his followers, at this time, could be said to be a true adherent of a world religion in any modern sense—not Buddhist, Muslim, Taoist, or Christian—yet steppe society had assimilated elements of all these religions swirling around them.

Despite owing allegiance to Ong Khan, Temujin was not a Kereyid, and certainly not a Christian. He was not ethnically a part of their group, and the vain and somewhat arrogant Ong Khan did not seem to want his uncouth band of misfits and renegades to come too close to his more refined and aristocratic court. Better to keep them out on the frontiers fighting off the Tatars and other marauding bands. Temujin and his men were like watchdogs guarding the periphery of Ong Khan's territory.

Temujin wanted to be recognized as the chief of a band of follow-ers and not merely the leader of a border detachment of varied strays. When he asked Ong Khan for recognition as a khan, so that he could become the leader of his own tribe, Ong Khan agreed. At this time, around 1189, Temujin was about twenty-seven years old. He gath-ered his followers at Blue Lake, near the Black-Heart Mountain, not far from Burkhan Khaldun, and his people proclaimed him khan and swore allegiance to him. "If we disobey in battle, take away our property and our families," they swore. "If we disobey in peace, exile us and throw us out into the wilderness."[5]

Temujin's followers were divided into thirteen main camps, each with its own grazing areas and subsidiary camps. They were orga-nized into three units of ten thousand, but in total, he probably had fewer than thirty thousand people under him. The women ran the main camps and cared for the animals while the men were away fight-ing. Borte operated the central compound as a mobile headquarters; her ger became the tribal ordu, or court, because her husband was khan. His mother lived separately with his youngest brother and had her own court and her own people assigned to her care and leadership.

Sometime between 1190 and 1193, while her husband was out on campaign, Borte gave birth to her fourth and final son, Tolui. She now had four sons. Among Mongols, the youngest son was known as otchi-gen, the prince of the fire. While the older brothers were expected to roam far away and establish separate families, the youngest son would have responsibility for the care of his parents.

Temujin arranged a marriage for his sister Temulun, but when her prospective suitor offered fifteen horses for her, he became outraged. "To arrange a marriage and to discuss wealth is to behave like a merchant!" he exclaimed. He quoted one of the ancient sayings of the Mongols: "a meeting of the minds is made firm by mutual need." All he wanted through the marriage was loyal friendship. "What mattered wealth?"[6]

As the newly emerging khan, Temujin began slowly to create new laws. Initially his laws were simply the customs that he knew and thought best, but gradually they began to grow and change as he adapted to new situations. He formalized the organization of his military and his staff, designating responsibilities corresponding to each man's talents. "I appoint each of you to offices in different places," he proclaimed, and then he designated them cooks, quiver bearers, commanders, messengers, equerries, horse herders, and overseers of carts.[7] In most regards, his organization resembled a large household more than a nascent nation. Although each follower and staff member still belonged to a separate lineage and clan, they were now united as part of an emerging tribe, with a new, yet unnamed, identity—Temujin would not formally declare the Mongol nation for another fifteen years.

At his installation as khan, Temujin thanked heaven and earth for bringing him to this point in life, but no other religious ceremony is mentioned in the accounts. Ong Khan sent a message encouraging Temujin's followers to remain loyal, coupled with a not-so-subtle admonition that the new khan remain loyal as well. "Do not break your word. Do not break your bonds," he said. The steppe people frequently referred to their leaders as a collar, and he warned them, "Do not tear off your collar."[8]

Temujin thanked his followers for choosing him over Jamuka, but his ascension to the office of khan only stoked the rivalry between the two men. Temujin dispatched messengers to inform Jamuka of his new office. The message seemed intended as an invitation for Jamuka to recognize Temujin as his khan, one that he would not accept. Jamuka accused the messengers of provoking hostility between the two leaders. They were "poking the flanks, pricking the ribs."[9]

Soon the two Eternal Sworn Brothers were fighting each other again. The excuse was that one of Jamuka's "younger brothers" stole a horse herd from one of Temujin's men, who then went in pursuit of the thief and shot him with an arrow that "split apart his spine."[10] Under this pretext, each man rallied his troops and raced to battle.

Steppe warriors fought fiercely in battle, but they detested wanton cruelty. Mercy was valued as highly as valor. When the battle ended, the victors often adopted the children orphaned by the fight. But in his dealings with Temujin, Jamuka did not balance ferocity with charity. At one point, after unexpectedly defeating his rival, Jamuka followed his victory with a reign of terror, displaying unprecedented cruelty against his prisoners. He cut off the heads of some of Temujin's captured officers, and others he had boiled in large cauldrons.[11] Both forms of execution appalled the Mongols, not just for the grisly nature of the physical torture but also for their spiritual cruelty, for they believed that the soul would run out onto the earth through the spilled blood of the beheaded men and be eternally doomed. Similarly, by boiling the body, all the soul-bearing fluids—blood, bile, mucus, semen, and perspiration—were destroyed. Jamuka's cruelty suggested a deep desire for emotional retaliation against the man he had once loved.

The battle and its grisly outcome did not settle the matter of who would be the true leader of the Mongols. The rivalry grew sharper a few years later when, possibly at the urging of Ong Khan, Jamuka's supporters also proclaimed him khan. They gave him the title Gurkhan, an ancient and popular designation used by different groups at various times in steppe history. Now Ong Khan had two rival khans claiming leadership over his Mongol vassals, and he was mistakenly confident that he could balance the egos and ambitions of these two relentless rivals.

Despite Jamuka's victory over Temujin, more of his followers deserted him and came over to Temujin. One of those was Monglik, who had been sent to summon Temujin back from Borte's family when Yesugei had been killed. Monglik came with his seven sons to support Temujin. Soon after he began to live with Mother Hoelun and thereafter he was usually referred to as Father Monglik, giving him and his sons a special position within Temujin's growing tribe. Temujin later recalled the union with Father Monglik as "fortunate and happy," and promised to consult with him before making decisions every year and every month.[12] This would later prove an unfortunate choice of words.

𐌅

There were many greater dangers and more important enemies than Jamuka. For the next ten years Temujin, then in his thirties, and his fluctuating band of followers fought their way back and forth across the Mongolian steppe in never-ending feuds, raids, and battles in fragile alliances that were broken as easily and quickly as they were made. Most of these campaigns were in the service of the Kereyid ruler Ong Khan, but it became increasingly clear to Temujin that Ong Khan was an incompetent, petty, and avaricious leader with no goal beyond loot from the next raid. He was deceitful and often jealous of the success of his younger vassal.

The Kereyid's traditional enemies, the Tatars, still threatened from the east. Ong Khan organized a war against the Tatars, and Temujin led the army. He was tiring of fighting the same battles against the same enemies again and again. He would defend Ong Khan's interest in war, but after he won the battle, Ong Khan inevitably lost the peace, rekindling animosities with old enemies while making new ones.

Temujin began to act more independently, neglecting to consult Ong Khan or vet his actions with him. After defeating the Tatars in 1202, he held a meeting of his top men to decide how to avoid constant warfare with the Tatars. He chose to use two drastic and seemingly contradictory solutions to end the fighting with the Tatars permanently. To eliminate any future threat, he killed most of the men who fought against him, particularly their leaders. But he also incorporated many of the Tatars who had not been fighting against him into his tribe, including all the women and children.

By this time, Temujin was forty years old and he had been married to Borte for almost a quarter of a century. To cement the union of his tribe with the Tatars, he took Yesui, the youngest daughter of the defeated Tatar khan, as his wife, but at her urging he also agreed to marry her elder sister Yesugen. Borte took the news stoically. "One who is born a man takes both the older and younger sisters together," she said. "A caftan with two layers will keep you from freezing. . . . A rope with three strands does not tear."[13] The Tatar sisters never replaced Borte, but Yesui was to play an important role as a counselor in the future, and, much later in life, she became a mediating force among his contending children. Despite the fact that their new husband had destroyed their tribes and annihilated their families, the two women remained loyal to him throughout their lives.

In addition to marrying the two Tatar sisters, Temujin set an example for his people by adopting a son from a prominent Tatar family. He gave the boy, Shigi-Khutukhu, to his aging mother to raise. Hoelun would eventually have four adopted sons and an unknown number of such daughters as her son conquered and defeated ever more tribes. These adopted children remained fiercely loyal and eventually held high offices. Of them, Shigi-Khutukhu, the abandoned Tatar boy, was to play the most important role.

Large gaps occur repeatedly in the record during these early years. The *Secret History* offers special details and even intimate conversations at some points, and then suddenly the narrative breaks off with whole years passing without remark. The gaps could occur for many reasons, but at least some seem to have been intentional. Either information was deliberately omitted in the original, or the text was censored and edited by unknown hands during the later decades, when the Mongols ruled China. What would later Mongols not want us to know about Temujin's early years?

Whoever censored the document did not hesitate to leave a very detailed account of his killing his half brother or to spell out cases of contested paternity and adultery in the royal family. A hint of the missing chapters, however, was inadvertently provided in the first foreign report drawn up on Temujin and the Mongols. It was written by an ambassador from the Sung imperial court named Chao Hung, and his observations were transcribed during Temujin's lifetime. He provided his emperor with a thorough ethnographic overview of the Mongols and their recent history.

His observations and reporting are generally excellent (though he made a few notable errors), but he includes one story that can be found in no other source. He wrote that in his youth, Temujin "was taken prisoner by the Jin," referring to the Jurched, a Manchurian group then ruling northern China, and they "kept him as a slave."[14] This reputed enslavement occurred at a time when the Jin had attempted to wage a war of extinction against the Black Tatars, killing off the men and bringing the women and children to China as slaves. Even the poorest families in northern China reportedly had a few such slaves. Temujin may have been one such victim. Chao Hung maintains that through this experience, Temujin had an intimate understanding of the Jin court, and then describes him "fleeing home," indicating that he had not been freed, but had escaped.

The story of enslavement, while possibly true, seems difficult to explain in light of Temujin's later alliance with the Jin during his war on the Tatars. It was after this campaign that the Jin emperor awarded Temujin the military rank of *Jautau*, or pacification officer, in the border guard.[15] Temujin certainly knew a lot about Chinese life and culture, more than he would have learned from hearsay and lore alone. While he admired and later adopted many aspects of Chinese technology and administration, gathered Chinese advisers and engineers, and showed a special interest in Chinese spiritual traditions, he sustained a lifelong hostility toward the Jin dynasty and their allies the Tatars.

Although the Tatars had killed his father, Temujin never cited this as the reason for his hatred. Instead, he attributed his feelings to something that had occurred around the year 1150, more than a decade before Temujin's birth. At that time, Temujin's ancestors were ruled by Ambaqai Khan, and they had good relations with the Tatars. Ambaqai Khan took his daughter to them on the assumption that a marriage had been arranged with a Tatar man. Before he arrived, however, another group of Tatars, probably border guards for the Jin dynasty, captured him. Although he had committed no offense, it was said that someone in the area had recently murdered a messenger of the Jin emperor and Ambaqai had been seized as revenge. It seems a flimsy pretext. A more likely explanation is that for the first time in many generations the Black Tatars, as the Chinese called these steppe nomads who lived farthest north and had a reputation as the most savage of all the tribes, were beginning to unite, and Ambaqai was one of their leaders. An effort to make a marriage alliance with a Tatar could have begun a dangerous unification of steppe tribes against the Jin. Whatever the reason, the Jin officials wanted to be rid of him. Determined to expand their influence deeper into the steppe, they sought to exterminate any who refused to become vassals.

While in captivity, Ambaqai managed to send a message to his clansmen. "I have been seized by the Tatars," he said. Mongols often used specific poetic forms of alliteration and meter, similar to a limerick in English but much more serious in tone, to convey messages as exactly as possible in a way that could be easily memorized not only by the messenger but also by everyone who heard it. He used such a form to demand revenge:

> Until the nails of your five fingers
> Are ground down,
> Until your ten fingers are worn away,
> Strive to avenge me.[16]

The *Secret History* then falls silent, with no explanation other than that Ambaqai had been captured. For Mongols, the silence speaks louder than words. They know that Ambaqai suffered a horrendous fate beyond mere capture and imprisonment. Mongols felt a deep discomfort at the thought of mentioning the gruesome details of a death, for fear of summoning the injured party into the present, and so the account descended into ominous silence.

The Muslim chroniclers felt no such fear of gory details and seemed, in fact, to delight in them. Rashid al-Din, the great Persian historian, filled in some of the missing details.[17] He wrote that the torture of Ambaqai began when the executioners nailed him to a special frame commonly called a "wooden ass." Then he slowly died. Other accounts maintained that his executioners slowly peeled away his skin until he had been totally flayed, or they ordered death by a "thousand cuts," first chopping off his fingers and toes and then more small chunks of flesh until, finally, he mercifully died.[18] If true, this would explain his command to his descendants to wear away their fingers in pursuit of revenge. Whichever form of torture was used was also meted out to another of his male relatives who was captured about the same time. Usually, after an execution, the head of the victim was cut off and put on a pole in the market as a warning to all.

The winners joyfully exaggerate their victories, but the losers pick their sores, and, unable to move beyond the shame and anger of their loss, they use history to feed hatred. History nourishes the memory of past enemies and sharpens the hunger for revenge. Horrific as the story was, Ambaqai was only indirectly related to Temujin, and the events happened well before his birth. Furthermore, it was the two widows of Ambaqai Khan who had expelled Hoelun, Sochigel, and their children while making their spring sacrifice to their lost husband and other departed ancestors. What would make Temujin so determined to avenge the death of their husband? Unless some future scholar finds new Chinese or Persian records related to these events, the mysterious gaps in Temujin's youth will continue to haunt us and be filled with mere speculation.

Temujin's sons were growing up, and now he began a new phase in his political life. He recognized the value of marriage for making peace among tribes and creating lasting friendships and alliances, and he was ready to secure more formally his position of power. In a bold move, he proposed a dual marriage to his overlord: he offered to marry his son to Ong Khan's daughter and offered a bride from his family for Ong Khan's son.

Ong Khan refused. Temujin's lowly family was not worthy of such an honor as to marry into the royal clan of the Kereyid. In the early years, Temujin had served Ong Khan as a faithful vassal, as his "dry son." But Ong Khan treated him as little more than a mere convenience. Despite having risked his life repeatedly to help Ong Khan maintain power, Temujin remained a practical tool, nothing more. Temujin's success in battle and growing popularity among his followers only fueled Ong Khan's disdain. Thus far, he had been faithful to his lord, but as his power and confidence grew, the justification for remaining loyal began to wither.

Ong Khan grew increasingly suspicious of Temujin's ambition and popularity. Having himself overthrown the ruler of his tribe, he knew all too well that today's seemingly loyal subordinate could become tomorrow's usurper. His sniveling son Shiremun resented the Mongol upstart's military success and popularity and fed his father's paranoia. Pétis de la Croix described Shiremun as "one of those obstinate Persons, who when they have taken a thing into their heads to believe or do are not to be convinced of their Error."[19]

In the end, after so many years of service, Ong Khan betrayed Temujin and tried to kill him. He justified his plot by saying it was the correct path, using the same word—*arga*—that the old women had used when they had expelled Temujin's family from the tribe.[20] Temujin gathered his loyal followers and told them that the time had come to revolt against Ong Khan. According to Pétis de la Croix, he made a religious appeal to his followers for the first time: "Knowing the Power Religion has over the People's Minds, he finished with assuring them that this important Enterprise which he now proposed to them, proceeded not from himself alone, but that the Almighty had inspired him with these Thoughts, and sent him to deliver them from the heavy Yoke of Slavery."[21]

As Temujin prepared for revolt, many of the Kereyid deserted Ong Khan. Even the old khan's younger brother Jaqa Gambu joined Temujin's side.[22] After a protracted and difficult struggle, Temujin defeated Ong Khan and his bumbling son, both of whom fled from the battlefield and died. As the chronicler Bar Hebraeus wrote, in an effort to explain the defeat of a Christian king by a non-Christian: "God took away the kingdom and gave it to one who was better than he; and his heart became right before God."[23]

Temujin decided not to decimate the Kereyid as he had done to the Tatars. Instead, he encouraged liberal adoption and intermarriage between his followers and the defeated enemy. He accepted Ong Khan's entire guard, the Torguud, as his own personal guard, in recognition of their unswerving loyalty to their defeated lord. Instead of breaking up families and destroying clans as he had done with the Tatars, Temujin initially allowed a majority of the Kereyid to stay together as a tribe and remain in their traditional territory.

News of Ong Khan's defeat rippled across the steppe and eventually reached Europe. Until this time, no one outside of the Mongolian Plateau had taken any notice of the Mongol warrior unifying the tribes on the steppe and the constant warfare surrounding him. The news carried not because of his success, but because he had defeated the most distant king then known to the Western world. It tapped into a long-held hope in Europe that a Christian king from Asia would invade the Islamic world from the east and destroy the relatively new religion. Some western Christians hoped Genghis Khan might be that king.

This dream dated back to the twelfth century, when a letter, a forgery that may have been sent by Crusaders seeking more commitment from their Christian brethren, arrived in Europe with a romantic tale of a rich and powerful Christian kingdom in Asia.[24] In every generation, it seemed that a new king in a different location was hailed as the possible savior of the Christian world. This mythical Christian king, sometimes called Prester John, sometimes King David, was thought to be a direct descendant of the three kings who had come from the East to honor Jesus at his birth.

It did not take long before the Christian ruler Ong Khan became identified as the mysterious Prester John. Not knowing who had defeated him, the Crusaders hoped that this new conqueror might turn out to be another, even more powerful, Christian king. No one had yet heard the name Temujin or his future title, Genghis Khan. It would be another generation before the Europeans understood the truth about the Mongols, at which point they would switch their focus from Asia to Africa and pin their hopes on the Ethiopian emperor of Abyssinia.

☫

Once Temujin had incorporated the Kereyid tribe into his own, his erstwhile brother and enemy Jamuka joined the Naiman, a confederation of eight tribes in central and western Mongolia. Their aging Christian king Tayang Khan both feared Temujin and resented his success. To the Naiman, long established as a power comparable to the Tatars and Kereyid to the east, the Mongols were savage upstarts. Tayang referred to the Mongols as "these people with their quivers" and asked mockingly, "do they now want to rule themselves?" With the urging of his family, he planned a preemptive strike against them before the Mongols grew too strong. "Let us go and bring here those few Mongols," he said, hardly realizing what he was up against.

The Naiman queen cautioned him to reconsider. "What could we do with them?" she asked. She then answered her own question by saying that the Mongols were too wild for almost any task. They smelled bad and wore dirty clothes. Even if she wanted to use one of their women to milk her animals, she would make them "wash their hands" before touching one of her sheep or cows.[25]

Tayang Khan gathered an army, but he soon lost his bravado. Having seen the Tatars and the Kereyid fall to the new vigorous conqueror, the Naiman khan defeated himself before the battle began. He trapped himself and the major part of his army on a mountain, thinking it impregnable, but when Temujin covered the steppe with hundreds of campfires at night, he made the Naiman think that he had raised an army far larger than he actually had. The Naiman warriors deserted during the night, many of them dying by falling and pushing one another as they descended the mountain in a panic.

Unable to hold his army and filled with resignation at the transitory meaninglessness of everything, Tayang Khan's words seem as much a curse as an epitaph. "Life dies," he sighed. His words echoed those inscribed on the Turkic monuments nearly four hundred years earlier, "A body suffers. It is the same for all."[26] During Temujin's attack the next morning, Tayang Khan was killed. After the quick Mongol victory, the defeated khan was buried on the mountain where he made his strategic mistake and lost his kingdom.

Temujin had barely finished with the Naiman when he made a final strike against their remaining ally, the Merkid, whom he had first fought after they kidnapped Borte. He quickly crushed them, executed many of their leaders from the aristocratic lineage, and then incorporated the majority of the Merkid into his tribe. He divided them and placed them under the command of many different leaders, so that they could not form a united faction in any one territory, but he allowed them to keep their Merkid identity. They became loyal followers and played important roles in the future empire.

By 1204 Temujin, now in his forty-second year, had annihilated the three tribal confederacies surrounding him—Tatar, Kereyid, and Naiman—as well as most of the smaller tribes. For the first time since the fall of the Uighur Empire nearly five centuries earlier, one man ruled the entire Mongolian steppe. He controlled the entire Turkic homeland, the ruins of ancient cities, and the heart of what had once been a great nomadic civilization.

Now that he held total power over the steppe, Temujin took revenge on some of those who had betrayed him early in life. He captured two of the men who had first abandoned his mother and siblings
on the steppe. After thirty years, rage still gnawed at his heart. The
teeth in his soul had grown stronger and sharper, particularly against
his uncle. "I will wipe him from my sight," he declared.[27] He then
condemned both men to death for having violated the sacred principle of loyalty to kinship.[28]

With the fall of all three tribal empires on the steppe and the execution of those who had betrayed him, only Jamuka remained at
large. One by one, he had lost almost all of his followers, and finally
the few who remained turned on him and took him captive to Temujin. In 1205, after a public trial, Temujin ordered the execution of
Jamuka and of the men who betrayed him. He had killed one brother
to assert his dominance over his family and his future. Now he had
overthrown the man he had called father and executed another whom
he had loved as his brother. No one remained to dispute Temujin's
rule over all the tribes on the Mongolian steppe.

PART II

Becoming Genghis Khan

Genghis Khan invented himself from the page of his own mind.

~*Ata-Malik Juvaini*, The History of the World-Conqueror,
Baghdad, thirteenth century

5

Messenger of Light

I n the nearly twenty-five years he spent consolidating the steppe
tribes and bringing them under his leadership, Temujin had encountered no khan worthy of imitation, no successful ideal to
follow, no contemporary heroes who could compare with the near
mythical glory of the ancient Hun and Turkic khans. He had seen
little to emulate in the courts of Ong Khan and Tayang Khan, but the
one thing that had caught his attention was the importance of writing. It enshrined laws and seemed to offer both a connection to the
past and the promise of future recognition. Led by the desire to create
a writing system for his emerging nation, Temujin ended up connecting the Mongols to one of the most unusual cultural and religious
traditions in the world. It would play a crucial role in the political and
spiritual orientation of his future empire.

Modern Uighurs live in western China, are Muslims, and write
their language in a script derived from Arabic; but much earlier the
Uighurs had lived in Mongolia, had followed the Manichaean religion,
and had written in an alphabet derived from ancient Syriac. They had
presided over the third and final Turkic empire on the steppe, from 744
until their defeat and flight to China in 840. Unlike the purely nomadic

Mongols, the Uighurs had built cities on the edge of the steppe and introduced agriculture in the river valleys, while never abandoning the long-standing practice of herding. By 1204, when Temujin acquired their former territory from the Naiman, their cities were little more than ruins, but Uighur civilization lived on, preserved by those who had chosen not to flee after the ravaging of their land, and by their written language. The abandoned ruins of the former Uighur capital at Kharbalgas, on the Orkhon River, were at once majestic and mysterious. The first Hun Empire had originated here, and later it was where the Turks had built their first steppe city.

Though small compared with cities in China, the Uighur city nonetheless accommodated the full array of cosmopolitan life, with a temple, palace, citadel, monastery, and market as well as a massive city wall and monumental gates. The Uighurs dug irrigation ditches, planted gardens and orchards, built warehouses, and worked to turn the inhospitable terrain of the icy plateau into agricultural land extending for a month's walk in every direction. Whereas the prior Turkic Empire had sought to shut out all foreign influence, the Uighurs forged a strong diplomatic and military alliance with the Tang dynasty of China. The Chinese emperor recognized their unique military skills, which he credited to their upbringing in the harsh Mongolian climate: "Severe frost reveals the strongest pine; harsh wind reveals the toughest grass."[1]

Not wanting to depend solely on an alliance with one foreign power, the Uighurs vigorously pursued close commercial connections with the Sogdians, descendants of the ancient Persians who now lived and traded around the city of Samarkand in what is today Uzbekistan. The Sogdians once controlled a great empire in Central Asia, and had sent caravans into China and all along the Silk Route to Constantinople long before the birth of Christ. The Sogdians had been conquered by Alexander the Great in 327 BC and thereafter incorporated Greek words, beliefs, and philosophy into their culture.[2] They blended Hellenic culture with Persian traditions and

Indian influences and transported their sophisticated hybrid to the Mongolian steppe. Through the centuries, they had been stripped of most of their political power, but they had endured as an ethnic group of merchants operating an elaborate mercantile network connecting China and Central Asia through a string of oases and routes leading south to India and west to the Middle East. While China had a fully developed civilization, with everything from an army and royal courts to manufacturing and massive engineering projects, the Sogdians were a remnant of a civilization with few institutions of state and no nation to call their own.

For centuries, the Sogdians had trudged back and forth across the desert with their camel caravans. "Then come the merchants," wrote an eleventh-century Turkic observer, "they never rest from trading and seeking a profit." Despite the implicit criticism, he quickly went on to acknowledge their value: "They provide all sorts of silken stuffs, and all the world's rare and wondrous things. . . . If there were no merchants roaming the world, when could you ever wear a black sable lining? If the China caravan ceased to raise dust on the roads, how could these countless kinds of silks arrive? If the merchants did not travel around the world, who could ever see a string of pearls?"[3]

The Chinese maintained a harsher, and much more suspicious, perspective on the Sogdians, particularly the merchants who were their rivals, and resented their constant search for goods of the highest quality at the lowest price. "Sogdian children get rock sugar in their mouth at birth," wrote one Chinese critic, "so that when they grow up they can talk sweet." They were similarly inculcated to a life of greed: "Glue is pasted in their palms so that money received would never leave their hands."[4]

Despite these objections, the Sogdians were acknowledged by their critics to be highly literate as well as numerate, and they had produced an ancient and sophisticated culture, literature, and religion. "They roam the world for a living, while they keep mind and heart devoted to God," wrote a Muslim observer.[5] The pious

Sogdian merchants also acted as missionaries, spreading their faith as they traveled.

Through their contact with many different religions, the Sogdians followed varied faiths and maintained commercial ties with all of them, but most adhered to what they called the Religion of Light; history has called them Manichaeans after the name of their prophet, Mani. Today in English and many other languages, *Manichaean* is a derogatory word, referring to a narrow-minded division of the world into good and evil. The name is generally applied as an insult to people with a simple vision of right and wrong, and is closely related to *Machiavellian*, with which it is sometimes confused. Recently it has been commonly applied to religious fundamentalists of all types and to Muslim terrorists in particular as well as loosely to any type of political, religious, or business activity deemed unscrupulous, devious, or evil. Yet originally, the Manichaeans were a vibrant, albeit highly unusual religion.

Mani was born in the third century near Baghdad to a Persian family belonging to a small Jewish sect that practiced baptism. He received his first prophetic vision as a child and wrote several books of scriptures, which survive in some long but incomplete texts as well as numerous fragments. Dissatisfied with the religion of his birth, Mani sought to combine the major religions around him into one. He believed that God first appeared in human form in Persia as the prophet Zoroaster, was reborn as the Buddha in India and Jesus in Israel before finally taking the form of Mani. His followers worshipped all of these divine incarnations and believed that the divine spirit appeared in different lands to teach in various languages. In addition to combining elements from India, Persia, and Israel, Mani considered the teachings of Greek philosophers to be divinely inspired.

Mani presented his philosophy in the *Shabuhragan*, the *Book of the Two Principles*, the only work he wrote in Middle Persian. Although he dedicated the book to the Sassanid Persian shah Shapur I, his teachings did not succeed in converting the shah, and his creed, while popular, never became an official state religion in Iran. He wrote his other works in Syriac, a language closely related to Hebrew and to Aramaic, the language of Jesus.

According to Mani, the universe originally consisted of pure light, spirit, and wisdom. All that was good was set apart from the material world of darkness and evil, but evil managed to seduce light and the two became mixed. Everything spiritual was good and part of the world of light; everything material, including the human body, was wicked and part of the world of darkness. Mani taught his followers to separate the divine spirit within them from the darkness of the material world. His goal was to allow humanity to reenter the light by abandoning earthly desire, including sex and the eating of meat. His was a harsh and unequivocal portrait of a world in which evil is personified as a malevolent spirit that "scorches, he destroys . . . and he terrifies. He flies on wings of air. He swims with fins as in water. And he crawls like a being of Darkness. . . . Poisonous springs gush from him, and he exhales fog; his teeth are like daggers."[6]

Although Persia boasted a history of religious tolerance in long-ago epochs such as the rule of Cyrus the Great in the sixth century BC, by the time of Mani, the religion of Zoroaster dominated and its leaders recognized Mani as a major threat. The Zoroastrian priests urged Shah Shapur to stamp out Mani and his heresy. The shah attempted to comply, declaring Mani and his teachings "useless and pernicious," chaining him up for nearly a month and then executing him just before springtime of the year 274.[7]

Mani and his followers had sought to unite all religions; instead, they incurred the fury of the older faiths, as the leaders of each religion portrayed their beliefs and practices as totally comprehensive and perfect and therefore not needing to be augmented by foreign ideas. A ninth-century Arab chronicler denounced the Religion of Light as "even worse than Christianity."[8] Dislike turned to persecution at the beginning of the fourth century, when the Roman emperor Diocletian outlawed the followers of Mani completely. "We order that the authors and leaders of these sects be subject to severe punishment," he wrote in his decree of March 31, 302. Manichaean worshippers "together with their abominable writings" were condemned to be "burnt in the flames."[9] This repression intensified in the fifth century when the Manichaean Augustine of Hippo denounced his faith and converted to Christianity. Augustine wrote vehement theological condemnations of the Religion of Light and charged its adherents with immorality. Although Augustine did not go so far as to call for a crusade against them, the newly powerful Christian hierarchy quickly turned his philosophical disagreement and charges of crime into grounds for vicious persecution.

And yet each round of martyrdom caused the fleeing Manichaeans to spread their ideas ever farther, as they were driven out of Europe, Africa, and the Middle East. Their faith spread throughout Asia all the way to India and across China, where they sometimes were absorbed into other religions and even when tolerated often received scorn, as in the Chinese description of them as disgusting "vegetarian demon worshippers."[10] Their final refuge was on the Mongolian steppe in Kharbalgas, one of the most remote cities on the continent. Here at last they found support among the Uighurs, and for the first time in their long history, a government not only tolerated their presence but also accepted them as the official religion of the court and nation.

By the time Temujin was born, the Manichaean religion had been circulating on the steppes for more than four centuries. While the nomads never followed Manichaean restrictions regarding meat and sex, many of the ideas about light, the sun, and water had so saturated traditional culture that it was nearly impossible to ascertain which ideas originated where. Manichaean cosmology and theology blended seamlessly with traditional steppe spirituality. Like the Huns before them and the Mongols after them, the Uighur nomads had a profound spiritual connection to light. Dawn is the most sacred moment of the day. The sun rising over the expansive and nearly tree-less and cloudless steppe casts a special light across the land as it reflects off small patches of ice or snow in the winter and makes the grass shimmer like gold in the summer. The daily miracle of warmth and light is honored in hymns to the morning sun. Even today, Mongols frequently emerge from their warm *gers* at sunrise to stretch out their arms in respect and to sprinkle milk in the four directions in appreciation as they soak in the sun when its golden rays impart the purest blessing.

"Let the people accept the Religion of Light," read the stone edict of the Uighur khan recorded in 763. The inscription commanded the Uighurs to abandon their barbarous customs so that they may "change into one people," and "let the state where men kill be transformed into a kingdom where good works are encouraged."[11] The Uighur khan proudly proclaimed that he had chosen this unusual foreign religion as a means to unite his people.

Once ensconced in power, these somewhat puritanical and intolerant Manichaeans destroyed many of the images and much of the shamanic paraphernalia revered by the Uighurs.[12] While they had incorporated older classical religions and Greek philosophy, they had no room for the animistic practices of the steppes. The traditional family worship of the fire under control of the elder women had to compete with new ideas of fire worship coming from Zoroastrian practices also introduced from Persia by Sogdian merchants. The Manichaeans explained their religion using precisely the same words that the Turkic tribes had been using for centuries: God was Tengri, and now to this they added the name of the old Zoroastrian god Ahura Mazda, which they eventually pronounced in Mongolian as Qor-Muzda or Khormusta.

☞

While most religions depend largely on a single sacred language—such as Sanskrit, Hebrew, or Arabic—the Religion of Light taught that wisdom came at different times in different languages. "Wisdom and deeds have always from time to time been brought to mankind, by the messenger called Buddha to India, in another by Zoroaster to Persia, in another by Jesus to the West," proclaimed Mani in his sacred script. "Thereupon this revelation has come down, this prophecy in this last age, through me, Mani, messenger of the God of truth to Babylon." Mani believed that worshipping in different languages was as important as being able to sing songs with more than one note.[13] "The religions of the ancients were in one land and one language," he said, "but my religion is such that it will be manifest in all lands and in all languages and will be taught in distant lands."[14]

In this newly introduced worldview, water, wind, and light constituted the primary substances of life. The Manichaeans borrowed an ancient Babylonian idea that the earthly sphere was the "ocean of water" and the heavenly was the "ocean of light," where the God of Knowledge lived.[15] The Uighurs commonly referred to their religion as the World Ocean—*Thalassa* in Greek, *Samudra* in Sanskrit, *Tengis* in Turkic, and *Dalai* in Mongolian—as it combined the rivers of all prior religions into one great sea. In a deliberately synergetic effort to unite all religions of the world, the Uighurs compared their Manichaean beliefs to the great World Ocean into which all rivers or knowledge flow.[16] The World Ocean was believed to represent purity, knowledge, power, and peace, and actual treasures from the ocean, such as pearls and coral, were thought to embody the supernatural power of the ocean itself.

Despite the theological appeal of their teachings, Manichaean monks and nuns maintained a bizarre style of life. They strove to eat only food that they designated as filled with light. Water in flowing rivers and streams sparkled with light that passed into the person drinking it, but well water came from deep within the earth and held only darkness, so they argued that humans should avoid drinking it. Green plants, fruits, and vegetables grown above the ground absorbed light, but roots and tubers grown beneath the ground had none and should thus be shunned. They ate fruits, vegetables, and the leaves of plants, but avoided onions, garlic, carrots, radishes, and other underground parts. They refused to eat meat because it did not grow in the sunshine and therefore had no light to offer. They liked grapes but shunned wine because the light was pressed out of the grapes to create wine. The Manichaeans preferred green and yellow vegetables, which they considered to be the ones with the most light. They also ate seeds. In keeping with their belief that a plant has a soul, they thought that seeds contained millions of souls. Consuming these souls filled the person with light and helped to concentrate the souls together and thus move toward the ultimate concentration of all souls in one light-filled entity.

The Manichaean religion of the Uighurs was cloaked in mystery and ceremony. The priests told magical stories of gods and men in faraway places. Where Jesus spoke in parables, Mani trafficked in veiled allusions. One of his scriptures quotes Jesus, who in the Uighur tradition was called Jesus Burkhan, as saying that to "save you from death and destruction . . . I shall give you what you have not seen with the eye, have not heard with the ears and have not touched with the hand."[17] Only the highest officials claimed a full understanding of the religion and its guarded rituals. Because of their emphasis on secrecy, the Manichaeans were known as Gnostics, from the Greek *gnosis*, for knowledge, which became *bilig* in Uighur and Mongolian.[18]

The Religion of Light combined practices and ideas from other religions, but it strictly forbade some important ones such as the Christian rite of baptism, the Jewish ritual of circumcision, and the Buddhist rite of cremation. Despite the demand for celibacy, the Manichaeans did not approve of castration as practiced voluntarily by some Christians or imposed as punishment by others to create eunuchs as servants.

Mani also forbade the ritual bathing prescribed by Hinduism. He taught that entering any body of water was a sin, because it polluted the living water on which all life depended. Fire can purify itself and all that it touches, but water is vulnerable and can be easily polluted.

In a document known as the Cologne Manichaean Codex, the story is told of a man about to enter a river to wash himself who is rebuked by the soul of the water, which asks him, "Is it not enough that your animals injure me, but do you yourself also mistreat me without reason and profane my waters?" The man replies, "Fornication, defilement, and impurity of the world are thrown into you and you do not refuse them, but are you grieved with me?" The water reminds the man that he is supposed to be righteous and above such foul acts. Another time he is admonished that people and the water are one, and what we do to one drop of water we do to the whole ocean.[19]

Only members of the religious elect had to abide by the strict rules of chastity and vegetarianism, abstinence from alcohol and fermented foods, and the prohibition of roots and tubers or parts of plants cultivated underground, where there was no light. These rules did not apply to aristocrats or to the common people.

The elect dressed in white robes and wore white turbans to show their purity; white thus became the symbolic color of their religion. By contrast, Buddhism became known as the Yellow Religion and Christianity as the Black Religion because of the color of the robes worn by their priests. Muslims were identified as people of the turban. The white robes of the Manichaean priests indicated that they performed no type of work that involved dirt. Unlike shamans, who participated actively in daily life, Manichaean priests formed a class apart from the ordinary people. Later, when Temujin formed his own government, he appointed shamans in similar white robes as his spiritual counselors.[20]

The priests' authority over the Uighur populace came not just from the power of their ideas and the appeal of their public rituals but also from their power to tax. In addition to the annual tribute to the khan, used to fund the state and military, the people now had to pay a new tax called the "soul service" specifically for the operation of the monasteries and care of the clergy. To enforce compliance, the Uighur khan revived an ancient steppe military tradition, organizing the people into units of ten. He further ordered that one person out of every group had to attend to the spiritual welfare and proper conduct of the others.[21] The soul monitor served as a spiritual teacher, ideological police, and religious tax collector, forcing people to pay required alms and fees to the church and reporting on sins and misdeeds.[22]

Temujin ultimately rejected the idea of a religious tax, but he adopted the underlying social principle, organizing his military into units of ten and putting one man in charge of each unit. These tens were in turn organized into larger units of one hundred, one thousand, and ten thousand, giving the Mongol army a precise decimal organization. Animals were also counted in clusters. To count sheep, cows, goats, horses, yaks, and camels separately was too cumbersome, so the Mongols came up with a simple unit based on the horse. Five goats or sheep equaled one horse. Five cows or yaks counted as four horses, and four camels as five horses. Thus, all the animals could be combined and reduced to one number.

The Uighurs were by one account "strong and invincible" because "the differences between the Princes and the people were not very great."[23] But Mani believed in the existence of a superior elite, and he deliberately omitted references to the egalitarian ideas in the teachings of Buddha, Jesus, and other religious leaders. He taught that a small minority, the elect, had superior qualities to the masses, and he believed this small superior group should rule the others. As the Uighur state grew powerful and its leaders became more involved with the Manichaean religion, elite families yielded to the temptations of this philosophy that justified, in their opinion, whatever they wanted. Confusion over the real meaning of the scriptures (in part deliberately obscure) offered them an excuse to indulge themselves in ways that Mani had never intended.

The Uighur ruler built splendid palaces filled with imported luxuries, fine clothes, sweet foods, coral, and turquoise. "The women had powder, color for their eyebrows, and clothes decorated with embroidery."[24] Such luxuries were "made in China," and their import created a decisive "break with barbarian customs."[25]

As history affirms, decadent societies can persist for a long time until some unexpected incident causes their demise. That fate befell

the Uighurs in the deadly winter of 839, when a severe blizzard resulted in mass starvation of the animals—a phenomenon known as
the "white famine." Disaster for one is often opportunity for another.
With the Uighurs temporarily impaired by the famine, the Kirgiz
from the Yenisei River in Siberia poured into Mongolia by the tens of
thousands to pillage. The Kirgiz killed the Uighur khan and his family, and for more than five years they ravaged the land, looted the
temples, burned the cities, stole the animals, and enslaved the people.

At the end of their wave of destruction, the Kirgiz did not create a
new empire, rebuild the city, or install another dynasty. Instead, they
began to drift away from the devastated nation, taking with them
whatever they wanted and searching for new lands to plunder. As the
ash and dust settled over the burned-out temples and palaces, a few
survivors crawled out of the ruins, abandoned their former cities, and
wandered out into the steppe to find a new life. Some fled south across
the Gobi to Turpan, Hami, and other oases along the Silk Route in
western China, where their Uighur descendants remain today. Others
joined the migrating nomads, abandoned their urban civilization, and
followed the herding life that had flourished for millennia.

Not all Uighurs fled, and not every Kirgiz moved on. Some of
them remained behind to form new tribes on the steppe. Their descendants sometimes returned to the site of the old cities to graze their
goats and horses among the ruins, lean against the walls of the old
temple, or climb atop the ruined mound of the former citadel to look
out over the steppe in the hopes of spotting a missing animal or
friendly *ger*. As Manichaean Uighurs joined other tribes, they en-
riched their new neighbors' traditional animistic beliefs by adding a
new layer of spiritual practices.

Temujin understood one clear message from the Uighur civilization:
for an empire to become successful, it needed a system of writing. He
recognized that the first step in transforming his band of nomadic

warriors and their followers into a nation was to introduce writing like the Chinese and the Turkic empires, but at first, it was not clear which type of writing he should adopt. Although the Mongolian language was closely related to Turkish in grammar and vocabulary, the original practice of writing with runes had already fallen out of fashion. Sanskrit, also used on some stones, was too remote and incomprehensible. Chinese characters required extensive familiarity with the Chinese way of life and thought, making them difficult to adapt to other languages. Temujin's highly unusual choice of a script proved to be one of the most important and enduring ways in which he shaped the future culture of his emerging empire.

Suddenly, by one command, Mongolian became a written language. The Mongols called their new form of writing *Uighur* script because the clerks spoke the Uighur language, but they were actually connecting themselves to a wealth of past civilizations. Uighur writing was derived from the Sogdian alphabet, based on ancient Syriac and related to Aramaic as well as to Hebrew and Arabic, which were written from right to left. To further complicate things, the Uighurs and Mongols turned the alphabet vertically, writing their sentences from top to bottom in the Chinese style. Their writing system drew on roots from Asia to Europe, and in this way it brought a cosmopolitan flair to steppe life. The Chinese ambassador Chao Hung from the Sung court described it as resembling Chinese musical notes for the flute.[26]

"Chinggis Khaan" in Mongol script.

This hybrid script became the Mongols' new window on the world and a prized link to history. Unlike the Sky Turks' attempt to reject foreign influences, the Uighurs had welcomed them, but they picked precisely which foreign elements to incorporate into their culture. Temujin recognized in the Uighurs the kind of society he wished to make for the Mongols. But he wanted his empire to be larger and longer lasting. He set out to learn the secrets of Uighur success and, just as important, the lessons taught by their failures.

In 1204, two years before the official founding of the Mongol nation, Temujin adopted a clerk by the name of Tata Tonga from the Naiman court and instructed him to adapt the Uighur alphabet to the Mongolian language.[27] Tata Tonga recruited other scribes into the thus-far quite small Mongol court and began tutorials for the younger men, including Temujin's sons and his adopted Tatar brother Shigi-Khutukhu. These seemingly small steps were to have profound ramifications in the coming decades as the clique around Temujin transformed into an imperial court. With each future victory on the battlefield, the number of scribes increased as men literate in other languages and cultural traditions were added to the administration. They grew from a simple corps of clerks into language schools that gathered clusters of intellectuals trained in philosophy and literature from rival religions and contrasting intellectual traditions. From this meager beginning would emerge a group of steppe scholars, a sort of new intelligentsia that would become increasingly important in the decades ahead.

By choosing the Uighur script and the chancellery practices associated with it, Temujin accepted the world's first and only Manichaean state as a model for his emerging nation and gave his formerly illiterate tribe access to the civilizations of the world. Juvaini wrote somewhat snidely that the Mongols "consider the Uighur language and script to be the height of knowledge and learning."[28] The Uighurs may have been peripheral players on the world stage, but the Mongols suddenly enjoyed access to information about Sogdian business practices, Chinese philosophy, Turkish literature, Hebrew scriptures, Greek history, Hindu mathematics, Persian fairy tales, and the major precepts of the great religions.

The abundance and variety of new influences can be seen in some of the words introduced into the Mongolian language by means of the new script: *crystal, sugar, candy, alcohol, steel, crown, dagger, soap, pomegranate, parrot, chess, diamond, emerald, book, bell, fig, and jewel.*[29] The Uighur script also brought in new terms for dealing with the larger world and for creating a government with words such as *sang*, signifying a warehouse or storehouse but quickly expanded to mean treasury and finance. With the increased vocabulary came knowledge of a different way of life.

Temujin absorbed some Manichaean religious laws directly into his legal code, such as the protection of water. Both Christian and Muslim observers later expressed bewilderment and disgust at Mongol laws concerning water, particularly those forbidding the washing of people or clothes in rivers or lakes, but in reality these were simply imported from the Manichaean rules of the Uighur state.

The Uighur language and Manichaean teachings introduced a new worldview, particularly the notion of life as a perpetual war of light against darkness. Evil and good were separate and could not be combined any more than the sun could shine at night. Temujin began to see himself as an embodiment of the Will of Heaven, engaged in a constant struggle with those who would not submit to his will. People were either good because they sided with him and heaven, or evil because they opposed him and represented darkness.[30] His mission was to spread peace by subduing rebels and bringing them into submission.

The Uighurs provided the Mongols with a new ritual language for explaining the world, the law, and the state. Much of this language was incorporated into the *Secret History*, elevating the prose from tribal myth to official ideology clothed in metaphors of gold and light. Manichaeism offered a strong religious endorsement of the ruler, whose power was deemed to come directly from heaven, more specifically from the sun and the moon. Under traditional practice, the khan was the strongest man on the steppe, but now, burnished by Manichaean belief, he became "the beautiful, lovely, noble, luminous, valiant, sublime, mighty khan."[31] In one Manichaean hymn, the elect are told to "put on a bright garment and clothe yourself with light." Only then can they deserve to rule and have God "place the diadem of kingship on your head."[32] This image of the man of light would eventually become a part of the glorification of Genghis Khan. In a story with direct Manichaean connections, it was said that one of his ancestors, Alan Goa, had been impregnated by a golden man riding a ray of light, and from this miraculous event, she prophesied that her descendants would "become the rulers of all."[33]

The Sogdians brought to Mongolia a sophisticated ideology of kingship based in part on Persian ideas but embodied most dramatically by Alexander the Great. They did not condemn Alexander as an invading menace or tyrant; they celebrated him as a hero. The *Romance of Alexander* and *Aesop's Fables* were two of the earliest literary works translated into Mongolian using the new alphabet. Although Alexander ruled for only a brief period in the long history of the region, his kingdoms had a profound cultural impact with their blending of civilizations, languages, and ideas. Through Alexander, the Sogdians, Uighurs, and eventually the Mongols acquired a rich background in art, aesthetics, and philosophy, and a correspondingly expansive vocabulary.[34]

Mani borrowed many of his ideas directly from Greek philosophy. His teachings regarding the spiritually superior class of the elect corresponded closely with Plato's advocacy for rule by elite philosopher kings in the *Republic*. Plato described the guardians as "brought into this world to be rulers."[35] Through their education and their determined effort to master themselves, they acquire the talent to rule others. Guardians were expected to abstain from the luxuries of the world and empty honors, things of importance only to those who prefer to live like pigs. They regarded justice as the greatest and most necessary of all things.[36] The Turkic and Mongol khans sought to portray themselves as wisdom-loving guardians of their people even before Temujin, but he embraced this identity with new scope and commitment.

Temujin's struggle was more than an effort to enact his own individual fate; he was creating a nation and enjoyed the blessing of heaven in this endeavor. Mani himself had claimed aristocratic ancestry, and he attempted to win royal converts by offering a justification of the power of ruling monarchs. He and his followers wrote several books of advice to kings, explaining how to make decisions, conduct public rituals, and build support from the people and from heaven simultaneously. A strong army is necessary but not sufficient alone to create a strong nation, he advised. The duty of the ruler, he wrote, is to subject "his jewel-like, noble body to torture in the service of the kingdom, for the sake of religion within and the whole realm without."[37]

Manichaeans had introduced to the steppes a strong ideology of the state and rationale for the power of the ruler. They also provided a decisive explanation of the relationship between government and religion in their theory of the two principles: the inner law and the outer government.[38] Just as each individual had a soul, each state had a leader. The khan was the soul of the state. According to Mani, the khan reigns supreme over both the divine and the secular realms. He is "perfect in both types of the good." He is master of both types of happiness, "of both sovereignties, of the body and the soul."[39] He is "worthy of both kinds of bliss, of both kinds of life, of both kinds of dominion: the body and soul."[40] The khan's domain may have extended over the body and the soul, but matters of faith remained internal and personal, while external matters belonged to the government. Temujin adapted this idea to the steppe by designating personal problems as matters of the *ger* and public behavior as matters of the steppe. [41]

More important than the army for Manichaeans was the law, often called the pure law (*arig nom*). To follow their religion was to "walk the pure path." They called their religion and God *Nom Quti*, combining the Greek word for law and the Turkic word for majesty. The Uighurs embraced this great emphasis on the law, drawn from both Greek and Manichaean traditions, and in time Temujin would too. Greek law, *nomos*, had a long philosophical and legal tradition, and the Uighurs thought of the law in the larger sense almost as a written scripture.[42] The law was both natural and spiritual. The Mongols already had words for law, but they adopted the Greek term *nom* to designate books of divine law and spiritual morality.

For Manichaeans, the law of the khan was divine. Manichaeans viewed God as "king of the whole law" and the khan as "clothed by the majesty of the law."[43] One of their hymns refers to God as "King of the Law, Jesus the Buddha!" and in another he is "all-wise King of Law, Mani the Buddha."[44] He is perfect in both the spiritual and earthly realm. "Because he has established the law of the Burkhan, we are saved from sorrow and wretchedness."[45]

In Book IX of his *Laws*, Plato compared laws to stones that were necessary for the building of the state. Some are already in place when a ruler is born, but others must be gathered and added to the structure over time. In proclaiming new laws, the ruler is not so much creating them as finding them and using them for the appropriate purpose at the right time.

From the Uighurs and the Turks, Temujin acquired the simple idea that religion and the law could not be separated. What was right was sacred, what was holy was legal. The ruler could not rule without support from heaven, and to build that support his laws had to conform to the laws of Mother Earth and Father Sky.

The Mongols already recognized *tor* as the unwritten moral code of the universe, but *nom* added a new element by introducing written laws. All people were connected by the same tether like camels in a long caravan crossing the Gobi Desert. Temujin called this binding thread "the golden cord."[46] It connected people to the golden stake, as the Mongols referred to the North Star. As long as they stayed connected, they could easily find the way to their goal, but if they broke that cord, they would drift and die alone.

֍

When Temujin began to conquer the steppe tribes, his Mongols appeared to be so akin in religion and culture to the Uighurs and Sogdians that many foreigners simply called them Uighurs, Sogdians, or Manichaeans and did not recognize them as a different people with their own unique culture.[47] Ibn Khaldun, the great Arab historian of the fourteenth century, stated that the Mongols followed the religion of the fire-worshipping Magi of Persia and were Manichaeans.[48] The Uighurs called their priests *bogu*, using a Turkish term, but they were sometimes called by the older Zoroastrian name of *magi*. The distinction between Zoroastrianism and Manichaeism—two religions born in Persia, though bitter enemies—was often muddled.[49]

The Mongolian word for shaman, *boo*, was derived from the Uighur *bogu*, which was applied to holy men in other tribes such as the Kereyid but not to Mongols until later.[50] The use of this same term for Manichaean priests and steppe shamans led Bar Hebraeus to write that the Mongols borrowed many of their religious ideas from the Uighurs, particularly the use of "enchanters" or shamans. He also accused them of sexual impropriety (as the Manichaeans were considered sexual deviants). He wrote that when in trance their "secret conversation with devils was not complete until after they had been defiled by other men, because the greater number of them were women-men."[51]

Eventually the Manichaeans were cut out of Mongol history by most Christian, Muslim, and Chinese scholars. Centuries later when converting the Mongols to Buddhism, the Buddhist monks censored any mention of the hated religion. Yet, despite the monopoly that scholars maintained over written history, the people preserved these censored parts of history in their myths and tales.

Thus, a strange and intriguing Mongolian story connects Temujin to the prophet Mani in a supernatural figure known as Mani Khan, described in Mongolian prayers as having "a body of gold and silver."[52] The Prophet Mani preached vegetarianism and forbade the slaughter of animals, and Mani Khan became the protector of wild animals, "the lord of all beasts," who has "tens of thousands of wild animals in his power."

The contrast between the vegetarian Mani and the meat-loving Mongol hunters was addressed in a mythical account of how Temujin came to strike a bargain with Mani Khan. According to a legend, probably composed much later, he was hunting black sables, white foxes, and spotted snow leopards on the Bogd Khan Mountain when Mani Khan cast a heavy fog around him. As his horses were unable to find the path down the mountain, Temujin made camp and built a fire to cook the deer and antelope he had killed. A wizened old man with a wrinkled face and long beard appeared before Temujin. He introduced himself as Bayan Khan Mani, the Rich King Mani, and claimed that the animals here belonged to him—antelope, hare, deer, fox, tiger, panther, and others. "I offer a few of them to you," he said to Temujin, but "please, save the life of the others."

The old man's request moved Temujin, who offered to let the wild animals from the mountain roam out on the steppes controlled by him. But in return he wanted enough meat to feed his people. Mani Khan agreed to always furnish Temujin with enough meat, skins, and fur to help his people to survive. Temujin asked that he not give the meat as a gift but instead allow the hunters to take it so that they might keep their skills sharp, and Mani Khan agreed. Having made this compact, old Mani Khan drove out many evil beings, including "fox-demons, riotous animals, yetis, and one-legged demons." This is how the mountain became safe for humans and for animals. Mani

Khan reigned thereafter as the spiritual protector of Mongol herders and hunters so long as they hunted justly.

When any society adopts a religion, they change it to conform to their own culture. And so the vegetarian prophet of the Manichaeans became the lord of the hunt for the Mongols.[53]

6

Jesus of the Steppe

After Ong Khan fled and was killed by his Naiman enemies, Temujin installed Jaqa Gambu, Ong Khan's younger brother and frequent rival, as a khan over the Kereyid. At first, he allowed the Kereyid a loose rein under their new khan. Although he had killed most of the aristocratic men who had fought against him, he recognized something unique and useful in their women. The Naiman and Kereyid women were some of the most sophisticated and cosmopolitan women he had encountered. They were very much women of the steppe—riding horses, shooting arrows, drinking fermented mare's milk, and participating fully in political life—but their Christian faith gave them knowledge of a world beyond the steppe and connected them to some of the most important centers of civilization.

Temujin arranged a double marriage between his family and that of Jaqa Gambu. He took the new khan's daughter, Ibaqa Beki (Princess Ibaqa), as his wife, and married his youngest son, Tolui, to her sister Sorkhokhtani Beki.[1] He also took a Naiman princess, Toregene, from her Merkid husband and married her to his son Ogodei. Temujin and two of his sons now each had a Christian wife, and although no Mongol man of that era was known to have converted to

Christianity, having a Christian wife became a popular practice over the next generation.

Temujin also arranged Christian marriages for some of his daughters. Alaqai Beki married the khan of the Onggut, another Christian tribe south of the Gobi in Inner Mongolia, who joined the Mongols voluntarily and remained loyal throughout his life. After his death she married several more times, and each husband seems to have been Christian. Chinese envoys reported that she frequently read religious scriptures, but the nature and language of the scriptures was unspecified.[2]

The appearance of Temujin's daughters at this time is complicated, as no record survives of their birth or of their mothers. The *Secret History* originally contained information about them, but this section was cut out of the text sometime during the Mongol rule in China. Six women can be identified as Temujin's daughters, but whether they were born to him and one of his official wives, were adopted, or bore some other relationship to him is unclear. During Temujin's lifetime, these daughters occupied powerful positions, though their influence was eclipsed after his death by his daughters-in-law.[3]

For almost a century from the time of Temujin's marriage until 1294, every Mongol khan either came from a Christian mother or had a Christian wife. The *Secret History* suggests that he favored Christian spouses for his children and deliberately chose them because he thought they would make good parents for his grandchildren. He showed keen interest in their skills, knowledge, and connections to the larger world, but dismissed their faith as the failed experiment of a defeated people.

Several Christian chronicles reported that Temujin's wife was Christian and identified her variously as the daughter of the mystical King David or Prester John. According to one imaginative account, Temujin dreamed that a messenger had promised him power and success, and when he related this strange dream to his Christian wife, she recognized the messenger as Mar Denha, a Christian bishop. He reportedly summoned Mar Denha to interpret the dream, and the bishop told him that he could find success only by being "milder toward the Christians" and by giving them "many distinctions." Thereafter, according to the French monk Vincent of Beauvais, Temujin favored the Christians and went so far as to ask a Christian monk to forecast the future and make divinations for him.[4]

Mar Denha was an important leader of the church in Baghdad, but he lived at the time of Marco Polo and had not yet been born when the Mongol nation was founded. No record of a religious conversation between Temujin and a Christian can in fact be found in any reliable source. Yet for most of his adult life he had an intimate association with Christians, first as the vassal to the Christian king Ong Khan and then as husband and father-in-law.

Christians lived on the steppe for more than two hundred years prior to the rise of the Mongols. When the Uighur Empire collapsed in the ninth century and most Uighurs fled into the desert oases of western China, Manichaeism lost its status as an official religion and withered into a small and irrelevant sect. In their new homeland, the Uighurs became Muslims, but the remaining steppe tribes in Mongolia wanted to be neither Muslims nor Buddhists, although both religions had dispatched missionaries to convert them. Instead, they chose a religion that had never sent a missionary to Mongolia. Manichaeans had recognized Jesus as one of their main prophets, and even after the fall of the Uighur state and the flight of the Manichaean priests, the people continued to honor him as a god. Unable to find new Manichaean priests, they sought out distant Christians who also worshipped Jesus.

The conversion of the steppe tribes from Manichaeism to Christianity occurred at the start of the eleventh century. In Baghdad in the year 1009, Catholicos Yohannan V, the patriarch of the Assyrian Christian Church of the East, received a strange letter from the metropolitan bishop Abdisho of Merv, a small city just over a thousand miles from Baghdad, in what is today eastern Turkmenistan but was then a part of Persia. The church in Persia considered itself the oldest of the Christian branches, closest to the teachings of Jesus in both language and spirit, but times were growing steadily more difficult for its followers. Cut off from other Christian communities, they battled oppression first by the Zoroastrian elite and then by the conquering Muslims, who suspected them of being covert allies of the Europeans.

The news in the metropolitan's letter was as welcome as it was strange. He reported that in the far northern steppe, a warrior tribe of 200,000 had converted to Christianity. This was the Kereyid tribe, later under the leadership of Ong Khan. The bishop informed the patriarch that the conversion had occurred two years previously, around the year 1007, and he related a standard Christian narrative of a pagan king in distress being rescued by a Christian saint. According to Bar Hebraeus's account, written two centuries later, the Kereyid khan went hunting in the mountains and was lost in a blizzard. An apparition said to be Saint Sergius offered to rescue the khan if he converted to Christianity, a religion that was known to him from itinerant merchants along the Silk Route. The khan agreed and followed the teachings of one of the Christian traders as best he understood them. After the rescue, the khan sent a request 2,500 miles away to Metropolitan Abdisho in Merv, requesting missionary priests to conduct a mass baptism of the entire tribe.

Christianity fit the Kereyid pastoral lifestyle. The steppe nomads understood the biblical references to shepherds and herding, appreciated the importance of law for a dispersed people operating in a harsh environment, and were themselves engaged in an eternal search for a better life. The Kereyid traveled with a portable shrine (or chapel) and priests, called *rabban*, or teacher (from the Hebrew *rabbi*), who foretold the future, read the stars, healed the sick, located lost animals, and controlled the weather, chanting their Christian scriptures in Syriac. Dressed in flowing robes, they performed elaborate rituals with incense and lamps and glorified the khan and his rule.

As part of their conversion, some aristocrats accepted Christian names such as Yahu (Jesus), Shiremun (Solomon), and Markos. They performed the Christian ritual of communion by drinking fermented mare's milk in lieu of wine, though they did not take bread, which was largely unknown to them. Their communion continued the traditional steppe practice of combining ritual occasions with the drinking of fermented *airag*, and thus the Christian service frequently ended in drunkenness.

The *Book of the Tower*, written by an Arab Christian in the twelfth century, described the unusual form of Christianity among the steppe tribes. According to this account, the Kereyid worshipped in a tent and kept special mares nearby to produce the milk used for religious services. Prior to their absorption into Temujin's camp, the Kereyid khan performed most of the religious services for his people himself, saying what prayers he knew, and placing the milk on the altar before the Bible and a cross.[5] For this reason, some reports described the khan as a priest.

The steppe tribes appreciated Christianity because it permitted eating all types of meat and used alcohol in its religious services. Muslims and Jews abstained from pork, Hindus from beef, and Buddhists from all meat, and all but the Christians forbade or severely limited the consumption of alcohol. One aspect of the Christian liturgy, however, they found repulsive. During their religious service, the Christians claimed to be eating the flesh and drinking the blood of their prophet. In 1453, the year that Constantinople fell to the Turks, Nicholas of Cusa described an imaginary meeting with representatives of various faiths. The Tatar complained that the Christians "offer bread and wine and say, it is the body and blood of Christ. That they eat and drink this sacrifice after the oblation seems most abominable. They devour what they worship."[6]

Catholics prayed with their hands folded in front of them, Orthodox with their hands together on their chest, but the steppe Christians raised their outstretched arms to the sky in the Mongol fashion. They threw a small piece of food into the air before eating and poured a drop of their drink onto the ground in the traditional Mongol offering to the sky and earth.[7]

The steppe Christians mounted no crusades against the Europeans and no jihad against Muslims. No one persecuted them as heretics or forced them to believe anything. They wandered freely in their land, with few constraints on their religion, not confined to special buildings or trapped in seemingly incessant arguments over the exact meaning of words. For arguably the first time in its thousand-year history, Christianity found nearly total freedom on the steppes of Mongolia.

The steppe Christians maintained a flexible attitude toward other beliefs. They used shamans to control the weather, important for both herding and warfare,[8] and invoked whatever power they believed might work. Christianity served as an official religion, and Christians assisted with correspondence and translation as well as some healing, but Christianity operated not so much as a court religion as a religion attached to a court. Even the royal family turned to traditional spiritual healers and shamans when needed. Both Ong Khan and Tayang Khan of the Naiman had difficulty fathering sons; they both turned to shamans in order to secure the birth of an heir.[9]

The established church hierarchy in Baghdad maintained a persistent mistrust of the sincerity of the steppe Christians and their fidelity to the church. As one bishop of the Syrian Orthodox Church wrote of Ong Khan, God rejected the Kereyid ruler, "but he was not rejected for nothing, but only after he had turned aside his heart from the fear of Christ His Lord, who had magnified him, and had taken a wife from a tribe of the Chinese people which was called Kara Kitai." In so doing, Ong Khan "forsook the religion of his fathers and worshipped strange gods."[10]

Temujin's Christian wife did not come to his camp alone. Ibaqa Beki brought with her a contingent of two hundred retainers and vassals in addition to her household staff of cooks and servants.[11] Together they formed a floating community of Christians at the center of the Mongol court. The new Christian princesses and their numerous subjects brought the Mongols into a complex religious and commercial network that stretched across Europe and Asia and connected the Mongols to a long and tortured religious history that spanned across Russia, the Byzantine Empire, most of Europe, and many outposts in the Muslim world.

In addition to the princesses, Temujin recruited the help of many Christian clerks because of their strategic and bureaucratic skills. Some became officers and commanding generals, and Christians were among the first foreigners to hold office in Temujin's government. The first and one of the most important Christian scribes, variously identified as Uighur, Kereyid, or Onggut, joined him by 1202. He was called Chinqai, from the Chinese *Zhenhai*, meaning True Ocean. Through him, Temujin strengthened the Uighur model of civilization, and he became a high official in the future Mongol imperial court.

Later, Juvaini criticized Chinqai for his persistent favoritism of Christianity. He wrote that Chinqai "went to great lengths in honoring the Christians and their priests, and when this was noised abroad, priests set their faces towards his Court from Damascus and Rum and Baghdad and the As [Ossetians] and the Rus; and for the most part too it was Christian physicians that were attached to his service." He held power of "the tying and untying of affairs" and was "responsible for good and evil, weal and woe." Consequently, "the cause of the Christians flourished during his reign, and no Moslem dared to raise his voice to them."[12]

Chinqai concentrated on building trade relations with China and along the Silk Route. Because the Uighurs knew much more about commerce, agriculture, and the organization of city life, Temujin relied heavily on his advice and delegated responsibilities in these areas to him. In his administrative capacity, he founded a new city, usually called Chinqai City, which served as a military garrison, wheat growing area, and craft production center. During Chinqai's time of prominence, the Mongols revived one of the Manichaean centers on the Selenge River in northern Mongolia. Founded as Rich Town, Bai Baliq, in the year 757 by the Uighur ruler Moyun Chur, the city served as a northern trade center with the tribes of Siberia and housed artisans who produced gold jewelry and other items for the Mongol aristocracy.[13]

Given the large number of Christian priests and portable chapels among the Mongols, some foreign observers assumed that Christianity was the chosen religion of the Mongol court. Bar Hebraeus wrote, with proud exaggeration, that the Mongols preferred Christianity over other religions. "And having seen very much modesty (or, chastity) and other habits of this kind among the Christian people, certainly the Mongols loved them greatly at the beginning of their kingdom, a time ago somewhat short."[14]

Despite the tremendous influence of Christians at the Mongol court, Temujin showed little interest in Christian theology. For him, the defeat of the rich, powerful, and prestigious Kereyid clearly illustrated the powerlessness of the Christian religion. Either it was a false religion from the start or its members had drifted so far from the true faith that heaven had turned against them. Ong Khan was a Christian and yet he had betrayed him. If the Christian religion could not persuade its members to act morally, then the Mongols had little use for it.

Furthermore, Temujin upheld his animist beliefs that spirits were everywhere, while Christians believed the word of God was in their books, as though they had trapped God and now contained him in a small, portable box bound in leather. Only the Christian priests could read the holy scriptures or hear the voice of God. The priests controlled access to God, but they greedily sold this access to those with money and power. In contrast, Mongols believed that heaven spoke directly to them on mountaintops and from trees but not through a book. They communicated with gods and spirits regularly and were frustrated when Christians failed to answer basic, practical questions about the scriptures they quoted and memorized.

Did you have to go to heaven to receive God's words or did God come to you to deliver them? If you did not receive these words your-self, to whom did God give them? Was that person your ancestor? Did God speak the words, write them, or deliver them through signs? Did these meetings with God take place in a dream, a trance, or in person? Were you alone or with other people or gods? What language does God use to communicate? What happens if you do not speak that language?

The nomadic Christians of the Mongol steppe did not share West-ern Christianity's fondness for paintings or sculpture. They had little use for icons. They particularly rejected Christian art because it de-picted the worst imaginable human acts of torture and martyrdom (people being beheaded, boiled in pots, crucified, eaten by savage beasts, strangled, tortured on the rack, broken on the wheel, pulled asunder by animals, shot with arrows, pierced with lances, starved, fed to lions, sealed alive in tombs, whipped, raped, skinned alive, eviscerated, burned at the stake, roasted on a spit, nailed upside down, drowned, hung by ropes, thrown from high places). Western Christians not only wrote stories, sang songs, and made pictures of suffering; they eagerly collected the blood, broken bones, dried skin, hair, and other body parts of their holy martyrs and prayed to them.

The nomads, in contrast, believed that to mention evil or depict suffering only created more evil and suffering. They particularly ab-horred depictions of Jesus nailed on a cross, bleeding from his crown of thorns, or with his side pierced by a spear. Images of a tortured God defied their moral sensibility. To the steppe Christians, the idea that Jesus could be killed as he triumphantly rose to heaven made no sense. Unlike the Kereyid and the Naiman, the Mongols perceived a clear separation between the divine and the earthly. For them God was the sky, or heaven, not a person.

The Christian notion of individual salvation mystified and fright-ened the Mongols because it conflicted with the strong communitar-ian ideals of steppe culture. Most Mongols did not dare even to sleep alone at night, and so to imagine eternity in a supposed paradise without their family or close companions was horrifying. To become an orphan was considered life's worst fate, and getting separated from the group terrified them; indeed much of their magic, rituals, and customs were used to protect family members until they could safely return home. Why, the Mongols wondered, would a religion reward believers with a heaven that their parents, grandparents, and ancestors had not been allowed to enter?

ॐ

No direct dialogue between Temujin and a Christian has survived, but there is an interesting one written by the first French envoy, William of Rubruck, who arrived at the court of his grandson Mongke Khan in 1254. William traveled to Mongolia at the behest of Louis IX, a fervent Christian, to convert the Tatars and explore the possibility of an anti-Muslim alliance. The French king had organized and led a crusade to the Holy Land and was eager to learn more about the community of Christians that was said to lie between Persia and China.

Mostly on horseback, but sometimes on foot or in oxcarts, William and a handful of carefully chosen companions endured a nearly four-thousand-mile trek from Constantinople to the Mongol capital on the Orkhon River. The presence of so many Christians in the Mongol camp, including some from Paris, surprised him and gave him both great hope and tremendous frustration. He hoped with so many Christians already present that the other Mongols might easily convert, but he quickly found that their very familiarity with Christian faith made them resistant to it.

Although William compiled an excellent account of what he saw, he dismissed Mongol religion as ignorant and impious superstition. William of Rubruck's writings illuminated the profound and persistent differences between the Mongols and the Christians, despite so many Mongol men having Christian wives and mothers. William incorrectly believed that the felt figurines the Mongols made to honor their ancestors were also their gods. "The Mongols, though they believe in one God," he explained, in his invaluable account of his journey, "made nevertheless images of their dead in felt, and dress them in the richest stuffs, and put them in one or two carts, and no one dare touch these carts, which are under the care of their soothsayers." William thought that if they worshipped these idols with a human form then they could understand that God had also made his son into a human.

"I asked them what they believed concerning God," he recorded.

"We only believe that there is one God," they answered.

"Do you believe that he is a spirit, or something physical?" Rubruck asked.

"We believe that he is a spirit," they said.

William then tried to convey the heart of his Christian belief, that God had created his son Jesus, who was both a God and a man. "Do you believe that God never became human?" he asked them.

"Never!" they answered.

William challenged them by pointing out that they worshipped idols, gods in a human form. If you believe that God is only spirit, then "why do you make Him in the form of bodily images?" And, he added, "Why do you make so many of them? Furthermore, if you do not believe that He became man, why do you make Him in human shape rather than in that of some animal?"

The Mongol shamans insisted that the figures they made and honored were not gods. "We do not make images of God!" they declared emphatically. The images are made in honor of the dead—"a son, or wife, or someone dear." The image was only to revere the memory of such a loved one.

William ridiculed this as vanity and false piety. "Then you make these only out of flattery," he charged.

"Then they asked me, as if in derision," he wrote, "where is God?"

William began delivering a sermon on Christian belief and the soul in very abstract terms, but he soon lost his audience. "Just as I wanted to continue reasoning with them," he wrote in his official report, "my interpreter got tired, and would no longer express my words; so he made me stop talking."[15]

Already exasperated by his dealings with shamans and animists, William became even more frustrated by his dealing with the Christians, who showed no interest in his teachings or in the pope in Rome. The freedom of the steppe Christians irritated their Catholic observers, who believed in a rigid conformity to doctrine and a powerful church hierarchy. William expressed extreme hostility to these Asian Christians. They claimed to be Christians, he wrote, "but that lord of theirs had abandoned the worship of Christ, and taken to idolatry, having about him priests of the idols, who are all evokers of demons and sorcerers."[16] William complained that the priests among the steppe Christians made statements that are "ten times more than was true" and "out of nothing they will make a great story." Even the Buddhists led a "more innocent" life.

The Christians "know nothing," William complained in his account of his journey. Their priests perform the rituals haphazardly. They "have books in Syrian, but they do not know the language; so they chant like those monks among us who do not know grammar, and they are absolutely depraved." William claimed that the priests were more interested in alcohol, women, and making money than in religion. "In the first place, they are usurers and drunkards." Some have several wives. "They are bigamists, for when the first wife dies these priests take another." They are mercenary, and people have to pay for their Christian rituals, "for they administer no sacrament gratis." They are "more intent on the increase of their wealth than of the faith."[17]

☧

Temujin's connection with Christians remained important throughout his life, but his marriage to his Christian wife, Ibaqa Beki, did not endure. The marriage had been made for political reasons, and through politics it was severed. Soon after being named khan, her father, Jaqa Gambu, defied Temujin, still considering his Kereyid people masters of the Mongols. Temujin sent a detachment of soldiers to defeat and execute him. The general who performed this important service received Ibaqa Beki as his wife. Temujin made it clear in a public statement that he was not giving her away because she was ugly or displeased him; he was forced to do it for political reasons, because he could not be married to the daughter of a traitor. He allowed his son Tolui to keep her sister Sorkhokhtani as his wife, and he further honored Ibaqa Beki by permitting her to retain her title as princess along with all her property and all the people assigned to her, and added the command that she always be treated with respect.[18]

While politically justified, Temujin's motives may not have been purely political. He wanted a different wife—Khulan, the daughter of the defeated Merkid chief. She had the name of the onager, the wild horse of the Gobi.[19] The onager is extremely swift and avoids humans. Unlike other species related to the horse, the onager had never been tamed, and that perhaps indicated something about the personality of Khulan and what attracted Temujin to her. Aside from Borte, who remained his primary wife as long as he lived, he loved Khulan the most, and had one son with her.

According to the *Golden Chronicle*, Temujin was reluctant to tell Borte about the new wife. He had earlier taken the two Tatar queens as well as Ibaqa Beki as wives more as a political decision than one of passion, but he exhibited stronger feelings for Khulan. Instead of taking Khulan home, presenting her to his wives and family, and then consummating the marriage, Temujin seemed overcome with desire for her and wished to sleep with her while still out on campaign. "If you united on a pillow with her in the field, it would not be customary," warned one of Temujin's unnamed companions. "How about uniting on a pillow with her once we reach home?"

But Temujin "did not follow these words, and united on a pillow with the Lady Khulan in the countryside and was delayed."[20]

He had known Borte since childhood and still loved her. "It will be difficult to see her face," he said to one of his retainers after the encounter with Khulan. "I did not discuss it with her," he explained. "When I enter the house it will be narrow," and if "she is angry and enraged, that will be something shameful and frightening." So instead of going to tell Borte of his new wife, he sent a messenger.

"Why have you come?" Borte asked the messenger. He told her that Temujin had a change of heart, and that desire had overcome his own will and he had ignored the advice of his companions. His words through the messenger were simple and direct: "I have indulged in the beauty of the tiger-skin house," he said, referring to his nuptial tryst. "I have slept with the Queen Khulan."

Borte received the news with the resigned dignity of a true queen. "He is the desire of all Mongols," she exclaimed. "He is the desire of them all," she repeated. "On the banks and rivers are many swans and geese. My Lord will know how to shoot them from on horseback until his thumb is worn out. In the ordinary people are many girls and women. My Lord will know himself how to find and take them." She seemed understanding and forgiving of his having started his relationship with Khulan while out on campaign and contrary to custom. She quoted the proverb, "Let a saddle be placed on an unbroken horse."

Then, cryptically, Borte wondered aloud, "Is it bad to have too much? Is it good to have too little?"[21]

After sending Ibaqa Beki away and taking Khulan as a queen, Temujin never married again. He now had four wives, counting the two Tatar sisters, and he never saw a political or emotional need for another.

☫

With the death of Jaqa Gambu, Temujin ended the loose reins of the Kereyid. He decided that his nation would not be a confederacy or league of tribes like the Tatar, Kereyid, and Naiman whom he had defeated; he intended to unite all of his various clans and tribes into one single nation with himself as the sole khan. All tribes and clans would be part of a new Mongol nation and would thus become continuously less important. Their main identity now was Mongol; everything else was secondary.

Now in his forties, Temujin shifted his focus from conquest to administration. He had destroyed every government on the steppe and now it was time to build up a new one. The elite systems of the Tatars, Kereyid, and Naiman had collapsed totally when he had killed off the aristocrats and redistributed the survivors among his own followers. He had successfully created a powerful army, but now to stay in power he realized he would need a functioning government with systematic and publicly known laws, with a division of labor and responsibility, and a means of settling disputes. His days were increasingly devoted to the practical concerns of deciding who gets what pastures, mediating family squabbles and settling inheritances, feeding the growing number of officials and clerks around him, and other such issues big and small. He was mired in practical concerns, but he did not want to govern like other khans. He wanted to start something new.

Temujin had failed to achieve the power he sought through marriage into the Christian royal family of the Kereyid, and he had failed in his effort to rule through the puppet khan Jaqa Gambu. Although not the son of a khan, he decided that he himself must be the khan of his own nation, but it would become a nation unlike any other in the history of the steppe or the world. And he would become a ruler unlike any other. At age forty-four, he was at last ready to step into the arena of world history.

7

The Making of the Mongol Nation

With an alphabet and an army, Temujin was ready to create a nation. To mark a distinctly new beginning he chose a short, yet august, title for himself. He had no interest in the traditional title *Gurkhan* because too many wicked men with that title had come to bad ends, and in the words of a Christian priest, "its glory was forever tarnished."[1] Instead, he chose to call himself *Chinggis*, a new Mongol title that represented firmness, strength, constancy, and commitment—some of the same qualities suggested by his name, Temujin. The Mongolian word *chin* meant "determined" or "strong willed," so he became the "Sovereign of the Strong" or "Khan of the Strong." The earliest Chinese mention of his title, in a 1221 report to the Sung monarch by his envoy Chao Hung, says that his title meant "granted by Heaven."[2]

To his Mongol followers Temujin became *Chinggis*, but to his Turkic followers he was *Tengis*, which meant "ocean," a designation that had carried great meaning since the times of the Huns, as it was the name of Attila and his son. For centuries, steppe rulers had used such water titles for their leaders. These occurred in many forms, such as the Uighur *Bilge Kol*, meaning "ocean of wisdom," or *Dalai Khan*, meaning "ruler of all within the sea."[3]

When the time came to establish a base for his new empire in the summer of 1206, Genghis Khan chose to return to the foot of his sacred Burkhan Khaldun, along the headwaters of the Onon River. Nearly four decades earlier his mother had found refuge there. She had run up and down the river with a black stick in her hand, digging roots to feed her brood.[4] Now, in choosing this place as the seat of his new nation, he was honoring both his spiritual home and his mother, who had witnessed his lifelong struggle and was still alive to see his triumph. Despite the honor, she was quite displeased that he awarded her only five thousand vassals for her new court.

No foreigners were present to witness the creation of the Mongol Empire, but later chroniclers created a variety of informed, and sometimes imaginatively invented, descriptions of the events. In the *History of the Nation of Archers*, the Armenian chronicler Gregory of Akner wrote that the Mongols prayed to God for salvation from their poor, miserable lives. God heard their prayers and sent an angel who appeared to Temujin in a vision as an eagle with golden feathers. The eagle angel stood out in the open, about one bow shot away from Temujin, as it proclaimed his new title and then proceeded to dictate the laws of the new nation.[5]

In another Armenian account, *The Flower of Histories of the East*, Hethum claims that the Mongol people did not initially believe that Genghis Khan's title had come from a divine source, given the misfortune that had afflicted him as a child and the fact that the divine vision had not come from a holy, educated, or aristocratic man. In response to people's skepticism, God sent a dream to Temujin, but still no one believed it. "The following night these same leaders saw the white soldier and the same vision which old Genghis had related to everyone. And they received the decree from immortal God to obey Genghis and to make everyone obey his orders. Thus those seven leaders and grandees of the seven Tartar peoples gathered in an assembly and agreed to obey Genghis as their natural lord."[6] Others described a royal seal descending from heaven, a mist of perfume filling the countryside, a precious stone blown in by the wind, a five-colored bird perched on a rock loudly proclaiming the title for all people to hear, and a divine light shining down from heaven.[7]

The Persian chronicler Rashid al-Din added that a shaman flew to heaven on a white horse to get the name. The more reliable Juvaini reported that the shaman had not given the name Genghis Khan, but rather that heaven had bestowed the name on him, saying, "God has spoken with me and has said: 'I have given all the face of the Earth to Temujin and his children and named him Genghis Khan. Bid him administer justice in such and such a fashion.'"[8]

Each of these stories points toward a special divine mission, an anointment by God. "Their king is a relative of God," reported the Armenian chronicler Kirakos of Gandzak in a clear echo of the Biblical account of the Virgin birth of Jesus. "God took heaven as his portion and gave earth to . . . Genghis Khan," who "was not born from the seed of man but that a light came from the unseen, entered through a skylight in the home, and announced to his mother: Conceive and you will bear a son who will be ruler of the world."[9]

If Genghis Khan's father had been an emperor, a khan, or a king, his legitimacy would have been understood and accepted. As he lacked such a political pedigree, his followers embellished his life story with supernatural signs and explanations. His legitimacy did not come through blood or bone, but through the golden light of heaven. Despite the manifold supernatural elements in foreign accounts of Genghis Khan's rise to power, the *Secret History* itself mentions nothing overtly religious in the choice of name or in the events related to the creation of the Mongol Empire. No shaman, priest, or other religious official is mentioned as participating in the anointing ceremony. The text mentions no prayers, no beating of drums, no sacrifices to the sky, no reference to God or the heavens, and emphasizes that this act—Temujin's elevation to Genghis Khan—was simply the will of the people. The people gathered together, raised the white horse-hair banner of the nation, and gave him the title

Chinggis Khaan. The *Secret History* offers loquacious descriptions of horses and things important to nomads, but regarding ceremony the writing tends to be quite blunt. "After Genghis Khan brought order to the people who live in felt walls, the people gathered at the Onon River in the Year of the Tiger and made him khan."[10]

In addition to claiming a title for himself, Genghis Khan decided to give his nation a new name. The Chinese, although aware of many of the ethnic divisions on the steppe, referred to all the nomadic tribes as Tatars. Genghis Khan's group, and most nomads north of the Gobi, had been known as the Black Tatars, whom the Chinese considered the least civilized and most dangerous, in contrast to the White Tatars who lived closer to China, south of the Gobi, and had acquired a semblance of Chinese culture. Genghis Khan wanted to break with all the names of the past (Hun, Turk, Tatar) and thus named his people "Mongol." Many explanations have been offered, but he himself never explained the meaning of the term. Like so much in his life and government, the real meaning remained a secret; it was part of the power of knowledge reserved to only a select few.

Mongols are fond of the saying, "unity creates success."[11] Simply calling a diverse people by one name, however, did not create a unified state. Genghis Khan faced the enormous task of uniting and integrating a nomadic people, who lacked fixed abodes and cities, into one cohesive state. Even the concept of *state, country, nation,* or *government* so common to agricultural societies seemed incongruous when applied to nomads. They were what the Chinese called "moving states" or "states on horseback."[12] In their own eyes, the Mongols were simply *uls,* a nation.

The longest section at the heart of the *Secret History of the Mongols* describes the proceedings of 1206. It records in detail each person who helped Temujin in his rise to power, and explains precisely how that assistance was rendered and how he was rewarded. Special honors went to those who had performed feats of bravery and heroism in war, as well as to others who were not battle heroes but who had reported seeing signs or had dreams legitimizing his right to rule.

Mongols say that a dream is a letter left on a pillow, a message from somewhere for someone, and they believe most important events were portended in dreams. When Temujin was eight years old, Dei-Sechen, his future father-in-law, supposedly announced: "Last night I had a dream of a white gyrfalcon clutching the sun and the moon, and he flew to my hand."[13] Since Hun times, the gyrfalcon symbolized power for the steppe tribes. It had served as a family emblem for Attila, and Temujin adopted the white gyrfalcon to represent his family as well.[14]

Another revelation came from Qorchi of the Baarin, one of Jamuka's followers who had deserted him in order to follow Temujin. Although Jamuka and Temujin shared no male ancestors, they were deemed to be children from one womb and of the same water because they both descended from an Uriyankhai woman captured by their mutual ancestor Bodonchar the Fool. Qorchi described how in a dream he had seen a powerful ox pulling the great cart of state along a broad road across the earth. As it moved forward, the ox bellowed out to the people that Father Heaven and Mother Earth had chosen Temujin to rule as Lord of the Nation and commanded the people to follow him. All the warriors should come and serve him, he cried; all the steppe tribes should turn to him and follow behind his cart.

After he revealed this dream, Qorchi offered Temujin certain teachings on moral principles.[15] The dream about his rise to power was a prelude to the receipt of the secret spiritual knowledge he would need to rule. These teachings were called the Great Tor (*Töre*), and they embodied the most profound principles and truths of life. Their contents remained secret. In recognition of the importance of these teachings, later in life Genghis Khan referred to Qorchi not as a teacher or shaman but as *nendu khutukh*, extremely blessed.

Not long after the naming ceremony, Genghis Khan announced the organization of his new government, outlining the nature of the offices and who would hold them. He named each person who had given him exceptional service or performed a heroic deed during his twenty-five-year struggle to unite the tribes, and he rewarded them with an official office, exemption from taxes, or whatever seemed appropriate to their contribution. "All the tribes were of one color and obedient to his command," wrote Juvaini. "Then he established new laws and laid the foundation of justice."[16]

After the festivities the young people wrestled, raced horses, sang, played anklebones, and flirted. The elders drank *airag*, feasted on marmot meat boiled with hot stones, visited relatives not seen in many years, and laughed with erstwhile enemies. Men and women competed in archery and wrestling. Spectators enjoyed the show, and delighted when an overlooked horse unexpectedly won the race, or a small woman flipped a much larger man in wrestling. There was no gambling for money, but participants gambled with their reputations, which could be made or broken in a few dramatic moments of competition that the Mongols called *naadam*.

The creation of the Mongol nation was a compact between Genghis Khan and his people. No other blessing was needed. He had returned the Mongol people to their proper path according to the laws of heaven. In the words of the *Secret History*, he had "straightened" them or "put them into the right."[17]

The summer of 1206 on the steppes was one of the most peaceful in generations. No feuding of clan against clan. No kidnapping of women. No revenge killings. The people gathered between the Onon and Kherlen rivers and luxuriated in the freedom of not having to stare at the horizon for raiders or wonder at night whether their family would be alive in the morning. The steppe nomads were accustomed to summer gatherings of hundreds or sometimes thousands of people, but never had so many people assembled as for this unprecedented event, the unifying of all the tribes. They quickly erected a city with hundreds of structures, all made of felt blankets stretched over wooden frames. Unlike the haphazard nature of most villages and cities, their winding streets jumbled with buildings, the layout of the Mongol camp had a strict military discipline, with straight lines and broad, open avenues. The *gers* were arranged according to a specific plan, with the home and court of the Great Khan at the center, markets on the periphery, and designated locations for the equipment repair neighborhood, the horse holding area, the meat distribution center, doctors, or the lost-and-found. Any stranger arriving for the first time would have known instantly where to find everything and everyone of importance.

When Temujin first became tribal khan in 1189, he had fewer than thirty thousand followers, but by 1206, when he became Genghis Khan, the number had grown to a million. He was not the khan of a tribe, he was now emperor of a new nation that had outgrown the old tribal structure whereby the khan acted as lawgiver, military leader, shaman, judge, and tax collector.

Genghis Khan was well aware that the fall of the Tatars, Kereyid, and Naiman was the result not just of his tactical superiority on the battlefield, but of internecine power struggles and frequent rebellions, pitting brother against brother and father against son. He knew that as long as the old tribes, clans, and aristocracy existed he would never be safe. Since his defeat of the Tatars he had made sure that men of the aristocratic clans either fled or were killed, for they could never be trustworthy or loyal to him. He was determined to establish a new political organization to prevent such treachery in the future.

Genghis Khan permitted some groups that had been consistently loyal to remain together under their traditional leaders, but his new empire would not be a collection of tribes with their own khans ruling over their traditional territories. He abolished all of the old tribes and clans that had resisted or betrayed him and redistributed the conquered subjects throughout his territory into new units of one hundred, one thousand, and ten thousand. He carefully blended his followers into mixed groups, placing former enemies or less reliable individuals into groups with people whom he trusted. These new units, adopted from the system used to ensure loyalty and conformity among the Uighurs, cut through kinship and class lines. Loyal men from the lowest families now ruled over descendants of khans and queens. To prevent the kinds of desertions and factionalism that characterized steppe life, he forbade any of his subjects to leave the units of ten warriors and families to which they had been assigned.

Genghis turned to members of his own family to enforce the law and to "decide on judicial matters."[18] He assigned his half brother Belgutei the authority to determine who was guilty of theft or falsehood and to adjudicate quarrels.[19] Because of the great value he placed on writing, Genghis Khan wanted his laws to be carefully recorded, but Belgutei was illiterate. The old Uighur court had had an office of Master of the Law, and Genghis Khan created a similar position for his adopted Tatar brother Shigi-Khutukhu.[20] He took pains to explain the importance of the law, and dictated that it should be written in Uighur script on white paper and kept in blue binders. "Let no one alter the blue writing," he warned. These were laws that were to last for generations to come. He said that the new laws would be based upon existing custom, but as he wrote them down, Shigi-Khutukhu should "judge the judgments"[21] and recalibrate them to fit current needs and concerns. Genghis Khan declared that Shigi-Khutukhu would be his "eyes to see with, ears to hear with." He apportioned out responsibilities, but no one could change his laws or his words. Later, Genghis gave Shigi-Khutukhu the highest rank and the assignment to judge all: "curbing theft, and discouraging falsehood, execute those who deserve death, punish those who deserve punishment."[22] In time, these laws became known as the Ikh Yasa, the Great Law of Genghis Khan, and judges were known as Jarguchi, a title with the same linguistic root as the name of Genghis Khan's first teacher, Jarchigudai.

Under Genghis Khan's guidance, Shigi-Khutukhu created a new judicial system to ensure that the law was known and enacted throughout the Mongol nation. The law forbade torture and intimidation by officials. The accused "must not confess out of fear and anguish." "Do not be afraid and speak the truth," Shigi-Khutukhu inveighed.[23] According to the testimony of Rashid al-Din, as the empire grew Shigi-Khutukhu sought to extend these legal procedures into China and into Muslim lands, where torture was routinely used against witnesses as well as the accused. As written laws gradually replaced the Ancient Sayings, a new network of express horse riders was established to deliver the law and other imperial orders. Genghis Khan's central court could now make decisions formerly left to local chiefs. His vast but highly centralized system relied upon speed and communication rather than tradition and custom.

Temujin was now Genghis Khan, ruler of the entire Mongolian steppe, and just as he had sworn to do as a young boy on Burkhan Khaldun, he had made a name for himself. Now he was ready to take on any enemy or to make new ones, and he was confident he could prevail. He was not prepared, however, to be challenged from within his family. The new Mongol nation emerged as a massive experiment in social engineering, one that for most people, weary of the constant feuds and grateful for this new stability, proved successful. Like all happiness, however, the rejoicing at the creation of the new nation was temporary, and not everyone shared in it equally. Some inevitably resented that they had not been given enough power. Bitterness mounted among a minority of Genghis Khan's more traditional subjects, who resented being cut off from the Great Khan even as Uighurs and other foreign advisers seemed to be coming and going into his *ger* in increasing numbers. They felt threatened by the fact that the power and prestige of their elders had been usurped by the rapid rise of a battalion of clerks writing letters and stamping the seal of approval. Younger brothers sometimes held rank over their elder brothers or clan uncles, and clerks consulted strange almanacs to forecast the movement of the stars and planets and foretell eclipses of the sun or moon. Others resented the destruction of their tribe or the killing of some of their relatives during the conquest, and many begrudged being ruled by the upstart Mongols, who had never before ruled an empire and had always been the vassals of the other, more cultured, steppe tribes. For them the change from tribe to empire was difficult to endure.

Opposition soon coalesced around one man who became Genghis Khan's main rival.

Kokochu Teb Tengeri was the middle of seven sons of Monglik, the faithful companion of Temujin's father.[24] The two families had close ties of an imprecise nature. Temujin and Monglik came from different clans, but they had lived together during some of the more turbulent parts of Temujin's life. The *Secret History* credited Monglik with saving Temujin from "whirling waters" and "blazing fire"—a reference to his help in defeating Ong Khan and Jamuka. Although Monglik and Temujin had called Yesugei *father*, and Yesugei had called them both *son*, Temujin showed deferential respect to Monglik.[25]

Genghis Khan rose to supremacy through military might, but Kokochu Teb Tengeri had attracted a following thanks to his spiritual powers. The *Secret History* does not refer to him as a shaman or state that he gave Genghis Khan his title, but several foreign chronicles have made both of these claims. The Chinese specifically referred to him as a magician, and the Persians wrote that he was a prophet. How he acquired the title Teb Tengeri, with its suggestion of a special divine consecration, is unclear, as scholars cannot agree on the origin and meaning of *teb*. Although shamans were known in the court of the defeated Tayang Khan and Ong Khan, none is specifically mentioned in the court of Genghis Khan. Some reports state firmly that no "trance shamans" appeared in the lineage of Genghis Khan.[26] Mongol shamans communicated specifically and exclusively through their ancestors, and the old women who had barred Hoelun and her family from the ancestral ceremonies had severed Temujin's connection to those spirits. So he worshipped the mountain and formed a direct connection to heaven without going through another medium.

Male shamans were treated with cautious respect, but they evoked suspicion and even disgust. As one saying put it, "the worst of men become shamans."[27] The word *boo*, Mongolian for "shaman," is part of a cluster of words with loathsome connotations: foul, abominable, to vomit, to castrate, an opportunistic person without scruples; it is also the general term for lice, fleas, and bedbugs.[28]

Teb Tengeri's followers, who are referred to in the *Secret History* as the "nine-tongue people,"[29] seem to have included everyone who bore a grudge against Genghis Khan. They grew increasingly convinced of Teb Tengeri's superior power and spiritual authority, and this created a tension that needed to be resolved. The vehemently anti-Mongol but usually perceptive Persian chronicler Juzjani may have been right in thinking that he was a fake who took excessive advantage of his close kinship with Genghis Khan. "The imposter was so puffed up with his own importance," wrote Juzjani, "after the success of his pretended revelation that he began to entertain ambitious views for himself."[30]

While outwardly feigning loyalty to Genghis Khan, Teb Tengeri used his growing spiritual authority to gather his own following. Whatever his inspiration, he vastly underestimated his rival's skill, strength, and popularity. And he underestimated his ruthlessness. Without attacking the Great Khan directly, Teb Tengeri provoked repeated confrontations with family members around him, particularly stoking his rivalry with his brother Khasar by encouraging his ambitions while at the same time putting suspicions about him in Genghis Khan's mind. Genghis Khan was emotionally vulnerable to threats from Khasar, as Khasar was larger, stronger, and much better with a bow and arrow. Khasar had also betrayed him in the past by siding with Genghis Khan's rival Ong Khan.[31]

In the first years after the founding of the Mongol state, Teb Tengeri's power grew and grew, until sometime around 1208, he triggered a crisis that Genghis Khan seemed unprepared for and uncertain how to contain. Knowing the significance his rival ascribed to dreams, Teb Tengeri told him he had had a revelation in a dream in which Khasar had become the Great Khan of the Mongols. After word of this threatening dream spread, Khasar fled the camp, further provoking the suspicion that his brother had plotted some form of treason. Some chronicles state that Khasar joined Teb Tengeri and his brothers in a conspiracy to overthrow Genghis Khan.[32] Others suggest that Khasar had attempted to seduce Khulan, Genghis Khan's beloved new wife. One chronicle stated delicately that Khasar went hunting and shot the wrong bird, but one of Genghis Khan's retainers reported more bluntly, "When your brother Khasar was sitting drunk, he took lady Khulan's arm."

Genghis Khan never completely trusted Khasar. He seemed to be afraid of him. Jamuka had once described Khasar in supernatural terms of a sort he never used for Temujin. "He was born a coiling dragon-snake" and had the power to shoot enemies "who are beyond the mountain," and "beyond the steppe." His magical fork-tipped arrows could kill ten or twenty men with a single shot. He also had the power to swallow men and make them disappear "complete with quiver."[33]

Still trusting Teb Tengeri and already suspicious of Khasar, Genghis Khan believed that his brother posed a threat and used the dreams as an excuse to move against him. He seized Khasar, stripped him of the men he had placed under his command, and was debating what to do with him. Only Hoelun's intervention saved Khasar's life. Upon hearing of Khasar's detention, she rode in her camel cart all through the night, entered her son's *ger* at daybreak, and demanded that he release him. At one moment she even exposed her breasts to remind him that he needed to protect his brothers who had nursed from the same breast as he. Genghis Khan reluctantly obeyed his mother and freed his brother, but he gave him command of only 1,400 followers and kept a close eye on him thereafter.[34]

Hoelun was so exhausted by the tensions and fighting among her sons that soon after this incident, though she was only in her mid-fifties, she "completed her age" and died. Her death gave Teb Tengeri a new opportunity to expand his power and increase his personal following. As *Otchigen*, or Prince of the Fire, Hoelun's youngest son, Temuge, inherited her property. Indeed he had already been administering it, as he had been living with his mother prior to her death. Teb Tengeri now persuaded many of Hoelun's followers to leave Temuge and come to him. When Temuge Otchigen confronted him, Teb Tengeri and his men publicly humiliated him, making him kneel down to apologize and assume submission as a vassal.

Temuge fled to his older brother's court and tearfully begged for help. Borte was still in bed when he entered the *ger*, and when she heard his plea she became outraged at what had happened. She sat up in bed and, covering her breasts with a blanket, gave an impassioned plea to her husband to protect his children from Teb Tengeri, this evil shaman. If Teb Tengeri was willing to harm Genghis Khan's younger brothers while Genghis Khan still lived, she said, what would he do to her children after Genghis Khan was gone? Borte had suffered a great deal in her life, but the only time in the *Secret History* that we see her crying is when she pleaded with her husband to take action against Teb Tengeri.[35]

After Borte's urging, Genghis Khan allowed his younger brother to dispose of Teb Tengeri in revenge for the theft of his followers and the public humiliation. Temuge Otchigen waited for the next time Teb Tengeri appeared in Genghis Khan's *ger* and challenged him to fight.

When the two men went outside, Temuge's companions were waiting. According to Juzjani, they grabbed Teb Tengeri "by the throat and dashed him to the ground with such violence that he never rose again."[36] The *Secret History* records that they broke his back and left him on the edge of the camp to die. Later Genghis Khan publicly announced his final judgment: "Because Teb Tengeri slandered and beat my brothers," he proclaimed, "Heaven no longer loved him and took away his life."[37]

To Teb Tengeri's father and brothers he spoke more directly, placing the blame on them. "You thought that you were equal to me, and now you have caused Teb Tengeri to die. If I had known this earlier I would have dealt with you as I did with Jamuka and the others." Because of the debt he felt toward Monglik, he spared him and his remaining six sons, but he removed them from power. He permitted no rival for political power thereafter, and allowed no religious leader to exert too much influence. After Teb Tengeri's death, no Mongol openly questioned the authority of Genghis Khan.

Genghis Khan strove to mix followers of different religions in the same way that he combined disparate clans and tribes into new military and political units. In this way, each religion would be represented in his court without any one forming a powerful bloc. Teb Tengeri's overt challenge to his authority crystallized Genghis Khan's suspicion of men of religion who promoted themselves as closer to the Will of Heaven than other people. He continued to use shamans for special purposes, such as forecasting the future or controlling the weather, but he never again allowed a man to come between him and heaven.

Teb Tengeri's killing set a bloody precedent. This was the first, but far from the last, time that the Mongol khans would kill a religious leader who claimed a higher authority than the state or the khan. Later this policy would be invoked to justify the execution of the Islamic caliph and his sons in Baghdad in 1258, and of the imam of the Ismaili Assassins, whose followers considered him divine. Subsequent Mongol rulers repeatedly but unsuccessfully summoned the pope to examine his behavior and very likely would have killed him as well if he had accepted their invitation. Just as they tolerated no rival political leader, they killed religious leaders who defied the Great Khan. Genghis Khan was heaven's representative, and to defy him was to disobey God. Buddhist, Sufi Muslim, and Orthodox Christian leaders understood the Mongol policy and quickly adapted their ways to accommodate this new force.

Rather than selecting a court shaman, he maintained the tradition of appointing wise elders as spiritual counselors, or *beki*, around him. "In the Mongol tradition," he proclaimed in 1206, when he created the Mongol nation, "it is customary for a senior ranking person to become a *beki*."[38] He bestowed that title on Old Usun Ebugen of the Baarin, who had been consistently loyal, never "hiding or concealing" anything, and made him a counselor with special honors. Genghis

Khan allowed him to dress like the old Manichaean priests. "He shall wear a white *deel*, ride a white gelding, and when in the *ger* he will be given a seat waited on by others."[39] Although greatly honored, these counselors offered advice but had little independence and no room to interfere in the affairs of state. They could never exercise power or become a threat like Teb Tengeri had. The ruling elite in Genghis Khan's new nation would not be men of religion or tribal aristocrats. That privilege was reserved exclusively for his band of warriors.

Every story, whether factually true of not, has something to teach. One of the most interesting accounts of Genghis Khan's founding of the Mongol Empire and creation of his code of law was recorded by an Egyptian scholar, Shihab al-Din al-Nuwayri, at the beginning of the fourteenth century. According to al-Nuwayri, early in his life Genghis Khan turned to a Jewish rabbi for guidance and asked him what gave Jesus, Moses, and Muhammad their power and fame.

"Because they loved God and devoted themselves to him, so he rewarded them," the rabbi answered.

"If I love God and devote myself to him, will he reward me?" asked Genghis Khan.

"Yes," replied the rabbi.

After a lengthy discussion of the teachings and laws of Moses, Jesus, and Muhammad, Genghis Khan retreated into the mountains to meditate. Sometime later, he emerged singing and dancing; he had contemplated the various religions around him, and in the end he chose not "to obey any religion and did not belong to any religious community." Instead, he "just had love for God, as he claimed," and "he stayed like this as long as God willed, and this was his beginning."[40]

It seems doubtful that Genghis Khan ever met a rabbi, but the story combines aspects of his long spiritual training on Burkhan Khaldun with elements of his meetings with various religious scholars. Because he worshipped the *Tore*, Mongolian law, many observers frequently equated this with the Torah, which the Jews recognized as the Law of Moses, or with the *Tawrat*, which the Muslims recognized as the law of all prophets, including Jesus.[41] For Mongols, the *Tore*, Torah, and *Tawrat* blended together into a search for the laws of truth and the proper way to live.

Genghis Khan taught his people to worship their nation as other people worshipped their gods, spirits, prophets, and saints. The Mongols made sacrifices and promises to the Spirit of the State, *Toriin Sulde*, and the national banners precisely as other peoples did to their gods.[42] They treated the authority of the state, its *Tore*, as a god. The nation alone was the highest of all authorities and faiths. This idea was expressed clearly in the law as written by Genghis Khan's descendant Altan Khan in the sixteenth century, whose law code placed the state above religion. "The laws of religion are like knotted silver ribbons," he decreed, but "the laws of the emperor are like a golden yoke."[43]

For centuries, observers sought the secret to Genghis Khan's unparalleled conquest and imperial expansion. Was it the composite steppe bow, the sturdy Mongol horse, the diet of the warrior, the harsh life of the herder, some simple fluctuation in weather or climate, or was it, as the Mongol chroniclers wrote, simply fate or a reflection of the Will of Heaven above? Genghis Khan had no doubt as to the source of his many victories. His success came from his search for truth and unfailing effort to uphold the ultimate principles and the laws of the highest order. "My dynasty sits on the throne of many countries," he said in the *Secret History*, "because I think constantly of the sacred way of truth, the *Yeke Tore*."[44]

8

Guardians of the Flame

History shows repeatedly that one person, no matter how strong or dedicated, cannot exercise total control. Often rulers rely on their family to extend their reach, suspicious of all outsiders, but having been betrayed repeatedly by his relatives, Genghis Khan turned instead to a small circle of close companions known as the *Nokor* (*Nökör*). The *Nokor* were mostly men he had known before the founding of the nation whose loyalty had proven unshakable. They usually came from lower-ranking clans and had joined him at a young age, sometimes with the consent of their families, but some had run away from home to join him, proving that their loyalty to him was greater than to their families. Like self-made men in many societies, they honored achievement and disparaged birth and nobility. They owed their success to bravery, discipline, and total commitment to their fellow warriors and to Genghis Khan.

The *Nokor* became intimate companions, closer than family. "You are my strength," Genghis Khan told them. He knew that they were the ones who had helped him in the decades-long struggle to obtain power and create a new nation. "Lying down around my tent under the stars at night, you made sure that I slept peacefully," he said. "You never rested and stood at my side in the swirl of snow and the cold of rain."[1]

Throughout his career, Genghis Khan took new men of exceptional qualities, including former enemies, into his inner circle. Some were selected in highly unusual ways. During one battle, an enemy warrior shot Genghis Khan's horse through the neck. Genghis Khan survived and won the battle, and demanded of the captured soldiers, "Who shot an arrow and severed the neck bone of my tawny horse with the white mouth?" One man stepped forward and confessed to the killing, fully expecting that he would be executed "and left to rot."

Instead, Genghis Khan honored him as a brave hero, rewarded him, and explained that most defeated warriors concealed their prior actions and held their tongues out of fear. This man was brave enough to tell the truth. "He is a man to have as a companion."[2] Thereafter, he called him Jebe, the name of the particular type of arrow he had used to kill the horse, and asked him to "keep by my side." Jebe, proud of his new name, became one of the great Mongol generals.

In time Genghis Khan formed a group known as the Nine Companions. They included his trusted friends Jelme and Subodei of the Uriyankhai, Jebe, and Khubilai Noyan, who together were known as the Four Dogs. They swore their loyalty to Genghis Khan and never wavered. Subodei promised to be as diligent as a rat or crow in getting whatever his lord needed. "I will cover you like a felt blanket; I will shelter you from the wind," he vowed.[3] Genghis Khan honored their loyalty above all else. He rarely took credit for anything and even went so far as to lavish praise on others for his own achievements, great and small. He said of Subodei and Jelme, "When I said to go there, you crushed stones to get there. When I said to attack, you split open the rocks, shattered the shining stones, and parted the deep waters."[4]

Subodei became his greatest general, but Genghis Khan's closest spiritual bond was with Old Jarchigudai's son Jelme. Later in life, looking back on his youth, Genghis Khan said that Jelme had appeared at precisely the moment "when Heaven and Earth increased my strength and took me into their protection."[5] He described Jelme as sharing in his divine mission. He quoted from the ancient sayings, and speaking directly to Jelme in a public assembly, he said, "[You] brought peace to my mind," and, "You brought peace to my heart." The two men remained exceptionally close. Jelme seemed to materialize unexpectedly when the greatest dangers confronted Genghis Khan or those whom he loved.

Jelme saved his life several times and helped to save the life of his grandson Tolui. On one occasion after an arrow wounded Genghis Khan in the neck and he had been unable to stop the bleeding by pressing on the wound, Jelme stayed with him on the battlefield and constantly sucked the blood from his neck throughout the night. Another time, in an effort to get food for his master, Jelme walked naked into the enemy camp undetected, an ability frequently attributed to those with supernatural powers.

On another occasion, according to a chronicle known as *The Golden Summary of Genghis Khan*, Jelme accompanied Genghis Khan and a few of his companions on a hunt to the Ongi River in the north Gobi. While riding monotonously through the river gorge, the "repetitive bobbing" of the horses lulled Genghis Khan into a dream. He saw the Tayichiud, the great enemies of his childhood, coming to attack, and when he awoke, he saw a military detachment approaching them in the distance. Jelme climbed to the top of the gorge and, "beckoning from the top of a high ridge," called in a fog that settled over the gorge.[6]

Jelme maintained a post right outside Genghis Khan's door and served as his most loyal guardian. With hundreds of guards around the perimeter of the khan's residence, there was little chance that an intruder could reach the entrance, but the doorway carried a special spiritual meaning. Whoever stepped on the wooden threshold of the door was deemed to have trampled on the heart of the entire lineage, disgracing both the ancestors and the generations waiting to be born. Protecting the entrance implied a spiritual responsibility. Jelme was stationed on the right side, a special place of honor symbolizing the spiritual protection of the imperial lineage.

Hoelun had accused Genghis of having "no friend but your shadow, no whip but a horse's tail." Perhaps because of this maternal taunt Genghis Khan designated Boorchu, one of his earliest followers, as his shadow and Jelme as his whip.[7] Jelme's unique role in the life of Genghis Khan was similar to the role that Old Man Jarchigudai had played in the life of young Temujin.

He singled him out as *oljetu khutukhtu*, "fortunate and blessed,"[8] a phrase used primarily to indicate the spiritually powerful forest people. Both words later became popular names for Mongol rulers in Persia, Russia, and China. Genghis Khan later took Jelme's son and gave him the distinctive title of "Great Quiver Bearer."[9]

In addition to the Four Dogs, another four companions became known as the Four Horses. These included Boorchu, who as a boy had been the first to leave his family and join Temujin; Muhali, who eventually led the campaigns in northern China; Boroqul, who once saved the life of Genghis Khan's son Ogodei in battle, but was destined to be the first to die in a treacherous fight against Botohuitarhun, queen of the Tumat, in the area between lakes Baikal and Hovsgol; and Chilaun, who served faithfully but with less acclaim than the others. Together the Nine Companions (Genghis Khan himself was the ninth) stood at the apex of the empire, in command of the army, government, and nation.

For some of these men, such as Muhali, who was born a slave, the rise in social status was incredible and something that would have been nearly impossible for them to achieve on their own. Muhali was destined to become the military ruler of all of northern China, but he never forgot or hid his humble origin. He even named his son Bol, meaning "slave."

☫

Genghis Khan was the supreme ruler of his nation, surrounded by eight companions, the Four Dogs and the Four Horses. These men, his generals and commanders, did not camp regularly with him. They were usually out with the army on campaigns, guarding the borders and overseeing the most distant parts of his territory. Normally, Genghis Khan traveled with only one of his four wives, and she ran the *ordu*.[10] The other wives would be encamped in more distant territories, each with her own court, responsible for overseeing the people and ensuring the continuity of government in her area during Genghis Khan's absence.

The *ordu* in the main camp was encircled by and separate from the Left Wing and the Right Wing; it formed a distinct area known as the *gol*, or center. This inner circle of guards and companions was always at the center, whether in camp, on the move, or in battle. Wherever Genghis Khan was by day or night, they surrounded him. Few people, even his highest ministers, could enter this area without permission, and an elite corps of warriors carefully and constantly guarded it. They were the *Keshig*—literally the Chosen Ones, or Sacred Guardians— who protected the nation.[11] More than bodyguards, they formed the most powerful body within the government. Their job was not temporary: they were Genghis Khan's companions for life.

Marco Polo referred to this elite guard as *Questian*, a name close to *Equestrian*, an order of aristocratic mounted knights in the Roman Empire. Because of this similarity between the Latin and Mongolian names, he described the Mongol *Keshig* as "the Faithful Knights of the Lord."[12] The Chinese envoy from the Sung emperor marveled at their total devotion to the khan. He wrote that the *Keshig* attributed all good things to him, and would often be heard saying "thanks to the Eternal Sky and spiritual blessing of the khan," and "if my khan sends me into the fire or into the water, I will go for him."[13]

Genghis Khan specified that his guards had to be imbued with the highest physical and spiritual qualities. He insisted that they have a good appearance and be wise, skilled, and spiritually strong. He chose the *Keshig* himself and sometimes rewarded men who least expected it. The *Keshig* numbered 150 in 1202, but inclusion of Ong Khan's bodyguards expanded it to about 1,000. After 1206, with the official founding of the Mongol nation, Genghis Khan increased them to 10,000. By this time, most of them were bodyguards, servants, and administrators, but the inner core from his earlier days remained the elite within the elite.

Within the group a strict hierarchy prevailed, and yet each person shared equally in the responsibilities of the group. The officers were expected to be the bravest and hardest working of all the men. Because protecting Genghis Khan was their most important function, even the commanders had to stand guard on their day or night shift like every other warrior in the *Keshig*.

In order to uphold the law and to maintain the mystique of the elite court, fraternization outside the *Keshig*, even with family members, was discouraged, and when on duty totally forbidden. Most members of the *Keshig* were illiterate, and no written messages were used inside the group. "Explaining by teeth and mouth," Genghis said, according to the *Secret History*, "we shall believe."[14] Despite the strict restraints on nearly every aspect of *Keshig* life, he encouraged them to find fulfillment within the group and to enjoy life with one another. "In deeds of familiar life and laughing together," he told them, "be friendly, like the lazy black two year old bull."[15]

The *Keshig* constituted the highest power in the government. Despite the fact that he had adopted a written language for legal and judicial matters, Genghis Khan forbade his army to write things down. Information and messages had to be transmitted and stored orally, so that they could not end up in enemy hands. A Chinese observer noted with amazement that in the entire Mongol army of 100,000 men there was not a single slip of paper with any writing on it.[16] Writing was strictly for legal affairs and civil administration, but no written order could become official until it was stamped and dated with the permission and name of the *Keshig* officer in charge of that shift.

Although it was the administrative hub of the nation, the *Keshig* operated much like an extended household. Ever mindful that the Tatars had killed his father by feeding him poisoned food, Genghis Khan charged his inner guards with preparing what he ate and drank and guarding the pots and dishes from which he ate. They carefully monitored the serving boys and girls who came and went, oversaw the fermentation of *airag*, and supervised the distribution of alcohol, a substance that grew increasingly problematic as the empire expanded. Genghis Khan saw the unlimited use of alcohol as a threat not just to the individual but to the whole nation. "Wine is an enemy," warned the author of *Wisdom of Royal Glory*, the handbook for Turkic rulers. "While princes of the world enjoy sweet wine, their lands and subjects suffer bitter ills."[17]

Traditionally the Mongols fermented mare and camel milk in the fall when milk was most widely available. The supply of milk regulated the amount of drinking, and when the cows dried up in the winter, the herders no longer had milk with which to ferment alcohol until the following fall. With merchant contacts and invasions of new countries, however, the Mongols found a seemingly inexhaustible source of alcohol made not merely from milk but also from grapes, rice, honey, and other exotic sources. Instead of an outright prohibition against these many forms of intoxication, Genghis Khan sought to instill moderation in the army, the people, and his family by teaching them the dangers of alcohol. In this area, he had little success, and it seems that in time all four of his sons as well as other descendants suffered from severe alcoholism.

The powers of the *Keshig* extended far beyond control of the camp, alcohol, and food. They enjoyed the right to go more or less wherever they pleased, and all people had an obligation to supply them with horses, food, or whatever they might require without explanation. No one could quarrel with them or question them, and they outranked other soldiers in the army, including unit commanders. They could go after anyone who raised a spear against them, and then they would kill them, "strip them of their bloody clothes and take their valuables."[18] Despite their special powers, the warriors of the *Keshig* lived and died by an exceptionally harsh and unyielding code. A guardian who did wrong was not merely violating a law; he was betraying a moral principle. Such an act threatened the identity and spiritual power of the entire group.

In general, Genghis Khan did not distinguish between degrees of crime when punishing his subjects; stealing a horse or telling a lie was no different from murder or betraying one's family, in his view. He did not establish gradations of offenses; all crimes were equally wrong. To commit one such crime was to violate the moral principles of life. The person who would lie or commit adultery would surely steal or kill. Such people should not live in society, and thus the punishment, regardless of the infraction, was usually death. His rules were even harsher for those close to him. A guard who fell asleep on duty, the thief who took a horse, a subject who rebelled against his khan deserved equal punishment because they had all proven themselves unreliable and unworthy and could not be trusted members of society. Despite the fact that death was the prescribed penalty for virtually every crime, in practice Genghis Khan recognized that everyone was guilty of a crime at some time in his life. He usually showed mercy for the first few infractions and mostly executed habitual offenders.

Genghis Khan frequently instructed his men in the precise duties and characteristics expected of members of his elite force. His teachings revealed much about his personal view of life and what had propelled him to such a high level of success and power. He emphasized the necessity of steadfast determination and decisive action. In any crucial matter, action mattered above thought. The time for consideration was before an action was taken, but once it was decided and done, thought had to be pushed aside. Determination and will were paramount in Genghis Khan's view. If there was a pass that others said was too high and impossible to cross, "it is only necessary to wish to cross it and already you have passed through." If there was a river that could not be crossed, "do not think of how to cross it," he warned. "You must only want to cross it and you will pass through!"[19] Success always waits on the other side of the impossible obstacle. If something bad happens, you can find a way out.[20]

Such words from a lesser man might have seemed a hollow form of idealism or empty rhetoric, but Genghis Khan demonstrated their truth repeatedly by achieving seemingly impossible tasks. For the men of the *Keshig* and his other warriors, their first duty to one another was feroc-ity in battle. He charged them to be as fast as the falcon, as precise as the hawk, as hungry as the tiger, as fierce as the wolf, and, by night, as invisible as the crow. The important aspect of any deed or action is not intention but successful completion. No matter how good the plans, how strong the desire, how great the effort, in the end, success alone matters. Many "made an oath," he said to one of his followers in praise, but you "carried out the task." Such determined effort, without regard to the hazards, can change fate itself, Genghis Khan believed. Because of your actions, he said of his faithful followers, "the door was opened and Eternal Heaven gave me the reins."[21] Heaven does not need prayers, offerings, and chanting; it needs action.

ॐ

In organizing his government, Genghis Khan relied on steppe tradi-tion, common sense, and his own innovative genius for combining the best of the old and new. He had not read any of the many Turkic books on statecraft and certainly not the works of Greek philosophy; yet the ideas from both had penetrated the steppe via the Manichae-ans and Uighurs.

The *Keshig* combined elements of the Chosen Ones, the *magi* or *bogu* of Manichaeism, and the Guardians of Plato's *Republic*. Plato described the Guardians as "warrior athletes" who would "take care of themselves and of the whole state." The rulers should take their soldiers, live separately with them, "and contain nothing private, or individual."[22] The role of the guardians was to "preserve us against foreign enemies and maintain peace among our citizens at home."[23] He described them as "noble youth very like a well-bred dog in re-spect of guarding and watching . . . quick to see, and swift to over-take the enemy when they see him; and strong too."[24] Plato compared the guardians to "watchdogs of the herd."[25] They must be "wide-awake dogs, and must also be inured to all changes of food and climate." Like Homer, Plato claimed that true warriors should avoid vegetables and live primarily on meat.[26]

Plato's words echoed poetically and far more graphically in the *Secret History*, where Jamuka described the men around Genghis Khan as his dogs "with foreheads of hard copper and chisels for snouts, awls for tongues, and hearts of iron." These dogs charge forward "feeding on dew and riding the wind, and on days of battle they eat human flesh."[27] Jamuka singled out the Uriyankhai men—Jelme, Subodei, and the archer Jelme of the Besud clan—as the fiercest of these dogs of war.

Their training consisted of constant physical exercise. Plato too had stressed the importance of physical training for the body and music for the soul.[28] He explained that "musical training is a more potent instrument than any other because rhythm and harmony find their way into the inward places of the soul."[29] As the soldiers were forbidden to write down messages, Genghis Khan required his men to learn the discipline of musical rhythm and harmony in a practical way. They had to memorize detailed songs of the laws of the nation and the army, and musical formulas for making message songs. His men had to be able to repeat verbatim long texts, and to do this they had to be able to use preformed song formats into which a new message could be fit. Similarly, Plato said of the ideal guardians that they had to study music in "the essential forms, in all their combinations, and recognize them and their images wherever they are found."[30]

Although Genghis Khan's *Keshig* was made up primarily of soldiers, they played an important spiritual role in his court and shared in the divine mandate of their leader. They also shared the power and rewards of their achievements. Under no other circumstances could men of such humble birth have risen to power within the steppe tribal aristocracy, much less over foreign nations.

Members of the *Keshig* maintained a direct and personal connection to the divine through their proximity to Genghis Khan. They required no sacred books, priests, or magic to intervene in worldly affairs. They followed the code of right behavior simply because it was right. The Mongols believed that everyone had an innate inclination to self-preservation and comfort, but each person also had an innate attraction to honor and correct behavior. They were free to decide for themselves which of these instincts they would allow to dominate. For his inner circle, Genghis Khan selected people who chose the path of honor. For a person to achieve this moral discipline, a spiritual disposition was essential.

The inner sanctum controlled by the *Keshig* was the sacred center of the empire. Foreigners could never sleep there. Before entering the presence of the khan, they and their gifts had to be purified by fire. "When we were to be introduced at his court," wrote Friar Carpini of his arrival at the Mongol camp in 1246, "we were informed that it was previously necessary for us to pass between two fires." This requirement extended to their religious paraphernalia, including Bibles, letters from the pope, and crosses. "We refused at first, but were told there was no danger," he explained. "The fire would remove all evil."[31] Carpini obeyed the order. "Having kindled two fires at a convenient distance, they fix two spears in the earth, one near each fire, stretching a cord between the tops of these spears, and about the cord they hang some rags of buckram [felt], under which cord, and between which fires, all the men, and beasts, and houses must pass; and all the while, a woman stands on each side, sprinkling water on the passengers, and reciting certain verses."[32]

The area was so sacred that even when the camp moved, the space it had occupied remained taboo. For months or years, no person dared cross it or enter it until all traces of Genghis Khan's camp and fire had disappeared.

Genghis Khan flung a veil of mystery around himself and his inner court. This secrecy extended to all religious activities. Unlike kings and emperors who publicly displayed their religion and flaunted their personal piety, he permitted only rare public glimpses into his spiritual practices. He believed that knowledge was precious, to be shared only when necessary and even then cautiously. Of all forms of knowledge, that about heaven and the supernatural world was the most precious and therefore the most secret. Sharing it would dilute it, and revealing it to foreigners and strangers posed an extreme danger.

Because of the constant concealment, some otherwise reputable observers asserted that the Mongols lacked an organized spiritual life. "There is no religion or worship among them," wrote a perplexed Armenian chronicler in the thirteenth century, "but they frequently call on the name of God in all matters. We do not know, nor do they, if this is to thank the God of Being or some other thing that they call God."[33] The Mongols "know nothing of eternal life or perpetual damnation," claimed Friar Carpini. "They believe, however, that after death they live in another world, that flocks multiply, that they shall eat and drink and do other things which living men do in this world."[34] "Formerly the Mongols had no literature and no Religion of their own," wrote Bar Hebraeus, "but they knew one God, the Creator of the Universe, and some of them confessed that heaven was God, and they called it so."[35] The Arab writer al-Nuwayri recorded a similar sentiment, saying that the Mongols "did not obey any religion, and did not belong to any religious community, but just had love for God."[36]

Law and religion were generally intertwined at this time; most societies attributed a divine origin for their laws. But the Mongols "differ from all the nations in the world," wrote the Dominican monk Riccoldo da Monte di Croce in his *Liber Peregrinacionis*. He had been sent as a missionary to convert the Mongol Christians to Catholicism and allegiance to the pope, but he failed in his mission. He wrote *Liber Peregrinacionis* as a guide for future missionaries in the hope that they might have more success. "They do not boast of having any law warranted by God, as many other nations falsely do, but simply by some instinct or movement of nature, say that there is something sovereign above all things of this world, and that that is God."[37]

The claim that Mongols lacked a religion irritated Genghis Khan's descendant Injannasi. Writing much later in the nineteenth century, he explained in *The Blue Chronicle* that observers dismissed Mongol theology as primitive or nonexistent. "Those who think that no Mongolian words express deep and profound concepts are like one who bathes himself on the bank of an ocean and thinks the sea is shallow."[38]

Religion provided a major source of political strength and enabled Genghis Khan to maintain the support and morale of his troops, but in protecting the privacy of his spiritual life, he prevented others from stealing or limiting his power. Not having participated in the ceremonies of his tribe as a child, he pursued religion in his personally unique way while incorporating elements from many sources. The ever-insightful Juvaini wrote that Genghis Khan invented himself, "without the toil of pursuing records or the trouble of conforming to tradition." His achievements in life arose as "the products of his own understanding and the compilation of his own intellect."[39] Not only did he conquer on the battlefield, but he administered law and justice derived from his belief in the power of heaven. "In accordance and agreement with his own mind he established a rule for every occasion and a regulation for every circumstance; while for every crime he fixed a penalty."[40]

Even his enemies and those who hated him believed that such incredible success by a man with no formal training was a miracle of God. With a small army, carrying no supplies, he "reduced and subjugated the lords of the horizons from the East unto the West," wrote Juvaini.[41] Although a devout Muslim throughout his life, Juvaini wrote that Allah had chosen Genghis Khan, a non-Muslim, for a unique mission on Earth. "God-Almighty in wisdom and intelligence distinguished Genghis Khan from all his coevals and in alertness of mind and absoluteness of power exalted him above all the kings of the world."[42]

Genghis Khan closed the entire area around Burkhan Khaldun and the headwaters of the Onon and Kherlen rivers. Only members of the royal family and his closest associates could go to the mountain, while common people and foreigners were prohibited from passing within sight of it. As long as he lived close to the sacred mountain, he cultivated a spiritual relationship with the landscape and sky, but as his conquests took him farther afield for increasingly long periods, he had to find a different means to connect with God. Given his life as a nomadic warrior, his religion needed to be portable and easily adapted to new places. It could not be centered on buildings and could not depend on statues, bells, or other large ritual objects that were impractical to transport. His religion needed to remain agile, durable, and practical.

Traditional Mongol religious practice focused on the fire in the center of the *ger* to which family members, usually the mother, made daily offerings of fat in the belief that the spirits of the family, past and future, resided in the fire. Royal camps of previous khans worshipped the fire as a symbol of the royal family, but Genghis Khan did not follow this tradition. His fire was the place where the men around him worshipped. Because they belonged to different lineages, their worship of the fire in the army camp expanded from honoring one lineage to honoring them all. It became a way to worship the nation and thereby to cement their bond and unity. Under Genghis Khan, the fireplace in the center of the *ger* became the focus for this cult of the state. It symbolized the law and the moral authority of the army and the nation.

In the family home, women held responsibility for most rituals, such as starting the fire in the prescribed way and extinguishing it respectfully when the camp moved. They honored everyday objects such as the milk pail used to sprinkle libations to the sun and the cardinal directions each day. Male rituals centered on objects from their daily domain of herding, hunting, and fighting, such as horses, weapons, and the accoutrements of military life. Bows, arrows, and saddles belonged to a particular man, but the drums and banners of Genghis Khan's army belonged to all warriors collectively and in time came to symbolize the whole group. The *Keshig* kept a close eye on these sacred objects, principally the drum and banner. The care of and responsibility for these items remained the duty of his elite soldiers; no priest or shaman had power over them.

Old Jarchigudai first came to Temujin with his drum strapped to his back, and the drum was the ritual center of his spiritual life. Beating the drum carried messages to heaven and brought back messages as well. It spoke with the voice of heaven on Earth and the voice of humanity in heaven. This spiritual attachment to the drum increased its efficacy in battle. The effect can be felt in the words of an observer of the Mongol army invading China: "the sound of drums rose to heaven and on every side could be seen smoke and dust."[43] Injannasi wrote that "at the first sound of the drum, the spirits of the men are aroused and they will charge with great energy." Often the Mongols began the battle in silence to make the drums more frightening to the enemy when they suddenly sounded later in the battle. "We beat our drums at the time when the enemy's spirit is exhausted; this is how we were victorious."[44]

At home on Burkhan Khaldun, Genghis Khan spoke to the earth through the trees, particularly to trees that stood alone, rose above the others, had an unusual shape, or stood in an unusual spot. He prayed to the tree, hung strips of cloth on it, offered gifts and sacrifices, and sometimes sang and danced around it. The drum could easily be carried everywhere the army went, but the tree could not. Instead, the Mongols carried a spirit banner, a long pole or spear at the top of which was attached horsehair. They honored this spirit banner, worshipped it, and sacrificed to it. Their secret rituals had the banner of Genghis Khan at their center. Wherever it stood became the center of the Mongol Empire and thus the center of the Earth.

There is no record of Genghis Khan's taking anyone with him when he wanted to commune with the Eternal Blue Sky or perform a private spiritual ceremony. He listened to his heart for inspiration and then told people what he had heard. A record of his prayers did not survive, but some echo can be heard in a more recent shamanic ritual prayer from the area:

We play on the rays of the sun
We ride on the rays of the moon
We rise into the heavens
We descend onto the hills.[45]

The tasks of assembling warriors as disciplined as the Mongols and fashioning an elite fighting force as loyal as the *Keshig* took decades of effort. Many mistakes occurred along the way, and it was not until he was in his late forties that, having defeated every foe on the steppe and learned his most important lessons through failures as well as triumphs, Genghis Khan was ready to set out against the world. By then he had united all the nomadic tribes solidly behind him and extinguished any possible dissent from within their ranks. With a united Mongol nation and thoroughly experienced and loyal warriors, the time had come to focus his elite fighting force on more distant horizons.

Before setting out to battle, the Mongols sprinkled a milk libation on their banners. The words used by Genghis Khan's men are not known, but at one such ceremony, the words of Jamuka had been recorded. "I have made offerings to my standard that waves in the wind, and held it high overhead for all men to see. I have beaten my ox-hide drum and made it sound like a thousand men charging. I have mounted my warhorse with the black stripe down its back. I have laced up my breastplate of leather. I have raised my sword from its sheath. I have placed on my bowstring an arrow I have marked with my enemy's name. Let us all die together fighting."[46]

PART III

Becoming the World Conqueror

God has severed his love from the kings of the Earth and the light of His face has fallen on Genghis Khan. He has given him kingship over all lands.

~Hulegu, 1258, Baghdad

9

Two Wings of One Bird

At the start of the thirteenth century, China consisted of more than a dozen kingdoms, some large enough to claim to be an empire and others too restricted to be concerned about anything beyond petty rivalries and local strife. Northern China was in political turmoil while southern China was in a protracted period of decadent decay. A so-called barbarian group, the Jurched of Manchuria, ruled the north as the Jin, or Golden, dynasty. Farther south, the Sung dynasty, which had once ruled a united China, continued as a truncated empire teetering on the brink of collapse. In what are now Tibet and Yunnan, a handful of isolated Buddhist kingdoms drifted along with none successfully dominating the others for long.

In the upper reaches of the Yellow River and around the Ordos, in what is now Inner Mongolia, the Tangut people maintained a Buddhist court and controlled the Gansu Corridor, China's entryway onto the Silk Route. The western part of the Silk Route was ruled by the Kara Khitai ethnic group, whose ancestors once ruled northern China as the Liao dynasty but had been chased out by the Jurched and now held a much smaller kingdom in the Tien Shan Mountains and adjacent oases. Along the southern edge of the Gobi, several tribal kingdoms of mostly Christian Turks patrolled the border region separating the Mongols from the large production centers and trade routes.

The kingdoms of China may have been disunited, but they were rich, and their people enjoyed a high standard of living and even luxury compared with the meager lifestyle offered by the steppe. Every form of known merchandise moved along the trade routes that knitted the Chinese kingdoms together with the Muslim centers of Central Asia. Aside from metal, the most important product was silk. Today it is thought of primarily as a luxury item, but for the Mongols it was a highly practical commodity. Chinese weavers produced silk so tight that lice and other vermin could not penetrate it, and even on lesser qualities of silk, the strands were so slick that lice could not attach their eggs to it. In the cold, dry environment of Mongolia, where bathing was difficult, these characteristics made Chinese silk uniquely valuable. Silk had another, even more important, lifesaving quality. When penetrated by an arrow, the strong, slick fibers wrapped around the arrowhead even as it sank into the flesh. The silk greatly reduced the severity of the wound and, most important, allowed the arrowhead to be gently extracted without doing further damage and with decreased likelihood of infection. For a warrior, silk was a magic fabric.

Despite the great appeal of Chinese goods, trade across the vast Gobi was limited by the distance that needed to be covered over a harsh landscape. The Mongol nomads grew no crops, wove no cloth, mined no metals, and made no pots, yet they required all of these things to continue in their nomadic way of life. To be herders and warriors they needed the trade goods of China. In times of strength, the Chinese carefully controlled the flow of these goods out onto the steppe and demanded steady payment in animals, furs, leather, and wool. The Mongols offered little, however, that could not be supplied more easily by Koreans, Manchurians, Tibetans, Uighurs, and smaller neighboring nationalities. These others far surpassed the Mongols at commerce, but the Mongols were better warriors. Now united and no longer fighting one another, they looked south toward the tempting wealth of China.

While Genghis Khan had been consolidating his power on the steppes, the kingdoms of China remained mired in disarray. As soon as he united his people, he sent out a series of raids on cities just south of the Gobi belonging to the kingdom of Xi Xia and inhabited by the Tangut, a people culturally related to the Tibetans. These raids seemed to be nothing more than typical attacks by nomads whenever settled kingdoms weakened or lowered their guard. For Genghis Khan, however, these early forays were probes to test the resistance and resolve of his neighbors and to locate their weak points.

Instead of encouraging these agricultural and commercial kingdoms to rally together and mount a united front against the steppe nomads, the probes only increased tensions. This turmoil produced a small and irregular stream of refugees from the losing factions. Genghis Khan welcomed them. At first, they trickled in as small groups of families, but then whole tribes began to defect. One of the first to do so was the Onggut, a semisedentary Turkic tribe in alliance with the Jin dynasty charged with patrolling the northern border to keep out the nomads. Genghis Khan accepted them and made a marriage between their khan and his daughter Alaqai, thereby adopting the tribal nation into his empire.

In the summer of 1208, two years after the founding of the Mongol nation, four Chinese officials of the Jin dynasty fled to his court with their families, seeking protection and offering to serve the Great Khan. They encouraged Genghis Khan to overthrow the emperor of the Jin dynasty.[1] Their presence among the Mongols was thought to demonstrate the shifting Will of Heaven, and they convinced Genghis Khan that his duty was not merely to unite the warring tribes of the steppes but to liberate and unite China as well. The flight of such educated and respected men inspired and emboldened the disgruntled soldiers in the Jin army, many of whom fled to join this new nation that awarded much higher respect and far greater rewards to the military than did the Chinese. They convinced Genghis Khan that the Jin dynasty was a dying dynasty that offered new lands and new people for the taking.

Genghis Khan did not immediately respond to the suggestion of attacking China. At first he continued to consolidate his power at home. A Chinese chronicler described the chaos in the decades prior to his arrival. Civil wars ravaged the land and desperate citizens "jumped into wells and rivers when the terror approached, and there were those who cut their own throats or hung themselves when the situation became critical." It was an era when "soldiers and civilians alike were slaughtered indiscriminately; the virtuous and the evil died in the same manner. Corpses filled the city, blood covered all the roads and streets."[2]

Genghis Khan had spent all of his adult life fighting, but up until now his enemies had been other nomads. He understood how to fight nomadic tribes who lived and fought like him. Though the tribes he had battled previously might have varied in size, the differences were minor compared with the Jin dynasty of the Jurched, who had some fifty million subjects against Genghis Khan's one million. Altogether, the Chinese kingdoms totaled about 120 million people. In China, for the first time, Genghis Khan had to confront people who lived in cities, behind massive walls, with many more powerful weapons, including gunpowder and exploding devices. He could not fight them the way he had battled nomads on the steppe.

Having been encouraged by the refugees and warriors who had come to him across the desert to descend from the Mongolian Plateau, and having tested the defenses to the south, Genghis Khan decided to escalate his cross-border raids to a full military campaign, which he would lead. To take on these new enemies, he returned to the most basic lessons he had learned as a hunter on Burkhan Khaldun. His military strategy was to approach the enemy like a wolf. Wolves never attack the strongest member of a herd; they do not go after the stallion or the mare, ready to fight to the death to defend their colt. Instead, they pick the weak ones, the slow ones, the young or old, and attack the vulnerable while letting the others flee. Thus, Genghis Khan did not initially move against the Jin dynasty or the more distant Sung; he chose the Tangut, a smaller and weaker independent kingdom in what is today western China, as his first prey. Early in 1209, he crossed the Gobi Desert with his army while the weather was still cool, and attacked. In the words of the French historian René Grousset, "The Mongol and his horse were to hunt the Chinese, the Persian, the Russian, and the Hungarian just as they hunted the antelope or the tiger."[3]

His new war strategy drew from the organization of the great Mongol hunts called *mingan ava*, or "taking a thousand." For this type of group hunt, hundreds and sometimes thousands of hunters spread out to form a large circle surrounding a vast area. Beating sticks and making noise, they slowly converged, driving all the wild animals before them.[4] As the noose tightened around the frightened animals, they panicked and ran in all directions with no hope of escape. After corralling them, the hunters could leisurely pick them off one by one.

The Mongols used this same tactic as they approached the Tangut territory, terrifying the people in the countryside and villages and forcing them to flee toward the cities. Some foreign observers were mystified by the apparent lack of coordination among the Mongol warriors, who seemed to be dashing back and forth across the countryside, attacking one place, then leaving their work unfinished to race off to attack another. They even sometimes retreated in the midst of a victory without following through. The Mongol warriors were intentionally stirring up the population and driving people from their homes. Their goal was not to kill people but to use them as a weapon for the coming campaign against the capital city. Once amassed behind the city walls, the fleeing population quickly began to consume supplies of food and provoke panic and discord in populations living in crowded conditions, ripe for outbreaks of illnesses and rapidly spreading epidemics. Unable to escape the Mongol siege, the Tangut turned like animals ferociously on one another.

When Genghis Khan reached Yinchuan, the capital of the Tangut kingdom, and saw its massive walls, it appeared impregnable. He knew there was no point in throwing his men against the heavily fortified walls of the city. At first, he was uncertain what to do next, but he quickly discovered that he could control the flow of water by building dams, diverting rivers away from the city or flooding them to undermine the walls and further weaken the morale and capability of its defenders. He ordered his men to construct a series of canals and dams to divert the river, but the dams were too weak to hold the massive flow of water and he ended up flooding his own siege camps instead.

One of Genghis Khan's most important attributes was his ability to turn apparent defeat into triumph. By this time, his campaign had been under way for nearly a year. In early 1210, he ordered a lifting of the siege and withdrew from Yinchuan. Overjoyed at their apparent victory, the Tangut soldiers rushed out of the city to attack the fleeing warriors, not realizing that this was a trick to make them open their gates and to lure them out. The Mongols ambushed the weakened and euphorically overconfident army and defeated them. Their king surrendered, swore allegiance to Genghis Khan, paid an enormous tribute, and promised to send more each year in return for keeping his throne.

This victory, Genghis Khan's first in urban territory, encouraged the border tribes to join the Mongols. Just as the Onggut had voluntarily united with them, soon the Uighurs in the oasis cities of western China enthusiastically broke away from the Kara Khitai and joined the growing Mongol nation. The Karluk Turks on the western steppe followed soon thereafter. Genghis Khan arranged marriages for his daughters to the leaders of these tribes, as well as to the Oirat of southern Siberia, who also joined him. Then, leaving these four kingdoms under the control of his daughters, he summoned their leaders to bring their armies and join the Mongol forces.

Bolstered by the rich bounty taken from the Tangut and by his growing army of vassals, Genghis Khan was now ready to turn his attention to the Jin dynasty and their capital of Zhongdu, which is modern Beijing. He justified his attack on the Jin on different grounds depending on his audience. To his own people he called for revenge, denouncing the Jin for having brutally crucified their ancestor Ambaqai Khan. To the Khitai people who had been deposed by the Jurched and now suffered under their rule, he reminded them of their close kinship to the Mongols and told them that they had a common enemy in the Jurched. He dangled the hope of restoring the Khitai to the power they had once occupied. To the Han people who chafed under the barbarian rule of the Jin, he offered hope of liberation from foreign rule, or at least replacing the choking reign and constant exploitation of the Jin with the looser reign of the Mongols.

The Mongols considered the Golden Emperor of the Jin a usurper, and in deference to the Khitai, who had previously ruled the area, they always referred to China as *Khitai*. This name was also used by Marco Polo with a different spelling—*Cathay*. Despite Genghis Khan's defeat of the Tangut and his alliance with the Onggut, Oirat, Uighur, and Karluk, Jin officials initially showed little fear of their formerly low-ranking vassal and treated him arrogantly, even demanding his renewed submission. The Jin emperor remained unimpressed by Genghis Khan's victory over these smaller kingdoms fringing the Gobi. He sent a challenge to Genghis Khan: "Our empire is like the sea," he said, "and your empire is nothing more than a handful of sand."[5]

Genghis Khan used these insults against him to rally his people. He mastered the art of magic ritual as well as spiritual showmanship. When he faced the daunting mission of attacking the Jin dynasty, he needed the firm and complete commitment of his people. Juzjani reported in detail how he achieved it. Genghis Khan gathered his nation in the steppes around one of the sacred mountains. He had the people divide into separate groups of men, women, and children. "And for three whole days and nights, all of them remained bareheaded; and for three days no one tasted food, and no animal was allowed to give milk to its young. During this time, Genghis Khan prayed alone as the people prayed together and loudly calling of the name of heaven, " 'Tengri, Tengri.' They did not pray for victory; they prayed to honor the sky."

Genghis Khan prayed for guidance that he might follow the Will of Heaven and not impose his will on heaven. Finally, "after three days, at dawn, on the fourth day," he emerged with the message that Tengri had promised him victory. "For the space of another three days, in that same place likewise, a feast was held. At the end of those three days, he led forth his troops."[6]

Soon a song circulated in Chinese territory:

> The Tatars come.
> The Tatars depart.
> They hunt the emperor.
> He has no escape.[7]

In 1211 at nearly fifty years of age, Genghis Khan crossed the Gobi once again—this time to teach the Golden Khan a lesson. The Mongols crisscrossed northern China, attacking one city and another, routing people from their villages, pillaging the smaller cities. Finally, in 1214, after accepting the Golden Khan's surrender, Genghis Khan was eager to return home with the great wealth his army had seized.

As he had done with the Tangut king, Genghis Khan told the Jin emperor he could remain in office and keep his capital city if he swore obedience to him. He quickly regretted this magnanimity. As soon as the Mongol army withdrew, the Golden Khan revolted and fled south to create a new capital at Kaifeng, which he foolishly thought was too far away to be susceptible to Mongol attack. Genghis Khan returned in the following year, 1215, to lay siege to Zhongdu.

On his return to Zhongdu, Genghis Khan set up a camp about ten miles southwest of the city, near a bridge of remarkable beauty. The bridge was relatively new and spanned 874 feet across the modest Yongding River. In the shimmering light of the morning mist, its white marble floated serenely in the air, a phalanx of carved lions guarding its balustrade. The bridge looked like an arched stairway connecting one cloud to another. The Chinese called it the *Lugou Qiao*, but foreigners later called it the Marco Polo Bridge. The bridge still stands today, frequently repaired due to flood damage and war, but much the same as it was in Genghis Khan's time.

He had shown little interest in the walls and moats built by the Chinese, as they were only impediments to him, but in this bridge, he saw something of not only great beauty but also great usefulness. He had never needed bridges for the shallow rivers of Mongolia. Except on the rainiest days of the year, people and animals easily forded them, but the larger rivers of the coastal plain proved too wide and powerful for even the hardiest horses to swim. The bridge construction appealed to his sense of nomadic mobility, and he realized, perhaps for the first time, that massive structures could facilitate movement of people as well as hinder it. From this time, he became a dedicated bridge builder, and he organized units of Chinese builders to accompany his army on future campaigns.

While he was camped near the bridge, a large contingent of the Jurched soldiers, who had been left to defend the Jin capital when their emperor fled to Kaifeng, now defected to the Mongols. Genghis Khan could have easily won without them, but their presence made the victory quicker. He easily captured the dispirited city, deserted by its own royal court and left as a victim to the invaders.

In keeping with the pattern of Mongol conquests, those who survived the battles and forced migrations soon found unexpected advantages under Genghis Khan's rule. Marco Polo, who was no specialist in military affairs, was nonetheless quick to spot the Mongols' difficult dilemma: they were so few in number that they would never have enough soldiers to effectively occupy their conquered lands. To prevail and endure, the Mongols would either have to win the support of the local population or else expel them. "When he conquered a province he did no harm to the people or their property, but merely established some of his own men in the country along with a proportion of theirs, whilst he led the remainder to the conquest of other provinces."[8] As Marco Polo wrote in reference to Genghis Khan's conquests across Asia, "when those whom he had conquered became aware how well and safely he protected them against all others, and how they suffered no ill at his hands, and saw what a noble prince he was, then they joined him heart and soul and became his devoted followers."

After Genghis Khan's defeat of the Tangut kingdom in western China in 1209 and the Jin dynasty in northern China in 1215, he insisted that everything of value be counted. As soon as he took a city, plunder and tribute had to be carefully recorded and distributed. A census was then made of all material goods and movable property—animals, buildings, mines, factories, and forests. Shigi-Khutukhu, in his capacity as the supreme judge of the Mongol nation, was responsible for overseeing the looted goods in the Jin capital and recording the information.

Genghis Khan was eager to ensure that all of his followers received an appropriate share of loot. Each member of the royal family—along with soldiers and administrators, even orphans, widows, and the elderly back home—was guaranteed his or her specific portion. He tried to be as careful and thorough in peace as in battle. He knew that his continued popularity rested on the scrupulousness with which he shared everything.

Voltaire, who wrote a fanciful play about the conquests and life of Genghis Khan in China, offered up a pithy interpretation of the

view of the vanquished toward their conqueror. "This northern tyrant, whom the wrath of heaven hath sent for our destruction . . .
these wild sons of rapine, who live in tents, in chariots, and in fields,
will never brook confinement 'midst the walls of this close city; they
detest our arts, our customs, and our laws, and therefore mean to
change them all; to make this splendid seat of empire one vast desert,
like their own."[9]

But Genghis Khan did not intend to destroy Chinese civilization.
He had not crossed the Gobi and fought so hard only to rob the Chinese and devastate their country. Every nomad understood the value
of a good herd and knew you could not get milk from a dead cow.
Even the hunters recognized the error of killing too many animals in
the forest and leaving none to reproduce for the following year. China
was a valuable resource, and Genghis Khan was determined to exploit it, yet protect it.

Genghis Khan conquered every city he saw. In defeat, all looked
alike—crumbling towers, broken gates, dangling timbers, burned
palaces, dying soldiers, devastated markets, lost children, and looted
shops. Scavenging dogs stalked the streets and carrion-eating birds
haunted the temples. The shrines where gods were once housed,
where wealth and offerings were collected from the rich and poor,
where explanations of the past and prophecies of the future ema-
nated, and where commandments for living came from, were now
cracked and crumbled like the walls that had failed to defend the city.
The temples formerly adorned with paintings of the other world and
citations from scriptures, hung with rich tapestries, lit with butter
lamps, decorated with marble and gold, smelling of juniper incense,
and filled with the chanting of monks and the prayers of the faithful,
now stood naked and empty as the wind whipped the few remaining
shreds of a once vibrant spiritual life. The sacred scriptures were now
scorched pages blowing in the dust, shredded by mice for their nests

and gnawed by starving goats. The monks who once knew the secrets of righteousness and eternal life lay in a pile of corpses undistinguishable by age, education, or profession. The priests who spoke to and for the gods, issuing orders in the name of heaven, were dead or had fled in fear. The astrologers, who could forecast the future in the flight of birds or read cracks in the shoulder bone of a sheep, were now war captives hauling the machinery of battle from one defeated city to the next.

Accustomed to the open steppe, the Mongols became easily disoriented in urban areas crisscrossed with roads, walls, fields, ditches, and canals. The Mongolian language lacked words to identify different types of structures, which they classified by their materials as wood, stone, mud, or grass but with little understanding of their function. Similarly, they could not identify most crops, which were simply "grass" or "greens" to the Mongols. They lacked knowledge of the various modes of dress, ranks, and social organization of the people they had set out to conquer, did not speak their languages, and could scarcely differentiate one nationality from another.

Although the Mongols easily defeated the Chinese armies, they feared the vengeance of unknown spirits in this alien landscape. Mongol soldiers often became sick and seemed to suffer emotional pain and spiritual longing. The *Secret History* declared that the spirits "of the lands and rivers of the Chinese are raging violently" against the Mongol invaders "because their cities and towns are destroyed."[10] The Mongols had entered a spiritually hostile land, filled with unknown dangers. They did not know the songs and chants of these foreign spirits and could not ascertain what type of offering they might like or what acts they might punish. This was not the land of their ancestors; it was filled with the ghosts of the slain. In the alien Chinese landscape of dusty roads, tall walls, plowed fields, arched bridges, high buildings, animal sheds, symmetrical orchards, stinking outhouses, gleaming temples, mounds of rotting garbage, and noisy markets, they did not know what, where, or how to pray.

It had taken Genghis Khan a quarter of a century to conquer one million nomads, but now suddenly, in only a few years in China, his subjects had increased twentyfold. He lacked experience managing sedentary civilizations rooted in agriculture and elaborate tradition. As a warrior of the steppe, Genghis Khan knew how to conquer, but he did not yet know how to rule a sophisticated cosmopolitan civilization. It did not take him long to apply lessons he had learned while hunting on Burkhan Khaldun or herding animals on the steppe to master warfare against this sedentary people, but nothing in his experience of tribal politics had prepared him for the task of ruling cities, managing vast stretches of farmland, organizing networks of merchants, overseeing factories of craftsmen, or governing small villages of peasants. The nomads' centuries-old skills failed to transfer to this alien environment of farmers and city dwellers.

It was obvious that he could not succeed by force alone. His army may have had fewer than 100,000 men and certainly not more than 110,000. Having now conquered tens of millions, his forces were not sufficient to occupy all the lands they conquered. Genghis Khan could defeat any army and capture any city, but he needed his army to move on to the next stronghold and fight the next battle. He could not leave his soldiers behind as an army of occupation, and he certainly could not trust the promises of fidelity from his subjects. As soon as his army passed over the horizon, the vanquished subjects could and often did revolt. He punished them severely for each such revolt, but he needed their loyalty, or at least their cooperation, to maintain his empire.

Genghis Khan improvised several strategies for ruling his vast and varied empire made up of different languages and religions. Early in his career, he was content to accept submission from conquered people and let their old rulers continue to administer their lands. This failed. As soon as the Mongols withdrew, the renegade rulers acted as though they had defeated the Mongols. To address this problem, he instituted a policy of routinely executing all rebels, so they would never have another chance to revolt. But this too was not enough.

Next, he tried placing his military generals in charge of local administration, but this diverted them from their military tasks of conquest. Besides that, great generals do not tend to make good administrators. He looked briefly at the native bureaucracies and wondered whether he could make use of the highly educated Chinese mandarins or the less educated but clever eunuchs who ran the imperial courts, but he concluded that if they were not competent enough to save their own countries from his aggression, what good would they be to him? They had demonstrated their ineptitude by offering bad advice to their rulers; there was no reason to believe they would do better for him.

This attitude of suspicion appears in *Autumn of the Palace Han*, a Chinese play written anonymously during Mongol rule in the thirteenth century.[11] In the opening act the villain, the chief minister of the Chinese emperor, explains that a government minister must have "the heart of a kite, and the talons of an eagle. Let him deceive his superiors, and oppress those below him. Let him enlist flattery, insinuation, profligacy, and avarice on his side. And he will find them a lasting assistance through life." The government minister then describes how he rose to power in the royal court. "By a hundred arts of specious flattery and address I have deceived the Emperor, until he places his whole delight in me alone. My words he listens to, and he follows my counsel."

Initially, Genghis Khan showed disdain for the scholarship of his new subjects. If their holy men could see the future and God designated them to speak for Him, why had they not seen his army riding across the desert and over the mountain? If they knew the secrets of the scriptures and stars and could read the omens of flying birds and fluttering leaves, why had they not fled their city to avoid the Mongols? If God taught them what to eat and wear and how to pray, why had He not taught them how to speak the Mongolian language so that they could prepare for their fate? If their religion was so powerful, why had the Mongols been able to pull down their idols, pry out their jewels, and melt their gold into nuggets?

Ten years earlier, with his first conquest of the Naiman, he had begun to take clerks from his defeated enemies. By now he needed more than a handful of clerks. He needed a large corps of administrators to manage the hundreds of cities and thousands of villages under his control. To fill the administrative requirements of his rapidly expanding empire, he turned to religious leaders, who typically were highly educated, familiar with writing, and good at interpreting and implementing written law. They claimed devotion to principles and ideals well beyond the greed and graft of traditional aristocrats, and they knew how to lead and communicate with the masses. Genghis Khan looked to the Chinese religious establishment for possible assistance and guidance. He made it known that he sought religious personnel to "assist the Court in promoting culture and education and in realizing the way of goodness, so that fine customs and benevolent rule may excel those of former ages."

He broadcast a general appeal to scholars and religious leaders to "submit plans to the Court" designed "to fix the laws, to deliberate upon rituals and music, to erect ancestral temples, to build houses, to found schools, to hold examinations, to seek out retired scholars, to search for the ministers of the previous dynasty, to promote the worthy and the good, to seek upright men, to encourage agriculture and sericulture, to suppress indolence, to moderate punishments, to reduce taxes, to honor moral integrity, to castigate profligacy, to dismiss superfluous officials, to expel oppressive officers, to exalt filial and brotherly devotion, and to relieve poverty and distress." If these things are done, then people will "yield to reform like grass bending to the wind," or like "water flowing downward." Thereby, a "Great Peace" will settle across the land.[12]

He quickly recognized that the city scholars lacked a deep understanding of life in the countryside or in distant provinces. To gain a fuller view of the entire country, he sent messengers throughout the newly conquered territories, summoning scholars and priests to "our Mongol land so that I, the Khan, can complete the great deeds of the state."[13] According to the Buddhist chronicle *The Pearl Rosary*, Genghis Khan invited scholars with training to instruct him in "the good customs of the Chinese *nom*," their law and religion.[14] *The Book of the Golden Wheel with a Thousand Spokes* and the *History of the Golden Lineage of Lord Genghis*, both Mongolian chronicles of the eighteenth century, each relate in nearly identical wording that "when he had assembled in his power the many people having other customs," Genghis Khan summoned learned men to his military camp to learn about the customs of his new subjects. He inquired about the manner in which one might support and uphold the *Tore*, the principles of good government, in order to "protect and support living beings."[15] Only after examining these laws and customs did he appoint officials to govern in his name.[16] After conquering northern China, Genghis Khan "then chose the wisest ministers of the external peoples to make and sharpen the empire's laws."

In his desperate need for men to help him count and catalog what had been seized, he turned to a special class of former advisers to the Jin court who entered Mongol service after the fall of Zhongdu. One of the first new recruits was Yelu Chucai. By 1218, although he was only twenty-eight years old, Yelu Chucai was appointed clerk to the nomadic court of the khan and served as an astrologer searching for signs in the night sky. Upon meeting the lanky youth, Genghis Khan was struck by how tall he was compared with the Mongols and also what a fine beard he had for such a young man. He often gave nicknames to officials whose foreign names were difficult to remember, and thereafter he called the young scholar *Utu Sakhal*, Long Beard.

ॐ

Yelu Chucai descended from the royal family of the Liao dynasty and was a member of the Khitan ethnic group, a steppe tribe closely related in language and culture to the Mongols. When the Liao were overthrown by the Jurched tribe, many members of his family had continued to serve the new rulers, just as Yelu Chucai had chosen to serve Genghis Khan. As a member of a family that had originated in

Mongolia but had lived in China for three centuries, Yelu Chucai displayed a keen understanding of both nomadic and sedentary life. This combination of backgrounds made him an effective conduit of Chinese ideas and culture in the early Mongol Empire. His subsequent writings became a valuable source of information on Genghis Khan and, more generally, on the laws and structure of the Mongol empire.

The *Secret History* relates that Genghis Khan "thought of establishing order over his many people, climbing high passes, crossing wide rivers, and waging a long campaign," but he knew clearly that "living beings are not eternal." Soon after the conquest of northern China, his wife Yesui Khatun reminded him, as Borte had once earlier, that he would grow old "and like a great old tree, will fall down." Even the stone base of a great pillar will eventually collapse, she told him. Grass is not forever green. Now fifty-seven years old, an age when most Mongols would step back from active life, he knew he would need a new system of management for his rapidly expanding empire if it was to outlive him.

On May 15, 1219, he sent a letter to the elderly Taoist Qiu Chuji, a renowned sage, requesting a meeting. Although Yelu Chucai may have written it for him, to conform to Chinese literary style, the letter makes clear his objective in summoning the religious leader. His words reveal a candid picture of a man at the height of his earthly power but facing the long, irreversible decline into old age, and hoping that his empire might endure.

Instead of bragging about his conquests, he matter-of-factly explained why he had succeeded and his enemies had failed. His victory came because of the feebleness of his enemies, he wrote. "Heaven had abandoned them," he claimed, because of their "haughtiness and extravagant luxury." The government of the Jin dynasty "was inconsistent, and therefore Heaven assisted me to obtain the throne." Consequently, "in the space of seven years I have succeeded in accomplishing a great work uniting the whole world in one empire." He showed a keen awareness of the uniqueness of his conquest. "It seems to me that since remote time, such a vast empire has not been seen."

As for himself, his virtues were by his own account modest. "I have not myself distinguishing qualities" other than that "I hate luxury and exercise moderation," he went on. "I have only one coat" and "I eat the food and am dressed in the same tatters as my humble herdsmen."

After introducing himself as he wished to be seen, he described his paternalistic but benign system of rule based on merit. "I consider the people my children and take an interest in talented men as if they were my brothers." He cited the philosophical and spiritual unity of his people as important factors in his government and observed that religious ideology tore other societies apart and made them vulnerable to conquest. As the Mongol Christian priest Rabban Bar Sauma wrote, dogma "makes bitter the soul."[17] By contrast, Genghis Khan claimed that in his Mongol nation, "We always agree in our principles and are always united by mutual affection."

He seemed almost to regret the burden that heaven and history put on him, acknowledging that he needed help to fulfill it. "As my calling is high, the obligations incumbent on me are also heavy; and I fear that in my ruling there may be something wanting." Just as in "crossing a river we need boats and rudders," he needed "sage men . . . for keeping the empire in order." However, "Since the time when I came to the throne . . . I could not find worthy men." He then asked for help, saying, "have pity on me. . . . give me a little of your wisdom. Say only one word to me and I shall be happy."[18]

Genghis Khan's signed his letters without the long and flowery titles beloved by monarchs and tyrants. His triumphs spoke for themselves, without the need for frivolous ornamentation.

By the time Qiu Chuji could respond, Genghis Khan had moved on to another campaign. Two years would pass before the sage and his disciplines finally caught up with the Mongol army in Afghanistan in the spring of 1222. Although he would become the most famous of the many religious scholars to meet with Genghis Khan, he was far from the only one. Wherever Genghis Khan went on campaign,

Mongol officials eagerly sought out other sages. In this early phase of his effort to master his new empire, the most detailed account of his quest to find Chinese holy men appears in the report of two Buddhist monks found wandering about Lanzhou in 1219, shortly after the Mongols had captured the city. The Buddhist master, who was about sixty years old, told his teenage disciple Haiyun to flee and save his life. "I am an old monk," he told the boy. "It would be natural if I were to die in this war. You, however, are still young and you should therefore try to escape the disaster."

The disciple stubbornly refused. "Life and death are a matter of destiny," he told his master, echoing what he had been taught. "How can I abandon my own teacher at this critical moment?" If I escape, he said, "what will I tell my friends when I meet them afterwards?"[19]

A Chinese officer in the Mongol army came upon the two monks tranquilly going about their sacred duties amid the devastation of war around them. When asked why they did not fear the Mongols like the others, the younger monk cleverly replied that they knew the Mongol soldiers had come to protect them. The surprised officer asked him what kind of monk he was, a Chan or Zen Buddhist, devoted to meditation, or a devotee of one of the more ritualistic sects known as Tantric Buddhism.

At first Haiyun said that both branches of Buddhism deserved equal importance, "like the two wings of a bird." It soon became clear that the two monks practiced the meditative Zen type of Buddhism, but they had practical knowledge as well. While some monks condemned violence and had little interest in the martial arts, Haiyun said that "warriors and scholars" are like two wings of a bird, "with neither of whom a State can dispense."[20]

Impressed by their story, Muhali sent a message to Genghis Khan recommending the two monks as true "speakers to Heaven."[21] The Mongol leader was too far away to meet with them, so he asked them to gather together and pray with others for the success of heaven and protection of the Mongols. He said he hoped that he might meet them in the future. "Feed and clothe them well, and if you find any others of the same sort gather them all in and let them speak to Heaven as much as they will," he instructed. He further ordered that "they are not to be treated with disrespect by any one and are to rank as *dark an*,"[22] a category of freeman that exempted them from taxes, military conscription, and obligatory service such as road repair and other forms of manual labor demanded by local officials in the name of the state.

Muhali took the two men to his headquarters in northeastern China to care for them as he had been instructed to do. He bestowed titles on them, calling them Senior Venerable and Junior Venerable, but the two men declined the worldly honors and continued to live simply among the people, begging for food.[23] The elderly Zen master died soon afterward, in the summer of 1220, and his disciple Haiyun was destined never to meet Genghis Khan, but the young monk would later play an important role during the reigns of his grandsons.[24]

From his earliest conquests, Genghis Khan had been interested in identifying men of talent, but in the earlier days, he focused predominantly on recruiting loyal fighters and men who knew how to fashion weapons, work with metal, or serve as guides, spies, and scouts. Later his interests expanded to include doctors, weavers, carpenters, jewelry makers, translators, engineers, potters, and a variety of craft workers. Following the campaigns in northern China, he began to collect a menagerie of priests and spiritualists as well. Monks, astrologers, magicians, prophets, alchemists, soothsayers, sages, fortune-tellers, and charlatans traveled for months, crossing the widest rivers and traveling from beyond distant borders to search out his nomadic camp. "Now that the world from one end to the other is under one or the other branch" of the Mongols, wrote Rashid al-Din at the end of the thirteenth century, "philosophers, astronomers, scholars, and historians of all sects and religions connected with China, ancient India, Kashmir, Tibet, Uyghur, as well as other people like the Turks, Arabs, and Franks are before our eyes in large numbers." Furthermore, he elaborated, "Every one of them has books containing the history, chronology, and religious thought of those countries."[25]

Genghis Khan's court attracted Mongol shamans with magical stones, Taoist alchemists, chanting Buddhist monks and astrologers, praying mullahs, singing Christians, Confucian masters of ceremony and court ritual, Tibetan soothsayers, and a great variety of freelance spiritualists and charlatans renowned as conjurers or simply able to delight with magic tricks. Genghis Khan's camp combined aspects of a nomadic university and a spiritual zoo with scholars from a multitude of languages, cultures, and religions. The camp bustled with fluttering robes in bright yellow, pure white, iridescent orange, oxblood red, and stark black. The days began with the sounds of clanking religious beads, drums, gongs, whistles, and wooden bells and ended with feathered shamans dancing into a trance by the fire, sorcerers reading the cracks on the burned bones of sheep, astrologers calling to the night sky, and soldiers tossing anklebones.

From the beginning, this recruitment of foreign scholars and men of religion was not universally well received, as Mongols tended to mistrust all things foreign. Bar Hebraeus explained that when Genghis Khan invaded China he heard that the people revered images and had "priests who were lords of wisdom." Therefore, he "sent ambassadors to them, and asked them for priests, and promised to hold them in honor. And when the priests came Genghis Khan ordered them to make a debate on faith and an inquiry into it with the Enchanters [shamans]. And when the priests spoke and read extracts from their Book, which they called 'Nom' in their language, the enchanters failed and were vanquished, and they were unable to reply because they were destitute of knowledge. And from this time, the rank of the priests increased among the Mongols, and they were commanded to fashion images, and to cast copies of them as they did in their home country, and to offer to the full sacrifices and libations according to their customs. And although they honored the priests greatly, the Mongols at the same time did not reject the enchanters. And both parties remained among them, each to carry on its own special work, without despising or holding the other in contempt."[26]

Religious personnel seemed an appropriate choice to tap in the task of organizing a new society, as they were already experienced in many cases in supervising the collection of taxes and codifying law. In Genghis Khan's perspective, all priests venerated heaven in some form or other. He had not yet witnessed the great animosity that often separates one faith from another and one worshipper from another. Having gathered together men of different religions to assist him in governing, he quickly came to see the problematic way that they sowed distrust, suspicion, or even hatred of those whose spiritual beliefs or practices differed from their own.

Though he did not know it, Genghis Khan was about to be pulled into his first war of religions.

10

God's Omnipotence

Soon after the success of his campaign against the Jin, Genghis Khan received an urgent and unusual request from a group of Muslims living in the Kara Khitai Empire, along the eastern shadow of the Tien Shan Mountains, bridging modern-day China and Kyrgyzstan. Having seen the Uighurs and Karluks, both fellow Muslims, break away from the Kara Khitai to join Genghis Khan, the group beseeched him to come liberate them from their current master and to rule over them. They appealed to the Mongol leader in part because their current ruler happened to be an old nemesis. He was Guchlug, the son of Tayang Khan of the Naiman.

When Genghis Khan had conquered the Christian Kereyid and Naiman tribes nearly a decade earlier, both khans had been killed, but their sons had fled. Ong Khan's son, who was initially granted refuge among the Buddhist Tangut, died wandering in the southern Gobi, abandoned by his followers. Tayang Khan's son Guchlug almost met the same fate, but he finally succeeded in making his way to the capital of the Kara Khitai, the westernmost of the Chinese kingdoms, around the year 1208. The Kara Khitai leaders received him warmly; after all, they too had once been refugees from tribal upheaval.

Their ancestors, the Khitai, had ruled northern China and the tribes of Mongolia from 907 to 1125 as the Liao dynasty, but over time they had lost their former glory and they now ruled a much smaller kingdom known as the Kara, meaning "black" or "western," Khitai. They created their new empire around the former Sogdian trade center of Balasagun, near Issyk Kul, the magnificent deepwater lake high in the Tien Shan mountains, close to the modern Kyrgyz capital of Bishkek. Clinging to the remnants of their old imperial style and their staunch Buddhist faith, the ruling family lost contact with their subjects, who increasingly converted to Islam and began to break out of the reins that had once controlled them. As happens at the end of so many regimes, those in power became trapped between a generalized fear of their subjects, whom they no longer understood, and an inability to comprehend a world in which they themselves would no longer be in power.

The Gurkhan, emperor of the Kara Khitai, fantasized that with Guchlug's support he might defeat his upstart rival Genghis Khan and return the steppe tribes to his control. He saw in Guchlug a dynamic barbarian who could be useful in helping to restore the power and glory of his sclerotic dynasty. Guchlug nourished the emperor's delusions and happily renounced his Christianity and converted to Buddhism, the official court religion of the Kara Khitai royal family. Guchlug "changed from the religion of Jesus to the practice of idolatry," in the words of one Muslim chronicler, and he tried to impose his new religion on the people. "He changed the lights of the true path into the darkness of unbelief, and the service of the all merciful into the serfdom of Satan."[1] The grateful emperor gave his daughter in marriage to Guchlug, made him a khan, and allowed him to begin gathering a private army of steppe soldiers from the dispersed enemies of Genghis Khan.

In a lifetime of inept rule, poorly planned wars, and inconsistent laws and commands, this decision proved to be the Gurkhan's worst and final mistake. Once empowered with control over the army, Guchlug turned against his father-in-law and "fell upon him like lightning from a cloud."[2] In 1211, the year of Genghis Khan's invasion of the Jin territory, Guchlug deposed the Gurkhan, imprisoned him, and seized control of the capital, treasury, and government. Two years later, in 1213, the Gurkhan died, and Guchlug became sole ruler. With the vitality of a rebel on a mission, he launched a campaign to regain the former territories of the emperor in the fertile oasis cities of western China, noted for their production of grapes, melons, and wine.

Although Guchlug was now a Buddhist, he initially appointed Muslim officials to preside over his Muslim subjects, but discontented locals quickly repudiated them as collaborators and assassinated the new appointees. Guchlug first responded moderately, orchestrating public debates among Christian, Buddhist, and Muslim scholars to soothe religious tensions, but these emotionally charged spectacles only sharpened the differences among his subjects and heated the anger among the rival religions. At this point Guchlug decided that because the Muslims had rejected the officials he had sent to preside over them, he had no choice but to repress them completely. He closed the mosques and forbade instruction in the teachings of Islam. Finally, in a desperate attempt to bring religious homogeneity to his fractious people, he demanded that Muslim converts return to their original religions of Christianity or Buddhism and abandon Muslim dress, adopting the traditional clothes of the Kara Khitai Empire. To enforce his strict new policies against Islam, Guchlug stationed one soldier in each Muslim home to monitor behavior and force compliance. "Oppression, injustice, cruelty, and depravity were made manifest," wrote Juvaini, "and the pagan idolaters accomplished whatever was their will and in their power, and none was able to prevent it."[3]

Although Shah Muhammad II of Khwarizm, based in what is today Uzbekistan, was the closest powerful Muslim ruler in Central Asia, the persecuted Muslims under the Kara Khitai received no assistance from him. He and Guchlug were, at least temporarily, allies. So the beleaguered and desperate Muslims sent emissaries instead to Guchlug's archenemy, Genghis Khan. "Before the rumors of the conquests of the Emperor of the World, Genghis Khan, had been spread abroad," wrote

Mirza Muhammad Haidar, a fifteenth-century Turkic historian of Central Asia, the Muslims turned to the Mongols for salvation. "Under the protection of the Emperor of the World Genghis Khan" they "obtained immunity from the evil acts of the Gurkhan Guchlug."[4]

Genghis Khan received the Muslim embassy with dignity. Convinced of the sincerity of their cause, he accepted their plea and sent Jebe, who had become one of his best commanders, with an army to free them in 1216. In Juvaini's words, their "arrow of prayer hit the target of answer and acceptance." Genghis Khan set out "to remove the corruption of Guchlug and lance the abscess of his sedition."[5] For the Mongol leader, the campaign offered a seemingly simple way to expand his empire to a people eager to join him. It also provided him with an opportunity to seek revenge on Guchlug, the last surviving enemy of his earlier steppe wars.

The mission proved easier than Jebe had anticipated, due to the unintended consequences of Guchlug's tactic of spreading his soldiers out of their central garrison in the mountains and stationing them in dispersed homes in the desert oases. As the Mongol army approached the towns and villages, the Muslims spontaneously rose up and attacked their resident guards. Thus, "all his soldiers that sojourned in Muslim houses . . . were annihilated at one moment, like quicksilver upon the ground." Guchlug fled south through the mountains toward India with the rapidly dwindling forces that were still loyal to him. The Mongols chased him "like a mad dog" across the modern borders of Tajikistan, Afghanistan, and Pakistan, where they finally caught and killed him in 1218.

The liberated Muslims of the Kara Khitai and their allied tribes flocked to the banner of Genghis Khan. Juvaini called the arrival of the Mongol army "one of the mercies of the Lord and one of the bounties of divine grace."[6] The Kara Khitai were surprised when the disciplined Mongol warriors seized no booty and asked for no tribute from them. Jebe "demanded nothing of them but news" about his enemies. Looking toward the future, Genghis Khan particularly wanted information about Shah Khwarizm, who ruled most of Persia and Central Asia between the Tien Shan Mountains and the Caspian Sea. After liberating the Muslims and killing their usurper khan, Jebe returned triumphantly to central Mongolia. He brought one hundred white horses as a gift to Genghis Khan, to replace the horse he had shot out from under him more than a decade earlier.

Conquering the Kara Khitai, with its mixed population of Muslims, Buddhists, and Christians, was Genghis Khan's first encounter with the disruptive power of religious factionalism. His response was simple and just. He once again permitted "the call to prayer" not only for the Muslims, who had begged him for liberation from the Kara Khitai, but for followers of all religions. Genghis Khan sent messengers to each city and village throughout the newly liberated lands to announce his law so that every person would hear it and know it. He decreed that "each should abide by his own religion and follow his own creed."[7] This became a founding principle of his conquests thenceforth, and he remained true to it for all his subjects throughout the remainder of his life.

Religious tolerance, although rare in history, was not completely new in the thirteenth century. In addition to the implicit religious tolerance of exceptional leaders such as Cyrus the Great and Alexander the Great, at least once before an emperor had issued an explicit Edict of Tolerance. That was the Roman emperor Julian, commonly known as Julian the Apostate because he had been born a Christian but rejected the faith in the year 361, when he became emperor. The following year he issued the Edict of Tolerance, allowing all types of Christians freedom of practice, restoring the Greek and Roman gods as the state religion, and naming himself, like previous emperors, the Pontifex Maximus, high priest of the empire. He offered to restore the Jewish Temple of Solomon in Jerusalem, but despite his leniency toward some religions, he remained devoutly anti-Christian, just as the Christians remained antiemperor. The edict, although justifiably famous for its unique intent, did not create religious freedom. The following year, while on campaign in Iraq, the thirty-two-year-old emperor was assassinated by one of his own troops. According to Julian's former teacher Libanius, the assassin was a dissatisfied Christian who considered the emperor a pagan.[8] Upon his death the empire reverted to Christianity and to even more vigorous religious persecutions. Julian's edict had applied to temples, churches, and priests. It granted tolerance to these Christian and pagan sects to operate within certain limits.

Genghis Khan's law was unique because it did not merely allow religious clerics to practice their profession; it allowed each individual to choose which religion or belief seemed most appealing. Freedom of religion, under the Mongols, was an individual right. Much later, in the eighteenth century, this distinction between religious freedom as an individual right versus a group right would have important philosophical and political implications in Europe and America.

Juvaini was the first to point out the importance of Genghis Khan's new law. In part he did so because it was his first international edict. Genghis Khan had created a law code for the Mongols in 1206, and he had issued various military and administrative edicts on his campaigns in China, but this was the first general law that stated a firm legal and moral principle that would extend to the entire new Mongol Empire. This was the first of what became known as the Great Law, a set of international laws that went beyond those of any one nation within the empire. Later scholars, including Pétis de la Croix, whose biography was so influential to Thomas Jefferson, called this the first law of Genghis Khan.

౩

At the time, Genghis Khan had no way of knowing how important his new law would become. His encounter with the Muslims of Kara Khitai had given him a new understanding of the boundaries between the great religions—how different from one another they perceived themselves to be, and how much animosity existed between them. He believed all forms of worship tended toward the same goals and spoke to the same divine presence. One was neither right nor wrong; they simply varied in the means they used to teach their form of morality. He did not view rival faiths as equal so much as he viewed them as all the same. There was one universal religion, but it found different forms of expression, just as there was but one universal empire, his Mongol Empire, but within it, people could speak different languages, follow varied customs, and adhere to various forms of government, according to their traditions and the teachings of their ancestors.

With the subjugation of Guchlug and subsequent annexation of the former Kara Khitai Empire, Genghis Khan unexpectedly became a champion of religious freedom and defender of the oppressed. Among the steppe nomads, kinship and tribal affiliation formed the natural cleavages in society, but in sedentary societies, religious fault lines crisscrossed the nation like flaws in a diamond, waiting to be shattered with one strike. Genghis Khan recognized the benefit of turning one faction against another, but he realized that the only way he could bring peace to his growing empire was to neutralize these potentially explosive divisions.

Marveling at how receptive Genghis Khan was to foreign faiths, al-Umari, a fourteenth-century Arab historian and official in Damascus, mistakenly reported that each of his sons chose a different religion. He claimed that one converted to Judaism, another to Christianity, while some remained faithful to their native religion and others worshipped various idols, but none was fanatical or tried to impose his beliefs on the others.[9] He wrote that according to Genghis Khan's law, the penalty for killing a person because of his religious belief was execution.[10]

Juvaini also placed a naively benign interpretation on Genghis Khan's commitment to religious freedom. "Being the adherent of no religion and the follower of no creed, he eschewed bigotry, and the preference of one faith to another and the placing of some above others," he wrote. Instead of persecuting them, "he honored and respected the learned and pious of every sect, recognizing such conduct as the way to the Court of God."[11] While this may have been true, he also had clear political motivations for his religious policy.

Genghis Khan had a logistical flair for exploiting his enemy's weaknesses, and for transforming his enemies' presumed strengths into liabilities. He discovered that religious freedom could be used as a political and military weapon against the civilizations around him. He understood clearly the power that religious belief had over people, and just as he had channeled rivers to knock down the walls of the city, he used the people's faiths to his strategic advantage.

"Men are difficult to rule because they are quick in doing evil and slow in practicing goodness,"[12] Yelu Chucai wisely observed. The army and government alone could not guarantee good behavior. Genghis Khan understood that he would need religion to control his diverse subjects. His policy of religious freedom offered a practical solution to the pressing problem of factionalism within his growing empire. In the slowly developing Mongol worldview, heaven chose Genghis Khan to revive the proper world order, correct wrongs, restore natural justice, and lead the lost nations back onto the "white road" by uniting them into a single empire under Mongol control. To fulfill his divine mission in a forceful yet sincere manner, Genghis Khan had offered each nation he was about to invade an opportunity to voluntarily submit to his command. Their cities would remain unmolested, their markets would continue to function, and their rulers and religious leaders would be reconfirmed in office. The Mongols promised to protect them from enemies inside and outside their nation, manage their trade routes, and enforce uniform and fair taxes. Genghis Khan did not offer them political freedom, but he offered them protection and stability and total freedom of religion.

His policy attracted the persecuted Muslims and gave them a theological excuse for supporting a pagan leader. Juvaini wrote that whoever promotes Islam, "though it be not his own religion, advances day by day in prosperity and consideration."[13] Buddhists and Christians found the same freedom, and instead of turning against one another or denouncing the pagan conqueror who had savaged their land, they found a reason to see his rule as offering a form of liberation.

According to one Muslim chronicle, early in Genghis Khan's career he had a dream in which he was winding a turban around his head, but the turban continued to grow larger and larger and the cloth grew longer and longer, seemingly without end. As only Muslims wore such turbans, the khan sent for a learned Muslim merchant to interpret the dream. The merchant explained that the turban clearly symbolized power for the Muslims, and the size of his turban in the dream meant that he would conquer all of the countries of Islam and one day rule the Muslim world.[14]

Muslims proved to be Genghis Khan's closest allies, his fiercest enemies, some of the earliest benefactors of his rule, and, in the end, the ones who suffered the most from the Mongol conquests. Eight centuries later, Islam still struggles to recover. Genghis Khan seemed to understand Islam more intuitively than he understood other religions, and he respected the cultural and intellectual achievements of the Muslims, who shared a nomadic core at the heart of their culture. Both Mongols and Muslims were herders with a long and respected military tradition, and both detested eating pigs and dogs. As Juvaini wrote, "In those days the Mongols regarded the Moslems with the eye of respect, and for their dignity and comfort would erect them clean tents of white felt."[15]

Unlike the mystical and magical religions that dominated earlier empires in Greece, Rome, Egypt, India, and China, Islam offered a clear message focused on law contained in a single relatively short book, the Holy Quran. The Arabic script was curving and beautiful, like the Mongol script, with which Arabic shared a common origin. In the view of some of his Muslim defenders, Genghis Khan shared a mystical connection with Islam. The ninety-sixth sura of the Quran relates that Allah created the first man from a clot of blood, and Genghis Khan was born clutching just such a clot in his hand. Genghis Khan represented the beginning of a new age for humanity.

☧

Having conquered the kingdoms of northern and western China, the Mongols now controlled the world's richest trade route from the cities of northern China, through the Gansu Corridor and across the Uighur oases of western China to the cities of the Tien Shan Mountains, connecting the two great mercantile civilizations of China and Islam. Everything was in rapid flux. Prisoners were becoming princes, and princes becoming prisoners. Genghis Khan's daughters now administered the three primary trading kingdoms of Onggut, Uighur, and Karluk, and their husbands served in his army. The Great Khan issued new laws promoting trade, lowering taxes, abolishing local tariffs, and protecting merchants; he posted guards along the trade routes so "that whatever merchants arrived in his territory should be granted safe conduct."[16]

Looting the cities of China had overwhelmed the Mongols with booty. They had so much precious silk, lacquered furniture, tortoise-shell combs, jade vases, gold, silver, turquoise, coral, dishes, pots, medicines, weapons, and wine that they now suffered from a severe scarcity of camels to transport it all. In the bitterly cold climate of Mongolia, the nomads could wear only so much silk and carry only so much jewelry, and their *gers* could accommodate only so much furniture. The excess goods filled the storehouses and strained the Mongols' ability to continue in their nomadic ways.

Hearing of the surprising success of the Mongols and their vast wealth, enterprising Muslim merchants from Khojent, a trade city on the Syr Darya River in modern Tajikistan, collected a variety of cotton, wool, and other fabrics, which had always been desirable to the steppe nomads who did not weave, and organized a caravan. "Does this fellow think that fabrics have never been brought to us before?" Genghis Khan asked of the head of the caravan.[17] He asked that the merchants be shown the Mongol storehouses bulging with silk fabrics and other wares. The unprecedented display of such wealth so overwhelmed them that rather than trying to sell their goods to the Mongols, they offered them as a gift, in the hope that Genghis Khan would share his wealth with them.

This turned out to be a wise decision. The Muslim merchants had brought some nice cottons that appealed to Genghis Khan, and a type of gold-embroidered fabric he had never seen before. Chinese weavers used silk threads to create exquisite pictures of mountains, birds, trees, and elaborate scenes, but these Muslim weavers used threads of gold to create elaborate geometric patterns with swirling floral designs and an occasional bird, lion, or other animal.

Genghis Khan liked what he saw and decided he would use his new wealth to buy goods that he could not obtain from China: the sumptuous gold cloth brought by the merchants from Khojent, but also high-quality steel from Damascus and sweet-smelling sandalwood from India. He did not need to send an army into Central Asia to get these goods, as it seemed that he could just send a trade caravan. His newly acquired Muslim subjects were adept at trading and had a long history of organizing trade caravans across the deserts. The expense of sending a caravan was a fraction of the cost and effort of equipping an army. With honest partners and a respectful relationship, the Mongols could acquire whatever they needed simply by purchasing it with gold or silver or bartering for other foreign goods.

༖

In 1218, Genghis Khan sent a diplomatic mission to the shah of Khwarizm to negotiate an opening for trade. Khwarizm, the wide and fertile river delta where the Amu Darya flowed into the Aral Sea, was the home of the royal family. The shahs of Khwarizm had modeled their country on earlier Persian kingdoms, making them the heirs of the ancient Sogdians. Their territory included many great trading cities but also inhospitable desert and mountain lands, stretching from the Aral Sea into Afghanistan and north into modern Kazakhstan and including much of modern Iran, Turkmenistan, and

Uzbekistan, southern Kazakhstan, the eastern half of Azerbaijan and western halves of Tajikistan, Kyrgyzstan, and Afghanistan. The shah's empire bordered the Arab lands of the caliph of Baghdad to the west and the former Kara Khitai Empire to the northeast. Somehow the shah managed to maintain hostile relations with all his neighbors, large and small.

Even Juzjani, who was harshly critical of all things Mongol, admitted that Genghis Khan had initially sought peace when he went to Khwarizm. He quotes the message that the khan sent to the shah: "I am master of the lands of the rising sun while you rule those of the setting sun. Let us conclude a firm treaty of friendship and peace. Merchants and their caravans should come and go in both directions, carrying the valuable and ordinary products from my land to yours, just as they do from your land to mine."[18]

The shah responded positively and, citing the Mongols' success in freeing Muslims from Buddhist persecution in the Kara Khitai kingdom, suggested that Genghis Khan had fashioned a permanent alliance with Islam. He invited him to send a caravan of goods. In order to assemble a large caravan, Genghis Khan ordered each of his daughters and sons to select one of their Muslim retainers for the expedition and to equip him with "a brick of gold or silver."[19] In addition to gold, the Mongols sent sable furs, musk, jade, and textiles of fine camel wool.[20] This was both a trade and a diplomatic mission to the largest kingdom in Central Asia.

"We have dispatched to your country in their company a group of merchants," Genghis Khan informed the shah, in the hope that they may acquire "wondrous wares," and at the same time "the abscess of evil thoughts may be lanced by the improvement of relations and agreement between us."[21] The *Secret History* records that the caravan consisted of one hundred merchants under the leadership of a man named Uquna,[22] who may have been from India because at least one Indian had a major role in leading the caravan. Juvaini puts the total number of retainers at 450 plus their animals and wares, with more than five hundred laden camels.[23] Whatever the number, the caravan was the largest and most valuable caravan ever to have come out of Mongolia.

Genghis Khan sought to rule an empire in which trade formed the basis for prosperity not only for the Mongol nation but also for the vassals under his rule, from the lands of the Chinese to those of Muslims and Christians. However, as Juvaini poetically pointed out, it is sometimes difficult to tell whether the bird nesting quietly on one's roof is the Phoenix of Prosperity or the Owl of Misfortune. Genghis Khan may have been momentarily resting on the roof of the world, but he was about to unleash a great terror on those who underestimated his remaining strength and resolve. Before the "waters of prosperity" could flow with "their rivers of desire," the Muslims of Khwarizm would endure an "army of affliction and sorrow."[24] The bloodshed, when it came, was unrelenting, but it did not have to be.

In the winter of 1218–19, an official who was a maternal uncle of the shah raided the Mongol caravan as soon as it reached Khwarizm territory at Otrar, a city near the modern borders of Kazakhstan and Uzbekistan. He imprisoned the merchants leading the caravan, and then, with the approval of the shah, who was also anxious to seize the wealth, he executed all save one, who managed to escape and report back to Genghis Khan. The attack was more than opportunistic theft of a typical merchant's caravan. It outraged Genghis Khan and, more important, shook his confidence in the trust he thought he had cultivated with the Muslims. This hostile act jeopardized the trade network he had envisioned connecting East and West.

He took the raid as a deliberate and unprovoked act of betrayal by the shah. In the words of Juvaini, "the whirlwind of anger cast dust into the eyes of patience and clemency while the fire of wrath flared up with such a flame that it drove the water from the eyes and could be quenched only by the shedding of blood."[25] But initially Genghis Khan showed remarkable restraint: he sent an ambassador to the shah to ask that he punish the governor of Otrar. The shah scoffed at demands from this distant barbarian, who might terrorize the nearby Chinese but posed no threat to his heavily fortified Muslim cities protected by a powerful army many times the size of Genghis Khan's. Rather than responding to the message, the shah executed the envoy. In a lifetime of inept and vacillating rule, this was the worst decision he ever made.

The shah of Khwarizm had not simply betrayed Genghis Khan. From the Mongol point of view, he had violated the Will of Heaven by straying from the path of correct behavior. In the words of Genghis Khan, the shah had broken the sacred bond that tied humanity to the moral path and to heaven. "How can the Golden Cord be broken?" he asked, and then he prepared his nation once again for war.[26] He justified his invasion of the Muslim countries of Central Asia as an effort to put them back on the right path. He was coming with the explicit mandate of the Eternal Sky to "return them to righteousness."[27]

The Mongol army set out in the winter of 1219–20, less than a year after the attack on the caravan. Genghis Khan's campaign against the shah and the Muslim cities was a family affair—in both the best and worst senses. His sons and sons-in-law accompanied him on campaign while Borte Khatun remained in charge of the Mongol nation and his daughters ruled the mercantile cities of the Silk Road. At the start of the campaign, Genghis Khan called a meeting with his sons to settle on his successor. He was now fifty-seven years old, and at his age, it was possible he might not return alive. After a bitter family discussion, his sons agreed to support Ogodei, his third son, as the next Great Khan. The other three would all be khans in charge of parts of the territory. Genghis Khan had preferred his eldest son, Jochi, who was the smartest of them all, but questions about his paternity had kept the other brothers from supporting him.

Genghis Khan carefully gathered the men of his extended family and his army and set out on the long path to Central Asia. He chose his fourth wife, Khulan Khatun, to accompany him and manage his mobile military headquarters while his other three wives remained at the imperial court in Mongolia. He was accompanied on campaign by his five sons—the four sons born by Borte and one younger son, Kolgen, born to Khulan.[28]

Just before leaving the Mongol heartland and crossing the Altai Mountains into Central Asia, Genghis Khan and his army stopped to offer a sacrifice to the imperial banner. This ceremony was one of the most important ones performed by the *Keshig* at the beginning of a long campaign and held deep symbolic value for everyone involved. Although the ceremony was held in July, three feet of snow fell immediately afterward.

"The emperor was perplexed," wrote his adviser Yelu Chucai, who, like any skilled reader of signs, interpreted the snow as a favorable sign: the Water Spirit was responsible for the snow, and his appearance "in the height of summer is a sign that you will defeat the enemy."[29] The work of a good astrologer was not so much to predict the future as to be able to give a positive interpretation of whatever situation the soldiers or common people might perceive as a bad omen. Genghis Khan did not need the interpretation himself so much as he needed his people to hear it. Throughout the remainder of his life, Yelu Chucai proved adept at turning potentially negative signs into positive assurances of success and victory for Genghis Khan. He became skilled at propaganda and at the important task of managing public opinion for his master.

More snow lay ahead, and at this point it was a real problem, not just a matter of symbols. "At that time it was just the height of summer," reported Yelu Chucai, "but snowflakes were flying over the mountain peaks and the mass of ice was deep."[30] He described the mountain pass as nothing more than a "woodcutter's track,"[31] but the Great Khan "ordered that a road be cut through the ice so that the army could pass."[32] Nothing would impede him now. "When a man of character has made up his mind, he stands firm as a mountain in his resolve," Yelu Chucai wrote. "He is not affected by times and circumstances."[33]

Although this would turn out to be one of the bloodiest military campaigns in history, it began as something of a lark for the young

Yelu Chucai. Leaving home with the Mongol army offered him a liberation he might otherwise not have had. Crossing Mongolia, western China, and Central Asia exposed him to new sights and ideas. He had spent most of his life studying and learning about the world from poems, books, pictures, and calligraphy. Suddenly he had a chance to discover for himself how the mist looked on the mountains, how the sun reflected in a glassy lake, or how the birds flocking on a hilltop could make it appear almost snow-covered.

With the enthusiasm and indefatigable curiosity of a schoolboy, he jotted down numerous short poems that he called "my bag of poems full of sun and wind."[34] Yelu Chucai also described Genghis Khan's mobile imperial capital in Mongolia, where "mountains and streams interlaced and the vegetation was dense and green." In the camp "carriages and tents were as numerous as clouds; officers and soldiers as numerous as raindrops. Horses and oxen covered the fields and weapons brightened the sky. Dwelling faced dwelling and camp followed camp in streaming succession. Of past splendors, none could rival this."[35]

Life was a sensuous discovery. As he crossed the mountains and entered the lands of the shah of Khwarizm, Yelu Chucai delighted in Muslim gardens and orchards of pears, almonds, and apples, and rhapsodized when he saw pomegranates "as large as two fists and of a sour-sweet taste." He saw watermelons so large that "a long-eared donkey could only carry two of them at the same time." In other places, the melons grew as "large as a horse's head."[36] Sometimes the simplest of things puzzled him, such as the lack of a hole in the center of Muslim coins, in contrast to Chinese coins, which had such a hole so that they could be strung together for easy counting and transport. He loved grapes and wine and, with the ingenuity and innocent rebelliousness of youth, soon learned to make wine himself, "so that I did not have to pay the tax."[37] Throughout his life, he continued to enjoy wine, sometimes excessively, and frequently referred to it in his poems.

Amid the descriptions of almonds, pomegranates, and duty-free wine, it is sometimes hard to believe, in reading Yelu Chucai's account of his travels with the Mongols, that there was a war around him. He was participating in one of the greatest conquests of history, and although at first he seemed quite unaware of the significance of this venture, he gradually understood its momentousness and realized that it was important for him to record what he saw. The Mongol campaign against the shah of Khwarizm gave him exposure to new lands and ideas, provoking him to think more about his personal background and to clarify his beliefs. He found his identity. Despite his fierce loyalty to Genghis Khan and the Mongols, the farther Yelu Chucai traveled from home, the more Chinese he became as his early education continually bubbled up from inside him.

Word traveled ahead warning of the Mongols' approach, but the shah had little idea what to do. He seemed to simultaneously fear the Mongols and believe that Allah would protect him from the foreign brutes. He sent reinforcements to Otrar, knowing that it would be the first city attacked. When the Mongols arrived, they surrounded Otrar and set up a siege that was to last for several months. Under the false assumption that the Mongols would either give up the siege or be satisfied with sacking the city as retaliation for the raid, the shah remained woefully unprepared when the Mongols sent out smaller armies in different directions to attack several cities at once. Similar to the Mongol strategy of frightening animals at the start of a big hunt, the scattered and seemingly disorganized attacks confused the shah and prevented him from making a coordinated response. He did not know which way to go to counter the Mongols, and least expected what happened next.

The Mongols struck at the heart of the Khwarizm Empire before taking the border city of Otrar. If they had stuck to the trade routes followed by most armies since the time of Alexander the Great, they would have passed through a series of cities, including the great trading and arts center of Samarkand, before reaching cities such as Bukhara or the capital at Khiva, also called Khwarizm, near the modern city of Urgench, in Uzbekistan. Instead of taking this route, Genghis Khan and his youngest son, Tolui, took some five units of ten thousand men each and, with the help of local nomads as guides, crossed the Kyzylkum Desert early in 1220, while the weather was still relatively cool. In February, the Mongols leapt upon Bukhara like a pack of wolves on unsuspecting sheep and in two weeks conquered the city.

Within a month they had arrived at the gates of the much better fortified Samarkand, but despite the large army quartered there, the Mongols quickly took the city. The Mongols unleashed their outrage on Otrar, the city of revenge. Knowing the fate that awaited them, the people resisted in every way possible. As the defenders exhausted their arrows and then fell, girls came forward and began dismantling the bricks from the palace in order to hurl them at their attackers, but the Mongols were determined to win. As Juvaini put it, the Mongols slaughtered those who wore the veil as readily as those who wore the turban.[38] The "citadel and walls were leveled with the street," and the haughty governor who had seized the caravan and began the war had "to drink the cup of annihilation and don the garb of eternity." Juvaini quoted from the Persian classic *The Shahnama*, the Book of Kings: "Such is the way of High Heaven; in the one hand it holds a crown, in the other a noose."[39]

The Mongol victories in Khwarizm were bloody and dreadful, particularly for the defeated warriors, whom the Mongols usually slaughtered en masse or saved for some worse fate such as serving as shields for future battles or as filler to be thrown alive into moats. With only a small invading army, Genghis Khan wanted to ensure that no potential enemy army survived between him and his Mongol homeland, to which he might need to retreat. Alive, such soldiers posed a constant threat, and he eliminated them. His treatment of civilians was more variable, sometimes severe and other times markedly benign. In the long campaign ahead, his policy toward the defeated soldiers remained the same, but his treatment of civilians grew starkly harsher as he moved deeper into Central Asia and farther from home.

After the dramatic fall of Bukhara, Samarkand, and Otrar, Genghis Khan offered every city a chance to surrender. He sent Muslim envoys to them and urged them "to draw out of the whirlpool of destruction and the trough of blood." If they resisted, he promised to annihilate them in a sea of blood. "But if you will listen to advice and exhortation with the ear of intelligence and consideration and become submissive and obedient to his command, your lives and property will remain in the stronghold of security."[40] Genghis Khan always honored his word. Those who surrendered suffered no harm, and he treated them well. In turn, he used this fair treatment as a means of encouraging other cities to surrender.

Though some cities surrendered, others chose to rise up against their oppressive shah even before the Mongols threatened them, and thus as some refugees fled to escape the invaders, others raced to join them. Some of those seeking out the Mongols were fellow nomads who preferred the rule of Genghis Khan to the oppressive exploitation of the shah. Others were from pagan, usually Turkic, tribes who resented the pressure from the Muslim majority to abandon their traditional religion and convert to Islam. Those who resisted faced a fate that grew worse with each new battle.

Nothing could stop the Mongols now. When they came to the great rivers, they built bridges of boats and constructed dams of stone and earth. When the enemy attempted to escape on the river by barges, the Mongol cavalry chased them down, fired flammable petroleum-based naphtha at them, and pulled a massive chain across the river.[41] The Mongols filled the moats around cities with stone, dirt, and captives. When they came to great walls, they built ladders and had their Chinese engineers fashion battering rams, catapults, and other ingenious siege machines while prisoners tunneled under the earth.

Shah Muhammad II was terrified. "Satan the Tempter had caused fear and dread to gain such a hold upon the mind," wrote Juvaini of the shah, "that he was seeking a hole in the ground or a ladder to the heavens in order to place himself out of reach."[42] He began to quarrel bitterly with his eldest son, Jalal ad-Din, who wanted him to fight because the Mongols had not yet reached his capital. "To scatter the armies through the lands and turn tail before an enemy whom one has not encountered," he said to his father, "is the mark of a craven wretch, not the path of a mighty lord."[43] Jalal ad-Din recognized that his father had failed to organize a united response against the Mongols. Every city and province had to face the invading army on its own and defend itself without coordination and guidance. He asked his father to let him command the army. Otherwise, "we are chewed like gum in the mouth of reproach and drowned in the flood of repentance before the eyes of all mankind."

The shah tried to justify his position by turning to philosophy. "Every perfection has a defect, every full moon a waning and every defect a perfection," he said airily. There were times when not fighting was the wiser course of action, as "it is well known and an established fact that agitation in the noose of the rope only precipitates death and that from the union of conjecture and fantasy there can spring naught but madness."[44] Jalal ad-Din left in anger, determined "to gallop on to the field of manliness" and fight, even if he had to defy heaven itself.

The Mongols pursued the feckless shah while he fled toward the Caspian Sea from his capital of Khiva, leaving his mother, wives, and children to fend for themselves and face a life of misery as Mongol prisoners. His deserted capital, near the border of modern Uzbekistan and Turkmenistan, was a city of unrivaled riches. "It was the site of the throne of the Sultans of the world and the dwelling-place of the celebrities of mankind," wrote Juvaini. "Its environs were receptacles for the rarities of the time; its mansions were resplendent with every kind of lofty ideas, and its regions and districts were so many rose gardens through the presence of men of quality."[45]

The shah's mother organized the evacuation of the harem and the royal treasury. She killed all the hostages accumulated in the city for fear that the Mongols might liberate them and that they would join the enemy. The people of the city were now abandoned, for "no leader had been appointed to whom they might refer upon the occurrence of untoward events and for the administration of affairs of state and the business of the commonweal, and by whose agency they might resist the violence of Fate."[46]

Genghis Khan sent Subodei and Jebe, two of his best generals, west with twenty thousand warriors in pursuit of the fleeing shah and the treasury, but he did not besiege the city. Instead, he put his three eldest sons in charge of it so that they might have the honor of taking the capital while learning to work together. They proved as uncoordinated in their efforts as the people of Khiva were in their defense. Jochi expected that he would inherit the city eventually, and therefore he wanted it taken with minimum destruction. Chagatai and Ogodei wanted only to destroy it and loot it. They "arrived with an army like a flood in its onrush and like blasts of wind in the succession of its ranks. They made a promenade around the town and sent ambassadors to call on the inhabitants to submit and surrender." When they received no response, "they busied themselves with the preparation of instruments of war such as wood, mangonels, and missiles . . . and since there were no stones . . . they manufactured these missiles from the wood of mulberry trees. They plied the inhabitants of the town with promises and threats, inducements and menaces; and occasionally they discharged a few arrows at one another."[47]

The Mongol attacks proved disjointed and disorganized. The troops filled the moat and almost took the city after firebombing it with naphtha and setting it on fire, but then, in an attempt to save the buildings, they botched the effort to divert the river. Genghis Khan had to remove Jochi from command and replace him with Ogodei. Despite the bungling efforts, the city finally fell. Then, in their greed, the brothers seized everything of value and divided it among themselves without sending the imperial share to their father, the Great Khan.

When Genghis Khan invaded the Khwarizm Empire he found that, in contrast to the Muslims of the Turkic tribes of the steppe and desert oases of western China, the urban Muslims of Central Asia saw no allure in him and expressed no spiritual affinity for the Muslims accompanying him. To them he was merely the latest in a long line of barbarian raiders who descended from nowhere, took everything they could, and disappeared back into nowhere. They discovered too late that this particular ruler had no intention of disappearing.

The people of Khwarizm did not welcome the Mongols as liberating heroes, as had the Muslims under the Kara Khitai. In turn, the Mongols showed contempt for their new enemies. "The dwellers in houses and towns were," according to a Muslim description of the Mongols' perception, "a degenerate and effeminate race—the tillers of the soil, slaves who toiled like cattle, in order that their betters might pass their time in luxury."[48] In the Mongol view the people of Samarkand, Bukhara, and Otrar were like herds of goats or sheep, quickly frightened, easily led, and completely disposable.

Even those Muslims who sided with the Mongols and served them struggled to understand what had happened to their empire and society. For these devout believers, the unprecedented destruction of the jewels of Islamic civilization was at once puzzling and unprecedented. Only an ally of God could possibly have so much power. But why would God sanction such destruction? They were accustomed to Muslims fighting, raiding, invading, and killing one another as well as to fighting Christians and nonbelievers, but pagans had never before conquered them on such a massive scale. Strange as this conquest was, somehow it had to be the will of God. Genghis Khan must have had some unseen connection to God. As a fourteenth-century Kurdish historian put it, "Even though he was not a Muslim, he had a true friendship with God."[49]

The Mongol army raced across Khwarizm and the lands of the ancient Persian civilization, conquering one city after another. One of the important cities was Ray, southeast of Tehran. Religious conflicts over competing versions of Islamic law so divided the city that it could scarcely mount an effective defense against the Mongols. According to the sixteenth-century Persian historian Muhammad Khwandamir, followers of two rival schools of Islam met with Jebe, and each pleaded with him to kill the other. He executed both, asking, "What good can be expected of men who plot to have their own countrymen's blood shed?"[50] Khwandamir's report cannot be accepted as factual, coming so long after the conquest, but it illustrates the religious hostility at the time between Muslim factions.

The rivalries and hatreds within Islam proved so deep that many of the Muslim enemies of the shah sided with Genghis Khan and the Mongols and delighted at the spectacle of horsemen crushing the shah's armies. Both the caliph in Baghdad and the head of the Nizari Ismaili cult better known as the Assassins were accused by other Muslims of surreptitiously aiding the Mongols in their campaign. Whether they did or not, they did not help the shah.

Genghis Khan certainly had mysterious dealings with the Ismailis. He was visited by ambassadors of Hasan III, the twenty-fifth imam of the Nizari Ismaili sect, following his spontaneous offer of submission to the Mongols.[51] The shah of Khwarizm ruled most of the Persian world except for the large piece of mountainous territory controlled by Hasan III around his military base at Alamut, a mountainous region near the Caspian Sea. His Muslim sect, condemned as heretics by most Muslims, considered its leader to be a godlike figure. The Ismailis had a reputation for wild and unusual behavior, smoking hashish and taking other drugs, engaging in sexual abandon, and frequently radically changing their theology and religious practices. Confined to a small country surrounded by powerful neighbors—the shah to the northeast, the caliph of Baghdad to the west, and the Seljuk Turks to the northwest—they took advantage of the rugged terrain of their homeland to protect themselves from being annexed. Though they did not have a large or powerful army, they maintained a series of seemingly impenetrable forts built into the mountains.

In order to ally with the caliph in Baghdad against the shah of Khwarizm, Hasan III had renounced his Shia faith and declared allegiance to the Sunni. His followers accepted that such sudden shifts were due to the changing nature of God himself, but they also knew that it could just be a political strategy without theological meaning. Such tricks occupied a proud place in their religious and political traditions. They followed their leader blindly, without question, doubt, or remorse.

The Nizari managed to maintain a powerful role far beyond their size because of their highly refined and effective use of assassination and terror. Unable to defeat armies on the battlefield, they targeted their leaders in special surgical strikes. For this purpose, the Nizari had a corps of specially trained men known as *fedayeen*, those willing to sacrifice themselves for their religion. "These people were faithless and lived without laws," wrote an Armenian chronicler in 1307 in *The Flower of Histories of the East*. "These are men without any faith or belief except what their lord [imam], called the Old Man of the Mountain, taught them; and they are so obedient to their lord that they put themselves to death at his command."[52]

Each *fidai* was trained to master the language, culture, and dress of his neighbors, as well as the arts of disguise and stealth. The *fedayeen* were then sent to infiltrate the inner circle of a targeted enemy, working as slowly and methodically as needed until they were well placed to carry out their mission. For the most part they operated as spies, but when necessary they were prepared to strike and to sacrifice their lives. They worked as individuals or in small groups so that if one failed, another could quickly take his place.

Most of their targets were other Muslims, particularly Seljuk Turks, but they also killed prominent crusaders such as Raymond II of Tripoli and Conrad of Montferrat and claimed unsuccessful attempts against kings Philip II and Louis IX of France and Edward II of England.[53] Some of the murders blamed on the Nizari may well have been committed by rivals much closer to the victims, and some of the supposedly failed attempts may have been the embroidered war stories of returning Crusaders, eager to recount in glorious terms their exploits and near-death experiences.

Even a failed assassination spread terror. In the twelfth century, *fedayeen* carefully infiltrated the inner circle of the great Kurdish general Saladin, the Ayyubid sultan of Egypt, Yemen, and Syria. They managed to gain access to his private quarters and tried and failed twice to kill him. A story circulated that the would-be assassin had deliberately spared him; after creeping into his tent, instead of killing him, he had used his knife to pin a warning letter to the sultan's pil-low. Even the Nizari's allies were wary of their friendship. "Some as were on terms of agreement with them, whether kings of former times or contemporary rulers," wrote Juvaini, "went in fear and trembling."[54]

Usually the assassination was a suicide attack, as his targets' guards generally either killed assassins immediately or captured and then tortured them to death. But some managed to escape and return to the lands around Alamut, where they were invited to live a blessed life of paradise on Earth, meaning ample supplies of drugs and sex. It is from this practice of using hashish that they supposedly acquired their name of *hashshashin*, users or smokers of hashish. It is debat-able how much hashish was consumed, and this may merely have been an insult hurled by their enemies to explain their addled think-ing. Whether or not it was true, the term took on a new connotation in the West and became the modern word *assassin*.

The meeting between envoys of Imam Hasan III and Genghis Khan was certainly one of the more unusual meetings in history, but it was also one of the most secret. Although Juvaini offers a long his-tory of the Nizari in his biography of Genghis Khan, including within it a biography of Hasan III, he gives only a short and frustratingly cryptic summary of Imam Hasan's interactions with Genghis Khan. He reports that the imam sent letters to Genghis Khan prior to their meeting and concludes unhelpfully that in regard to these letters, "the truth is not clear."[55] He hints that Genghis Khan met personally with Hasan III, but he does not elaborate. He concedes only what was probably common knowledge at the time: "This much is evi-dent," he admits, "that when the armies of the World-Conquering Emperor Genghis Khan entered the countries of Islam, the first ruler on this side of the Oxus [Amu Darya River] to send ambassadors, and present his duty, and accept allegiance was Jalal-al-Din [Hasan III]. He adopted the course of rectitude and laid the foundation of righteousness." Juvaini went to some lengths to justify this Mongol alliance with heretics, stressing that, at least at that time, Hasan III was married to Sunni women and following the Sunni faith.

Whatever transpired in the meetings, the Mongols and Nizari reached an accord that both the Assassins and the forces of the caliph would stand back and let Genghis Khan destroy their enemy the shah.[56] The Nizari would not interfere with the Mongols, but they did not have to contribute warriors to Genghis Khan's army. They were free to attack Khwarizm themselves, so long as their attacks did not compete with the Mongol operations. Perhaps most important, throughout Genghis Khan's campaign in Central Asia all land occupied by the Nizari served as a safe zone for refugees fleeing either the Mongols or the shah. The land of the Nizari became a lifesaving corridor for many civilians, although not for soldiers.

The pact between Genghis Khan and the Nizari imam appears to have been political and strategic. At the time of their alliance, Genghis Khan was focused on conquest, and the imam was already nearing the end of his life. One reason that Genghis Khan did not need troops from the Nizari was that they had something much more valuable to offer. The Nizari operated an excellent spy network, gathering intelligence across Central Asia and as far as the Mediterranean. According to the chronicler Ali Ibn al-Athir, a Nizari official met with the Mongol general Chormaqan to offer information and encouragement in the search for Jalal ad-Din.[57] The alliance held throughout Genghis Khan's lifetime, and the Nizari continued to supply intelligence to the Mongols for more than a decade after his death.[58] The Nizari did not supply soldiers or offer tribute to the Mongols, but while the Mongol army conquered city after city, the Assassins sometimes launched their own raids against Khwarizm and kept their borders open to refugees of all sorts who were deserting the shah.

The tremendous rifts within the Muslim world offered Genghis Khan a simple path to conquer people by appealing to religious rivalries and sectarian feuds. While many Muslims accepted Genghis Khan's assertion that he was a punishment inflicted on them by God, some mystical Sufis claimed that they had actually summoned the Mongols in a holy quest to destroy their enemies within Islam and punish the decadence of the shah's court. According to one account, the Sufi leader himself allegedly guided the Mongol warriors into the city and encouraged them to kill all the Muslims, shouting, "O tribe of infidels, kill these evildoers."[59] The same story and phrase were used repeatedly by competing Sufi schools that claimed credit for bringing the Mongols into the Muslim world. Though numerous, these accounts were all written long after the fact and appear to be more myth than fact.

In a more credible account, Rashid al-Din claimed that in 1221, Genghis Khan had sought to rescue the great Sufi leader Najm al-Din Kobra and his disciples before attacking Khiva, the capital of Khwarizm, where the Sufi leader lived. The Mongols fired messages into the city on arrows, encouraging the Sufis to flee. Seventy Sufi disciples came out, but their master was too old to flee. According to some accounts, he had been praying to God for just such an attack. The old Sufi master refused Genghis Khan's invitation to abandon the city, replying that he had lived through "both bitter and sweet times" for seven decades, and fleeing from his home now would lack "manly honor and magnanimity." "I will attain the blessing of holy war and martyrdom from you," he reportedly said, "and you will obtain the blessing of Islam from us." He believed that after purifying Islam the Mongols would eventually convert to it.[60]

As soon as the city surrendered, Rashid al-Din tells us that Genghis Khan had his men search for the old Sufi, and "after much searching, his body was found among the slain."[61] A rival anti-Mongol Sufi leader then took credit for his death, claiming that he had ordered Genghis Khan to kill him and other deviant Sufi leaders for sins such as teaching the true faith to unworthy disciples and even to dogs.[62]

Genghis Khan recognized the general piety of Muslims, and he quickly devised an effective way to use their deep trust in God as a powerful weapon against them. In March 1220, after visiting the mosque of newly conquered Bukhara, he summoned the city's leaders. "You have committed great sins," Juvaini relates that Genghis Khan told them. "The great ones among you have committed these sins. If you ask me what proof I have for these words, I say it is because I am the punishment of God. If you had not committed great sins, God would not have sent a punishment like me upon you."[63] Just as he held defeated leaders accountable for misguiding their society, he considered religious leaders responsible for their actions and for the behavior of their followers.

He did not summon Muslim leaders in order to become their student or disciple. He called them to judgment. As heaven's representative on Earth, he felt it was his duty to examine the religions of the people he had conquered to determine what they were doing incorrectly and to correct their errors. He scrutinized the Muslim leaders as carefully as a merchant checking an apple for worms or a precious stone for flaws. His duty was to separate good actions from bad, to punish the wicked, reward the virtuous, and restore everyone to the correct path. Few of those who came to him really understood the meaning of the Mongol invasion. "Be silent!" a leading imam commanded his followers when he was asked how this could be happening. Genghis Khan "is the wind of God's omnipotence that is blowing, and we have no power to speak."[64]

Over the coming months, as he met with the self-proclaimed men of God and teachers of wisdom, he listened to them, asked about their practices, examined their achievements, and tested their morals. His quest was not the leisurely study of a scholar or a hermit meditating in an isolated cave; he approached his search as a man of action. The fighting that raged around him, the decisions regarding life or death, the physical and emotional turmoil of battle all added urgency to his spiritual mission. Ideas have to stand strong and clear to distinguish themselves amid war's choking smoke and to rise above the cries of the dying.

He had come to harness the wandering religions with a golden tether and to guide them into a single caravan that he would lead.

One lone camel cannot make a caravan, and so he felt that one single religion could not lead humanity to heaven. He proclaimed that it was his duty to make "the whole great people walk on the road of the true state of the law for the sake of attaining glory and honor."[65]

It was not so much religion itself that he mistrusted as the men who controlled it, those who used their power to promote their own goals rather than those of heaven. He held the wrongdoers accountable, executed some and banned many. To others he promised freedom and financial support if they would fulfill their duties to society and heaven. He encouraged religious freedom in the lands he conquered, but crushed religious extremism wherever he encountered it.

In his meetings with Muslim scholars in Samarkand, Genghis Khan asked that pious Muslims include him in their prayers wherever they might be. He approved of most Muslim practices, praising their commitment to prayer and to almsgiving, but he chastised them because "they drink and eat what they pleased, and pass whole Nights in Debauches," even in the holy month of Ramadan.[66] The Quran may have contained a valid message, but it seemed no more effective at promoting proper behavior than the scriptures of other religions. A book could be no more important than the deeds it inspired. If Muslims did not follow the dictates of their own holy book, why should the Mongols be interested in it?

He told the Muslims that there was no need to go to the mosque to worship or to make the pilgrimage to Mecca because God was everywhere. He criticized, but did not forbid, such practices and more strenuously discouraged the Muslim punishment of amputation, the ritual of circumcision, and the veiling or segregation of women. Just as he detested foot-binding among Chinese, so he condemned some Muslim practices as deplorable and unclean. In his judgment, they violated the higher law of morality. He objected strenuously, for instance, to butchering animals by slitting their throats and bleeding them to death. In Mongol eyes, the practice was cruel, wasteful, and unclean because it polluted the air and earth. Similarly, bathing in

streams or pools was thought to pollute the precious water that people and animals needed to drink.

☦

As fighting subsided and some cities chose to surrender, the Mongols
came to appreciate that Islam was more than the simple religion of
nomadic herders. They had encountered one of the great Muslim
civilizations and marveled at its beauty. The mosques of Bukhara and
Samarkand rose up like turquoise mountains, their floors adorned
with carpets that were like poetry on white marble.

Prior to entering Bukhara, the Mongols had not encountered a
society where men of religion exercised political power, acted as
judges, and performed the functions of offices of state. In the Buddhist kingdoms, the ruler reigned as a virtual god, but in the Muslim
states, it was difficult to ascertain who made the law and whether the
ruler ruled religion or vice versa. Such comingling of the two realms
seemed problematic. Mullahs, imams, and ayatollahs administered
the law, effectively becoming the state and removing the need for
secular rulers. The Mongol empire was based on opposite principles.

The Muslims immediately sought to convert the Mongols, but
Genghis Khan resisted, partly out of suspicion of Islam's intimate
connection to urban life. The Mongols saw Islam as an appropriate
religion for craftsmen, traders, and farmers. As one khan told a Muslim trying to convert him, "there are no barbers, smiths, or tailors
among my warriors." If they become "Muslim and follow the rules of
Islam, where will they gain their livelihood?"[67] Mongols were nomads, herders, and warriors; their beliefs supported their way of life.

Accounts of these moral discussions appear in the writings of the
mystical Muslim Sufis, but these quickly degenerate into self-serving efforts to persuade the Mongols to attack rival Sufi sects. The stories are
often undated and rarely tell where the meetings took place and sometimes omit even the author of the story, but taken together, they provide
insight into tone and topics of discussions. When Sufi leader Khvaja Ali

was brought before Genghis Khan, the Mongol leader was informed that the holy man's father was a saint who "used to give food to the people."

"Did he give food to his own people or to strangers?" asked Genghis Khan.

"Everyone gives food to his own people," said one of his disciples. "This man's father gave food to strangers."

"It was a good person indeed who gave food to the people of God," Genghis Khan responded. He then released the man and gave him a new cloak.[68]

For the Sufis the woolen cloak was a sign of faith, rendering this gesture, in the eyes of some Sufis, an endorsement of their religious practices. But Mongols scarcely seemed able to separate Muslims from Jews, much less one Muslim faction from another. It is hardly surprising that no Mongol record mentions meeting with Sufis or even knowledge of them, whereas Muslim writers record a long list of such encounters with Sufi leaders and their disciples.

There is little evidence to support any particular anecdote among the many reported encounters, but the Sufis did proliferate under the Mongols. The initial Mongol invasion sent thousands of Sufis, such as the family of the great poet Jalal ad-Din Rumi, into exile, carrying their brand of worship west toward Turkey and along the eastern Mediterranean. These refugees certainly had no reason to praise the Mongols, but the Mongol policies of tolerance gave Sufis the freedom to proselytize and to prosper.

Sufis frequently claimed Genghis Khan as one of their own. One Sufi account describes Genghis Khan as an ascetic prior to his rise to power, saying that he "left his family and tribe, and stayed up in the mountains." As related by the Egyptian encyclopedist al-Nuwayri, the story seems to reflect some knowledge of Genghis Khan's early years on Burkhan Khaldun. In the Sufi version, his fame spread and people "used to come to him on pilgrimage, and he would speak to them." He "did not belong to any religious community," but when people came to him "he signaled them to clap with their hands. As he danced they chanted 'ya Allah, ya Allah, yakshidir—O God, O God, he is good.' They did this, beat time for him, and he danced."[69] The Sufi schools frequently utilized unconventional means of communing with God, singing, chanting, twirling, or dancing, often accompanied by the beating of drums or the rhythmic clapping and pounding of feet on the floor. Such hypnotic rituals allowed the practitioners to put themselves into a virtual trance, much like the steppe shamans.

One type of Sufi, known as antinomians because they went against the norms of society, wore unconventional clothes and sometimes even went nearly naked. The indefatigable Arab traveler Ibn Battuta reported that they wore "iron rings on their hands, necks, ears, and even penises, so that sexual relations were not feasible for them."[70] Their bizarre behavior somewhat resembled the Turkic and Mongol shamans noted for going naked in the snow and sitting by blazing fires without being burned.

Yet, apparently, Genghis Khan took little notice of the Sufis. He did not need more shamans. He sought men with practical skills, and he found these in the more traditionally trained Muslim clerics, who could read and write foreign languages with unusual scripts, calculate numbers, compile records, make simultaneous translations, and in general had mastered the skills of bureaucrats. He drafted the best of them into the clerical service of his growing Mongol nation. Muslim scholars combined their philosophy and theology with practical matters of how to design buildings, construct irrigation systems, dig wells, transplant trees, breed animals, make dyes, cast metal, and handle many other issues of daily life.

With the Mongol obsession for making censuses of everything and everyone in the empire, they needed accountants, and the Muslims' ability to handle numbers impressed them greatly. Of all the people they had encountered, the Muslims had the highest mathematical skills. Genghis Khan needed clerks with strong math skills as he organized his empire based on units of ten combined into hundreds, thousands, and ten thousands. He needed men whose fingers were more skilled with an abacus than with rosary beads. He found the Chinese mandarin class to be educated in poetry, calligraphy, and etiquette and skilled in court politics, but they could not do arithmetic the way Muslim clerks could. Buddhist scholars focused on ritual and meditation, and got lost in endless discussions about the meaning of words. Muslim scholars, by contrast, offered more practical skills. After the conquest of Khwarizm, the Mongols created a completely new class of Muslim administrators and dispatched them to China to help manage their newly conquered territory there.

Despite the utility of Muslims as clerks, Genghis Khan deliberately limited the potential influence of any single religion by employing rivals of different sects and ethnicities and granting them overlapping responsibilities. These included Jews and Christians as well as a large variety of Muslims from normally contentious groups. He forced Sunnis and Shias to work together, alongside Zoroastrians and Sufis. The tensions between them kept any one person from achieving too much power. Their personal animosities were so strong that they often suppressed negative attitudes toward the Mongols.

By the end of 1220, the Mongols had chased the shah of Khwarizm to a lonely island in the Caspian Sea, where he died. Eager to fight and defend the dynastic honor, his son and heir, Jalal ad-Din Manguberdi, now became the nominal, but last, ruler of the crumbling Khwarizm Empire. Despite his lofty titles of shah and sultan, he ruled little more than the land occupied at any one time by his roving and shrinking army. Having lost all his cities, he fled into the mountains of Afghanistan in the hopes of finding refuge for his army and family in India.

Having devastated Khwarizm, Genghis Khan dispatched units across Iran into the Caucasus Mountains to take Armenia and Georgia and attack southern Russia. He himself then headed for Afghanistan in pursuit of Jalal ad-Din. He hoped to kill him before he could reach India and possibly find new allies there.

The next three years saw some of the bloodiest of the Mongol conquests as Genghis Khan's armies raced from the Himalayas to the Ural Mountains, from the Pacific Ocean to the Black Sea, fighting on fronts as distant as the Yellow River in China, the Dnieper in Ukraine, and the Indus in India. Fortresses and cities crumbled, armies evaporated, churches, mosques, and temples were left in ruin. The world had witnessed prior episodes of violence just as devastating but never on such a huge geographic scale.

Chronicles in many languages, written by men of many different religions, echoed the same astonished and devastated assessment of the blood and ruin. We can hear it in the anguished cry of the author of *The Novgorod Chronicle* after the Mongols defeated the Russians at the Battle of Kalka in the spring of 1223: "And thus, for our sins God put misunderstanding into us and a countless number of people perished, and there was lamentation and weeping and grief throughout towns and villages. . . . And the Tartars turned back from the river Dnieper, and we know not whence they came, nor where they hid themselves again; God knows whence he fetched them against us for our sins."[71]

11

The Thumb of Fate

Genghis Khan showed no sign of doubting his mission on Earth and his right to decide life and death for whole nations. His conquests were harsh and brutal, but harshness and brutality were typical of his era. Although he showed a remarkable ability to think outside of his time and context about many issues, no evidence suggests that he regretted killing so many men or questioned the morality of his conquests. People who died in war were fulfilling their destiny assigned by heaven; this meant that they deserved to die. In killing them, he was simply fulfilling his own destiny and following the Will of Heaven.

Ever since he had set out on his first foreign campaign against the Tangut in 1209, Genghis Khan had not lost a battle. He had conquered the cities of Khwarizm with much greater ease and speed than he had anticipated. With an unbroken record of success behind him, he fattened his horses in the summer of 1220 and headed off toward Afghanistan in an almost leisurely pursuit of Jalal ad-Din, the new Sultan of Khwarizm. He disliked the heat of the lower lands of Central Asia, so the highlands of Afghanistan offered a tempting respite for the aging warrior while his sons, sons-in-law, grandsons, and one of his daughters continued to lead the troops across the hotter zones.

As Genghis Khan approached sixty, he found that managing his expanding family took up more of his time. The problem of grooming his heirs and preparing them for future leadership of his empire became acute. As stated in the *Secret History*, "a body must have a head; a coat must have a collar."[1] Martial valor was well and good, but it had to be tempered by reason. Unfortunately, he did not see his middle-aged sons growing wiser or more capable. They enjoyed life too much, and they argued among themselves over the riches that would come when their father was gone and they were left in charge. Genghis Khan began to worry that his descendants might be so lazy that "even wrapped in fresh grass they would not be eaten by an ox."[2] One question plagued him, a terrible question that no parent wants to ask or answer: is it possible "that among my descendants not a single one will be born who is good?"[3] He asked, but no one dared to answer. There was only silence.

In the China campaigns, he sent his sons out on independent missions but kept them under his charge, always ready to send reinforcements if needed or to call them back at a crucial moment. In the Muslim lands, his forces had spread out over a much larger territory. He had armies fighting from the Indus River in what is now Pakistan to the Volga in the south of Russia. In these distant lands, his sons had to command on their own for longer stretches of time, and they had to coordinate with one another when they could not reach their father. They also had to make independent decisions. Although the older sons were now men in their forties, the rivalries and issues of their childhood frequently surfaced and seemed exacerbated as each one anticipated what he would soon be inheriting.

The presence of his adult children and grandchildren spread out across Central Asia, sometimes with him and other times in pairs or alone, gave Genghis Khan a chance to test them on the battlefield like an old wolf teaching the young ones to hunt. He taught them war tactics and ways to inspire their men. He explained his precepts for proper government and described the nature of the good life to his sons, but he was not simply issuing orders or edicts. He encouraged them to question him and to disagree with him so that they might find a better way.

The Armenian Christian chronicler Kirakos summed up the differences among the sons. He quoted Genghis Khan's description of his son Chagatai: "He is a martial man who loves war. But he is proud by nature, more than he should be." Ogodei, who would become the heir, he described as "gracious from his childhood, full of virtue, generous in gift-giving and, from the time of his birth, my glory and greatness has increased daily." Another unnamed son, either Jochi or Tolui, was "triumphant in battle, but stingy."[4]

Jochi's paternity continued to be an issue. His brothers wanted him barred from the succession because he had been conceived while their mother was married to the Merkid Chilger. However, isolating Jochi within the family only increased competition among the younger ones over their future patrimony. After they squabbled over how to conquer Khiva and whose property it would become, their father called them to Afghanistan in anger and disgust. He first refused to speak with them, but eventually he relented and made an effort to instruct them more properly. In one session with his eldest son, recorded in the *Golden Chronicle*, Jochi objected to his father's lesson. Jochi was not interested in the boring aspects of government administration. He wished to conquer, not merely to rule. He rudely told his father, "I expected that you would tell me to go to those people whom as yet nobody has reached in order that I may take into possession the people who are yet unconquered." He declared that his primary obligation to his father and to the Mongol nation was to expand the empire, not merely to rule already defeated people and their looted cities. "But it appears that you instruct me to rule a completely ready people," he complained. He then dismissed ruling a conquered state as nothing better than "eating prepared food."

Genghis Khan told his son that with this attitude, "you will not be powerful." He described in detail the difficulty of creating the "prepared food" that Jochi had so contemptuously dismissed. The chief cook must prepare his varied components, making sure that the ingredients and dishes are ready at the right moment, and that he has enough food for everyone. He must guard against poison or other dangers, all the while socializing, having a good time, and encouraging his guests to do the same.[5]

Success in battle is essential but not sufficient to make an empire, he explained. The warrior must also know how to use words to find wisdom and to rule effectively. Winning the war is futile if the victor cannot hold his new nation. "You will rule a host of lands," he told his sons, but a ruler must be more disciplined than his subjects. The key is to conquer the body with the mind. "Strong in body, one conquers units," he told his followers, but "strong in soul one conquers multitudes," and "if you wish to subdue before or after me, having seized the body, hold the soul. If you hold the soul where could the body go?"[6]

As a young warrior dedicated to fighting, Genghis Khan was distracted and not fully focused on nurturing his sons, but with maturity he had become a more loving and caring grandfather. Though he found his middle-aged sons to be recalcitrant and stubborn, he found greater pleasure and was more relaxed in his relationship with his grandsons, particularly his favorite, Mutugen, the eldest son of Chagatai and his wife Yesulun Khatun. While Genghis Khan sent his sons to distant fronts, he campaigned with Mutugen by his side in war, hunted with him in peace, and enjoyed a companionship that he had not shared with his father, brothers, or sons. He "tenderly loved him because he discovered in him all the marks of good conduct."[7] Mutugen was the joy of his old age.

Mutugen was always eager for a fight, full of enthusiasm and loved by his men. In his late teens, he had already proved himself a hero on the battlefield. Women adored him, and he frequently gave them opportunities to express their love, fathering children both with his wives and with other women, including the wives of his fellow soldiers. As a young man, he became enamored of the wife of one of his attendants. "He took her into a corner and had intercourse with her. It occurred to him that she might become pregnant, and he ordered her kept apart from her husband. It so happened that she did become pregnant and gave birth to a son, Buri. She was then given back to her husband."[8]

Despite the gossip generated by Mutugen's lack of sexual discipline, his grandfather loved him. Maybe he saw in Mutugen the man he himself would have been if he had been born into better circumstances. Instead of chasing rats, or fighting with his brother over a fish, he could have been enjoying life as the favored prince of a doting grandfather. In his eyes, Mutugen was as rare as a star at noon. Mutugen was "a marvelous hero, he had an elegant white face, his clear white eyes brimmed with tears like spring water, his body moved gracefully, he was like another man's wife."[9] His horse always led, and he never tasted dust.[10]

Genghis Khan saw something in his grandson that was missing in his sons; he devoted special attention to the military training of Mutugen and seemed to be grooming him to one day become the Great Khan. For the Afghan campaign in pursuit of Jalal ad-Din, he took his grandson as his companion. They conquered a string of cities with ease, but Jalal ad-Din eluded them. Early in 1221 Genghis Khan dispatched Mutugen to Bamiyan, a dry, cold valley in the mountains of central Afghanistan. More than seven centuries earlier, it had been inhabited by thousands of Buddhist monks, most of whom lived in caves, which they had filled with paintings. The monks had carved massive statues of Buddha into the cliffs overlooking the valley, which peered down on those who lived in their shadow. It was a place of austere beauty, rich history, and vibrant culture: just the right place for Mutugen to strike out and begin to apply some of the lessons of leadership his grandfather had taught him on his own.

The campaign to take the Afghan cities proceeded initially more benignly than the war in the low lands. Tolui took his time with the siege of Herat, which had been heavily fortified by troops sent by the shah to protect the entire region. As he had done in China, Genghis

Khan admonished his men to look for wise religious leaders who might serve or enlighten them, and during the siege of Herat a respected but clumsy imam, Kazi Wahid ad-Din, fell off the city wall and rolled straight into the Mongol camp. The warriors took him to Tolui and thereafter to the Great Khan who, upon finding that the captive was a religious scholar, held long discussions with him about Islam and morality. "In Genghis Khan's service, I found great favor," he later recalled. "I was constantly in attendance at his threshold, and he used continually to inquire of me the traditions of the prophets." Genghis Khan asked the imam if the Prophet Muhammad had foretold his arrival and that of the Mongols. The imam responded that the Prophet had foretold "the irruption of the Turk." He then criticized the Mongol leader for killing Muslims and warned him that if no one survived, there would be no one left to remember him or to tell his story.

Genghis Khan scoffed at this. "The remaining people who are in other parts of the world, and the sovereigns of other kingdoms that are, they will relate my history," he confidently informed him. Having tired of his new guest, he dismissed the imam from his court and sent him home.[11]

Meanwhile, despite the seemingly impregnable fortifications of Herat, the population decided to side with the Mongols and secretly opened the gates to admit the invaders. They had grown tired of the arbitrary ways and oppressive rule of the Khwarizm royal family, and despite being a fellow Muslim, Jalal ad-Din was nearly as foreign to them as the Mongols. They had no incentive to defend him when the Mongols offered them liberation at little cost. The Mongols slaughtered the soldiers, but spared the people of Herat.

Jalal ad-Din was still far away in the east, but he was preparing for war. The newly proclaimed sultan had managed to find allies in the Afghan tribes and to recruit Turcoman, Qanli, and other Turkic groups to his banner. After fleeing his father's dying capital at Khiva, he had made his way into the mountains of Afghanistan. In Ghazni, he made an alliance with the Qanli governor of the city by marrying his daughter. His new father-in-law brought fifty thousand pagan Qanli recruits to join the fight against the Mongols. The leader of the Muslim Khalaj tribe joined him with forty thousand, as did many local Ghuri warriors anxious for victory and the spoils of defeating the now treasure-laden Mongol army.

Jalal ad-Din set up temporary headquarters at Ghazni, in eastern Afghanistan, near the modern border with Pakistan. At an altitude above seven thousand feet, surrounded by the Hindu Kush Mountains, Ghazni's climate was harsh. The inveterate Arab traveler Ibn Battuta visited it and wrote, "It has an exceedingly cold climate, and the inhabitants move from it in the cold season to Kandahar, a large and prosperous town three nights journey."[12] Jalal ad-Din stayed in Ghazni during the winter of 1220–21, planning to launch a counterattack on the Mongols, liberate his lost kingdom, and send Genghis Khan back to the steppe from which he came. His "condition was now one of glory and splendor and he had a numerous army and following at his command," wrote Juvaini. Then, early in 1221, "in the first days of spring when the flowers began to bloom," he moved forward to Parwan to prepare for his campaign against Genghis Khan.[13]

The Mongols were not going to wait for Jalal ad-Din to attack. Genghis Khan always moved first, dictating the terms of engagement. When he heard "how the sultan [Jalal ad-Din] had mended his affairs and restored them to order," he decided to attack immediately before his prey could grow any stronger. All of his sons were on distant assignments, and for the only recorded instance, he sent his adopted son Shigi-Khutukhu, one of the orphans he had found abandoned at a deserted campsite while fighting the Tatars and given to his mother to raise. Shigi-Khutukhu was now the most educated person in the family, a judge and tribute collector skilled at writing the Uighur script, but he did not have a reputation as a warrior. Nevertheless, Genghis Khan was training him to lead like his other sons, so he placed him in charge of thirty thousand men and sent him to confront Jalal ad-Din. The choice seemed reasonable: the Khwarizm army had consistently folded in the face of Mongol attack, and Genghis Khan saw Jalal ad-Din, despite his new title, as a man on the run.

He sent two seasoned officers to accompany Shigi-Khutukhu, but they did not seem serious about the undertaking. Shigi-Khutukhu later complained to Genghis Khan about their "incessant joking and lightheartedness," and said, "people renowned for their wit, their pranks, and their clowning assume they are heroes—but on the day when courage is needed, such men achieve nothing and only cause trouble." According to Rashid al-Din, he called them "buffoons."[14] They proved of no help in the coming confrontation.

Jalal ad-Din's army was twice the size of his, but Shigi-Khutukhu knew the Mongol strategies and tactics and seemed eager to apply them. He arrived at Parwan, a narrow valley far more circumscribed than the battlefields to which the Mongols were accustomed, and ordered an attack aimed directly at the center of Jalal ad-Din's command. His warriors pushed hard on the center, but despite the Mongols' gaining some ground at first, Jalal ad-Din's troops, reinforced from the two wings, repulsed the attack. At the end of an indecisive day, the two armies made camp for the night.

Shigi-Khutukhu chose to apply an old trick that had worked many times for Genghis Khan. Because the Mongols always campaigned with a large number of relief horses, he ordered the men to make felt dummies and tie them on the unmanned horses. The next morning the Mongols rode back toward the battlefield with what appeared to be a massive number of reinforcements. Jalal ad-Din recognized the trick and ordered his army to stand firm, and again they repulsed the Mongol charge.

Finally, Shigi-Khutukhu attempted the oldest trick in the Mongol repertoire. He ordered an attack followed by a retreat in an effort to lure the enemy out and to break their ranks. Jalal ad-Din's men chased after the fleeing Mongols, and then, after luring them away from their base, the Mongols suddenly turned and attacked the men, who were now dispersed and no longer in fighting formation. The Mongols quickly killed some five hundred enemy troops, but Jalal ad-Din had been prepared for the counterattack. "At this very juncture the sultan rose up like a lion of the meadow or a leviathan of the raging sea."[15] He attacked with full force and routed the Mongols. Rashid al-Din reported that "the grassland in that region is full of holes and ditches, so that many of the Mongol warriors were thrown from their horses," but the sultan's horses seemed better able to maneuver through them.[16] For the first time, Genghis Khan's army had suffered an important defeat, a loss that would not be repeated for forty years, when an Egyptian Mamluk army would have a similar victory at Ayn Jalut, the Spring of Goliath, in what is today northern Israel near the borders with Lebanon and Syria.

Shigi-Khutukhu escaped with most of his men, but Jalal ad-Din captured many of the fleeing Mongols. Here at last was a formidable enemy who seemed as determined to win as his rival did. Jalal ad-Din was brave and resourceful, but he could not control the men supposedly under his command. They did not view themselves as his subjects so much as his rescuers, and their goal was not to restore the Khwarizm Empire but to plunder the Mongols. Some of his Muslim allies despised the pagans alongside whom they had been forced to fight, seeing them as no better than Mongols. They went wild capturing Mongol horses and stealing the loot that the Mongols had taken from the fallen cities and soon began to fight among themselves. Jalal ad-Din's father-in-law, who had commanded the pagan Qanli tribesmen on the right flank, began fighting over a prized horse with the Muslim commander of the left flank, whom he struck in the head with a whip. Victory turned to chaos.

Genghis Khan and his troops never tortured their enemies. They could be swift in meting out punishments and left cities in rubble, but they never inflicted gratuitous pain. In contrast, Jalal ad-Din ordered the worst possible executions for the Mongols. He knew the Mongols feared losing their soul at the moment of death by having it pour out on the ground with their blood. They preferred strangulation, suffocation, or any form of death that left their blood and other soul-bearing fluids inside their body and left their head, the locus of the immortal part of the soul, intact. Jalal ad-Din had the prisoners pulled out one by one and ordered his men to pound nails or wooden stakes into their heads and leave them to bleed to death as their souls flowed out and disappeared into the sand.

Jalal ad-Din fled toward India soon after his victory. Genghis Khan was too busy at first administering his empire to chase him, but he wanted to understand exactly what had caused the Mongol defeat. He traveled to the battlefield with Shigi-Khutukhu and some of his men. They explained precisely what had happened, and in the end, without chastising Shigi-Khutukhu, he explained his errors in tactics, beginning with his having fought in a narrow valley with limited means of withdrawal or escape. He then gave Shigi-Khutukhu an assignment more appropriate to his abilities, sending him to spend the rest of 1221 in Ghazni. As the official charged with taking a census of the people after the defeat, he was tasked with organizing the transportation of chosen craftsmen and looted goods to Mongolia.

News of the Mongol defeat by the forces of Jalal ad-Din spread quickly throughout the former Khwarizm Empire. Compared with their own losses over the past two years, it was only a minor defeat, but it heartened them that the barbarians finally proved vulnerable. Defeating even this small army and then killing the survivors exposed the Mongols' weakness. As the news traveled with refugees and merchants from village to village and city to city, the people still holding out against the Mongols felt greatly encouraged, and many of those who had previously surrendered now revolted. They killed the officials left in place by the Mongols, even when they were Muslims and fellow Turks or Persians. The conquered people of Khwarizm resisted the Mongols at every opportunity and raided their baggage trains crammed with looted wealth.

The Mongol army had never been spread out over such a large area, and it was vastly outnumbered by the urban populations around it. At this point, a coordinated rebellion or organized army could have defeated it. Genghis Khan moved quickly and violently to put down the uprisings before they could become an organized campaign against him.

The people of Balkh, another city noted for its wealth and scholarship, famed as the home of the Bactrian princess Roxana, who had married Alexander the Great, rose up in rebellion. Juzjani informs us that afterward, "the few remaining people, for the period of a full year, had to sustain life on the flesh of dogs and cats and human beings, for this reason that the forces of Chingiz Khan had burnt all the stores, barns, and granaries leaving not a grain of corn, and no cultivation whatever existed."[17] Some fifty thousand were killed, but one of the many families to escape was that of one of the greatest of Persian poets and mystics, Jalal ad-Din Muhammad Balkhi, better known in the West as Rumi. He spent much of his life fleeing the Mongols through Nishapur, Baghdad, and Damascus, and finally settled in Konya in modern Turkey, where he became a renowned scholar and Sufi teacher.

Despite his suffering at the hands of the Mongols, Rumi, noted for his generosity of spirit and deep spirituality, seemed accepting, almost forgiving. Finding some good in everything that happens, he even seemed to appreciate the peripatetic life that resulted from being forced to flee his home as a refugee.

> Oh, if a tree could wander
> and move with foot and wings!
> It would not suffer the axe blows
> and not the pain of saws![18]

In 1221, in the beautiful valley of Bamiyan with its giant Buddhas sculpted into the living mountain, an arrow shot "by the thumb of Fate" struck Mutugen.[19] Muslim chroniclers wrote that because of

Mutugen's love of his grandfather and his frustration at the dogged resistance of the Muslims of Bamiyan, "he exposed himself to the greatest dangers."[20] According to one account, "the young prince fell dead at his grandfather's feet." It is unlikely that the end came quite so dramatically. He had simply been killed, like so many other soldiers, in the senseless crush of battle.

Genghis Khan was stunned. In a lifetime of fighting, none of his sons had fallen, none of his wives or daughters had died, and he had never lost a general. In his adult life, everyone close to him seemed to enjoy the same blessing of heaven that protected him. At this moment of unprecedented success and power, how could fate snatch away the most beloved member of his family? He could never again ride beside his grandson, smell his scent, hear his laugh, or see his eyes sparkle in battle. In a lifetime fighting, chasing, and fleeing, Genghis Khan had endured gnawing hunger, burning frostbite, piercing arrows, crushing clubs, and slicing swords, but to know that someone he loved was in agony and not be able to save him was the greatest suffering imaginable. The goals he had pursued, the dreams he had followed, the hopes he had nourished began to melt like snow falling into fire. He was drunk with sorrow and drowning in grief.

He began to fear that his whole family stood in danger and there might be no future for his empire. His life's work could abruptly be broken by a single arrow of fate. Genghis Khan did not believe the assertion of some philosophers that pain and pleasure were simple illusions or that suffering might be alleviated through meditation, compassion, sacrifices, or denial. From his lifetime of experience, he knew that although pleasure was fleeting, misery poured down cruelly and abundantly from the sky. Humans could no more prevent it than they could stop the rain, wind, or hail. In childhood, he had watched those around him writhe and die in agony, but when he became a man, he learned to redirect this suffering away from himself and from those he loved onto others. He became the aggressor, never the victim, and thereby conquered the largest empire in history.

Throughout his adult life, his strategy of calculated aggression had protected his family and nation, but now suddenly pain came pouring in. He was no longer a great conqueror, he was nothing more than a hapless victim of fate. Voltaire quoted Genghis Khan as saying, "Fate conquers all."[21] Whether or not he actually spoke those words, he understood their painful truth. Mutugen's death threatened not only his plans for his empire but his deepest spiritual core. If heaven had truly blessed him and given him so much success, why had it denied him the love of his grandson? Why had his fate failed him in front of the cliffs of Bamiyan?

Fate determined death's hour, but he reasserted his will by channeling the grief inside him into revenge on the world. He forbade mourning. In keeping with Mongol tradition, the name of the fallen could not be spoken, but he went further and forbade any mention of his death, lest the enemy know that a member of the royal family had died. Even the Mongolian chroniclers who later wrote the history of the empire refused to mention Mutugen's death or the revenge that followed, so we must depend on Muslim observers to understand what happened.

By the order of Genghis Khan, no Mongol could cry or scream, not even the boy's father. Genghis Khan would not let his son shed one tear or mourn. Instead, he made the local people wail in horror, shriek in pain, and beg vainly for mercy that never came. Genghis Khan drowned the fiery anguish in his soul by making others suffer. In the explanation offered by Juvaini, he "dispatched to the right and the left to the East and the West, and subjugated it all." Suddenly, "with one stroke, a world which billowed with fertility was laid desolate, and the regions thereof became a desert and the great part of the living dead, and their skin and bones crumbling dust." Thus, "the mighty were humbled and immersed in the calamities of perdition."[22]

He "gave orders that every living creature, from mankind down to the brute beasts, should be killed; that no prisoner should be taken;

that not even the child in the mother's womb should be spared."[23] His troops destroyed city after city. Tolui raced to put down a rebellion in Merv, which overflowed with refugees. He did so and killed everyone. The general sent to restore rule over Herat, which Tolui had treated with such tender mercy, did the same. In city after city, the Mongols entered with drawn swords and left nothing but dust in their wake.

"It was a pitiful sight," wrote the Armenian chronicler Kirakos. "Dead parents and their children were heaped on top of one another, like a pile of rough stones—old, young, children, adolescents, and many virgins." Across the plains, "the land drank in the blood and fat of the wounded. Tender bodies, once washed with soap, lay blackened and swollen. Those who had not gone out of the city were led away barefoot into captivity." There was nothing left to say. "This was the end of the affair."[24]

They carefully targeted the aristocrats whose ancestors had ruled from the time of Alexander the Great, and sent refugees fleeing to India and Persia. "Mongols of those days," wrote Injannasi, "regarded warfare as joyous and beautiful."[25] They conquered every city that had revolted, put it to the torch and annihilated the people. No rebels could survive to threaten Genghis Khan again.

In the late summer, still in the fiery anguish of losing his beloved grandson, Genghis Khan moved forward with his campaign to chase down Jalal ad-Din. The only cure for pain was to make someone else hurt more. "Like a male dragon panting for vengeance, a clod of calamity," wrote Juvaini, Genghis Khan "went forth to defeat him and exact vengeance, like flashing lightning or a torrential flood, his heart filled with rage and leading an army more numerous than the raindrops."[26]

He caught up with Jalal ad-Din on the banks of the Indus River near Kalabagh in modern Pakistan, southwest of Islamabad. Having been deserted by his two quarreling allies, Jalal ad-Din still led his own much smaller army of around seven hundred men. They were preparing boats to cross the river. When he saw the Mongol warriors on the horizon, he knew he was trapped "between water and fire—on one side the water of the Indus and on the other an army like consuming fire," but instead of surrendering, "he saddled the horse of vengeance and chose to plunge into the fray."[27]

Genghis Khan's army pressed in harder and tighter around the beleaguered sultan. Jalal ad-Din immediately knew that he had lost. He called his wives and children and bade farewell to them "with a burning heart and a weeping eye."[28] In an act much heralded by Muslim writers in desperate want of a hero in the war against the Mongols, he forced his horse to jump from the cliff into the raging water and swim to the other side. Mongol archers rushed to the edge of the cliff to shoot the target of their hunt, but Genghis Khan stopped them. He allowed them to shoot the other fleeing men and ordered them to let the sultan escape.

What could Genghis Khan have been thinking as he sat on his horse high above the Indus River, watching the son of his greatest enemy, the only foreigner to have ever defeated the Mongols in battle, swim away? He was a man of great consistency, with little hint of sentimentality in war, but this unexpected act of mercy was not consistent with who he was and what he had done before in similar circumstances. After slaughtering thousands of innocent people across Afghanistan, he let this one man go free. Was he doing what he wished he had done for his bond brother Jamuka decades ago? Was he granting Jalal ad-Din a special gift of life that had been denied to his beloved grandson? Was he following the Mongol tradition to always free some of the animals at the end of a successful hunt? Or did the aging conqueror see in this reckless jump a quality that he wished to honor?

He watched in silence as Jalal ad-Din swam to India until, in the words of Juvaini, "crossing the great river like a fiery lion he reached the shore of safety."[29] He did not explain his actions, but he turned to his sons, who had been called to join the rampage across Afghanistan after the death of Mutugen, and said gravely, "Such sons should a father have."[30] Genghis Khan did not pursue Jalal ad-Din, and he never crossed the Indus River. Jalal ad-Din found safety in India and in the subsequent years he continued to harass the Mongol soldiers across Central Asia, but the Mongols never harmed him. In the end, he was killed by a fellow Muslim when a Kurdish assassin stuck him down in 1231.

12

Wild Man from the Mountain

Genghis Khan was beginning to feel what the Mongols call *nasand daragdax*—the inevitable triumph of age over body. Although he had defeated the last holdout leader of the Khwarizm army, he had little cause to celebrate. His army had lost only one battle, but combined with the loss of his grandson, the year 1221 marked a turning point in his life. He was tired and very far from home. His eldest son, Jochi, had ignored his summons and stayed as far away as he could, and his other sons continued squabbling among themselves as though their father had already died and they had taken charge of the empire.

After seeing the world, tasting the best and the worst of civilization, experiencing humanity's good and bad, rising to the pinnacle of power and sinking to the emotional depths of despair, he now embarked on a new personal spiritual journey that was to be his final campaign in life. He did not turn inward to engage in philosophical meditations or seek magic rituals to promote inner harmony and peace. Instead, his new quest took him out beyond himself into the world to seek out the most respected and renowned spiritual teachers and wisest minds of his time. He knew intimately his own spirituality and customs, but he set out to study other, more formally organized religions to find some soothing knowledge, some mystical secret that had eluded him. As with the most important quests in life, he did not know precisely what he was searching for, but he hoped that he would recognize it when he found it.

Mongols preferred fighting in the winter. The warriors and their horses tired less easily and responded to the cold with energetic enthusiasm. In the summer, the heat drained man and beast, and their bows lost their strength and sharpness. In the long summer days, the horses grazed to store up the energy needed for the winter campaign. The men enjoyed wrestling and drinking fermented horse milk in the day and singing during the night. The late summer evenings, after the heat of the day had passed, provided Genghis Khan an opportunity to sit and talk in a more leisurely fashion. Summer was the season for playing games and talking philosophy in the Mongol camps.

In the spring of 1222, a delegation of Taoist scholars arrived at his camp at the foot of the Hindu Kush near modern-day Kabul. A few weeks after the destruction of the city of Balkh, the Chinese sage he had summoned two years earlier and his disciples traveled past the city ruins. "Its inhabitants had recently rebelled against the Khan and been removed," one of his disciples wrote cryptically. "But we could still hear dogs barking in its streets."[1] The Taoists approached the Mongol camp just south of what the Mongols called the Snowy Mountains, when the almond and peach trees bloomed.

In the aftermath of the violence and suffering in Afghanistan, the blossoming landscape offered the promise of healing. "Thousands of cliffs vying in beauty purify a man's thoughts," wrote Yelu Chucai, who was still serving Genghis Khan so loyally. "Myriads of streams vying in swiftness strengthen my spirits." The mountain scenery inspired creativity, and his thoughts melded with the setting. "Now I think of the mountains; now I look at the poems."[2]

Taoism had arisen out of folk beliefs about spirits and forces of nature, but through the centuries, it had evolved into a full philosophy complete with accomplished monks, elaborate rituals, and competing sects with their rival grand masters. Taoism was the native religion of the common people in China while Confucianism was the prescribed way of life for the educated elite. Both were indigenous to China, in contrast to Buddhism, Christianity, Islam, and Manichaeism, which were foreign imports. Taoism lacked the philosophical sophistication and prestige of Confucianism or the mystical depth of Buddhism, but Mongols found its worship of nature and local spirits familiar, and many Taoist teachings aligned with their traditional belief.

Some of Genghis Khan's first Chinese allies had been Taoists. As early as the 1190s, members of the old Khitai royal family had fled from northern China to join him, bringing with them an excellent knowledge of Chinese literary and spiritual culture, including a keen appreciation for Taoism. They proved loyal during the dangerous vicissitudes of his relationship with Ong Khan.[3] From these early experiences with Taoists, Genghis Khan appreciated their loyalty and recognized their value in winning popular support among the common people in China.

To this end, in 1219 before embarking on his invasion of Central Asia, he summoned Taoist monks under the leadership of the most famous sage of his day, the elderly and venerable Qiu Chuji, whose followers honored him as the Wild Man from the Mountain.[4] Shortly before the Mongol invasion of China, Qiu Chuji had assumed the leadership of the Quanzhen sect, sometimes translated as Complete Reality or as Complete Perfection, one of Taoism's fiercely competitive factions. In an era of social violence and moral decay in China, he garnered notoriety as a backwoods poet and homespun philosopher who celebrated the nostalgic purity of rural life, far away from the political infighting of the royal court and the turmoil in the cities and villages. His devotees claimed that he knew the secret to everlasting life.

Genghis Khan recognized his need for good laws, and because the old sage "has much explored the laws" and is a holy man who lived according to "the rigorous rules of the ancient sages," he summoned him to leave his home and come offer counsel. "In this letter I have briefly expressed my thoughts and hope that you will understand them," he wrote to Qiu Chuji. "I hope also that having penetrated the principles of the great *Tao* that you will sympathize with all that is right and will not resist the wishes of the people."[5]

Qiu Chuji was not a natural traveler. His first major complaint on the journey came early on, when he realized that his travel companions would include young Chinese women entertainers who had been recruited to lift troop morale on the front battle lines in Afghanistan and Iran. As a venerated philosopher, he feared the scandal, or possibly the temptation for his disciplines, of traveling in such company. He wrote to the Great Khan that he felt it was best "not to see things which arouse desire." The Mongols indulged him with a separate escort in another caravan.[6]

As China's most famous sage, Qiu Chuji had met with an earlier Jin emperor, and recently both the new Jin emperor of the north as well as the Sung emperor of the south had summoned him to their respective courts. He had refused both, but recognizing that the Mongols were the new power, and would be likely to replace both courts and possibly reunite all of China, he wisely accepted Genghis Khan's invitation. He did not then know that it would be three years before he would return home from the mobile Mongol headquarters, which he referred to respectfully as "Dragon Court." He was advanced in age and had little to gain personally from the long trip, but he wished to secure assurances from the Great Khan that his sect and disciples would be well treated.

The sage's disciple kept a diary of the journey that reveals a man too old and settled in his mental habits to see much that was new. Whatever Qiu Chuji encountered merely reinforced conclusions he had reached years earlier or matched long-held prejudices and frequently voiced complaints about everything from the cost of wheat in the desert to the poor quality of the roads. Qiu Chuji had never before ventured from northern China, and at his age, he found little comfort in anything new or unfamiliar. He made the prosaic observations of a tired old man who

commented on the weather and the landscape more out of boredom
than from interest in the places, culture, people, or history around him.
The mountains were high, the desert dusty, the sun hot, the rivers wet,
the snow cold, and the marshes filled with evil spirits.

The sage succeeded in identifying something disagreeable in the
most unlikely situations, as when he passed over a mountain and spotted a large lake that resembled a rainbow. "It was dreadful to look
down to the lake in the depth," he observed. He composed poems by
day and passed them around to his students to enjoy in the evening. He
reserved his greatest admiration for his own deeds, no matter how
trifling. En route to Genghis Khan, he addressed one poem to three
young geese that he had set free on a lake. "They tended you to no
purpose," he wrote addressing the goslings, "save to bring you to the
kitchen; and only my kind interest saved you from becoming a meal.
In a light skiff I took you out and set you among the huge waves, there
to wait till autumn's end when your wings are fully grown."

The old sage's only comforts seemed to be the fresh fruits, wine,
and soft cotton fabrics provided along the way. One night after a din-
ner of good food and drink, he delighted in the entertainment of
some local boys dancing with swords and performing balancing
tricks on long poles. Beyond ample complaints and vain vignettes, we
learn only that those he encountered received him with joyous awe,
were deeply impressed by the old master's piety and philosophy, and
wept copious tears when he departed. He appears to have noticed
nothing about their customs or religious life, but for some unex-
plained reason, he noted with great pleasure how amazed the foreigners were by the quality and ingenuity of his water pail.[7]

By the time Qiu Chuji finally reached the Mongol camp, Genghis
Khan had suffered the death of his favorite grandson and witnessed
quarreling among his heirs. Driven by a growing sense of despair
over human nature and his own mortality, he hoped to find some

ultimate truth or primary principle to guide him and his empire. Like the Uighur and Turkic leaders before him, he adhered tenaciously to the principle of *Tore*, the ideal of just power, a concept that was also central to Taoist teachings. Although the Mongols generally invoked the concept of just power in relation to the state and the khan, the Taoists showed greater concern for the individual spiritual quest. Early Taoist scholars translated the Mongol term *Tore* into Chinese as *Tao li*.[8] Their quest for the Tao resembled Genghis Khan's search for the correct moral principles of *Tore*.

It is hard to imagine the impression that the Mongol camp made on the Chinese visitors. They politely and politically refrained from recording any negative opinions. Some of the experience of entering a Mongol camp appears in the works of other writers. With a mixture of awe and contempt, Kirakos of Gandzak described life in the Mongol camp: "Whenever possible they ate and drank insatiably, but when it was not possible, they were temperate. They ate all sorts of animals both clean and unclean, and especially cherished horsemeat. This they would cut into pieces and cook or else roast it without salt; then they would cut it up into small pieces and sop it in salt water and eat it that way. Some eat on their knees, like camels, and some eat sitting." Accustomed to marked status difference among members of most royal courts, the Armenian was surprised by the egalitarian way of the Mongols. "When eating, lords and servants share equally." When drinking fermented mare's milk, "one of them first takes a great bowl in his hand and, taking from it with a small cup, sprinkles the liquid to the sky, then to the east, west, north and south. Then the sprinkler himself drinks some of it and offers it to the nobles."[9]

The records of Genghis Khan's philosophical discussions with the Taoist sage survive in more detail than those of any other of his religious conversations, as bitterly opposing accounts written by two primary participants, both of whom were about thirty years old and well educated in Chinese history, philosophy, and culture. Qiu Chuji's perspective was recorded by Li Zhichang, one of the eighteen disciples who accompanied the master on this long journey, whose fitting name translates as Perfect Constancy.[10] As the old master's scribe, Li Zhichang attended the meetings with Genghis Khan, listened carefully to the translation of his words into Chinese, and recorded the conversation.

Li Zhichang published his *Account of Travels to the West (Xiyou ji,* not to be confused with a more famous Chinese novel of a similar title about the Monkey King) seven years later, in 1228, soon after the deaths of both Genghis Khan and Master Qiu Chuji.[11] Almost immediately afterward, Yelu Chucai wrote a dramatically contrasting account of the scholar's visit in *Record of a Journey to the West (Xiyou lu)*. Yelu Chucai wrote a memoir of his service with the Mongols in Central Asia in an effort to correct what he claimed were the lies of the Taoist sage and his disciples.[12] For seven hundred years, Li Zhichang's account was accepted as the sole record of the discussions between Genghis Khan and the sage, as Yelu Chucai's report had disappeared from the libraries and archives of China and scholars began to suspect that it had never existed. Then in 1926, a meticulous scholar, Professor Kanda Kiichiro, discovered a copy in the imperial library in Japan.

Among the many religious scholars who had flocked to the Mongol court, some had been spies. One such group of Buddhist monks arrived from Japan under the pretext of seeking religious manuscripts from China for the edification of the thriving Buddhist community in Japan. Instead, they collected whatever information they could about the Mongol court. Because Yelu Chucai's book fulfilled both criteria of their mission, touching on religion and politics, the spying monks brought a copy back with them to Japan, where it enjoyed a protective inattention while the vagaries of religious politics and neglect gradually destroyed the limited edition of the book in China. Suddenly, with the unexpected discovery of the manuscript, a new firsthand account of conversations with Genghis Khan, scholars could compare Taoist and Mongol perspectives.

Yelu Chucai was a cultivated scholar of aristocratic disposition and courtly manner who was proud of his ancestry as a descendant of the rulers of the deposed Liao dynasty in northern China. He had enjoyed a classical Chinese education in Confucian thought and harbored a nostalgic longing for a lost past. The way forward, he believed, was always to go back in time to some earlier state of social and spiritual harmony. This accounted, in part, for his having joined the Mongols soon after Genghis Khan's conquest of the Jin capital, where he lived: he had hoped that they would restore the glory of his Khitai ancestors.

☫

Yelu Chucai had enthusiastically supported Genghis Khan's decision to summon the Taoist sage to the Mongol court, but he quickly regretted that decision. When he met the old man, admirable by reputation, he found him to be disgusting. "At the beginning of our conversations—at the time when we were exchanging verses—I openly approved of him to some extent," he wrote. "Then, as our acquaintance deepened, I got to know him thoroughly. . . . I disapproved of him in my mind and laughed at him in private." Yet he voiced no such criticism at the time. "Had I attacked him it would have created a dispute," he explained in his defense.[13] He considered Qiu Chuji not merely a religious deviant but a greedy, materialistic hypocrite posing as a sage. In short, he was a fake.

The Mongols showed polite deference to the Taoist delegation, but their reaction as reported by Yelu Chucai differed markedly from the Taoist account. Without contradicting the venerable sage directly, Genghis Khan gently teased him and lightheartedly joked in a way that the sage misunderstood or that his disciples chose not to mention.[14] He had summoned the sage for the purpose of "preserving life"[15] for his empire and seeking his wisdom regarding the key to an efficient and moral government. But the sage quickly confessed, "Affairs of warfare and statesmanship are not within my capability."[16]

Genghis Khan was concerned with immortality, but as he made

clear on many occasions, it was the immortality of his empire and the survival of his lineage that preoccupied him—not that of his mortal body. Another Mongolian chronicle connected the visit of the Chinese sage directly to the need to rule "many people having other customs."[17] He sought to learn "the manner in which one might hold the government and one might protect and support living beings." He understood the rules guiding nomadic herding life and the way of the warrior, but he sought assistance in administering the agricultural and urban parts of his empire.

Instead of practical principles governing public affairs, Qiu Chuji and his sect specialized in spiritual quackery, mainly selling longevity through magic. The sage sought to prolong life through chemical transformations in the body, replacing forbidden foods with magic elixirs concocted by the monks and by developing secret techniques to preserve semen inside the body of men. (Women did not seem to be in need, or deserving, of immortality.) Unlike healers who crafted medicines and potions from plants and animals, the Taoist alchemists used hard substances that did not decay and concocted their elixirs from cinnabar (red mercury), jade, pearls, gold leaf, and other precious stones that seemed to last forever. If the soul of gold could make it endure eternally without tarnishing, the logic went, eating it might make humans live longer as well.

To promote their craft, Taoist healers and sages circulated stories of monks facilitating miraculous cures and living to incredible ages. Some, like Qiu Chuji, were said to be immortal. Qiu Chuji's followers asserted that he was more than three hundred years old and still vigorously active. Rich men throughout China sought the services of his disciples to prolong their lives.

In contrast to the heavy formality and rituals surrounding most royal courts, entering Genghis Khan's inner court was much like stepping into the tent of a Mongol herder. The monks did not have to kowtow or kneel in his presence; they simply "inclined the body and pressed the palms of the hands together on entering his tent."[18] The Chinese monks marveled that this meeting with the great world conqueror was more like a chat. Li Zhichang remarked that their Mongol hosts even offered bowls of fermented mare's milk to relax them. When the sage complained that he did not eat meat or drink mare's milk, the khan indulged him with melons, fruits, and vegetables as well as ample wine made from grapes.

The relaxed informality of the Mongol court allowed Genghis Khan to put his guests at ease while he made quick and decisive evaluations of their character. He judged them by their answers to the easiest and seemingly most innocent questions before listening to their prepared speeches and philosophical discourses on the topics they considered most pressing. Queries about their name, age, family, and origin were not humble politeness or small talk. How visitors answered these questions played into his evaluation. He used the deceptively simple tactic of preceding a question with sweet words of flattery so that while the mind of the guest savored the taste of the compliment, the tongue began to wag freely.

The interview began, according to Li Zhichang, with an expression of appreciation for the long journey the master had undertaken and for his willingness to visit. "I take this as a high compliment," Genghis Khan told the sage. He then asked Qiu Chuji by what name he should call him, as he had various honorific titles. The sage seemed blissfully unaware of his host's dislike of fancy titles. "People call you *Tengri Mongke Ken*,"[19] the interpreter said, using the Mongolian equivalent of his Chinese title, literally meaning Heavenly Eternal Person but akin to Immortal Sage. The Taoist's title seemed to bestow an air of divinity on the sage, as if he claimed authority to speak for God. Genghis Khan seemed skeptical of such supernatural claims. The only Mongol previously to have claimed such a title was Teb Tengeri, who had ended up abandoned by heaven.

"Did you choose this name yourself or did others give it to you?" asked Genghis Khan.

The sage responded as if this were no more than an extension of the compliments he had just received. "I, the hermit of the mountains, did not give myself this name," he said in boastful humility. "Others gave it to me."

The Mongol emperor, a man who had grown up in the thickets of Burkhan Khaldun and had lived among the Uriyankhai mountain men, did not ask the city sage why he was also known as the Wild Man from the Mountain, but later he sent an official to ask the monk again for his real name. "What were you called in former days?" Again, the Chinese sage avoided giving his real name and replied that people called him "the Immortal Sage or Eternal Master."[20]

Genghis Khan next addressed the absurd claims that the old man had been alive for centuries. Qiu Chuji was born around the year 1148 and became a monk in 1166 at age eighteen. He had reached his early seventies when he met Genghis Khan, who was fourteen years younger. When asked directly how old he was, the sage demurred, claiming that he did not know his age. Not long thereafter, however, the monk's disciples celebrated his birthday with a party in a large orchard. "The nineteenth day of the first lunar month [mid-February 1223] was the Master's birthday," wrote his disciple Li Zhichang, "and all the officials burnt incense-candles and wished him long life."[21]

Mongols often did not know their age and seemed not to care very much about it, but the Chinese used the twelve-animal zodiac cycle, and most people, certainly an educated scholar, knew their year of birth. For a monk concerned with telling fortunes, the sign corresponding to the year, day, and hour of birth held great importance. As Yelu Chucai wrote, "He falsely stated that he did not know it. How can an intelligent person not know his age?"[22] By this point, Yelu Chucai had formed a decidedly negative opinion of the sage, but Genghis Khan, accustomed to dealing with all sorts of men, was more tolerant of the evasive answers. Yelu Chucai claimed that if the sage could not be trusted to answer the simplest questions honestly, how could his advice be taken seriously? Whereas Yelu Chucai was angry with the Taoist's deception, Genghis Khan gently teased the monk and decided in jest to call him "the immortal."

When asked practical questions, such as the cause of thunder and lightning, the sage answered with theological mutterings that thunder and lightning arose as nature's punishment for improper behavior. He advised the Mongol emperor to practice Taoist rituals in order to appease the ancestral spirits, not knowing what a sensitive subject this was for a man who had not been allowed to worship his ancestors. Genghis Khan remained silent. Chatting on freely and seemingly delighted by how much he had impressed the Mongols with his wisdom, the sage then recommended that the Mongols bathe and wash their clothes, acts that they considered to pollute Mother Earth. He also recommended that they follow odd dietary restrictions to avoid earthquakes, being struck by lightning, and similar calamities.[23]

Because the sage's disciples claimed he had lived for more than three hundred years, Genghis Khan asked him to share the secret recipe of his life-prolonging medicine. He replied that the secret to eternal life did not come from an elixir but from following the correct path, which he then proposed to explain. As his entire reputation and the prosperity of his sect derived from selling elixirs that promised longevity, rival monks later mocked the sage for this answer. The old man advocated the denial of bodily pleasure and the need to overcome physical longing through mental and spiritual discipline. The venerable sage had three often-repeated pieces of advice for Genghis Khan: stop hunting, stop having sex, and stop taxing the Taoist clergy. In the end, the Great Khan would agree to only one of the three recommendations.

In addition to their personal chats, Genghis Khan arranged for the sage to preach sermons to his advisers and to his sons, whom he desperately sought to educate with moral knowledge in addition to their military skills. One can scarcely imagine their reactions, sitting cross-legged on the ground after a day of fighting as they listened to this wizened old monk preach the virtue of restraint. Qiu Chuji delivered his most important lecture on November 19, 1222, and ten years later his disciples published it.[24] The sermon offered windy explanations of the origin of the universe that contained aspects of traditional Taoism combined with the dualism of the Manichaeans. "Tao is the producer of Heaven the nurturer of Earth," he began. "The sun and moon, the stars and planets, demons and spirits, man and things all grow out of Tao. Most men only know the greatness of Heaven; they do not understand the greatness of Tao. My sole object in living all my life separated from my family and in the monastic state has been to study this question."

His lengthy sermon outlined the history of the Taoist faith, introduced its great teachers, and offered anecdotes from his own life. He shared the Taoist creation story: "When Tao produced Heaven and Earth, they in turn opened up and produced Man. When Man was first born he shone with a holy radiance of his own and his step was so light that it was as if he flew." Life began in perfect spiritual harmony between body and soul, and between humans and nature. However, mankind made a fatal mistake, eating mystical mushrooms that disrupted the divine harmony and ended the original paradise on Earth. "The earth bore fungoids that were moist and sweet-tasting. Without waiting to roast or cook them, Man ate them all raw; at this time, nothing was cooked for eating. Man with his nose smelt their scent and with his mouth tasted their taste. Gradually his body grew heavy and his holy light grew dim. This was because his appetite was so keen."

The moral of this story was that people "must do without pleasant sounds and sights, and get their pleasure only out of purity and quiet. They must reject luscious tastes and use foods that are fresh and light as their only delicacy." His teaching reflected strong Manichaean tenets about the power of foods to destroy the spirit. "If the eye sees pleasant sights, if the mouth enjoys pleasant tastes or the natural state is perturbed by emotions, then the original Spirit is scattered and lost." Some wondered how he could preach about overcoming needs and the importance of austerity when his first action on approaching the camp had been to complain about the food served to him.[25]

He then turned to an even worse threat to the Original Spirit than food—sex. "The Taoist must, above all, abstain from lust," he said. He warned that "a licentious life wastes the fine particles of the soul and leads to a considerable loss of the Original Spirit." The Tao consists of two aspects: "The one, light and pure. This became the sky. The sky is male and belongs to the element fire. The other form is heavy and unclean. This becomes earth. The earth is female and belongs to the element water." Mongols understood the distinction, but for them earth and water were both pure substances, like fire. They could be made impure only through human action. The union of male and female seemed perfectly natural to them in the physical as well as the spiritual sense.

At this point, the sage directed his remarks more specifically to Genghis Khan. He told him that even a common man with one wife could ruin himself by having too much sex with her. "What must happen to monarchs, whose palaces are filled with concubines?" he asked. Although it was well known that Genghis Khan had sent envoys searching for wise men to counsel him, the sage accused him of actually ordering these men "to search Peking and other places for women." He specifically named the man who had first brought him to the khan's attention as one such procurer, having erroneously assumed that all the dancing girls in their original caravan were women for the khan's harem. He told his host that it was better not to see such women. "Once such things have been seen, it is hard indeed to exercise self-restraint. I would have you bear this in mind." He specifically recommended that Genghis Khan sleep alone for one month. "To take medicine for a thousand days does less good that to lie alone for one night."

He ended the sermon with another personal anecdote, possibly as a way to remind his audience that their leader was not the first emperor he had met. He recounted his audience more than thirty years earlier with the Jin Shizong emperor, who had been sixty-six years old at the time of their conversation. Genghis Khan was now turning sixty. At that meeting, the old Jin emperor could scarcely walk and could not get to his throne without an aide on each side of him. The Immortal Sage said that he offered the decrepit and feeble emperor the same advice he was now giving Genghis Khan about avoiding tasty foods and sex. The emperor had obeyed him and then "completely recovered his strength and activity," he said proudly, as proof of the wisdom of his message. Yet his teachings were not quite as miraculous as he suggested. As the sinologist Arthur Waley pointed out in his study of the sage's work, he "somewhat disingenuously does not mention that his interview took place in 1188 and that by 1189 the monarch was dead."[26]

In addition to proscribing sex and a variety of foods, the sage warned against hunting and other forms of vigorous exercise. Genghis Khan listened politely, but was unimpressed. Mongols do not like to say "no," so the khan accepted the advice graciously. "Habits are not easy to put aside, I have taken your words to heart," he told the sage.[27] Later he pushed back a bit. "Your advice is extremely good," he said, "but unfortunately we Mongols are brought up from childhood to shoot arrows and ride." He assured the Taoist sage that his words had been recorded in their original Chinese as well as in Mongolian translation for future study, but said he would continue to ride and hunt as before.

Genghis Khan mostly wanted to discuss practical matters of administration, and on this, the sage had little to offer other than to lament the Mongol destruction of ruling elites and claim that they had left the land without appropriate rulers. Referring to the modern world, he complained that "today it belongs to the common people." Rather than create a new form of government, he advised Genghis Khan to follow the model of the Jin dynasty and to appoint local Chinese governors until the Mongols could learn from them. Some of his recommendations reflected good common sense, including the suggestion that the Mongols appoint knowledgeable local administrators—"some talented official who knows that area well to manage it"—but most of his specific policies were nakedly self-serving. The most important of these was to declare a three-year tax holiday to stimulate economic recovery in the area of his hometown.[28] Genghis Khan gracefully declined, explaining that such a plan was simply too difficult to implement.

When he was back in China, the Immortal Sage composed a poem about his visit, expressing his frustration at not having a greater impact:

> For ten thousand *li* I rode on a Government horse,
> It is three years since I parted from my friends.
> The weapons of war are still not at rest.
> But of the Way and its workings I have had my chance to
>   preach.
> On an autumn night, I spoke of the management of breath.[29]

Later, a Chinese critic answered his poem with a shorter one, mocking the old sage's inability to give comprehensible answers to the questions he had been asked by the Mongols.

> He rode 10,000 *li* to the West
> but could not answer the question.[30]

Although Genghis Khan found little useful advice in the Taoist scholar's chattering, he tolerated the old man better than did those around him. Genghis Khan's indulgence for the sage infuriated Yelu Chucai, who complained that the sage's "replies were nothing but commonplace." Furthermore, "He touched upon matters like the *spiritual essence*, *spirit*, and *vital force*, and quoted stories such as that of Lin Ling-su guiding Hui-tsung of Sung in his mystical journey to the Empyrean Palace. These were the heights of His Excellency Qiu's preaching of Taoism."

"Surely you must have heard him say something remarkable?" asked a colleague. But Yelu Chucai could think of nothing. "When well informed people heard" his stories, he said, "they never failed to be convulsed with laughter."[31] Yelu Chucai added that despite feeling some sympathy for the elderly sage as a man, he "had no sympathy for his ideas." In the face of Genghis Khan's toleration and even favor toward the Taoists, Yelu Chucai proceeded cautiously. "I accepted his poetry, not his principles. At the time of his audiences with the Emperor, I found it difficult to criticize him. As our faiths were different, it would have created a dispute had I attacked him. This is why I disapproved of him in my mind and laughed at him in private."

☧

Yelu Chucai judged the Taoist sage on theological grounds, but Genghis Khan was not concerned with evaluating their validity or how his thoughts aligned with traditional Chinese philosophy. Recognizing the influence that religious men held over their followers, Genghis Khan wanted to enlist that power in the service of his new Mongol state. Religion is politics by another means, and behind the philosophical discussions, both Genghis Khan and Qiu Chuji had specific and highly important political agendas that only gradually emerged. Genghis Khan wanted the old sage's help building public support for the Mongols among the Chinese populace. He had thus far conquered only a third of China, and although he had won most of the Jin territory, he had not yet begun war against the Southern Sung dynasty. The Mongols had not established control over all of China; many years of hard fighting remained ahead. The sage's support could help solidify support for Mongol rule in the territory Genghis already controlled, and it might attract more support from the people living under the Jin and Sung rulers. Genghis Khan expected the Taoists to help him pacify the conquered people and to attract the still unconquered to his fold. As foreign rulers, the Mongols needed some form of Chinese legitimacy. The Confucians, intimately allied with the old elites, showed no sign of conferring any such blessing, but the Buddhists and Taoists did.

Qiu Chuji wanted to convert Genghis Khan and to make Taoism the official religion of his empire. Genghis Khan himself never considered conversion. "Why should I descend from lofty trees," he offered, according to Yelu Chucai, "to enter into a dark valley?"[32]

Failing to make Genghis Khan into a disciple, Qiu Chuji had a list of specific favors he wanted from the Great Khan. Before leaving to return to China, he begged for tax breaks and special concessions. Genghis Khan granted most of the old man's requests, with the expectation that in return the monks would provide a service to society. He asked him to promise that Taoists would recite the scriptures and pray earnestly for the well-being of the khan and his government.

Yelu Chucai had expected the sage to request the tax exemptions for all monks or all faiths, "whether it is a Buddhist monk or any other man who cultivates goodness."[33] Instead, "he requested to exempt from levies only the Taoists and made no mention of the Buddhist monks." The sage asked for a *gerege*, an oval disc, also called a *paiza*, worn on a cord, which would give him the right to use the Mongolian military system of posts and horses. It was like an all-purpose credit card that never had to be paid. The bearer of a *gerege* could demand virtually any type of goods or services without paying for them or even offering a rationale for needing them. Normally, only high-ranking officials received a *gerege* because it conferred tremendous prestige and power on the bearer. The front stated that the bearer had the blessing from heaven and from Genghis Khan, while the back carried the warning that whoever disobeyed the orders of the bearer "shall be guilty and die."[34]

Unlike Yelu Chucai's persistent enmity toward the Taoists, Genghis Khan, whether he agreed with everything the sage said or not, saw no harm in the Taoist teachings. To the contrary, they were compatible with Genghis Khan's own Mongol traditions, but more important, the khan had won the support of the sage. He wanted to build on that relationship, and so Genghis Khan granted his request and formalized it in an official directive. The sage was given the Golden Tiger *gerege* showing great imperial favor.[35]

Even when his meetings with religious scholars produced little spiritual or practical advice, Genghis Khan felt that they were useful on many levels. He knew that spies would report to his enemies that he was being initiated into secret knowledge, and in and of itself that held a certain value. In Central Asia, China exercised a powerful and exotic mystique as a land of non-Muslims who possessed great cunning and harbored secret knowledge, and the fact that an old and venerable monk had traveled so far to share his wisdom with the Mongol leader inspired awe in his new subjects and became a cause of caution for others.

Genghis Khan conducted a series of conversations with sages and priests of various faiths as his camp moved around Afghanistan. To emphasize their mysterious importance, he conducted these meetings in ostentatious secrecy. On some occasions, a special ceremonial *ger* was erected for the conversation, and nonessential people in the court were forced to leave the area entirely. The meetings were held at night, as "to the left and the right candles and torches flared."[36] Rumors spread that the Mongol leader was being inducted into secret rites and given knowledge that would grant him special powers. Occasionally he invited a select local official who had pledged loyalty to him to join these ceremonies. The official's inability to understand the Chinese or Mongolian language heightened the mystery and drama of what was being revealed.

These scenes provoked wild speculation among Muslim scholars as to what was taking place. Juzjani, whose credibility was occasionally diminished by his obsessive hatred of the Mongols, said that Genghis Khan had evil powers and was in frequent communion with malevolent spirits. He portrayed him as "adept in magic and deception, and some of the devils were his friends." Juzjani compared his actions and powers to those of a shaman. "Every now and again he used to fall into a trance, and, in that state of insensibility, all sorts of things used to proceed from his tongue," he wrote. During these times, he supposedly wore special clothes that he kept in a sealed box and donned only when he needed to prophesy. "Whenever this inspiration came over him, every circumstance—victories, undertakings, indication of enemies, defeat, and the reduction of countries—anything which he might desire, would all be uttered by his tongue." A scribe recorded his words during the trance. When he emerged, the scribe would read back his utterances to him, and "according to these he would act, and, more or less, indeed, the whole used to come true."[37]

Juzjani wrote that in addition to these trances, he "was well acquainted with the art of divination by means of the shoulder-bones of sheep; and he used continually to place shoulder-blades on the fire, and burn them, and in this manner he would discover the signs of the shoulder-blades." It is unlikely that Genghis Khan put on special clothes and fell into a trance or that he interpreted sheep bones, but Juzjani's descriptions record precisely the types of activities reported for steppe shamans and give some insight into what may have been occurring in the inner circle of his camp.

Despite Juzjani's vivid imagination, the meetings with sages probably produced more bewilderment than drama. In the end, Genghis Khan seemed little changed by the Taoist monk's visit, but Qiu Chuji left as a new man, invigorated by his newly granted authority. He carried papers from the Great Khan giving him the power to free his disciples from taxation, signed and sealed with the official stamps. To the Mongols such a paper was itself a sacred item before which they would bow in respect at the power of the khan and the majesty of the state. The edict was a direct connection to Genghis Khan in his words, straight from his mouth to the hand of the scribe. Content mattered little in a society where few people could read; what mattered was that the document demonstrated that its bearer had a direct connection to the Great Khan.

All too often in history, religious leaders, when provided with a modicum of political power, turn arrogant and haughty. As Qiu Chuji traveled farther from the Mongol court, he exercised his power to issue orders, requisition whatever he wanted, dismiss priests and monks from holy places, and replace them with his followers. He confiscated rival temples and forced the conversion of monks from other faiths. He attracted followers because he now had the power to recognize them as ordained members of his sect and therefore to free them from taxes. He became a petty tyrant whom no one dared to challenge.

The sage and his followers became greedy and boasted of their power. "Even if we make no appeal for funds, we shall certainly receive assistance," said one of his subordinates. "If by any chance sufficient help is not forthcoming—if we exhaust our own stocks of material and have come to the end of the temple-funds—all we have to do is go round with a gourd-bowl. We can collect as much money as we please."[38]

"When I think of returning to those numberless crowds," Qiu Chuji wrote in a poem on the way home, "deep in my heart are feelings too great to express."[39] Despite the loving tone of his poem, he changed his sentiments when he realized that all of these devoted followers of the Tao would have to be fed. He issued an order saying that because some of his followers "have shown themselves to be unruly and without principle," one of his disciples would be invested "with full authority to deal with such wherever he finds them, lest the disciples of Tao should themselves impede its mysterious power."[40] They were expelled.

In the coming decades, the powers of the sage and the scope of his order steadily expanded. He and his followers reinterpreted phrases in Genghis Khan's directive in order to grant their sect power over all Taoist monks, and eventually over their main rivals, the Buddhists. The Taoists extended the tax-free status of their clergy and buildings to include their diverse businesses, which expanded rapidly with their new tax advantage over other merchants. Each monastery became a virtual warehouse of goods to be sold tax-free.[41]

With the special dispensations granted them, the Taoists grew strong—so strong that in some cases they believed they were exempt from Mongol law. The monasteries operated as tax-free zones for commerce, banking, and manufacturing, with more space devoted to warehousing goods than to worship. They had become a chain of tax-free emporiums across the empire. Men who joined the order became exempt from military service and the onerous tasks of work brigades, highway construction, government transport, and other types of labor demanded by local Mongol authorities. In time, the expansion of the Taoists threatened the revenues needed to administer the realm and feed the massive Mongol army.

The Immortal Sage was so proud of his preaching to Genghis Khan that he convinced himself his brand of Taoism would soon receive sanction as the official religion of the Mongol nation and reach far beyond its original home in China. "Our temples will be renamed by Imperial Command," he told his disciples. "After my death our religion will see a great triumph. All parts of the world, far and near on every side will become homes of the Tao." He wanted his disciples to get "our Faith ready here and elsewhere to take control."[42] Like Buddhism, Islam, and Christianity, Taoism was ready to become a world religion.

Qiu Chuji was fortunate enough to have the most powerful man in the world as his patron, but he had also acquired an implacable foe. Yelu Chucai's rise to power had only just begun; his book was only the first round in a protracted religious struggle that would soon grip China and, in another generation, help to dismember the Mongol Empire itself.

13

The Confucian and the Unicorn

Mongol nomads rarely returned along the same route by which they came. Because Genghis Khan had entered Afghanistan from the northeast, he planned to return to Mongolia via another route, going south, crossing the Indus River, turning east, and making his way through the Himalayas or around them and across Bengal and Assam, and then turning north through China. If he took this route, he could continue to expand his empire along a course that would bring him back to the Tangut kingdom, where he could exact revenge on their ruler who had surrendered to him but then reneged on his promise and refused to send warriors for his campaign against the Khwarizm shah.

Instead of taking this adventuresome route, however, he turned back and returned to Mongolia the way he came. Practical reasons may have led to this decision. India was too hot for his men and horses. The humidity weakened their bows, and his warriors were exhausted after five years of fighting and wanted to return home. The routes through or around the Himalayas were long and extremely difficult—no known army had ever accomplished such a feat. So simple geography may have got the better of him.

Persian accounts offer an altogether different reason for the reversal of his plan, crediting something unusual that happened in Afghanistan. As the Mongolian army prepared to depart, Genghis Khan's elite bodyguards reportedly saw a mysterious figure emerging from the mist. According to their account, the apparition appeared to be a greenish animal with the body of a deer, a horse's tail, and one prominent horn protruding from its forehead.

The *Secret History* frequently refers to the power of heaven and Earth, but it relates no stories of unicorns or similar signs from heaven. One-horned mythical beasts appear frequently in mythology from China to Europe.[1] Some stories credit Alexander the Great with having encountered a unicorn in the same area, and one legend held that Alexander had died at a young age because of the curse from his having killed a sacred unicorn while hunting in Asia.[2] Marco Polo later reported that Alexander's stallion, Bucephalus, had bred with local mares to produce a unique type of horse with a special mark on its forehead.[3]

According to the story about the Mongol sighting of the unicorn, Genghis Khan's soldiers did not make the same mistake as Alexander. They had no desire to hunt or harm the mythical beast. For the Mongols, the appearance of any animal to a person, especially a wolf, is always understood as an honor and a blessing, not a threat. Whatever the animal may have been, the Mongols let it pass unharmed, and then they prayed and later made offerings to it in appreciation for its having appeared before them.

Although Muslim chroniclers repeated the story, Yelu Chucai may have been responsible for originating it, as the encounter parallels Chinese accounts of the life of Confucius. Any classically educated Chinese person would have known that a unicorn, described as a deer with one horn, appeared immediately prior to the birth of Confucius in 551 BC, carrying a message on a jade tablet proclaiming that his "doctrine will be a law to the world."[4] The appearance of the unicorn signaled the fall of an old dynasty and presaged that good government was about to be restored.[5] Another unicorn appeared shortly before Confucius's death in 479 BC. Whether or not Yelu Chucai created the unicorn story, he was the one credited with explaining the encounter and claiming that it demonstrated Genghis Khan's unique blessings from heaven. The incident, near the end of his long campaign in Central Asia, symbolized heaven's final approval of the life and achievements of the aging Mongol emperor. He had fulfilled his mission on Earth and had fully exhausted the great destiny conferred upon him. In the seventeenth century, an anonymous Buddhist monk in Mongolia offered a different explanation; that the unicorn had appeared as a warning to Genghis Khan, not as a blessing. He rewrote the incident in his *Yellow History* and claimed that the unicorn was sent from heaven to protect the holy lands of Tibet and India, the home of Buddha, from Genghis Khan's invading army.[6]

Genghis Khan and Alexander the Great both swept through Central Asia near the end of their lives and reached the height of their conquests in Afghanistan. Although separated by 1,500 years, their stories frequently intertwined. The *Romance of Alexander*, an allegory based on Arabic and Greek sources, was one of the first Western literary works translated into Mongolian. It related the myth of Alexander's search for the water of immortality. During the course of his epic journey, Alexander traverses the long bridge of life, climbs the mountain of effort, crosses the earth, and searches the floor of the sea in the quest for long life. Alexander narrates his own journey and tells us, "I followed the darkness in the direction of the setting sun."[7] Even though by then he was already "reaching the age of a thousand years," he wanted to live for three thousand. Now at the end of his life, Alexander said, "there are no people who have not yet been seen by me."[8] He finally obtained the sacred water of immortality, but then he reflected on what his life would become if he kept living forever, and he realized that perhaps he did not love life so much as he loved the people who shared life with him. Without them, there would be no pleasure in living. After having searched so diligently for this elusive elixir, he poured it onto a cypress tree that then remained eternally green. Giving life to the tree gave him the immortality he had sought. He said that no king had ever been happier than he was at that moment.[9] In the Mongolian version of the epic, he says, "I have become khan. On this very earth there has not been born a khan who has enjoyed life as I."[10] The story ended with a simple idea. "It is over, is ended, ended!" the text states. "Old men, be happy, all is vanity when one dies and comes to an end! It is ended. Be happy. When one dies and comes to an end, all is vanity! Let us be happy! Let us be prosperous."[11]

⚑

In part due to his ability to favorably interpret unusual events such as summer snow and the reported sighting of a unicorn, Yelu Chucai's role as Mongol imperial adviser and propagandist steadily grew. Those who knew him described him as dedicated to his work, constantly striving to learn, to improve himself, and to use what he had learned to improve the administration of the Mongol nation. "It was not his habit to talk and laugh heedlessly," wrote a colleague. "Thus, he may have appeared to be sharp and overbearing, but as soon as one was received by him, he became warm and affable, so that one could not forget him."[12]

Yelu Chucai was the vehicle through which classical Chinese thought and practice entered the Mongol court. Although he maintained respect for Buddhism and appreciated the utility of Taoism, he particularly valued Confucian philosophy and traditional Chinese ways. For all his travels and transformation, he remained an aristocrat at heart. When he first met Genghis Khan, he was an enthusiastic young man in his twenties with a special flair for divination and a desire for adventure and advancement. Yelu Chucai's transformation began almost as soon as he left China and entered Mongolia for the first time in 1219. He reflected on his greater appreciation for Chinese culture in the description of his initial arrival at the Kherlen River in Mongolia. "Iced is the river, although the spring has ended, soundless the water. Suddenly the far-away Southern Region seems like the butterfly's dream." The butterfly's dream alludes to a famous quote in Chinese philosophy, when the Taoist scholar Zhuangzi wrote that after dreaming he was a butterfly, he awakened only to wonder if he was then a man dreaming he was a butterfly or was now a butterfly dreaming he was a man. Was Yelu Chucai now a Chinese Khitan pretending to be a Mongol, or possibly something else? He ends the poem with a statement of his difficulty going forward. "Let me hold the whip for a while, and look towards the Northwest. My lean horse is facing the wind unable to proceed."[13]

The poet came as a somewhat naïve young man, but he left Khwarizm in his thirties as a fully mature minister to the Great Khan and a genius of court intrigue. Yet he still exhibited a nostalgic longing that had been a part of his classical Chinese education. Shortly after setting off on the long ride home from Samarkand, he composed a poem about the city, reflecting how much he had changed in four short years since he wrote the first poem about the ice and the butterfly by the Kherlen River:

> Yellow oranges are mixed with honey to fry,
> Plain cakes are sprinkled with powdered sugar.
> From the time I came here to the west,
> I no longer remember my own home place.[14]

The classical scholar within him had grown homesick, but he was not just yearning for the comforts of home. He longed for the spiritual simplicity of his youth. A few years later he wrote more somberly that no matter how "strong and determined" he was, he "could not help but feel sad and discouraged" being so far from home.[15] He was a changed man, and yet beneath the surface one could still find that young scholar eager to reclaim the core lessons of history's great spiritual teachers: Confucius, Buddha, and Lao Tzu. He believed that these original teachings had been corrupted by the arrival of the Manichaeans and the crass popularity of the Taoist sages. "To allow the practice of strange doctrines and heterodox principles will pervert the correct music and take away the luster of vermillion so that the people will no longer be able to distinguish right from wrong,"[16] he wrote. Among these degenerate sects, he specifically rejected Manichaeism, but he did not do so openly while Genghis Khan still lived. He elliptically referred to the Manichaeans and to related sects as "Incense Societies" or "Society of White Robes."[17]

Yelu Chucai recommended that one study only the primary sources in any given religion rather than the commentaries, but he recognized how challenging this could be even for the best educated of scholars. "It is simply that the more profound the writings of the ancients are, the more difficult it is to understand them."[18] He thought that all religions were compatible. While Genghis Khan sought to unite all the nations under Mongol rule, Yelu Chucai sought to unite the various religions of the empire into a single integrated voice. While Genghis Khan sought to preserve the diversity of religious beliefs within his empire, Yelu Chucai believed that only by unifying diverse faiths could humanity find a common cause and live peacefully within one harmonious empire.

While he supported all three of the established Chinese faiths—Buddhism, Confucianism, and Taoism—he did not treat them equally. He felt that Buddhism was the strongest and most meaningful, offering a highly personal form of moral guidance, a path toward enlightenment and peace of mind. To guide society and manage the state, however, Yelu Chucai believed that Confucius offered the best advice. The value of Taoism seemed a little less clear in his mind, but he seemed to view it as appropriate guidance for the common people.

Classically educated Confucian scholars were disorientated by and uncomfortable with Genghis Khan's Mongol rule. Confucian thought did not permit any foreign leader—let alone a barbarian from the steppe—to be considered equal to the Chinese emperor. During Genghis Khan's lifetime, China still had two royal houses, the Jin in the north and the Sung in the south, each with its own emperor. Confucian scholars taught that it was the constant duty of the Chinese royal court to conquer the barbarians. China had been ruled by foreigners before, but prior to the arrival of the Mongols all foreigner rulers had acknowledged the superiority of the Chinese language and culture. They had sought to become Chinese, offering Confucian officials a special role as cultural and spiritual guides. The Confucians had never been part of an empire that was larger than China, and certainly not one that considered the Chinese as vassals. For Genghis Khan, China was merely one country in his vast empire, which included lands about which Confucians had no knowledge. The scholars did not know what to make of such a previously unimaginable circumstance, so mostly they ignored the new reality and continued to think of themselves as the center of the world. They had no place for Genghis Khan and the Mongols in their worldview, and so it is not altogether surprising that he had no place for them in the administration of his growing empire.[19] Yelu Chucai had a doubly difficult task: to render Confucian thought and Chinese culture palatable to Genghis Khan, while making him, as their new sovereign, appear at least tolerable to the Confucians themselves.

If any man could accomplish such a difficult task, it was Yelu Chucai. His ancestors had been steppe nomads, and although they had adapted to Chinese language and culture, he retained a strong spiritual connection to his origins and was probably the last person to read and write in the Khitai language of his ancestors. He firmly believed that Genghis Khan had the mandate to rule all of China and the world. In a meeting with an envoy from the Sung emperor, he made this clear. "Our horses' hooves can reach anywhere," he told him, "be it heaven or sea!"[20] To his mind, the unification of China could not come quickly enough. This quest became a guiding principle for him and has made him a popular figure with Chinese scholars ever since.

Just as Genghis Khan had his *Keshig* to guard him, he gathered around him a cadre of intellectual guardians, some twenty highly intelligent men who served as his own Illuminati.[21] Most came from the steppe, or their ancestors did. All could read and write in Uighur script and Mongolian as well as other languages. One of these advisers was Chinqai, a Christian from one of the Turkic ethnic groups, who spoke Chinese as well as other tribal languages. Unlike the Muslims, who worked primarily in finance and taxation, or the Chinese, who excelled in technical services, medicine, and in some cases served as prized military commanders, these men were more difficult to identify ethnically or religiously. Their cultural orientation was tilted toward China, but they maintained a sophisticated cosmopolitan spirit, combining ideas from many cultures in a highly eclectic manner according to their personal styles.

Genghis Khan approved of some of the Confucian precepts propounded by Yelu Chucai, such as devotion to duty and consistency in life. He considered betrayal of duty, cowardice, lying, and laziness the vilest of all sins, and he praised those who put personal honor above their well-being, or even their life. He knew he could never depend on those who valued riches over honor. "Such people are base, craven, and they are slaves by nature," wrote Juvaini. "Genghis Khan despised and destroyed them without mercy."[22] He taught his sons to ignore the kings of history who stored gold and silver. "They were devoid of their share of intellect and strong understanding," he explained, "for no distinction could be made between that treasure and the dust." Such treasure was no "source of advantage" nor could it "ward off harm." "As for us, for the sake of our good name," he said, "we shall store up our treasures in the corners of men's hearts and shall leave nothing over the morrow."[23]

And yet, despite his affinity for these essential Confucian virtues, he did not share his adviser's deeper interest in Confucianism, and shunned some of its most basic teachings. This rejection was probably more emotional than intellectual. Confucian scholars objected vehemently to some Mongol customs, such as the expectation that a dead man's closest male relative should marry his widow. To refuse to do so seemed cruel and selfish in the eyes of a Mongol, but Confucians condemned such marriages as incestuous, particularly when a son married his stepmother. Genghis Khan considered this narrow-minded and felt it was a violation of the most basic law of compassion and responsibility, as a widow might otherwise have no source of support. The painful experiences of his abandoned mother certainly influenced his thinking on this issue.

Confucian philosophy had no real gods, and its priests had no ability to control weather, forecast the future, or cure illness. How could they speak to heaven if heaven did not speak to them? Their rituals were formal and inaccessible, alienating the Mongols, who were used to participating in ceremonies while seated on their horses, moving around as they pleased so that they could draw up close to friends and socialize while worshipping. Mongol rituals always concluded with food and alcohol, and even the most serious ceremonial gatherings offered men and women an opportunity to chat, eat, flirt, and above all, get drunk. A religious occasion was a celebration, not a solemn state ritual. It had to be interesting and entertaining and to fulfill some personal need. If the shaman or priest could not capture one's attention with his show, it was doubtful he would attract the attention of the spirits. By contrast, Confucian rituals were simply boring.

Genghis Khan respected Confucius as one of history's holy men, but he avoided scholars who claimed to be his disciples. Their teachings made little sense to him and they had little to say about imperial conquest and change. Confucius's writings stressed the importance of preserving the order of the past, while Genghis Khan wanted to destroy the order of the past and create a completely new society. They taught obedience to rulers at virtually any cost, whereas he had rebelled against his overlords and removed them. Confucianism stressed principles of patriarchy and obligations to relatives and ancestors, but these were precisely the people who had caused him the most trouble in his life. His clan had banished him and prevented him from participating in their ancestral worship, but he had overcome this cruel mistreatment to become the strongest leader in the tribe and indeed the world.

At some time in his life, he had violated most of the basic precepts of Confucianism. He had killed his half brother, defied his mother, and risen up and overthrown his sovereign, Ong Khan. Even Yelu Chucai, with his quick mind and skilled oratory, had difficulty reconciling his new master's actions with Confucian teachings. Confucius emphasized the priority of the male lineage in almost every aspect of society, but Genghis Khan, having been so poorly treated by his male relatives, depended on and empowered women. Mongol women owned property, including the *ger*, and a share of the animals. They inherited property from their families, but they also accrued it based on their service in peace or war, and they were often assigned control over men. Genghis Khan's mother, daughters, and wives each had her own royal court and administered her lands, waters, and men. With only a million or so Mongols to maintain control over an empire of more than a hundred million people, Genghis Khan had to maximize the talents of every person to the fullest extent possible. The men were primarily his warriors, so he relied on women to administer the homeland, to control trade and finance, and to rule over many of the conquered nations, particularly along the Silk Route.

Practices such as these contributed to the Confucian view that the steppe barbarians were the antithesis of civilized. In their view, the Mongols were a tribe who claimed descent from a wolf and a deer; they were scarcely human. The Mongols had no sense of the proper separation of generations, classes, or sexes, and no understanding of etiquette or tradition. The Mongol system of government completely violated the Confucian notion that men of formal education should rule and that warriors and merchants ranked low in the hierarchy. Genghis Khan ruled with the aid of his *Keshig* guardians, who exercised power over the military as well as over law, administration, and religion. To his mind, education and spiritual training were crafts, comparable to weaving rugs, making pottery, or farming. Each craft had its place in society, but these were not appropriate occupations for Mongols, who were born to hunt, make war, and rule over everyone else.

Fanatical followers of Christianity, Buddhism, and Islam evidenced a desire to reach a universal audience, but Confucian scripture remained stubbornly rooted within Chinese tradition. A person did not have to be an Arab to convert to Islam or an Indian to practice Buddhism, but it seemed necessary to be Chinese before one could practice Confucianism. Confucian teachings concentrated on social relations between people and adherence to a prescribed set of strict rules that a leader needed to learn and to obey. Genghis Khan felt that heaven endowed powerful leaders with the inherent right to rule over their subjects, especially over their conquered subjects. He had a genuine interest in hearing the advice of religious men, but he would decide on the validity and practicality of their teachings. He considered them to be recommendations, not commands. Genghis Khan was ultimately the one who would issue the orders, laws, and commands. He was not much interested in following another man's precepts.

Genghis Khan's attitude toward Confucianism appears to have been set well before he met Yelu Chucai, and he was not inclined to change his mind once it had been made. Yelu Chucai's position at court rose steadily, and over the course of his three decades of service to the Mongols, he persistently brought up Confucian ideas, references, insights, and practices as seemed appropriate to the problems of the moment. Over time, his influence was considerable.

"I wished to make Our Sovereign tread loftily in the footsteps of the ancient worthies," he wrote in his memoir of time in Afghanistan, written soon after the death of Genghis Khan. His aim was "to assist the Court in promoting culture and education and in realizing the way of goodness so that fine customs and benevolent rule may excel those of former ages."[24] To this end, he offered a long list of specifics: "to fix the laws, deliberate upon rituals and music, to erect ancestral temples, to build houses, to found schools, to hold examinations, to seek out retired scholars, to search for the ministers of the previous dynasty, to promote the worthy and good, to seek upright men, to encourage agriculture and sericulture, to suppress indolence, to moderate punishments, to reduce taxes, to honor moral integrity, to castigate profligacy, to dismiss superfluous officials, to expel oppressive officers, to exalt filial and brotherly devotion, and to relieve poverty and distress." Thus will he be able to create a "Great Peace."[25]

Because he was interested in Buddhist and Taoist teachings as well as Confucianism, Yelu Chucai sought to please Genghis Khan by combining the various religions. He referred to his training in different scriptures as bathing in "the immense ocean of the Law." Different religions are referred to as "laws," each one based on separate but similar scriptures.[26] "The Way of our Confucius is for governing the world, the Way of Lao Tzu is for nourishing the nature, and the Way of Buddha is for cultivating the mind. This is a universal opinion, in the past as well as in the present. Apart from these doctrines, the rest is all heresy."[27] Together, in his mind, these three faiths formed the three legs of philosophy and religion. "All that is needed is that the teachings of the Three Sages stand firmly in the world like a tripod without oppressing and robbing one another, each of them living peacefully."[28]

Despite his differences with the Immortal Sage, Yelu Chucai consistently preferred the three religions he thought of as Chinese—Taoism, Confucianism, and Buddhism. He dismissed Christianity and Islam as foreign and possibly dangerous. The Christians in the Mongol hierarchy were mostly women or the less powerful sons-in-law of the Great Khan, and Yelu Chucai initially perceived them as a lesser threat. By contrast, the rising influence of the Muslims in court greatly alarmed him. He seemed to enjoy finding small ways to diminish their supposed expertise in mathematics and science, the fields that Genghis Khan most admired. He reportedly once delighted in showing a Muslim prediction of an eclipse to have been wrong; the following year, his forecast was proved correct.

☯

Genghis Khan had exempted all monks from taxation and military duties, but he did not share Yelu Chucai's faith in them. He said that too many monks lived like parasites off the hard work of others without performing a useful function in return. It seemed gratuitous to exempt them from military service and taxes unless they could prove their mastery of the faith they claimed to follow. Having been through the classical Chinese education system with its emphasis on written exams, Yelu Chucai proposed that the Mongol government test the monks to make sure they qualified for the tax exemption by being, at the very least, able to read. The clergy resisted and angrily objected to even these simple standards, saying that reading was irrelevant to their work. They recited the scriptures that they needed from memory, and looked upon reading as a devious ploy for those not smart enough to memorize.

"How can the clergy be examined like young school boys?" objected one Buddhist leader. "I am a rustic monk," an illiterate lama complained. "I never look at scriptures and do not know a single word," he confessed. He pointed out that Mongol officials did not know how to read or write, and yet they performed their jobs without difficulties. So why should a monk have to read and write to perform his duties?[29] The law was never enforced.

Yelu Chucai encountered much criticism from his fellow Chinese scholars for helping the barbarians and, in particular, for bringing the Taoist sage to the Mongol court and granting him excessive privileges. To counter their criticism and assuage his conscience, he chastised the Taoists and confessed his error. "I was wrong. I was wrong!" he declared in his book. The experience increased his commitment to classical Chinese philosophy and to Confucianism in particular. He urged his master to adopt the Chinese system, which placed the administration of the empire in the hands of the best educated as selected through a rigorous system of national examinations. But Genghis Khan showed no interest in reinstating the Chinese system of state exams. He chose men based on their achievements in life and on the battlefield, not in the classroom. He valued men of courage and action over those of thoughtful deliberation.

Yelu Chucai failed in some of his more scholarly endeavors, but he managed to introduce many important Chinese administrative practices into the growing Mongol system of government. The Mongols viewed China as a collection of failed states, none of which had been able to protect itself from their arrival, and their leader had little interest in adopting their failed traditions and customs. Yelu Chucai often had to use delicate subtlety to hide the Chinese origins of some of the recommendations, which he presented as simple common sense. Rather than putting them forward as time-tested and proven Chinese or Confucian ideas, he described them in vague but spiritually uplifting terms, explaining that "the way of goodness" was "the essence of government and that however strong its army, no nation could survive without support of its people."[30]

Yelu Chucai advocated reforming and systematizing taxes so that state income would be consistent and predictable, but he faced opposition from members of Genghis Khan's royal family, who simply wanted more income from tax revenues. He remained at the center of a pro-Chinese faction at the Mongol court and was strongly challenged by a coterie of Muslim officials brought in after the annexation of Khwarizm. These Muslim administrators remained popular with the Great Khan's offspring because of their ruthless, and often cruel, efficiency in extorting every last cent they could from the Chinese peasantry. He described their method of tax administration as "a way used by villains, which is seriously harmful. I hope to stop it."[31]

Despite his efforts to bring a moderating influence to the Mongol court and to make it conform with Chinese traditional government, Yelu Chucai also changed during his lifetime at Genghis Khan's court. Once during a celebration at the royal court, according to the *Yuan Shi,* the official Chinese history of the Mongol reign, Yelu Chucai became drunk, wandered away from the festivities, and passed out in a cart. Genghis Khan's son Ogodei, also drunk, as he often was, saw Yelu Chucai in the cart, climbed in with him, and tried to rouse him. Without opening his eyes, Yelu Chucai became angry and demanded to be left alone. Ogodei chided him for being drunk alone instead of with the rest of them, and then dragged him back to the celebration. Disheveled, disoriented, and missing his hat, belt, and a few other items, the restrained Confucian scholar was just one more drunken bureaucrat.[32] Yelu Chucai came to Genghis Khan as a Chinese scholar, but over the years, he too became a bit of a Mongol.

By the time Genghis Khan departed from Afghanistan, he recognized that men of religion would have only a limited role to play in the administration of his vast empire. They had some useful skills, but they were stymied by an abundance of words with too little ability to act. Genghis Khan was looking for common sense; they were looking for enlightenment. The priests, monks, mullahs, and shamans brought into the Mongol court often frustrated Genghis Khan. They recommended preaching and teaching as the answer to every problem. Every problem required more thought, more study, more analysis, but Genghis Khan had to administer an empire of millions of people with pressing problems that needed immediate, even if not perfect, solutions. The religious men and scholars always wanted to wait, as one of Genghis Khan's advisers pointed out, for "favorable conditions" or a time of "tranquility before promoting culture and education." His problems were pressing, and he did not have the luxury of time to wait for enlightenment. "I say that this is very wrong indeed!" complained one Chinese minister. One had to do more than "delay and wait for the favorable conditions."[33] "Calm and self-satisfied, you put your hands in your sleeves and waited for tranquility," he complained of the Taoist monks, but such hypocritical inaction resembled the one who "wishes to relieve hunger and cold and yet throws away grains and silk."

Early in the twentieth century, a curator of Asian manuscripts at the National Library of France in Paris, while examining one of the oldest copies of Juvaini's book on Genghis Khan, found four brief inscriptions at the back of the manuscript. Each was a short poem written in the four languages used by the Mongol rulers in Central Asia—Mongolian, Arabic, Persian, and Uighur. The Mongolian inscription is one of the oldest Mongolian poems recorded—an elegant endorsement of the value of knowledge and law over wealth and jewels:

> Knowledge is an ocean, the jewel retreats before it,
> the law of knowledge, the wise man knows.[34]

Added as a postscript to the first book on the life of Genghis Khan, it seems a fitting summary of his quest in the final years of his life. By the time he left Afghanistan, he knew virtually everything there was to know about war and conquest, and he had accumulated more wealth than any other person in the world. But he was still restless; he was still searching for wisdom.

PART IV

Becoming a God

Khormusta, the emperor of the gods, was reborn in the fortunate holy Genghis Khan.

~Colophon on a Mongolian manuscript, seventeenth century

14

The Last Campaign

In 1224, at sixty-two years of age, Genghis Khan decided to head home, so that he could spend his final years along the Tuul River that ran down from Burkhan Khaldun. Unlike the lightning-strike speed with which he had begun his invasion of Central Asia, his trip home from Afghanistan was slow and leisurely, and included a long pause for one of the largest hunts known in history. During the four-year campaign, his army had conquered land from the Indus to the Volga, including what are today Kazakhstan, Afghanistan, Turkmenistan, Tajikistan, Kyrgyzstan, Uzbekistan, Azerbaijan, Iran, Georgia, Armenia, southern Russia, and part of Pakistan. His army had grown weary of fighting and plundering. They wanted to go home.

The return to Mongolia was followed by a full year of reunions with family and friends and riotous celebrations. War veterans told tales of distant places and heroic battles. Children met fathers they had never known or could not remember. Many young boys had grown into men and now, as victorious fighters, they were eager to parade their wealth and find wives. Courtships abounded as girls teased and flirted while friends taunted the young soldiers and laughed at them. The soldiers, in turn, showed off on horseback, wrestled with one another, played anklebones, and enjoyed their mother's home cooking.

Not everyone celebrated. The triumphant army also brought back many prisoners, including the mother and other family members of the defeated shah. Vilified for defying the Mongols, reduced to slavery and mockery, the shah's family members disappeared into obscurity and almost certainly endured a short life of terrific suffering in the harsh and unfamiliar environment of the steppe. With so many slaves, every Mongol was rich and none had to work. They spent the year celebrating.

By the time Genghis Khan returned to his homeland after the second of his long foreign campaigns, most of the people he had known from childhood were long since dead, but the places remained the same. His wives were thriving, and each presided over her court in her own territory. Borte controlled the Kherlen River and adjacent steppes in the area of her birth. The woman who had once been kidnapped into a forced marriage and near servitude among the Merkid was now a queen, with deposed queens and princesses as her servants. Khulan administered the upper Khentii and the Onon River, Yesui the Tuul River, and Yesugen the upper Orkhon and Khangai Mountains.

While Genghis Khan's conquests had changed the world, his homeland had remained nearly unaltered. When he was born, the steppe had no cities, fortresses, temples, or other signs of the sedentary life, and he deliberately left it precisely that way. His people continued to live in the felt walls of their nomadic *ger*, and they followed the seasons with their herds of horses, cows, yaks, sheep, goats, and camels. They studied the sky to know when to move on to their next grazing grounds.

He refused the role of a conquering hero, and gave all credit to his army and to the blessing of heaven. "I shall pray to Tenger, my divine father," he announced. Then, "Ascending a high mound, he spread out his felt saddle cloth, hung his belt around his neck and prayed." His words were simple, modest, and direct:

I did not become Emperor because of my manly virtues, I
   became emperor because I was so destined by my father,
   Tenger!
I did not become emperor because of my marvelous virtues, I
   became emperor because I was so destined by my father,
   Khan Tenger!
Heaven subjugated the foreign enemies for me![1]

Genghis Khan raised no monuments to his heroic conquests and
allowed no inscriptions. His deeds said enough. He was quick to give
credit to others, however, and he commissioned one monument to
commemorate the best archer of the summer Naadam games of 1225.
Using the Mongol measurement of an *ald*, the distance between the
fingertips of a man's outstretched arms, Khasar's son Yesungge had
hit a target from 335 *ald* (more than 1,600 feet).[2] No one had ever
achieved such a feat, and it was worthy of a monument.

In his decades of conquering people near and far, Genghis Khan
had carefully examined the foreign religions of the world and found
each of them—Christianity, Buddhism, Taoism, and Islam—to hold
valuable truths. Just as each land produces its particular crops and
fruits, each religion had its own unique customs and value. "The
books and writings of each nation follow the characteristics of their
respective nation and differ in their themes and views," wrote Injannasi in *The Blue Chronicle* many centuries later. "For example, the
most fragrant and beautiful thing in this world is a flower, but not all
flowers are the same. They all possess their characteristic colors. Fruits
are tasty, but they all have a different taste."[3] Poetry can be beautiful
in any language, but each country has its own method and discipline.
"While the Chinese use end rhyme, the Mongols use alliteration, the
Tibetans use rhythm and the Manchu use parallelism in their speech."

All religions made the same claims to teach and enlighten. They
loved good and worshipped God and heaven. They taught virtue,
honesty, duty, and righteousness. They decried evil and wrongdoing

and denounced greed, jealousy, acquisitiveness, and the instinct to harm others. Where they differed was in the details and in their understanding of how to do these things. Should the believer walk clockwise or counterclockwise around the holy place? Should he or she abstain from beef, fish, birds, or onions? Pray in yellow, black, or white? Remove their shoes to pray or their belt; wear a hat or bare their head; veil their face or uncover it? Should the dead be buried, burned, hung in a tree, or fed to the dogs and birds? Was it more honorable to execute a condemned man by cutting off his head or by strangling him? Would God prefer the sacrifice of a sheep, or rice and wine, a bouquet of flowers, or a piece of the believer's flesh? Did God prefer to hear them recite in Arabic, sing in Latin, chant in Tibetan, pray in Chinese, or merely dance?

Genghis Khan recognized that religious belief and practice fulfilled an important universal spiritual longing that transcended national and ethnic borders. The principle of universalism arose explicitly in Buddhism, Christianity, and Islam, and it seemed to underlie the beliefs of most religions. The universal message appealed directly to his desires to create a universal empire, but he decided his empire would not be based solely on one prophet, one scripture, or one set of beliefs.

At the conclusion of his many conversations with shamans, priests, scholars, monks, and mullahs, he reached one firm conclusion. While some demonstrated a genuine connection to the good, none, he believed, demonstrated adequate knowledge of morality, the meaning of life, or the nature of the divine. They were simply men, like him, struggling to make sense of the world. No amount of study had brought any of them closer to God. No scriptures, chants, dances, rituals, medicines, or prayers had revealed a secret way, a hidden path, to finding the right course in life. He believed that people did not need secret knowledge from prophets, teachers, enlightened masters, shamans, or their scriptures. Everyone possessed the same inner compass. Each person was born with the ability to discover and cultivate the moral way through careful thought, inner reflection, and simple common sense and awareness. Any faith might help along the path, but he found none that guaranteed exclusive access to the right way.[4]

The devout adherents of each faith wanted to be judged solely by the content of their ideas and not by the truth of their deeds or the consequences of their actions. They piously claimed credit for good deeds and consigned evil ones to those who had been mistaken, who had misunderstood the teaching, or to unbelievers who willfully committed evil. Genghis Khan was too pragmatic in his worldview to separate ideas from action. He did not judge by words, he judged by deeds. Stated goals mattered only when followed by proven achievement.

He found that each religion had its weak points and false teachings, its share of nonsense and trickery. Each one had flaws that appeared most starkly when its leaders remained unsupervised and were allowed to manage their own affairs and to slip into the chasm of authoritarian greed. He decided that promoting one religion above the others would harm his empire. Despite their claims to complete truth, each religion was local, rooted in a particular place, language, and culture, while he intended his empire to be universal, including all lands, peoples, and gods. Every religion contained some important truths, but neither their teachers nor their books contained the single, ultimate moral truth. Scholars of the same faith, reading the same scripture, constantly quarreled and even killed one another over issues big and small. While interpreting the same texts, they produced opposite judgments. How could any one of them be trusted with the all-important practical responsibilities of managing society? Only the firm rule of law and a strong ruler could prevent members of supposedly the same faith from tearing one another apart like starving dogs fighting over a bone. Was the answer a firmer hand or fewer restrictions? This was the central question bedeviling Genghis Khan as he entered the final years of his life.

Practicing virtue, like learning to shoot an arrow or ride a horse,

combines physical discipline and mental strength that did not originate in a list of rules and instructions. Ethics did not come out of a
book; it came from active practice. Morality is a skill that can only
be learned and perfected through doing. Genghis Khan did not acquire his sense of right and wrong from scholars, priests, or religious
teachers. He learned ethics and values from the people closest to him,
from simple people. In his childhood, these were his mother and the
Old Man Jarchigudai from the mountain. But as he grew older it
became the men around him, his companions and fellow soldiers.
"You urged me to carry out what was right; you persuaded me not to
do what was wrong," he said to men of lower rank but great wisdom
in the *Secret History*. "You pulled until my right proceeded; you restrained until my wrong subsided."[5] He publicly acknowledged that
the teachings of his humble companions such as Boorchu and Muhali
"made me gain the throne."[6]

Genghis Khan's refusal to embrace any one of the popular religions caused some scholars to believe that he was apathetic toward
religion, but Russian scholar Nikolai Trubetzkoy, writing in the early
twentieth century, understood clearly how much religion formed the
core of Mongolian success in Russia and the other countries they
conquered. "In order for a man to fulfill his duties fearlessly and
unconditionally," wrote Trubetzkoy, "he must believe firmly—not
theoretically, but intuitively, with his whole being—that his personal
destiny, like the destinies of others and of the entire world, is in the
hands of a higher being, a being infinitely high and beyond criticism.
Such a being must be God, not a man." Only a slave submits to the
authority of another man, but men of noble virtue submit to the will
of God in a hierarchy of beings. "A disciplined soldier who can obey
a superior willingly as he gives orders to a subordinate, who never
loses his self-respect, is by nature capable of submitting only to the
authority of an immaterial, transcendent first cause—in contrast to a
slave, who submits to the authority of earthly fear, earthly prosperity,
and earthly vanity." Throughout his career, "Genghis Khan regarded

only those people who were sincerely and deeply religious as valuable to his state."[7]

In his younger years, Genghis Khan's closest companions had been members of his *Keshig* who were around him every day. As he became the emperor of an ever-larger territory and as he and they grew older, most of these men were far away leading the campaigns scattered from China to Iraq and Russia. They had been replaced in the *Keshig* by their sons and grandsons and a growing number of sons from the khans of tribes incorporated into the Mongols. While their importance grew with the expansion of the empire, Genghis Khan had less of an emotional tie to these younger men who had not shared with him the long struggle to power. Increasingly, he turned to others, inside his inner circle of administration and outside the *Keshig*.

☃

In his final years, Genghis Khan seemed to be fully aware that his time on Earth would soon end, and he suffered from an increasing frustration that he had not fulfilled his heavenly mission to conquer the world. The Sung dynasty clung to power in southern China, and his soldiers had barely reached the edge of Russia, Tibet, Iraq, Korea, and India. Europe, Byzantium, Syria, and Egypt remained beyond his grasp.

One country, however, still obsessed him more than any other, keeping him awake at night and gnawing at him during the day. It was the "Great State of White and High," as the Tangut referred to their kingdom. They had surrendered to him more than fifteen years earlier, in 1209, and had sworn to obey him always, but soon after the Mongol army had moved on, the Tangut ruler had contemptuously mocked its leader when ordered to send soldiers to join the Mongol army for the campaign against the shah of Khwarizm. He sent a message saying that if Genghis Khan were truly the ruler of the world, he would not need Tangut help and he should not attack if he did not think that his soldiers could defeat the shah.

Genghis Khan was angered and humiliated by the Tangut ruler's refusal to fulfill his obligations, but he was unable to punish him at that time because of the pressing need to focus on his campaign against the shah of Khwarizm. He postponed action against the arrogant Tangut, but he never forgave or forgot. Now, nearing the end of life, he was determined to punish them for their treachery.

He set out in winter in early 1226. He chose his Tatar wife, the wise and respected Yesui Khatun, to accompany him. Her court would be his headquarters. For Mongols, a cold start to a campaign was a good sign, just as it was when he crossed the Altai Mountains during a heavy summer blizzard on his way to attack the shah of Khwarizm, but this year was particularly brutal. They had to wrap the horses in felt blankets to prevent them from freezing, and he ordered that his soldiers take sheep fleeces with which to line their already well-padded robes, some with capes made from wolf pelts.[8] He rode out from his camp on the Tuul River, in the Black Forest area near the modern Mongolian capital of Ulaanbaatar. The air was clear and sharp with tiny ice crystals sparkling in the winter sun like diamonds floating on the wind. The bellowing oxen pulling their carts, the grunting camels in a caravan, and the snorting and panting of so many horses created a fog around them like a protective cloud as the massive army moved forward.

After less than a week, the army headed south following the Ongi River, the only river flowing into the Gobi Desert.[9] Although crossing the gravel desert of the Gobi can be difficult in winter, it is easier for men and animals than in the heat of summer. The men chiseled out large blocks of ice from the Ongi, which they transported on oxcarts or on camelback. When they needed water along the route, they melted the ice in large pots over dung fires.

Before leaving the Ongi River, Genghis Khan decided to pause and hunt for *khulan*, a type of onager, the Asian wild ass, to provision the army before crossing the barren and frozen lands ahead. It was the last hunt of his life. He set out after the *khulan* riding a reddish-gray horse.[10] As he raced forward toward his prey, his horse became frightened by the stampeding *khulan* and unexpectedly bucked and bolted, throwing him to the ground and leaving him severely wounded and in great pain. For a leader to fall from a horse at any time is a bad omen, but to do it at the start of an important military campaign could be extremely disheartening to the soldiers under his command. Even clever Yelu Chucai could not construe such an accident as an auspicious sign.

Yesui Khatun immediately recognized the grave danger to a man of his age and frantically pleaded with him to delay the invasion and return to the Mongolian steppe to recuperate. He refused. Such a retreat would further frighten his people, weaken their confidence in him, and embolden his enemies. He ordered his army to move forward, across the Gobi, through the Gurvan Saihan Mountains known as the Three Beauties, and on toward Tangut territory.

Genghis Khan made his choice clearly and deliberately. Better to die on the verge of triumph than in the certainty of defeat. His life would not end on a sickbed at home, surrounded by chanting healers and mourning relatives while his whole nation idly waited, watching his every breath. He was going to die on the campaign trail, still fighting for what fate had promised him. If he could not fall in the midst of battle like his grandson Mutugen, then at least he would die close by, encouraging and inspiring his men with his determined presence.

The Tangut state subscribed to a national cult similar to Tibetan Buddhism, with a divine king who bore the name of God, Burkhan. The ruler at the time of Genghis Khan's invasion was Iluqu Burkhan, or Victorious God. Burkhan Khaldun was God's Sacred Mountain, but for the Mongols, it was idolatrous for a human to claim the name of God. Humans, even a king, could not become divine.

As a living god, the Tangut ruler cultivated a reputation for pious sanctity fortified by fierce magic. He was rumored to be a feared shape-changer. In the morning, he "becomes a poisonous yellow striped snake," and at noon, "a brown striped tiger." In the evening, he "becomes a beautiful yellow boy."[11] As befitted his name, he could become Khormusta, the King of Heaven.[12] He was accompanied by "a prophetic black muzzled fallow yellow dog named Kubeleg."[13]

The Tangut straddled the Silk Route and had grown rich on its wealth, surrounded by vast stretches of desert; they felt safe and secure enough to live in an illusory world of spiritual decadence. The Tangut rulers built magnificent temples and raised pagodas in their own honor, decorating them with larger-than-life statues and paintings in vivid colors. The smell of burning juniper and butter lamps drifted through their ceremonies, punctuated by the loud clang of cymbals, the groaning strains of the giant trumpets, and the throbbing of drums. Monks fluttered around in identical robes as bright as coral; they published illustrated books using the Tangut version of Chinese characters and printed their prayers on long silk banners that fluttered in the wind. The Tangut crafted beautiful jade vases, carved wooden altars, and sculpted images of their gods in precious gold and silver as well as more fragile images made of flour, butter, sugar, and sand. The Tangut religious rituals soothed the senses: sight, sound, and smell. The sweet words and soft chanting lulled the mind.

For a Mongol such as Genghis Khan, praying on the open mountaintop or in the vast expanse of the steppe emphasized one's unimportance while giving the worshipper direct contact with the Eternal Blue Sky. The Buddhists and Christians built temples of brick, stone, and wood covered by a heavy roof, as though they wanted to hide from the eyes of God or avoid personal contact with the sky. Only by going through a priest could an ordinary person connect to God. The magnificent art and architecture glorified the priest who stood on a raised platform, at the center of the universe.

The Tangut's Buddhist rituals and man-made temples glorified things artificial, such as statues, paintings, and pagodas. When they claimed to worship a mountain or a cave, they disfigured it by erecting man-made images and buildings. They revered their priests, monks, and saints more than the sky, and listened to the voices of men rather than to their gods. Their walls, closed to nature, amplified the human voice reverberating inside. Mongols preferred the open air, where the human voice, no matter how loud, never competes with the sound of the eternal wind that envelops the earth, the roar of the river, the howl of the wolf, the persistent call of the cuckoo, or the drumming of the black woodpecker.

Buddhist monks not only presided over faith and ritual, they occupied most of the high offices in the government of the Tangut kingdom, and served as messengers, clerks, diplomatic envoys, and spies. Because they could not marry and thereby accumulate wealth and power for their own offspring, they posed less of a threat to the king and royal family. The Buddhist church was a state institution. The government had to approve every religious appointment, and so all monks served effectively as state officials and received strict supervision over their sermons, preaching, and writing. No building or religious structure could be erected without state approval; not even a well could be dug on church property without written authorization. Punishments were swift and severe, and any act that threatened the state or welfare of the established clergy would be punished by execution.[14] The Tangut state and Buddhist faith were one and the same, making their god and king one and the same.

The state preceptor sponsored numerous Tantric texts, called "the practice in Pair," stressing the importance of sexual activities that he needed to perform to create the "body of supreme bliss." In *Brief Records of Black Tartars*, written late in the Yuan dynasty, an observer of the Mongol conquest of the Tangut reportedly stated, "Once I followed Genghis Khan in his campaign against the Tangut Kingdom of Xia," the state preceptor of the Tangut "was customarily served with great respect by all under the king." In particular, "every girl had to be recommended to serve the State Preceptor first, before she is allowed to get married to anyone."[15] This was not a practice that impressed Genghis Khan: "after Genghis Khan destroyed the kingdom, he first killed the State Preceptor. The State Preceptor was a Buddhist monk."[16]

During most of the campaign, Yesui Khatun ran the Mongol court and kept Genghis Khan's suffering and deteriorating condition hidden. He remained in her *ger* protected from public view. He shared leadership with his main general, Subodei of the Uriyankhai. Following their traditional pattern, they attacked the smaller cities first, but they encountered stiffer resistance than expected. When summer came, the heat impaired Genghis's recovery, and Yesugei evacuated him to the mountains. He remained in charge and ordered the pressure be kept up during the summer; several smaller cities were taken, but they waited for the return of cold weather before besieging the capital city, Yinchuan. When the rivers froze again, they besieged the capital at the beginning of 1227.

The Tangut, desperate but knowing the fate that awaited them if they surrendered, fought hard, but the Mongols fought harder. Having been unable to impress the Mongols with his religious power, Iluqu Burkhan decided to shower them with spiritual praise. He anxiously gathered his sacred scriptures, the statue of a golden Buddha, and other precious objects to take to the Great Khan, hoping to soften his anger and beg for his forgiveness. Genghis Khan was close to death when the Tangut ruler came to surrender, but he refused to see him or to allow his religious objects into his royal *ger*. At the moment of death, he did not need the scriptures or idols of his enemy. If they had not helped the Tangut king to follow the moral path and retain his kingdom, he had no use for them now. In the words of the *Secret History*, "Genghis Khan felt revulsion in his heart."[17]

He sent a message to the waiting Tangut king that the king had been abandoned by heaven, and therefore he could no longer carry a holy name, Burkhan. He was a mortal, not a god. He ordered him to take a new name, Shidurgu, meaning Surrender to Righteousness. Having nominally brought the Tangut ruler back to the moral path,

Genghis Khan condemned him to death. The Tangut Buddhists taught that in this world human fate is as fragile and fleeting as "summer flowers" or "autumn dew." The destiny of an individual or a whole nation signifies nothing more than "bubbles in the tide."[18] The end had come not only for the Tangut ruler but for his dynasty and his nation as well.

Because the Tangut believed in reincarnation, giving the king an appropriate name before killing him would allow him to be born into a new life with a fresh chance to do right. To make sure that the executed monarch could not be reborn into his royal dynasty and seek revenge against the Mongols, Genghis Khan ordered the execution of the entire royal family. "Exterminate the mothers and fathers down to the offspring of their offspring," he said.[19] He then had the golden bowls and gifts from the Tangut king gathered together and presented them to the executioner. The Mongol warriors then turned their fury against the Tangut and punished them with a fierce vengeance. They blamed the Tangut for forcing Genghis Khan to come out and fight and held them responsible for the accident that had put his life in danger. Not knowing whether their leader was alive or dead, the Mongol warriors turned their fear and mourning into rage.

Genghis Khan was too near the end of life to feel such rage. He put an end to the murderous rampage, spared the remaining survivors, and assigned the Tangut people to the care of his wife Yesui Khatun, who had ministered to him on that campaign. As the Tangut no longer had a royal family, she would rule them. He had accomplished his final mission and returned the Tangut nation to the path of righteousness. Some Mongolian chronicles erroneously report that he married the widow of the Tangut king, but if he was still alive at that point, he was certainly in no condition to marry. The same accounts say that she flung herself into the Yellow River and drowned, but the details of the story seem to have been borrowed directly from the fictional Yuan drama *Autumn of the Palace Han* rather than from the pages of history.

The *Golden Chronicle* states that as his death approached, Genghis Khan expressed the wish that his good companions around him might go with him to the next world, but then he reflected that they were needed to carry on the work of the empire. "Now, do not die," he ordered them shortly before he expired. Instead, he asked them to help his descendants rule the nation. He asked the learned ministers to show his people how to find "water in the desert places, and a road in the mountains."[20]

☨

The Mongols refrain from using words such as *death* and *dying*, and instead substitute the euphemism "becoming a god." Thus, in August 1227, Genghis Khan became a god. Yesui Khatun supervised the wrapping of his body in felt, and his personal guard prepared to take him home for burial. He did not die as a Buddhist, Muslim, Christian, Taoist, or disciple of any one religion. He died a Mongol. After carefully observing each of the religions known to him and after long conversations with both genuine and fake holy men, he did not condemn any one of these faiths, yet neither did he find comfort in any of them. No foreigners had attended his creation of the Mongol nation in 1206 and none were allowed to come near him at death. He chose to have his body returned to Burkhan Khaldun, the holy mountain where he had found refuge and spiritual renewal throughout his life. In death, as in life, a Mongol belongs to nature. He needed no tomb or mausoleum. Genghis Khan's memorial was not carved in stone or decorated with precious jewels; his monument was in the memory of the nation he created. His memorial stone was the *nom sang* of law.

His family gathered to honor him and bid farewell, but it was his loyal *Keshig* companions who accompanied his body for burial where he had first met Jarchigudai. Now Jarchigudai's grandson, Yisun Toe, commanded the guard that escorted the Great Khan home. More than half a century after Temujin left Burkhan Khaldun as an abused and abandoned child, he was returning home as the emperor

Genghis Khan, conqueror of the world. Old Jarchigudai had been his moral guide then, and Jarchigudai's grandson now was the guide to bring his body home.

Speaking for the entire Mongol nation, one of his warriors offered the final salute to their leader. Addressing Genghis Khan directly as though he still lived, he informed him that his men were returning him to the land and waters of his birth. "They are there!" he exclaimed emotionally to his departing soul, "your spirit banner made from the manes of your chestnut stallions . . . Your drums, conches, and whistles," they are there. And most important, "all your great laws, there they are!"[21]

He would die, but his nation would live on.[22] His mortal body was no greater than an *ald*, the span from the tip of one outstretched hand to the tip of the other, and although he had been a powerful khan, his life must end like every other and thus, in death, he carried no more importance than any other. His nation, however, could encompass the world. The Jewel Translucent Sutra offered a concise summary of his life: "Temujin was born by the Will of Heaven above, founded the sublime state from its beginning, brought the entire world under his power, and became famous as the holy Genghis Khan."[23]

In the Mongolian lament for Genghis Khan, a mourner addressed the deceased conqueror soon after his death to express the shared agony of his people, who had never before seen such a leader. "Have you left this great nation behind?" he cried. "Did you lose yourself, Lord?" Or "did you fly off with the wind?" Pleading on behalf of the whole nation, he asked: "Lord Genghis Khan, have you abandoned your old Mongol people?"

There was only silence as the mournful lament hung in the still air. But for those who cared to remember, Genghis Khan had already answered that question four years earlier in his last recorded dispatch from the battlefront.

"I have never forgotten you," he wrote in a letter from Afghanistan. "Do not forget me."[24]

15

War, Inside and Out

A life cannot properly be measured until it ends. One could argue that the greatest achievements of Buddha, Jesus, and Muhammad, or political figures such as Alexander, Caesar, and Cleopatra, lie less in what they themselves did, but in their legacies, in what they inspired their followers to do. Genghis Khan's most enduring impact came from the laws he created and the dynamic energy he infused into his large and ever-growing state. His empire continued to expand for more than sixty years after his death, and it survived another century after that.

In accordance with Genghis Khan's wishes, his people built no stone or wooden monument, tomb, or temple to honor their leader. After he died, most of his people continued to operate as if he were still in command. Each one of his four widows continued to hold court in the *ger* in which she had lived with Genghis Khan. Horses were put aside for his use and allowed to graze freely as though waiting for his summons. His heirs continued to issue edicts and letters in his name.

Under his instructions, each son would be khan over his territory, but Ogodei would be the Great Khan or emperor over all of them.

Each of his widows and daughters had already received allocations of land, water, and people. The lands had been distributed from east to west to his offspring according to their birth order, with the heir to the office of Great Khan in the middle. Tolui received the eastern portion including much of northern China, Manchuria, and eastern Mongolia, including Burkhan Khaldun. Ogodei received western Mongolia, adjacent to the lands of Tolui. To his west (or to his right, as the Mongols refer to the west) were the lands of Chagatai in modern Kazakhstan and Central Asia. Jochi had died shortly before his father. His death, as mysterious as the circumstances of his birth, simplified the succession plan; his heirs, soon to be known as the Golden Horde, inherited the westernmost part of the empire in what is now Russia.

In the spring of 1228, the Year of the Rat (according to the *Secret History*), or the summer of 1229, the Year of the Ox (according to Juvaini and later Chinese records), the Mongols gathered to install Ogodei as the new Great Khan. He chose the title Dalai Khan to distinguish himself from his father, taking the Mongol word for sea, *dalai*, so that, like Attila, he would be the emperor of all the land encompassed by the world's oceans. The first thing Ogodei did was to reaffirm the laws of his father. "The law of Genghis Khan should be maintained, and secured, and protected against the evils of change, and alteration, and confusion."[1] He kept his father's generals and important military officers as well as his Torguud bodyguard, but he prudently removed the late khan's *Keshig* from politics, appointing them eternal guardians of his father's grave.

With their new government in place, the people began to drink and feast. They slept by day and celebrated so much at night that "the brilliance of the fire of wine became like broad day."[2] Ogodei opened the warehouses that stored the wealth of the nation and lavished its goods on his followers. Juvaini wrote that it was a time of "herbs and flowers blossoming in the meadows," and thus "the world began to smile" with "the impurities of deceit and envy remote from their secret thoughts."[3] But deceit and envy seem rarely to be altogether remote from the thoughts of powerful men. Despite all the wonderful words and soaring metaphors, a struggle had begun. The drunken revelry of Ogodei's installation was a preview of the chaos to come.

ॐ

Genghis Khan's heirs had divided the land between them, but now they each wanted control of the future, and therein lay the problem. Should they send the army to attack China, Korea, India, Europe, or Iraq? Each brother was intent on extending the borders of his particular lands, not the empire as a whole. Unable to agree on a unified goal, they set out to conquer in every direction at once, with each brother in command of his own army. Their campaign was the closest history had come until then to a world war.

With the armies sprawled out in so many different directions stretching from Korea to Hungary, it seemed that the empire would quickly pull itself apart. Not even their founder Genghis Khan had fought on so many fronts quite so far apart or spread so thinly over two continents. The brothers showed a dangerous combination of stubbornness, arrogance, and reckless risk-taking, yet sometimes fate favors the fool. Surprisingly their audacious plan worked. Despite a few setbacks, the Mongol armies consistently triumphed over one enemy after another on every front. They appeared to be as invincible as they had been under Genghis Khan. During Ogodei's reign Mongol warriors conquered from Kashmir in modern India as far as the borders of Poland and Germany and from the highlands of Tibet to the suburbs of Vienna. Much of the conquest was more akin to a series of massive raids in which the armies looted wherever they went, but they were now spread out too far to effectively organize their vast land holdings into a single functioning empire.

While the Mongol army won its battles, it was not necessarily winning the war. Each son seemed eager, as Jochi had declared in his lifetime, to conquer and loot new territories rather than administer the old ones. Once Genghis Khan withdrew from Central Asia, his allies the Nizaris attempted to replace him and assume control over the former Khwarizm territory. The alliance between Mongols and the Assassins broke dramatically soon after Genghis Khan's death, when the Nizari assassinated a Mongol commander, Chaghatai Qorchi.[4] The target of the assassination was identified in some Muslim sources as the young orphan whom Genghis Khan had adopted at the end of the Tangut campaign, but Rashid ad-Din claims the boy was Genghis Khan's natural-born son with a Tangut woman.[5] Whichever was true, any such familial connection to Genghis Khan would have forced the Mongols to sever all ties with the Nizari.

Soon thereafter, in further plotting against the Mongols in 1238, the Nizaris joined with the caliph of Baghdad to send an envoy to the kings of England and France, attempting to create an alliance of the Nizari imam with the caliph and the pope against the Mongols.[6] The mission failed.

With the newly conquered territories, wealth poured back into Mongolia, but the heart of the empire had begun to rot. Behind the scenes the brothers squabbled. As Great Khan and therefore the most powerful, Ogodei snatched territory from his brother Tolui and ordered the building of border walls between them to keep the game, particularly the massive herds of steppe antelope, from migrating into his brother's land. While the brothers quarreled with each other and gradually absorbed the lands of their sisters, uncles, and their father's aging widows, a completely new generation of women was coming to power—the wives so shrewdly chosen by Genghis Khan for his sons, who had been left in charge of court life while the men campaigned. Over the next thirty years until the rise of Khubilai Khan in 1260, these women held the empire together.

One of the predominant figures among this rising matriarchy was Ogodei's wife, Toregene Khatun, a Naiman princess who had been married to a Merkid leader before she married Ogodei. She chose the ministers, administered the laws, allocated money, heard pleas, and ran the court which was, in essence, the imperial government. Although raised a Christian, she financed Islamic schools and generously donated money for the publication of Taoist scriptures. Most of the officials who had prospered under Genghis Khan continued to do so under Ogodei Khan and his wife Toregene Khatun. While the Taoists received slightly preferential treatment from the court, all faiths were allowed to worship freely.

During Genghis Khan's lifetime, Yelu Chucai had persuaded him to abandon some of the older Mongol traditions in favor of Chinese models of government. He had proceeded slowly but persistently in the belief, as he put it, that "things which are quickly made, quickly perish, and those that are achieved late, end well."[7] Yelu Chucai became more open in his promotion of Chinese ideas, and his policies flourished under Ogodei, who showed a more positive attitude toward Confucianism than his father had. In 1233, Ogodei Khan conferred on Confucians the same privileges and tax exemptions enjoyed by Taoists and Buddhists. He also built the first known Confucian temple in Mongolia at his capital city of Karakorum.

Yelu Chucai recruited capable Confucian officials to run the empire and helped to transfer power away from Mongol advisers. Over time, the *Keshig* lost the power to decide legal cases and no longer outranked commanders in the army and ministers of government. Koreans were eventually recruited to replace some of the Mongols in Ogodei's bodyguard. Just as Genghis Khan had kept a balance of power among his ministers by recruiting men of different faiths and cultures, in 1229 Ogodei recruited Yelu Chucai's old nemesis Li Zhichang, who as a young Taoist disciple had met with Genghis Khan in Afghanistan, and appointed Li to the office of state teacher.[8]

Despite the growing conflict within the Mongol royal family, the ameliorating influence of men such as Li Zhichang and Yelu Chucai helped make Mongol rule more acceptable to the Chinese and to adjoining nationalities who had an affinity for classical Chinese culture. Yelu Chucai's Chinese factions continued to conflict with the

Central Asian Muslims and Christians at the court, but at this point the frictions were more ethnic and cultural than religious. His insistence on introducing more Chinese clerical practices into the court and using Confucian phraseology in some documents improved the image of the Mongols in China by making them less foreign. In the end, Yelu Chucai had a much greater influence on the Mongol Empire than the religious leaders who met and sought to guide the Great Khan. Even his detractors recognized his importance. One was quoted as saying that Yelu Chucai's discourse "still rings in my ears, as clear as the stars and the sun."[9]

In the first years of his reign, Ogodei campaigned hard against the Jin in China, but he seemed to be in constant competition with his younger brother Tolui. Tolui appeared to have enjoyed his brief reign as regent and harbored desires to become sole ruler after Ogodei.

Ogodei could not have failed to recognize the danger that Tolui and his four dynamic and skilled sons posed to his rule. Whereas Tolui's sons remained united under their mother Sorkhokhtani's leadership, Ogodei quarreled with his sons and they with one another. Ogodei described his son Guyuk, who quarreled frequently with everyone, as a bad egg and, according to the *Secret History*, expressed the wish that he might rot like one.[10] His favorite grandson, Shiremun, who he hoped would inherit the empire, never showed as much promise as his grandfather saw in him.

Suddenly in 1232, on the verge of the final defeat of the Jin, Tolui died. Some claimed that he was simply drunk as usual and died in a coma, but the *Secret History* offers a lengthy and bizarre explanation that began when Ogodei became ill and lost his ability to speak.[11] The court shamans diagnosed his problem as having been bewitched by the guardian spirits of the Chinese lands and waters. The shamans offered the spirits gold, silver, cattle, food, slaves—anything they wanted to release their khan—but the illness only grew worse. Finally, they divined by "inspecting the entrails of victims" that the spirits would give up their paralysis of Ogodei only if they could have the sacrifice of someone in his family. Suddenly, Ogodei Khan supposedly woke up, asked for a drink, and wanted to know what had happened to him. When the shamans told him that the spirits had released him in exchange for the sacrifice of someone in his family, Ogodei looked around and his eye fell on his younger brother Tolui.

The shamans prepared "magic water" for Tolui, who dutifully drank it and died. The *Secret History* includes a long poetic speech supposedly given by Tolui just before he died claiming that he wanted to give his life for his brother. This episode with the victim supposedly asking for death resembled the events leading up to Jamuka's death, when Genghis Khan offered him freedom but instead he chose to die.

🐘

Unlike his father, who loyally accompanied his soldiers until the end of his life, in 1234, at nearly fifty years of age, Ogodei retired from fighting. He left the battlefield and returned home to Mongolia. His health was failing from rampant alcoholism and he seemed haunted by the ghost of his brother as he returned to the steppe for his final years. He appears to have suffered a stroke or some other severe impairment, so his wife Toregene administered his court just as Yesui had done in the final year of Genghis Khan's life. With the fall of the Jin dynasty, Toregene launched new campaigns in the name of her ailing husband against the Southern Sung, the kingdom of Goryeo (Korea), the Kipchak, and Tibet. While Ogodei's sons and generals went out to fight, Toregene and her ministers ran the empire, issuing edicts under her own name and authority.

Under Toregene's rule, the Mongol nation acquired its first capital, Kharkhorin, which became known in the West by its Turkic name, Karakorum. Built on the Orkhon River where it flows out of the Khangai Mountains, this was the place where the earlier Turkic tribes had built their capitals. But this was now the capital of a vast world empire. It housed metalworkers and weavers from Khwarizm and Persia, scribes and potters from China, soldiers from Russia, clerks and papermakers from Korea, maids who had once been ladies of the royal court, dung gatherers who had once lived in luxurious palaces, and even a goldsmith from Paris. Astrologers, monks, and priests of all religions flocked to the Mongol court. In addition to Christian chapels, Muslim mosques, and Buddhist and Taoist temples, a visitor could find a Confucian temple and school.

After Ogodei's death in 1241, Toregene became the regent, and for the next five years she ruled the largest empire in the history of the world. Although she is little remembered today outside of Mongolia, no man or woman had ruled as large a territory or as many people. Not until the reigns of Isabella and Ferdinand of Spain in the sixteenth century did an intercontinental empire come close to rivaling hers, and not until the British annexation of India and Burma under Queen Victoria in the nineteenth century did any monarch claim as large a domain or as many subjects.

Toregene's *tamgha*, the symbol branded on her animals, was a stylized archery bow, and that became her seal of office, replacing the S-shaped seal of her husband. Her bow was cast on coins, which boldly proclaimed her office and power in different languages depending on where they were issued. In Turkic, the most common language within the empire, the coins were inscribed with *Ulugh Mughul Ulus Beg*, Ruler of the Great Mongol Nation.

ॐ

After Ogodei's death, Yelu Chucai gradually lost favor. Though he was only fifty-four years old, he was a walking relic from another time. Respected but ignored, he was pushed to the sidelines of court life, replaced by other advisers who promised greater tax yields and more luxuries. These were men who had not been with Genghis Khan on the long campaign, had not helped in the march to victory, but now came wagging their tails, eager to exploit his subjects. Yelu Chucai died at Karakorum in 1244 reportedly of a broken heart, devastated by the direction taken by Genghis Khan's heirs.

Soon after Yelu Chucai's death, Subodei of the Uriyankhai, the nephew of Old Jarchigudai and the most respected surviving adviser of Genghis Khan's inner circle, retired. He was the last person to have known Temujin as a youth on Burkhan Khaldun, and he had continued fighting for nearly two decades after his friend's death. Having waged battles from China to Hungary, Subodei had conquered more cities than any other Mongol leader. Late in life, he was still begrudgingly honored by the younger members of the royal family but was otherwise ignored. He became so disgusted with Mongol politics that like Yelu Chucai, he withdrew. Friar Carpini reported seeing him in 1247, by which time he supposedly had grown quite heavy, but others said that he returned to Hungary, the scene of his greatest victory in 1241. He had named his son Uriyankhadai, in honor of their tribe of origin, and by this time Uriyankhadai had become an accomplished general, campaigning across Eastern Europe.[12] Some claimed that the old warrior wanted to die with his son by the Danube, but this romantic story is based solely on hearsay. While it could be true, it may also be a tale manufactured to disguise Subodei's disenchantment with the empire he had helped build. By 1248 Subodei was gone, and with him the Old Guard as well.

In time even the strongest rope begins to unravel, and the golden cord that was Genghis Khan's Mongol nation proved no exception. Beneath the surface of conservative continuity, political rivalries intensified within the family. By 1246, Toregene had solidified the empire and centralized power to the point where she was ready to hand it over to her unpopular and largely incompetent son Guyuk. The summer of his installation was dreadfully cold, with snowstorms, lethal hail, and floods in the area around Karakorum. Because of the damage from harsh winds, possibly even a tornado, the investiture ceremony had to be postponed until deep into August.

For the first time, foreigners were not only allowed but encouraged to attend the ceremony. According to different chroniclers, as many as two thousand foreign officials attended together with an equal number of retainers. Many were already vassals of the Mongols; others sought to curry favor with the new world power. Although they were not allowed to participate in the selection or to witness the actual installation, the foreigners were allowed to submit tribute and to offer their submission once Guyuk was installed. The 1246 Congress of Karakorum was the first international summit of ministers and heads of so many states. "Emirs, governors, agents, and deputies made their way to his *ordo* from north, south, east and west," wrote Rashid al-Din.[13] "No one had ever witnessed such an assembly nor has the like been read of in any history." They came from as far away as the courts of the sultan in Delhi, the pope in Rome, the Seljuk sultan in Turkey, and the caliph in Baghdad. Rival claimants to the throne of Georgia (both named David) came to pay their respects and plead for appointment as the new Georgian king, the brother of the Armenian king arrived, and the grand duke of Russia along with his son the great hero Prince Alexander Nevsky came. Two thousand tents had to be erected to house the vast number of guests.

It was feared that the foul weather at the time of the installation was an omen of a stormy reign, and so it turned out to be. Guyuk did not accept some of the ambassadors who were sent to him and pointedly refused all communication with the Nizari imam of the Assassins. "As for the envoys from Alamut, he dismissed them with contempt and disdain; and the reply to the memorandum they bought was correspondingly couched in harsh language," wrote Juvaini.[14] Guyuk was too busy to deal with the Nizari at this point, but their earlier treachery had sealed their fate.

We are lucky to have an exceptional eyewitness account of Guyuk Khan's selection and installation. Unexpectedly and almost entirely unnoticed, on July 22, 1246, amidst all the confusion of the election, the threatening armies, and the unprecedentedly large horde of foreigners thronging the Orkhon River valley, the first envoy arrived from Pope Innocent IV in Rome. Innocent had commissioned two Franciscan envoys and sent them east by separate routes. Their mission was to contact the Mongols, negotiate with them, and return with much-needed information on their political intentions and military capability. The pope dispatched Lawrence of Portugal, who apparently headed for Asia Minor and then disappeared into obscurity. The pope also sent out Friar Giovanni of Plano Carpini, who had been one of the early disciples of Saint Francis of Assisi. The sixty-five-year-old overweight friar set out from Lyon, France, on Easter Day 1245, accompanied by Stephen of Bohemia on the first successful mission from Europe to Mongolia. As any foreigner might, Carpini found Mongol politics and protocol quite bewildering. He apparently tried to approach Guyuk with the pope's letter, but he was politely referred to the court of Toregene Khatun, who still ruled. Carpini wrote with astonishment that Toregene Khatun had a massive white tent capable of holding two thousand people and that the area in front of her courtly tent teemed with officials and supplicants from all over the world. He stayed at her court for four weeks, and insisted that there were about four thousand people swarming around. Because of the language barrier, he was not sure what they were doing, but he thought that the Mongols were holding an election.[15]

The court included more Europeans than Carpini had expected. Fresh from their campaigns to Hungary and Poland, the Mongol court was filled with "many Ruthenians [Ukrainians, Belarusians, and Russians], Hungarians, people who knew Latin and French, and Ruthenian clerics and others who had been with the Tartars, some for thirty years, in wars and other circumstances, who knew everything about them because they knew the language and had stayed with them constantly, some twenty years, some ten, some more."[16]

With help from some of these Europeans working in the Mongol court, Carpini managed to have the pope's letter translated for Guyuk Khan. Given the fact that he had a Christian mother, Guyuk Khan knew significantly more about Christianity than the Christians knew about the Mongols. Indeed the khan had a private Christian chapel, and he maintained a "Christian choir before his largest tent, and they sang publicly and openly, and rang the hours according to the Greek custom."[17] From their reconnaissance, the Mongols were well aware that the pope represented neither Europe nor the Christians because he did not rule over all of Europe or have the allegiance of most of the world's Christians.

The Great Khan sought to send Mongol ambassadors back with Carpini to Europe, but Carpini strongly resisted. He did not want the Mongols to see how disunited the Europeans were, or to take responsibility for their lives. The Mongols did not insist. As a sign of good will, Toregene sent them back with coats made of fox fur sewn with silk to comfort them on their long journey home.[18] Mongols at that time rarely accepted "no" as an answer. Despite Carpini's refusal to escort Mongol ambassadors to Europe, they sent them anyway.

The English cleric Matthew Paris, who wrote a year-by-year chronicle of events in his lifetime, reported that Mongol representatives arrived in Rome in 1248. "In this same summer two envoys came from the Tartars, sent to the lord pope by their prince," wrote Paris, "but the cause of their arrival was kept so secret from everyone at the curia that it was unknown to clerks, notaries, and others, even those familiar with the pope." Because of the difficult language barrier separating the Europeans from the Asians, "the letters they brought with them for the pope were three times translated from an unknown to a better known language as the envoys approached the region of the West."[19] The Christian church was not receptive to the Mongol claim that Genghis Khan was heaven's representative on Earth and that by his law, the Mongols protected and honored all religions. Church officials anxiously suppressed all knowledge of this un-Christian message from pagans.

The court was soon splintered by arrogance, pride, and greed. Guyuk reaffirmed the laws of his grandfather and father, and he continued to use the title Dalai Khan, like his father. He may have done so not so much out of loyalty as sheer laziness. He greedily sought power and wealth and showed little interest in administration, referring officials and envoys to his mother's court and seeming content to allow her to continue to run the government. "He was, on most days," wrote Rashid al-Din, "engaged from morning till evening and from dawn to dusk with the quaffing of cups of wine and the contemplation of angel-faced, sweet-limbed maidens." Aside from the maidens, "he was in a melancholic frame of mind and had no inclination for conversation."[20]

A feud soon broke out with his mother, who had prepared the way for him to become Great Khan. As he purged her court, she tried to resist, but she was probably well over sixty years of age at this point and weakening. The fight between mother and son did not last long, as the Empress Toregene suddenly died. No information is given regarding the details of her demise. She could have died a natural death, but there may also have been a plot against her. We will probably never know the truth of this heroic empress's end.

Despite his avowed commitment to the laws of his grandfather, Guyuk executed some of the Muslim administrators Genghis Khan had assigned to help govern China. His hostility seemed less directed at the faith than it was an effort to clear out old ministers and take firm control over the government. The abrupt changes created an atmosphere of paranoia as each group felt itself to be, or about to become, unfairly victimized. Rumors and lies could scarcely be separated from fact. Each religious faction seemed to fear that its followers might be exterminated. Chinese and Persian chronicles relate how followers of different faiths attempted to have others banned. Some Chinese officials advocated banning Buddhism as well as Taoism.[21] The Catholics wanted to exterminate Asian Christianity, which they condemned as Nestorian heresy. The general mood of paranoia is reflected in the report, firmly believed by many, that some Buddhist monks proposed to Guyuk Khan that he massacre all Muslims under

Mongol control. When he would not do so, they purportedly persuaded him to prevent them from reproducing by castrating Muslim men. According to Juzjani's account, Guyuk drew up the order for castration only to rescind it when a dog unexpectedly attacked one of the Buddhist monks and ripped off his genitals.[22] This was supposedly a sign of Allah's determination to protect the Muslims. Such stories, however unlikely, further inflamed the passions and exacerbated the power struggles.

"By Virtue of God," proclaimed Guyuk, "from the rising of the sun to its setting, all realms have been granted to us. Without the Order of God, how could anyone do anything?"[23] The *Golden Chronicle* tells us that Genghis Khan's descendants enjoyed the fruits of his labor and undermined his life's work.

Guyuk's life was short and his death mysterious. After only eighteen months as Great Khan he died in the spring of 1248, while moving his army across southwestern Mongolia toward the land of his cousin Batu Khan in modern-day Russia. He was forty-two years old. Was it poison, alcohol, fever, a fight, exhaustion, a wound? There has been much speculation but no satisfactory answer. His widow, the Christian queen Oghul Ghaimish, perfectly matched both in temperament and ability, became the regent. Her reign lasted three years, twice the length of her husband's, but she lacked the skill and vision of her late mother-in-law, the Empress Toregene.

Oghul Ghaimish depended increasingly on her Christian advisers to run what little she controlled of the government, while she huddled with the shamans, turning to divine the future through astrology and by studying the cracks in the burnt shoulder blades of sheep.

In the words of Juvaini, she was closeted with the shamans, "carrying out their fantasies and absurdities."[24] She avoided the new Mongol capital at Karakorum and set up her nomadic court along the Emil River in western China, near the place where her husband had died and far from her main rivals, Tolui's family, in the east.

After Guyuk's death, the simmering conflicts within the royal family spilled into public view. The discord increasingly took the form of religious rivalries as his two sons set up rival courts, each hoping to become the Great Khan. Juvaini wrote that the wise men "struggled in the mire" and "could find no way out."[25] Differences over religion were not the underlying issue fueling the conflicts, but religion was the tool through which other rivalries were funneled and expressed. The Mongol Empire was at its height, and it would endure for another 120 years. But the decay had begun. The Mongols could defeat any foe but they could not control themselves.

Oghul Ghaimish's greed and lack of tact were fully displayed in 1250, when she received a Dominican monk, Andrew of Longjumeau, who had been sent by the French king Louis IX, also known as Saint Louis. The envoy had not come as a vassal to submit but as a possible ally eager to create a Mongol-European alliance against the Muslims. Although Oghul Ghaimish's armies had not attacked France or fought French soldiers on the battlefield, she arrogantly assumed that Longjumeau had come on behalf of his king in order to surrender Christian Europe, or at least France. Her letter of response to King Louis IX dispensed with flattery and did not even express appreciation for his having sent an envoy all that way. Instead she offered grandiose claims and puffed-up threats. She sent him a list of the rulers whom she claimed to have executed for failing to please her and then commanded the French monarch "to send us so much of your gold and of your silver each year, if you hold it back from us, we shall do what we did to those whom we named before." The French king simply ignored the letter. One surviving account of his reaction states simply: "he was very sorry that he had sent a mission."[26]

One person's failures often make room for another's strength. Oghul Ghaimish's weakness offered opportunities for others to step in, and it was another, far stronger woman who outmaneuvered all the men in the royal family. Ultimate victory in the bitter struggle for succession to the office of Great Khan went to Sorkhokhtani Beki, the sister of Genghis Khan's Christian wife, Ibaqa Beki. Sorkhokhtani

Beki was also Christian and was the widow of Genghis Khan's youngest son, Tolui, and the mother of four strongly competitive contenders—Mongke, Khubilai, Hulegu, and Arik Boke.

In the summer of 1251, Sorkhokhtani negotiated a secret alliance with Batu Khan, the heir to Jochi in the Golden Horde of Russia and an excellent leader, who would have been an excellent candidate for Great Khan had it not been for the questions of paternity surrounding his father. Jochi's lineage was thus united with that of Tolui against the weakened, fragmented, and alcoholic line of Ogodei. Through Sorkhokhtani's careful plotting and detailed guidance, her four sons seized control of the Mongol Empire in a carefully orchestrated coup.

Her eldest son, Mongke, took office as the new Great Khan, and, seizing territory already granted to other members of the royal family, his three brothers divided up most of the empire among them. Khubilai was given responsibility for most of the Chinese territory under Mongol control, including large parts of Tibet. Hulegu took Central Asia as far as Kashmir and western Tibet, and Arik Boke, the youngest, retained authority over the Mongolian homeland. The brothers controlled the entire empire with the exception of Russia. Because of Sorkhokhtani's alliance with Batu Khan, he and his family retained control of their lands, which they administered with increasing independence.

Sorkhokhtani, who had long served as regent for her dead husband, Tolui, over northern China and eastern Mongolia, could have followed the precedent of Toregene Khatun and Oghul Ghaimish Khatun and herself become queen. In her prime she almost certainly would have been the greatest of all the Mongol queens, but now she was in her mid- to late sixties, nearing what the Mongols call "the completion of her age." She refused the title of Sorkhokhtani Khatun and remained what she had always been, Sorkhokhtani Beki, a princess. She had fought all her life to prepare her sons for this day and she decided to put them forward instead.

In a protracted struggle of wills, Oghul Ghaimish Khatun, the legally elected regent, refused to participate in the election of Mongke Khan or to recognize him afterward. She insisted that only a person from the lineage of Ogodei could hold that office, which, in her view, had been vouchsafed to them in perpetuity by Genghis Khan. In the midst of this struggle Sorkhokhtani died in the spring of 1252, just as the young Juvaini arrived in Karakorum for the first time. As his father was already working for the Mongols, a twenty-six-year-old Juvaini had a chance to visit Karakorum only a few months after the installation. His eyewitness account of the new administration is valuable, if decidedly overwrought.

Juvaini's praise for Mongke Khan was even more exaggerated than it had been for Genghis Khan, whom he had never met. "The world was a rose garden and the season resplendent." he wrote.[27] "And when the World-Emperor had auspiciously seated himself upon the couch of the Empire, like the sun in the zenith of power," he decreed that "people should not engage in acts of hostility and enmity towards one another but should enjoy themselves and make merry."[28] Juvaini waxes on for a dozen pages about the beauty and perfection of Mongke Khan's reign until the celebrations have finished. "And the princes having departed and their business being dispatched, he [Mongke Khan] turned his attention to the administration of the realm, and the straightening of the crooked, and the righting of the wrong, and the chiding of the wicked, and the suppression of the seditious."[29] The ornate prose scarcely gave justice to the horror that was about to unfold at the Mongol court.

Until this point the struggle between the lineages of Ogodei and Tolui had been mostly one of words, political plays, and bluffing, but the death of Mongke Khan's mother seemed to have released him from all restraint. His first victim was his mother's long-term rival Oghul Ghaimish. He had her arrested along with the surviving widow of Ogodei Khan. Oghul Ghaimish was certainly guilty of many faults, including incompetence, arrogance, and greed, but she did not deserve the brutal fate that awaited her. Mongke Khan had her brought to court, stripped naked, and publicly tortured. Ravaged but still alive, she was then "wrapped in felt and flung into the river."[30]

Her formal charge was witchcraft, but privately in January 1254, Mongke told the French envoy William of Rubruck that she was the worst kind of witch, "more vile than a dog. She was a 'bitch.'" Thus ended the life of the last reigning empress of the Mongol Empire.

William of Rubruck was struck by the heightened state of paranoia and vigilance. He was surprised at the high security of the court and the suspicious nature of the Mongol khan and his officials. Upon arrival, every foreign envoy was summoned and interrogated about the details of his life and journey. "And they inquired most minutely whence we were, why we had come, what was our business,"[31] William explained in his account of his journey. He attributed this scrutiny to fear of assassination by the Nizari, with whom the Mongols were now virtually at war. "And this inquiry was made," he wrote, "because it had been reported to Mongke Khan that forty *Hacsasins* had entered the city under various disguises to kill him."[32]

Although a similar story of Nizari assassins was reported by other participants, it may well have been a rumor started by the Mongols as justification for the security. No evidence survives of anyone having been arrested. Alleged threats from Oghul Ghaimish or from the Assassins became an excuse for all types of additional security, but in truth the officials in Mongke's court were only persecuting their fellow Mongols and mostly just their own family members.

⚶

Having seized control of the empire, Mongke Khan needed to secure his hold on power. To do that he wanted to rid himself of all opposition. He interrogated nearly everyone associated with the reigns of Ogodei and his hapless son Guyuk and purged many of his cousins, their spouses, children, and allies. He "ordered them all to be bound and imprisoned, and for a while he reflected about their fate," wrote William. He presented himself as the defender of Genghis Khan's laws and traditions, but he lacked a legal pretext under Mongol law to torture the prisoners or punish them. Only a council of the whole royal family could order the execution of another member of the Golden Lineage. Instead, Mongke Khan chose to try them before a court with judges whom he controlled.

Shigi-Khutukhu, now in his seventies, still served as the supreme judge of the Mongol nation, an office he had held for forty years. Genghis Khan had specifically declared that no one could alter the laws recorded by Shigi-Khutukhu, whom he described as "eyes to see with, ears to hear with." Ogodei had also appointed him as the chief judge over northern China, the very land ruled by Sorkhokhtani. Shigi-Khutukhu was still alive at the time of the purges, and was almost certainly the most respected official in the government. He was quickly removed from office.[33]

Genghis Khan's half brother Belgutei had also served as a judge and was still alive, but he too was excluded from power, as were members of Genghis Khan's *Keshig*, who had been charged with enforcing and preserving the law, but now had only the authority to protect his grave. Mongke Khan seemed determined to destroy anyone with a closer tie to his grandfather than his own. He arrested Yisun Toe, the grandson of Old Jarchigudai, who had escorted Genghis Khan's body to Burkhan Khaldun. He too was killed.[34] Old Chinqai, the Christian minister who had served Genghis Khan so faithfully, had been abandoned. According to Rashid al-Din, he "was perplexed in the conduct of affairs, and no one listened to his words and advice."[35] Finally, on a flimsy pretext, Chinqai too was executed in the fall of 1252.

Mongke Khan appointed new judges and officials to carry out the prosecutions. He wanted no one around him with a direct connection to Genghis Khan. To override his grandfather's laws, he knew he would need to find some higher precedent. According to Rashid al-Din, he found this in the *Romance of Alexander*, a popular account of the adventures of Alexander the Great. One of Mongke Khan's advisers read a passage from the book that held that when faced with rebels, Alexander had sent a messenger to his former teacher Aristotle to ask "what measures he should take to deal with them." Rather than answering in words, Aristotle had uprooted a large tree to show that the old must be removed before the new can grow.[36] According to Rashid al-Din, Mongke Khan "was extremely pleased with this story and realized that these people must be done away with and others maintained in their place." It mattered little that the story was merely a myth or that it contradicted the explicit edicts and teachings of Genghis Khan. Mongke Khan issued his verdict.

$$ \maltese $$

Mongke brought the *ordu* of Genghis Khan, the tents that had belonged to his wives, from their resting place as shrines at Burkhan Khaldun and had them erected in the steppes near Karakorum, from where he now ruled. He used them as the venues for the trials of his relatives. According to Rashid al-Din, Mongke Khan "went to the *ordu* of Genghis Khan, sat upon a chair, and tried" his royal cousins, the princes and former heirs.[37] In the belief of the time, part of Genghis Khan's spirit lived on in the *ordu* and by not stopping the trials and punishments he was supposedly giving his posthumous blessing to the rule of Mongke Khan and to the trials.

Mongke Khan's prosecutors used an effective technique, beginning the questions circuitously before the accused realized what was happening. Like hunters who let their prey run until it tires and can be easily taken, the prosecutors proceeded slowly over several days to allow people to say as much as they wanted, knowing that ultimately they would reveal something incriminating. "They put the questions in an extremely subtle manner, so that in the end the contradictions in their words became apparent," wrote Rashid al-Din, and "no doubt remained" as to their guilt.[38]

The public prosecution of the cousins lasted for days, during which witnesses were beaten into confessing their crimes and betraying others. The trials degenerated into public torture sessions. When the Buddhist ruler of the Uighurs was brought in and denied the charges against him, "they so twisted his hands that he fell upon his face in exhaustion. A wooden press was then fastened on his forehead."[39] Others were brought in to testify against him, "and after sipping the unpalatable cup of the roughness of Tartar rods they vomited forth and declared what was hidden in their breasts." The Uighur ruler was then returned to his people for a public execution; his brother was ordered to cut off his head while his accomplices "were sawn in half."

"There were seventy-seven persons, all of whom were put to death," and hundreds received other punishments. Family members were killed in such a way as to prevent the shedding of blood, but Mongke Khan seemed determined to make their deaths as gruesome as possible. Two accused brothers had their "mouths . . . stuffed with stones until they died," and then their father was arrested and taken "to join his sons."[40] In this way, the condemned man could not call out his final prayer for his immortal soul to escape from his body.

Perhaps out of jealousy, knowing that Mutugen had been Genghis Khan's favored grandson, two of Mutugen's sons were singled out for particularly brutal treatment. For their interrogation and trial, Mongke Khan deliberately chose judges who hated them. "The agents of the Court arrived like so many Angels of Death," wrote Rashid al-Din.[41] One of them, Buri, who had fought in Europe and brought a regiment of Saxon miners from Germany to teach their skills, was ridiculed as a drunk bully and sent to his cousin Batu in Russia for an undisclosed disposal. Another son of Mutugen was brought to the court with his wife, who was tortured and tried in the presence of her husband. The judge had a "bosom filled with an ancient grudge," and after a perfunctory trial, "he ordered her limbs to be kicked to a pulp."[42] The manner of death of the two men was not specified, but the vengeful court seemed to delight in designing especially horrible fates for each person it condemned.

The original group of seventy-seven family members who had been arrested soon grew to hundreds as the prosecutions spread across the empire and more enemies were identified. After purging the royal family and high-ranking officials, Mongke Khan seemed determined to expand the scope of the purges and to remove anyone with a religious or spiritual connection to his grandfather. The new rulers were the sons of his blood and bone, and they wanted no one around who could claim a more direct, personal tie to him.

One of the court retainers, according to Juvaini, "was cast into bonds and chains and remained imprisoned for nearly two years, during which time, by reason of all manner of question and punishment, he despaired of the pleasure of life." Finally "he resigned himself to death and surrendering his body to the will of Fate and Destiny confessed to a crime which he had not committed. He too was cast into the river, and his wives and children were put to the sword."[43] Juvaini, like his father, was a strong supporter of Mongke Khan, yet he reported many such atrocities in the great purge of his ascension to power. To give one example, he wrote that Mongke Khan had ordered one accused "to be beaten from the left and the right until all his limbs were crushed; and so he died. And his wives and children were cast into the baseness of slavery and disgraced and humiliated."[44] While the Mongol royal family squabbled among themselves and plotted against each other, the edges of the empire continued to fray. Once he had completed his internal purges, Mongke Khan was determined to restore the empire of Genghis Khan. He sent the army on a new round of foreign conquest to take back lost territory and expand into new lands. His ruthless treatment of his family members was but a prelude to his plans for a much bigger and better Mongol Empire. His foreign enemies had ample reason to fear the worst. And Mongke Khan was already preparing to make their worst fears come true.

16

Burning the Books

Of all the religious scholars who had met with Genghis Khan, the young Taoist disciple Li Zhichang had benefited the most, lived the longest, and was destined to die in the cruelest manner. His sect had prospered after the meeting in Afghanistan and Li Zhichang had become an honored figure among the Taoists. He published a book on his discussions with Genghis Khan and, because of his intimate connection to the conqueror, he was revered by many younger Mongols.

In 1251, Mongke Khan placed Li Zhichang in charge of all Taoist institutions under Mongol rule and summoned him to Karakorum. Mongke Khan wanted to establish two things at once. He wished to appear loyal to the memory and laws of Genghis Khan, and inviting someone who had earlier worked with his grandfather would help toward that goal. At the same time, he sought to consolidate power over the various segments of his disjointed empire. Bringing Li Zhichang to his court was central to his effort to control religious groups in his newly centralized administration.

Although Karakorum was the capital of the Mongol Empire, when Li arrived it was little more than a steppe village of mud walls.

Preferring life in their *gers* out in the open land away from the town, none of the Mongol elite actually lived there. Karakorum was the servants' quarters, where they kept bureaucrats and artisans who worked for the court. The capital had a quarter for Chinese workers, a section for the Muslim markets, another for produce, and long warehouses filled with tribute and treasure. Despite its lack of monumental architecture or esthetic appeal, Karakorum, with its numerous houses of worship, was a living embodiment of Genghis Khan's policy of religious tolerance. The French envoy William of Rubruck arrived in Karakorum at about the same time as Li Zhichang, and he recorded seeing twelve religious buildings, including a church and two mosques. The city also had Taoist, Confucian, and Buddhist temples.

Despite the presence of these religious institutions and the fact that his mother was Christian, Mongke and his brothers relied on traditional shamans. The new khan and his court mostly lived within the felt walls of their *gers* out on the steppe, away from the city with its enclosed gods. Representatives of foreign religions who made their way to Karakorum from China, Europe, and the Muslim world frequently mocked the Mongol court for its dependence on these shamans and fortune-tellers.[1] "Their government of the people depends on divination," William wrote dismissively.[2] Mongke Khan told him "heaven gave us diviners, we do what they tell us, and we live in peace." William confirmed that whatever the shamans "say must be done is executed without delay." The shamans "predict lucky and unlucky days for the undertaking of all affairs; and so it is that they never assemble an army nor begin a war without their assent."[3]

Mongke Khan had so many shamans at his court that in 1253 he was compelled to organize them into two sections of healers and fortune-tellers. He appointed his favorite shaman, Aghucha, to oversee sacrifices. The shamans had many specializations: some were particularly good at controlling the weather, predicting the future, or conducting meat rituals and other ceremonies. William of Rubruck complained that Aghucha was the pope of the soothsayers whose *ger* was always "at about a stone's throw" from that of the Great Khan.[4] The shamans were much closer and had greater access than the assemblage of foreign monks, priests, and imams who made their way to the court.

Within the city of Karakorum, people of different faiths had no choice but to live together. This was deeply unfamiliar for the Christians, and William was not pleased to learn that he would have to live side by side with Orthodox priests from Georgia, Russia, Syria, Greece, and Armenia, and to practice Christian rites in compulsory harmony. They all claimed to worship the same God, yet none of the Christians seemed to like one another, and they had no experience of worshipping together in their home countries. For more than two hundred years the Orthodox Christians and Catholic Christians had waged nearly perpetual war against one another. Each had excommunicated the other and condemned their believers to hell. When the Catholics had not been able to defeat the Muslims in the Crusades, they had often turned their fury on the Orthodox, looting the churches and even the cathedral of Constantinople.

Contrary to Mongol court protocol, William had arrived from Europe with no gifts other than his own haughty claim that his branch of Christianity spoke for God. The Mongol Christians knew well that the first worshippers to acknowledge Jesus had been the three Magi from the East, making the Asian Christians the first followers of Jesus, not the Catholic Europeans. Furthermore, in their scriptures and rituals the Asian Christians used the same language that Jesus had spoken, unlike the Europeans who put his words into their own Latin tongue. Religious freedom, for all its vaunted good, seemed only to encourage members of different faiths to distrust their rivals all the more.

The shamans dominated the court, but the Taoists lorded over all other foreign religions. After Genghis Khan's meeting with the old sage in Afghanistan, the Taoists had enjoyed a special status. Toregene, Ogodei, and Sorkhokhtani had patronized Muslim, Christian, Taoist, and Buddhist institutions, but only the Taoists could claim that Genghis Khan himself had been their patron, and Li Zhichang was a living witness to that special bond.

In the thirty-odd years since Genghis Khan's death, the Taoists had become the wealthiest institution in the Mongol Empire—second only to the family of the Great Khan. Through Li Zhichang's leadership, they had sided closely with Ogodei's family. If Sorkhokhtani's sons wanted total power, they would have to break the Taoists in a highly visible way. To complete the revolution against Ogodei and his family, merely killing off the direct rivals was not enough. Mongke needed to destroy their network of allies outside the family as well. Li Zhichang would have to be eliminated. But his case required special handling as the rights he exercised came directly from Genghis Khan.

The fresh memory of the Mongol devastation of the Tangut and the constant Taoist assaults on Buddhist monks and monasteries within China had left the Mongol court with a strategic problem. Taoism was mostly a Chinese religion, but to conquer or forge an alliance with the several small kingdoms surrounding the Jin and Sung territories, Mongke would need to cultivate the support of the Buddhists. All the surrounding kingdoms were Buddhist: the Tibetans in the Himalayas, the Koreans, the Dali kingdom of modern Sichuan province, and farther south the Pagan of Burma and all the kingdoms of modern Vietnam, Laos, and Cambodia. If these kingdoms perceived the Mongols as anti-Buddhist, they might rally with the Sung emperor to overthrow them. To garner their support, or at least keep them neutral, the Mongols would have to appear to be pro-Buddhist. In addition to removing Li Zhichang personally, the extensive network of the Taoists throughout China would have to be broken if the Buddhists were to be mollified.

Mongke had another reason to favor the Buddhists over the Taoists: Buddhist monks were surprisingly skilled and highly innovative fighters. In 1232, during a battle in Korea, a Buddhist monk had shot an arrow and killed the Mongol commanding general. This was the first time that a monk had brought down a Mongol commander. The Korean monk, Kim Yunhu, admitted to only limited experience in warfare, stating perhaps too modestly, "at the time of the battle I was without bow and arrows."[5] That an untrained monk should bring down one of the mightiest Mongol leaders showed a powerful spirit that greatly impressed the Mongols. Regardless of whether the monk's success came from skill or from divine inspiration, it captured their attention. The elixirs of longevity offered by the Taoists paled before the martial skills of Buddhist monks who knew how to fight. The Mongols wanted them as allies, not enemies.

Unable to recruit the fighting monks from Korea to join him, Mongke Khan summoned Abbot Fuyu Zhanglao of the ancient Shaolin Monastery in the Chinese province of Henan to Karakorum to organize a branch of his martial arts monastery. Inviting both Li Zhichang and the abbot of Shaolin to the same small city was bound to trigger a confrontation, and that seems to have been precisely what Mongke intended.

The Buddhists could not claim a personal link to Genghis Khan— no famous Buddhist leader had ever met with him, and he had not granted any special privileges to Buddhism. But Buddhists had a patron god of fighting monks by the name of Vajrapani. Buddhists generally abstained from meat, but the monks of Shaolin not only permitted but insisted on the eating of meat, a belief in complete harmony with Mongol tradition. The monks justified eating meat based on an ancient story of how Vajrapani became their patron. One day, Vajrapani was said to have appeared to a Shaolin novice and asked, "Boy, do you wish to become strong?" When the youth answered in the affirmative, Vajrapani told him to eat meat.

"Monks are supposed to renounce meat," said the young man.

Vajrapani lifted a bowl of meat and "with his long knife" forced the meat on the monk, who refused to swallow it. When Vajrapani threatened to kill him with his thunderbolt club if he did not obey, the frightened monk gulped down the meat.

Suddenly, the boy flexed his muscles, "revealing his powerful sinews and bones. He looked practically like a god."[6] Vajrapani then taught him the sacred secrets of martial arts and thereby started a wholly new tradition of Buddhist martial arts experts devoted to defending their religion.

$$\maltese$$

Li Zhichang was unimpressed by Abbot Fuyu Zhanglao and his Shaolin monks. The Buddhists were fighting monks, but Li was a scholar. He had more confidence in the weapons of words than in the reputed skills of these newcomers. Until this time, Li's publishing career had helped him with each step of his advancement in the Mongol hierarchy. His book about meeting Genghis Khan had been the main source of his fame and prestige, but during the intervening decades it had faded in importance. He decided to write a new book. To counter the growing resentment against the Taoists, Li Zhichang published a vigorous scholarly defense of the superiority of his Taoist religion over all others, particularly over Buddhism. This proved to be a terrible tactical blunder.

His new book offered a reinterpretation of theological history going back to the beginnings of both Taoism and Buddhism. He had his disciples distribute copies of *The Scripture of Lao Tzu's Converting the Barbarians and Becoming Buddha*. He followed that book with *Diagrams of the Eighty-one Incarnations of Lao Tzu* to illustrate more clearly his startling claim that Buddhism was an offshoot of Taoism.[7] In his highly illustrated text, Li Zhichang identified Buddha as simply one of several western barbarians who had attained enlightenment, not on his own as claimed by his followers, but due to the teachings and work of Lao Tzu, who had been Buddha's teacher. Li depicted Buddhism as an imperfect copy of Taoism, the original and pure religion. The Buddhist monks from Shaolin were enraged by this blasphemy, and charged that fifty of the claimed eighty-one incarnations of Lao Tzu had been stolen from Buddhism and that in the entire series there was only one genuine incarnation, that of Lao Tzu himself.[8] To compare him with Buddha was like comparing a stag to a unicorn.[9] The war of words had begun.

Mongol authorities could not charge Li Zhichang or the Taoists with crimes committed at the time of Genghis Khan, because he had given his personal support to them. But the publication of this new book provided them with grounds for new charges. Li Zhichang's claim that one religion was superior to another directly contradicted the ecumenical teachings and laws of Genghis Khan, and this gave his enemies an excuse to charge him with violating that law.

Sensing weakness and seeing a way to minimize the relationship between Genghis Khan and the Taoists, the Buddhists attacked the Taoists' strongest claim to power: they began mocking Li's master, the old sage who had originally met with Genghis Khan in Afghanistan. The sage's disciples had piously claimed that the sage, who had died the same year as Genghis Khan, had ended life while in prayer, and that at the moment of his death "a strange perfume filled the room." The Buddhists countered that the Taoist master had died in the outhouse or toilet, where his bed had been moved because he had dysentery, which, despite allegedly being immortal, he had been unable to cure. They circulated a satirical poem playing on his name Eternal Spring and on Taoism's claim to be the *way* or the *current*.

> His body is but a bunch of dried bones.
> In one morning Everlasting Spring has turned to Autumn.
> In the midst of urine and covered with excrement he died in the
>   toilet.
> One Taoist current had become a double stream.[10]

Li Zhichang had hoped his new work would protect the privileges given to the Taoists, but instead he had fallen into a trap of his own making. Mongke Khan summoned him to prove the outrageous theological claims about Lao Tzu and Buddha in his new book. The enraged Buddhist monks demanded a public retraction of its lies, the destruction of all existing copies, and the transfer of Taoist properties to the Buddhists as compensation for his slander.

Unfortunately, although he was present in Karakorum at the time, Juvaini had little interest in the theological disputes of the Chinese. He was busy assisting his father with preparations for the new campaign in Central Asia, which sought to extend Mongol rule into the lands of the Nizari and on to Baghdad and Damascus. Juvaini seemed far more interested in the finances of the Mongol court and the transactions of the merchants at Karakorum than in the comings and goings of monks. In fact, no financial issue seemed too small to warrant his urgent and detailed attention; the monks were of interest to him only because they had been exempted from paying the taxes imposed on others.

Once Mongke Khan "had been firmly seated on the throne of the Khanate and his attention was no longer concerned with the case of the self-seeking and envious, he turned his mind towards the subjugation of the farthest East and West of the world," wrote Juvaini. In 1252 "he dispatched Khubilai to the Eastern parts" to continue the conquest of China, and he "proceeded to arrange and organize the affairs of his other brother Hulegu and charged him with the conquest of the Western parts" in Central Asia.[11]

Juvaini departed in the fall of 1253, but only a few months earlier another foreigner had arrived with a deep interest in the issues.

William of Rubruck reached Karakorum in the spring of 1253, and although these two great chroniclers of Mongolian history overlapped by nearly six months, we have no record of their having met or even having been aware of each other. In contrast to Juvaini, William not only witnessed the religious strife, he participated in it. He wrote that Mongke Khan had sent a message to the Christians, Muslims, Taoists, and Buddhists saying, "each of you says that his doctrine is the best, and his writings—that is books—the truest." The khan orders you to "meet together and make a comparison."[12] He had summoned them all to a great debate with clear rules: "This is the order of Mongke, and let no one dare say that the commandment of God differs from it," a Mongol official told the contestants. "No one shall dare wrangle or insult any other, or make any noise by which this business shall be interfered with, on penalty of his head." The monks listened in obedient silence.

Mongke Khan did not summon shamans to be a part of the debate because theirs was a religion of action, not of abstractions and ideas. As stated in a Mongol chant, theirs was "a religion without books, a religion not on paper, a religion without letters" that relies instead on "a scripture by drum and drumstick, a scripture kept by speaking."[13] The shamans claimed a direct connection to heaven and had no need to argue or debate. The debates would be only among the foreigners, the religions of the books. The shamans were mere spectators to this battle of the scriptures.

Prior to the formal debates, Mongke Khan gave the opposing scholars time to study, meditate, prepare their comments, and practice their arguments. The Mongol organizers assigned William of Rubruck to the Christians, but in their mock debate, he played the part of the Buddhist monk, arguing against Christianity. "We will suppose I belong to that sect, because they say that God is not, now prove that God is," he told his teammates. He knew that Manichaean thought had infiltrated Buddhist theology. "They all hold the heresy of the Manichaeans that one half of things is evil, and the other half good," he said, and believe that reincarnated souls "pass from one body to another."

The Mongols treated all of the competing sects as if they were one single religion. A Mongol official explained this carefully in a directive addressed to King Louis IX imploring him to treat fellow Christians equally, in accordance with the teachings of Genghis Khan. "The King of the Earth has decreed that in the law of God there be no difference between Latins and Greeks and Armenians and Nestorians and Jacobites, and all those that worship the cross. For all of them are as one to us. And this is what we require that the magnificent king not distinguish between them, but that his piety and clemency lord over all Christians."[14]

Much to the French envoy's disgust, when it came time to prepare for the debates, the competing Christian sects not only had to debate on the same team, they were lumped together with the Muslims so that there were only three competing factions: Taoists, Buddhists, and Christian-Muslims. No Confucians had been included. The rival teams had a hard time actually debating the issues or comparing beliefs because each team wanted to quote only from its own scriptures, which they believed sufficed as incontrovertible evidence. Reasoning only from their own premises, all three sides talked past one another.

֍

The debates began in the summer of 1254, the annual season of Naadam, the Mongol games. This year in addition to horse racing, archery, and wrestling—the three sports most loved by the Mongols—there would be theological debate, which would be more interesting to the foreign diplomats and envoys in the city. The real audience, however, was far beyond the Mongol capital. Mongke Khan intended that word of the debates would spread throughout his territories and beyond as an illustration of Mongol justice and religious tolerance, helping to win greater support from the Buddhist people throughout the Mongol Empire.

Unlike the other sports, which took place outdoors, the debates were scheduled in one of the newly erected palaces of the Great Khan. "The palace is like a church," wrote William of Rubruck, "with a middle nave, and two sides beyond two rows of pillars, and with three doors to the south. [The Great Khan] sits in a high place to the north, so that he can be seen by all; and two rows of steps go up to him: by one he who carries his cup goes up, and by the other he comes down." Nearby "stands his cup-bearer, and also envoys bearing presents; and he himself sits up there like a divinity." Men were seated on the western side and women on the eastern side. "To the south, beside the pillars on the right side, are rows of seats raised like a platform, on which his son and brothers sit. On the left side, it is arranged in like fashion, and there sit his wives and daughters. Only one woman sits up there beside him, though not so high as he."[15]

The rules of the debate largely followed the Mongol rules for wrestling. At the end of each round, a winner was declared, followed by a round of drinking *airag*. It was not long before the Christian-Muslim team was eliminated. They had not been serious contenders, but their initial presence made it appear that the debate was more robust rather than merely pitting the Taoists against the Buddhists.

The Buddhists emerged victorious from the first set of debates. To seal their victory, they brought criminal charges against the Taoists. These charges were sufficiently strong for Mongke Khan to order a judicial investigation. No sooner had the debate ended than the judicial inquiry began. The Taoists were now defendants, and the Buddhists were their accusers.

The primary charge was that of spreading false scripture, with additional charges of having destroyed Buddhist images and sacred objects, seized Buddhist property, and inflicted both material and spiritual damages on Buddhism.[16] Li Zhichang seemed not to appreciate the gravity of the situation. The Buddhists envied his privileged status, but the last two Great Khans and their officials had consistently stood beside him and protected him. He failed to grasp just how much things had changed, and he made little effort to construct a viable defense for his alleged crimes, other than to remind people repeatedly that Genghis Khan had given his sect special approval and had granted special rights to his order. When questioned about specific allegations that he and his followers had abused their power, confiscated Buddhist property, falsified documents, distributed false information, forced the conversion of Buddhist priests to Taoism, and abused their tax-exempt status, Li claimed to have no knowledge of any such wrongdoing.[17] If such things had occurred, others had done them without his cooperation or approval.

The Shaolin abbot challenged Li Zhichang on each of these points. How could Li Zhichang claim to be the head of his religion, he demanded to know, and not be cognizant of the wrongdoing of his subordinates? Either he knew and had approved of their wrongs, and was therefore also guilty of the crimes, or he did not know and was therefore guilty of dereliction of duty. In either case, he was clearly unqualified to serve the Great Khan. Unaccustomed to being publicly insulted by anyone, far less so in the presence of the khan, Li Zhichang suddenly grasped the danger he was in. He began to sweat heavily in the summer heat and turned red with frustration.[18] He had been thoroughly shamed before the court, and now he was about to face his first punishment.

On the twenty-ninth day of the ninth lunar month of 1255, an imperial edict from Mongke Khan decreed that all copies of Li's slanderous book had to be surrendered to the Buddhist lamas and that all destroyed or damaged Buddhist images must be replaced by new ones of equal value.[19] Having shamed the Taoists, Mongke's limited judgment did not completely resolve the issue of which religion would be dominant, and it did not satisfy the Buddhists. After this initial judicial inquiry, Mongke Khan decided that a full criminal trial under Mongol judges, like the ones he had conducted for members of his family, would not be convincing to the public. A Mongol trial might be interpreted as persecution of the Taoists, or even as an attack on Chinese culture. Mongke Khan sought to pit the Taoists against the Buddhists, such that each side would direct its animosity toward the other rather than toward their Mongol rulers.

Mongke Khan decided he could win Chinese public opinion more effectively if he organized a new round of open debates and let the religions rout one another. He would not be held accountable for putting a religious order on trial or disrespecting a faith esteemed by many Chinese. He could appear to support the Mongol policy of religious tolerance while the rivals wore one another down. As with any battle, whoever emerged victorious from this new round of debate would reveal the Will of Heaven and shape public opinion.

Thus far, the Buddhist side had been represented by the abbot of Shaolin, who practiced a type of Buddhism that was popular across northern China, Korea, and Japan. But Mongke wanted to build support in the southern regions and particularly in Tibet, which Ogodei's family had controlled until Mongke had snatched it away. The Tibetans practiced a more esoteric form of Tantric Buddhism, which was also popular in Bhutan and among many communities along the Silk Route. Following his strategy of sometimes forcing rivals to combine forces and work together, Mongke Khan chose Namo, a highly educated Buddhist lama from Kashmir, to work with the abbot of Shaolin.[20] Namo spoke fluent Mongolian, an advantage not shared by the abbot.

The Chinese were highly critical of this decision. One classical Chinese chronicle, *Zizhi Tongjian Gangmu*, revised and expanded to include the Yuan era, outlined the criticisms of Namo in a lengthy commentary. "The existence of a monarchy is founded on mutual duties, on those of a father to his son, of a sovereign to his subject, of a husband to his wife, of the young men to the old, and of friends to one another," it began. "As to this Namo, he was a stranger of low extraction . . . wandering about for a living, he could not fulfill the duties of supporting his father and mother. He shaved his head and opened his tunic, a proof that he did not know the duty a subject owes to his sovereign. Having a dispensation from being married he had no descendants; he knew not the duties either of a husband or a father. He sat on his heels; he did not therefore pay respect due to old age. He renounced society, and retired from the world; he did not therefore know the duties of friendship. He had none of the qualities therefore upon which a State is founded. He received the title of *Ho she,* but what could he teach? How could he be an example to others?"[21] The commentator concluded his assessment of Namo and the monks curtly, writing: "Brutes cling together."

༄

The next round of debate was scheduled for the seventh month of 1256, at the imperial camp south of Karakorum.[22] By taking the debate away from the Mongol capital, Mongke further distanced himself from its outcome. The debate had become a showdown, with the abbot of Shaolin leading the prosecution of the Taoist monks.[23] One Chinese religious scholar was pitted against another, with the Mongols as neutral bystanders. In fact, Mongke would not even be present at the event.

While Mongke was busy preparing for an invasion of southern China, his brother Hulegu had gathered up his army for a western campaign against Baghdad, the seat of the Muslim caliphate. As the outcome of the debates was now reasonably assured, Mongke Khan assigned control of the Mongolian homeland, left by tradition to the ruler's youngest brother, to Arik Boke, who would be staying behind while Mongke, Hulegu, and Khubilai left on campaign. All Arik Boke had to do was preside over the debate and then declare the Buddhist team the winner.

Arik Boke was the most traditional of the four brothers. He was a man of the steppe who loved the vigorous Mongol life in the open air. He showed little interest in theological dispute and was not happy to have to stay home and oversee squabbling monks while his brothers fought campaigns in distant lands. He saw himself as a warrior, not a referee. Under his control, the debates stalled while his brothers rode across Asia with their armies.

༄

Juvaini's writing was always vivid and colorful, but it came alive as he related the events he participated in during the campaign to destroy the Nizari sect in northern Persia. Not only was he present with Hulegu's army, he nursed an obsessive hatred of the Nizari. He describes the campaign in fascinating detail, offering up a quick history of the sect and relating the incredible conquest of the hitherto impregnable fortress of Alamut. He is open and honest about his hatred of the Nizari, despite their alliance with Genghis Khan.

After the seizure of Alamut, the Mongols began their usual thorough census of everything in it. As a scholar well versed in Persian and Arabic, Juvaini managed to get permission to take possession of the great library and archives, where books and records had been stored for generations. He "received and executed the command to examine what was deposited in their treasury and collected together in their library to order to extract therefrom whatever was worthy." He approached his assignment with great relish. "Now I was examining the library which they had gathered together over a period of many years, and from amongst the multitude of lying treatises and false teachings throughout their belief (which they had mingled with copies of the noble Koran and all manner of choice books, interweaving good and evil) was extracting whatever I found in the way of rare and precious volumes." From these records, he eagerly "copied whatever was to the point and suitable for insertion in this history, adducing whatever was confirmed and verified."[24]

Juvaini is the primary, and virtually exclusive, source for information on the history of the Nizari at Alamut and the interactions between Genghis Khan and Imam Hasan III. Historians sometimes alter the historical record to suit their own needs and beliefs, but rarely does one have the opportunity to completely destroy the evidence. In an indefensible crime for a scholar and a surprising moral lapse in one as talented as Juvaini, he destroyed much of the record.[25] It is not just barbarians who burn books: Juvaini burned many of the documents on the grounds that they contained heretical and blasphemous writings. He had strong political motivations to minimize the extent of the relationship between Genghis Khan and the imam, which appeared to be of considerable importance. Juvaini's destructive act only heightened the mystery.

Everything Juvaini chose to share with posterity pointed to the evil of the heretics whose defeat he celebrated. He quoted from the secret negotiations of the imam with the caliph, but made no mention of the alliance with Genghis Khan.[26] There were almost certainly records of the first meetings between the Nizari imam and Genghis Khan, and he certainly would have read them. But in his determination to minimize the relationship, he destroyed them all. He found the choice pieces and picked out what he wanted. Then, "As for the remaining books, which related to their heresy and error and were neither founded on tradition nor supported by reason, I burnt them all."[27] He almost seemed to be bragging. He portrayed the destruction of the Nizari sect and their library as great acts of God. "So was the world cleaned which had been polluted by their evil."[28]

ॐ

Hulegu captured the imam of the Nizari and brought him and his family to Mongolia, where they were executed. The imam's followers were killed and every effort was made to wipe out the sect. Having removed this obstacle, the Mongols were now ready to move on to Baghdad.

Unlike his brother's slow and frustrating campaign in China, Hulegu's campaign into the heart of the Muslim world was proceeding at a great pace. He had crossed territory that had been previously invaded by his grandfather as his army rode through Uzbekistan and across northern Persia. Now he would conquer new territories belonging to the Abbasid Caliph as a step toward his planned invasion of Syria and Egypt. Although some of the vassals conquered by Genghis Khan had broken away from Mongol rule in the intervening thirty years, none had completely recovered demographically, economically, or culturally. Hulegu was mostly reasserting Mongol rule over previously conquered lands. His primary target now was Baghdad, whose ruling caliph had maintained neutrality in Genghis Khan's war against Khwarizm and had been at least a tacit Mongol ally.

At this point, the caliph made a fatal mistake. Because the Mongols had not succeeded in taking Baghdad when Genghis Khan had invaded Central Asia, he did not believe that they could do so now. When Hulegu's armies threatened his degenerated but still luxurious capital city, the caliph, as head of the entire Muslim world, successor of the Prophet Muhammad and God's chosen representative on Earth, expected that hundreds of thousands of Muslims from all nations would rush to his defense. None came.

While the Mongols converged on Baghdad, the caliph raised only a small army with a Kurdish commander to defend him and the city. "The enemy has reached the gate, and we have but a few horsemen along with us in Baghdad, while the number of the infidels is 200,000," despaired the Kurdish general. He recommended that the caliph flee. "It will be well that the Lord of the Faithful should embark on board a vessel, and give directions for placing his treasures, and his family on ship-board; and we will likewise attend the Lord of the Faithful in the vessel." He urged him to hide in the islands near Basra "until such time as deliverance comes from Almighty God, and the infidels be vanquished."[29]

Moving like a firestorm across the land, Hulegu spread sheer psychological terror before the battle began. After crossing the Tigris River, his army dug a ditch and built a wall around the entire city of Baghdad, delivering a clear message that the inhabitants were trapped like birds in a net, with no escape. Then they slowly began assembling their siege engines and mighty weapons of attack while archers fired propaganda messages across the walls and into the city. Some of the arrows contained safe-conduct passes for all religious scholars and learned people of God, whether Muslim, Christian, or of any other faith.[30] The offer did not apply to the caliph.

The caliph had spent more on building palaces and collecting harem girls than on the military, but he nonetheless nourished the illusion that

"Allah has given us victory." He had neglected to pay his army, and many of them now deserted. An Arab poet decried his plight, living in a society where the "vizier is busy with his wealth," and "the chamberlain is at times intoxicated with drink and at times playing the harp and the lute." He complained that the caliph's heir was enticed by sex and "has in every direction a pimp and a prostitute." Baghdad was a city in which blasphemy was promoted as Islam, a city devoid of the just rule of law or a true religion.[31]

Unable to conceive that a pagan army could conquer the capital of the Muslim world, Baghdad's doomed defenders marched out of the city to prepare for the ultimate battle. Their first fatal mistake was to erect their military camp on low ground. The Mongols were masters of the unexpected and always optimized whatever advantage they could find over their enemies. Hulegu's engineers quickly diverted the river toward the low ground, so "floods of water poured down on them at midnight. And they began to flee from the waters, and their bows, and their arrows, and the sheaths of their swords were soaked with water." The men were defenseless.

The caliph offered the Mongols ample tribute—"money, precious stones, jewelry, brocade, fine clothes, gold and silver vases and other splendid objects"—and promised to make Hulegu a sultan if he would spare them.[32] He released some earlier Mongol envoys from the prison where he was holding them, dressed them in beautiful clothes, and gave them vast amounts of gold and a large number of Arabian horses before dispatching them to plead with the Mongols. He asked Hulegu to spare the lives "of his sons and daughters," and, in an effort to shift the blame to others, offered the sniveling excuse "that the things which had happened had taken place through evil counselors." If the Mongols agreed, the caliph promised that the Muslims "would become his slaves, and subjects who would pay tribute."[33]

Hulegu scoffed at the foreign title of *sultan*. Only the Mongol Great Khan had the right to grant titles, and only the Mongols had the full support of heaven. Hulegu's message to the caliph was crisp and unforgiving: "Unless the eyes of your soul have made you blind, look at what the sun and moon have done. Look at what the king of earth and time has given to Genghis Khan."[34] The Mongols captured the city and the caliph together with the caliph's sons. They "clasped iron fetters on him" and kept him in a tent for a week while Hulegu pondered the caliph's fate. Before sentencing his prisoner, Hulegu went "in person to the palace of the Caliph and had inspected the treasures, and the rich things, old and new, which were hidden away and laid up in stores, and he uncovered them all and brought them out."

Hulegu condemned the caliph and ordered his execution. Before stomping him to death under Mongol boots, his men sat the caliph on a felt or leather carpet and sewed it up around him like a sack, so that his blood would not touch the earth. The Muslims claimed that the Mongols feared shedding the blood of Muhammad's successor, but the truth was that they believed his blood was so evil it would pollute the earth and stain the light of day. Hulegu spared the caliph's daughters and youngest son, but he had the older sons executed in the same manner.

After forty days of looting, the dead filled the streets. The rains fell, bringing a pestilence to the city. So many flies hatched from the bodies of the dead that they filled the air and people could hardly breathe. The Mongols shattered the caliphate and established a new government made up of Christian and Jewish officials as well as Muslims of different sects, including Sunni, Shiite, and mystical Sufis, to rule Baghdad.

By the summer of 1258, word reached the Mongol court that Hulegu had taken the city of Baghdad and killed the caliph and his heirs. Once again, Juvaini took control of the city's archives and library. Books were of such high value in Mongol-ruled Baghdad that when food and money became scarce the survivors used them as currency.[35] Yet, despite their value, Juvaini destroyed what displeased him or contradicted the vision he wished to portray of history.

The destruction of Alamut and Baghdad, combined with the killing of the caliph and of the imam, made a mockery of Genghis Khan's edict of religious tolerance. Meanwhile, back home in Mongolia, yet another mortal blow was about to strike against religious freedom.

☫

While his brothers were out extending the empire, Arik Boke had been unable to settle the dispute between the Taoists and Buddhists. Finally, he convened the contending parties, but unaccustomed to playing an impartial role, he quickly made a mess of the debates. Rather than building confidence in the impartiality of Mongol rule, he strengthened the impression that the Mongols had no real religious sensibility.

The Buddhists appeared before Arik Boke and presented the severed head of a statue of the Buddha, charging that the Taoists had sawed it off. Arik Boke had one of the Taoist officials brought before him, and instead of questioning him in a calm manner, he became irate and screamed his questions, after which he suddenly began to beat the hapless monk with a whip to make him confess to the crime. It was not long before the khan grabbed the headless stone statue and began to pummel him with it. Arik Boke yelled in anger while the monk screamed in pain and blood gushed from his head.[36]

The chronicles do not identify the beaten Taoist monk, who was quickly taken away from court and died shortly thereafter. Only later was it revealed that the murdered monk was none other than Li Zhichang. His death presented a dilemma for all sides. The Taoists were shamed because, like his predecessors, Li Zhichang was believed to be immortal. The Buddhists, for their part, claimed that he had not died at all, but that this was merely a trick by the Taoists to avoid defeat in the debate.[37] To prove that Li Zhichang was indeed dead, Arik Boke had his body exhumed from the grave where his disciples had hurriedly buried him. After an impromptu autopsy, the Mongols declared that he had not died from wounds inflicted by a human. Just as the death of Teb Tengeri had been attributed to the anger of heaven, the official cause of death was now said to be a lightning strike. In Mongol eyes, this was the worst form of death, akin to a targeted execution from heaven. It portended badly for the Taoists.

Without their leader and in dire fear of the khan's wrath, the disheartened Taoists fell into confused disarray. They were too afraid to appear at the next scheduled debate. Rather than demonstrating the philosophical sophistication of the Mongol court, Arik Boke had reconfirmed the widespread suspicion that the Mongols were no more than savage barbarians who responded to every problem with violence. The Buddhists appeared to have won by brute force. The Mongol court sought to suppress the story of the debate's gory end and to refocus attention on the crimes of the Taoists rather than on the murder of their leader.

The debates could not be allowed to conclude on such a bloody basis. To sort out the mess and rectify the damage to the royal family's reputation, Mongke Khan, who was fighting in southern China and could not handle the situation personally, reassigned responsibility for resolving the debate from Arik Boke to his brother Khubilai, who had returned to his territories in northern China. Khubilai was the best educated of the brothers, but he had not distinguished himself on the battlefield with quite the glory of Mongke or Hulegu. He first sought a pause in the proceedings, then proposed a fresh start in a new location unstained by the prior fiasco.

Khubilai was determined not to be as hotheaded as his younger brother. He chose to move the debates out of Karakorum, where Arik Boke was in command, and south to his own capital at Shangdu (Xanadu) in Inner Mongolia. He designed the event to instill an aura of objectivity and thoughtful reflection, for he knew his reputation among the Chinese would depend on what ensued. The Christians and Muslims would not be invited; instead, Khubilai shrewdly asked the Confucians to join the carefully choreographed spectacle. Their inclusion signaled a new attitude toward Chinese tradition; by accepting the invitation, the Confucians, always the champions of the powerful, helped legitimize Mongol rule over the Chinese cultural and intellectual elite.

With three hundred Buddhists and two hundred Confucians united against two hundred Taoists, the outcome was certain, but this time every detail had to be precisely orchestrated. The abbot of Shaolin continued to lead the Buddhist delegation, and he chose seventeen monks as the primary speakers and leaders of his teams. Khubilai was careful to make sure that all the geographic areas, with as many major cities and monasteries as possible, were represented. In addition to the abbot, he brought in Namo from Kashmir, nineteen-year-old Phagspa from Tibet, who was destined to eventually become Khubilai's main lama, and others from Ordos, Yunnan, and oasis cities of the far west of China.[38] Given the presence of so many learned scholars, several accounts of the proceedings appeared, including *Debates Against Falsehood Held in the Chih-yüan Reign, Pien wei lu* (1264–84), published in 1291 by Hsiang-mai, another Chinese abbot who served as one of the seventeen leaders of the Buddhist team.[39]

In his opening speech, Khubilai explained that despite the condemnation and burning of Li Zhichang's theological works, many Taoists had not changed their minds or their inner feelings. He announced that the losing party would have to assume the lifestyle, food, and dress of the winning party, meaning that Taoists would have to shave their heads or Buddhists would have to grow their hair long. The newly joining Confucians seemed to be exempt from either of these degrading possibilities. Despite being grossly outnumbered, the Taoist monks believed that they were starting fresh and could defend the basic tenets of their religion. Hsiang-mai reported that they were eager to begin the fight and "danced with delight in their long blue skirts with richly embroidered sleeves."[40] Their delightful dancing did not last long as they debated point by point with the Buddhists, joined as ultimate arbiters by the Confucians.

The Taoists preferred to limit all discussion and evidence to the Chinese texts or Chinese translations of foreign scriptures. Khubilai ruled against them, asserting that the Chinese versions were only one among many great historic traditions. He admitted scriptures from any language as evidence in the contest. If the Taoists quoted Chinese emperors as authoritative sources, then kings of India could be quoted with equal authority. The Taoists, knowing only Chinese, had to confront the international assembly of Buddhist monks, who quoted texts from a variety of languages. Khubilai criticized the Taoists' ignorance of foreign languages. "Lao Tzu is only known here," he told them, "but Buddha's name is heard everywhere in the world. How can anyone be compared with Buddha?"[41]

The Buddhists and their Confucian allies easily refuted the disheartened Taoists in the final round of debates. The defeated Taoists were publicly humiliated for their alleged sins and crimes. Most of their books were banned and many of their scriptures burned in public bonfires. Their privileges were revoked, their monasteries seized, their monks expelled, and, perhaps most damaging of all, they would now have to begin paying taxes on commercial activities like any other business.

Khubilai was fighting a war of public relations while his two brothers continued to expand Mongol rule on the battlefield, with far different rates of success. While Baghdad was being looted, Mongke Khan pressed forward on his campaign into southern China. He fought a slow but steady campaign across Sichuan against the Sung army, which was technologically the most sophisticated on Earth, and probably the largest as well. Although their long confrontation cost the lives of a whole generation of Mongols and Chinese, neither side was willing to yield. In 1259, Mongke broke with the Mongol practice of fighting in the winter and decided to stay in the field through the summer. Mongols and their horses fared poorly in the summer heat; their bows became inefficient in the hot and humid south. Whether because of this or for some other reason, Mongke

Khan came down with a fever in midsummer and on August 11, 1259, he died, thirty-two years to the week after his grandfather had died on a similar campaign in China.

People who burn books can easily burn other people. Juvaini had become the censor and the propagandist for the Mongols and in 1259, Hulegu, in admiration for his devotion, appointed him governor of Baghdad. The scholar who wrote with such a passionate pen now turned into a conniving and power-hungry administrator. No trace remained of Genghis Khan's sense of justice or Shigi-Khutukhu's stern admonishment against using torture. Juvaini went so far as to have one of his opponents crucified inside a small portable cage in order to secure a full confession. An anonymous chronicler known as the Pseudo Ibn Fowati, who recorded daily events in Baghdad at this time, wrote that the interrogator slapped the accused man's face, "pummeled his head with a shoe and farted on him and peed in his face," all the while dragging the cage through the streets of Baghdad for people to see. His tongue was pierced with a metal rod so that "he could no longer make conversation," as retribution for his having mocked the authorities. Finally, "they cut off his head, they put a goat's head with a beard in its place, and again they rolled him around the town."[42] Other dissidents faced dismemberment, and one was anally raped in public before being flogged.

Many of those now living in foreign lands were no longer Mongols of a type that Genghis Khan would have recognized. They had become city dwellers. As the focus of the empire moved to distant cities such as Baghdad and Tabriz for Hulegu, or Khubilai Khan's new capital of Beijing, Mongols deserted the steppe. Karakorum reverted to pastureland, with goats and cows grazing where once ambassadors had trembled before the khan and wine had flowed from a giant silver fountain. Its temples, mosques, and churches crumbled into ruins and disappeared into the earth, buried beneath a new carpet of grass. The howling wind replaced the sound of chanting monks, the muezzin's call to prayer, and the singing of Christian hymns. The only prayers now came from the occasional pounding drum of a shaman, dancing and singing beneath the stars by the glow of the night fire.

The Muslim caliph was dead. The imam of the Nizari was dead. The Taoist Li Zhichang was dead. The books of Alamut had been burned. The books of Baghdad had been burned. The Taoist scriptures had been burned. The world empire that Genghis Khan had created was still expanding, but the spirit of his laws had been consumed in the flames of ignorance and intolerance.[43] Many of those who now praised him ignored his teaching. While honoring him, they forgot his words. While worshipping him, they broke his law. The Mongol Empire was now the empire of Genghis Khan in name only and already religious conflict was beginning to break it apart.

17

Life After Death

Genghis Khan built his empire with lightning speed, and it continued to expand until the death of his grandson Khubilai Khan in 1294. Then it began a prolonged period of decay, like a beached whale slowly rotting in the sun. Khubilai Khan, who united China and founded the Yuan dynasty in 1271, claimed to be the new Great Khan, whose empire extended to Russia and included everything between Korea and modern-day Turkey. Yet in truth he only controlled China and he had to struggle to keep a hold of his Mongolian homeland. He embraced a Confucian style of ancestor worship and honored his grandfather as the founder of the Yuan dynasty. In 1286, Khubilai assigned his grandson Kammala to administer Mongolia and build a temple on Burkhan Khaldun, and in 1292 he gave Kammala the new title of Jinong, or Golden Prince. Kammala assumed responsibility for the sacred area around Burkhan Khaldun and for control of the *Keshig*. He gathered the old *gers* of Genghis Khan's queens and made them into portable shrines. He also built a small brick and tile temple in the Chinese architectural style. He kept one thousand of the old guard, mostly Uriyankhai men, and instructed them to keep everyone out. The area became the official burial grounds for the Yuan emperors.

The Mongol territories in Central Asia fell into chaos as different Mongol clans and factions fought with one another. By the mid-fourteenth century, Mongol rule in Iraq and Iran withered. In 1368, the last Yuan emperor was overthrown by a rebel group led by a Buddhist monk, who formed the new Ming dynasty. Explanations for the Yuan dynasty's decline vary. Some attribute it to Chinese discontent at foreign rule, or exorbitant taxes, or a breakdown in social order, or floods and other natural catastrophes. But the truth is that a form of rot had penetrated deep into the soul of the imperial court and radiated throughout the country. The later Yuan emperors ignored the nation they were supposed to rule, consumed by political, religious, and sexual dramas inside the Forbidden City. One hundred and fifty-nine years after Genghis Khan had begun his invasion of China, his descendants returned to nomadic herding on the steppe, as if the century and a half had been a mere interlude. They went back to their old ways, but at night they told stories of their former greatness and dreamed that it might return.

Over time, Genghis Khan's influence began to surface in highly unexpected places. The Italian poet Dante Alighieri, best known for his *Divine Comedy*, completed in 1320, devoted an earlier masterpiece, *De Monarchia,* to the argument that all humanity was one and that mankind should thus have a single world ruler with power over religion. "The human race is most one when all are united together, a state which is manifestly impossible unless humanity as a whole becomes subject to one Prince, and consequently comes most into accordance with that divine intention," he wrote.[1] Dante struggled to bring forth a thoughtful critique of church power. He argued that the power of the ruler would come directly from heaven and not be dependent on intermediary religious leaders such as the pope. "The authority of Empire is not dependent upon the Church," he opined.[2] "The authority of the Empire derives from God directly."

In an era when the Christian church routinely tortured and executed its critics, to challenge the authority of the church was highly risky. Yet Dante prophesied the coming of a future world king who would banish evil and bring peace. This mysterious future conqueror bore marked similarity to the Mongol khans. He would be born "between two felts," and was referred to by the same term that his fellow Italian Marco Polo had used to designate the Great Khan of the Mongols—*Gran Cano*. Like Genghis Khan, this future Gran Cano would feed on "wisdom, love, and virtue."[3]

Dante was the first to publish a major work of literature in Italian rather than Latin, and his example inspired Geoffrey Chaucer to write in English. Chaucer, who lived farther away from the church in Rome, did not hesitate to name Genghis Khan and praise his religious laws. Chaucer lauded Genghis Khan as a hero, greater even than Alexander. Writing in *The Canterbury Tales* at the close of the fourteenth century, he proclaimed, apparently in a poorly veiled comparison with European kings of his era, that Genghis Khan was "hardy, wise, rich, pious and just to everyone."[4] He then went on to say that "as to the religion to which he was born, he kept his law to which he was sworn."

After the disintegration of the Mongol Empire, the steppe nomads once again dwelled in a closed and isolated homeland, where they continued to honor the mountains and rivers and to worship Father Sky and Mother Earth. Empires came and went, but the sun still rose each morning over Burkhan Khaldun. Flowers bloomed in the *khangai* and young people gathered strawberries, mushrooms, and cedar nuts, while the older ones sought out leaves and roots to make medicines and teas. In winter, snow covered the mountains and in summer, edelweiss. Life continued.

Through the centuries, the *Keshig* vigilantly guarded Genghis Khan's grave at Burkhan Khaldun. Though their role had diminished as the original members died, their sons and grandsons continued to patrol a vast area around the grave, as if Genghis Khan might return at any moment and wish to hunt in his forest again or graze his horses on the open pastures. Just as the Mongols believed that Genghis Khan's guards were reincarnated through their descendants, so too, they believed, was his horse. During earlier epochs on the steppe, mourners would sacrifice horses to honor the dead, but for Genghis Khan a new tradition was born. His favorite horse, with each new incarnation, could roam freely and was honored by everyone as the most holy horse in the world. When one horse finally died of old age, another horse matching his description, gait, and temperament was identified, and the nomad into whose herd the horse had chosen to be reborn was richly rewarded for this highest of honors.[5]

Although Ming emperors had ruled China ever since they expelled the Yuan Dynasty in 1368, the Mongols never officially surrendered and the descendents of Genghis Khan stubbornly claimed to be the legitimate emperors. At the end of the fifteenth century, Manduhai Khatun, Mongolia's greatest queen, decided to invade China. As her new second husband was still a young boy, she packed him up in a basket mounted on the side of a camel and headed off to war. To inspire her people and support her claim to be the heir to Genghis Khan, she removed his portable *gers* and a few relics and took them with her as she crossed the Gobi. When she returned, she reinstalled them in the Great Loop of the Yellow River, near the place where Genghis Khan had died fighting the Tangut. These *gers* and relics became the basis for the modern shrine, which can still be found exacty where Manduhai Khatun installed it. The area around the shrine became known as the Ordos, from the Mongolian *ordu*, or royal court.[6] Over the coming decades the Mongols under Queen Manduhai and her husband, Dayan Khan, managed to conquer large swaths of Inner Mongolia and parts of the Silk Route. She never really threatened China, but she succeeded in reestablishing control over parts of Genghis Khan's old trading network.

Custody of the shrine of Genghis Khan became a highly contested prize for any Mongol clan or foreign power who wanted to rule the area. One of the first foreigners to attempt to control the shrine was the fifth Dalai Lama. A large Tibetan entourage attended one of the shrine's main rituals in the tenth lunar month of the Black Dragon Year of 1652, when more than a thousand Mongol horsemen were present. As the Dalai Lama described in his autobiography, "when we arrived at Olan Bulag, I was received by the leader of the white palace tribe—the descendant of Chinggis Khan ordained by Heaven."[7]

The Buddhist dignitaries posthumously converted Genghis Khan from a Mongol animist into a Buddhist through an elaborate ritual that involved fastening his spirit to an invisible sacred string known as a *machig*. Genghis Khan and all of his companions and ministers were invited to sit "on the throne made of incomparable treasures, on the carpet decorated with eight lotus flowers,"[8] after which he was recognized as a reincarnation of the Bodhisattva Vajrapani, the patron of the martial monks of Shaolin. He acquired in the process a completely new genealogy, connecting him to the kings of Tibet and India.[9] The *White History*, a Mongolian chronicle, was the first to identify Genghis as an incarnation of Vajrapani, Lord of the Secret.[10] From that point on Genghis Khan could be worshipped either at the shrine or in a Buddhist temple as Vajrapani. To solidify his position within the Buddhist pantheon, Tibetan lamas, including the Dalai Lama and Panchen Lama, composed numerous sutras to him. These contained prayers and praises such as, "You are the best of 84,000 kings, who has the power like that of the universal king. You are the conqueror of the heretical enemies of Buddhism. We praise and prostrate to you, the all-powerful guardian deity."[11]

As the Mongols converted to Buddhism, they wrote new chronicles incorporating the life of Genghis Khan into Buddhist history and theology. "When I was born by the Buddha's decree," Genghis Khan was quoted as saying, "it transpired that I had a precious jade seal from the place of the dragons in my right hand. Now from the mighty deity Indra a jade cup full of holy liquor has been bestowed. Am I not the divinely destined Lord?"

New rituals were invented that Ghenghis had supposedly practiced

with his guardians in the *Keshig*. One such false ritual instructed worshippers to mix alcohol with the blood of a slain enemy, iron shavings
from a bar used to kill a person, flour, butter, milk, and black tea, and
to sprinkle the mixture or rub it onto a banner as a sacrifice. Participants
were instructed "to stir the enemy's white brain like sour milk, drink the
enemy's blood, utterly destroy the evil-doers."[12] Such descriptions were
pure fantasy of how life had been prior to the introduction of Buddhism,
but in time the identification of Genghis Khan with Vajrapani became
so close that blue, the color of Vajrapani, became the sacred color of
the Mongols.[13]

Others accepted Genghis Khan as a different deity, the ancient
Zoroastrian and Manichaean god Ahura Mazda, known in Mongolian as Khormusta. In one chronicle, Genghis Khan received his divine status when the god Khormusta offered him a sacred drink. In
another, he was simply the son of Khormusta.[14] As part of his deifica-
tion, the stories about him became more heroic and his shortcomings
less apparent. The poor boy in the *Secret History* who had managed
to fight his way to the top of the Mongol hierarchy thus became a
divine and holy agent sent to enact the Will of Heaven on Earth.

18

The Unfulfilled Law

As Europe progressed from the Renaissance toward the Enlightenment, consensus among intellectuals grew toward favoring some degree of religious tolerance, which mostly meant tolerance between Catholics and Protestants, and occasionally extended to Jews. Genghis Khan and the Mongol model were not mentioned in this context; no one seemed to have an interest in him. If Dante's views were truly inspired by Genghis Khan, that connection was lost on his audience, and the Mongols seemed to be fading from history.

The early Enlightenment philosophers who favored religious tolerance wrote logically, convincingly, and sometimes beautifully about ecumenism, pluralism, and freedom for all faiths, but none seemed to have any idea how to create a society or how to structure the laws to promote this. John Locke's proposals in The Fundamental Constitutions of Carolina of March 1, 1669, demonstrate this. Despite Edward Gibbon's claim that Locke had drawn his ideas from Genghis Khan, in fact Locke's proposed laws did far more to inhibit religious tolerance than to encourage it.

In a document of 120 clauses covering all aspects of civil

government, Locke devoted nearly a thousand words and fifteen clauses to the topic of religion.[1] While he generally affirmed the rights of all types of Christians, Jews, and "heathens" to worship, he saddled them with restrictions that severely limited these freedoms. He proposed that America should be governed by hereditary nobility and demanded that everyone participate actively in worship. "No man shall be permitted to be a freeman of Carolina, or to have any estate or habitation within it, that doth not acknowledge a God, and that God is publicly and solemnly to be worshipped," he wrote. Then he declared, in keeping with the English model, that the Church of England was "the only true and orthodox and the national religion." He concluded that taxpayers of all faiths must pay for the upkeep of its buildings and the salaries of its priests and officials. Locke offered no moral argument in his proposed constitution for religious freedom. Instead, he justified the decision to offer some limited freedoms to followers of other faiths by suggesting it was a clever way to convince them of the superiority of Christianity in the hopes of converting non-Christians. "Jews, heathens, and other dissenters from the purity of Christian religion may . . . be won over to embrace and unfeignedly receive the truth."

Locke proposed that members of one faith should be forbidden from criticizing or molesting others and that all should refrain from criticizing the government or its high officials. Any group that violates these rules "shall not be esteemed as churches, but unlawful meetings, and be punished as other riots." Finally, he strongly defended the rights of slaveholders of any faith to own slaves. "Every freeman of Carolina shall have absolute power and authority over his negro slaves, of what opinion or religion soever." Locke's law offered very limited religious freedom, and for only a few people.

Locke's inability to translate his lofty philosophical writings about liberty into simple laws was a general problem during the seventeenth century, and other political philosophers did little better. Despite the limitations of his model society, Locke received great praise from some philosophers looking for a blueprint for a new and more virtuous society. In his essay on religious toleration, Voltaire cited Tartary, as the Mongol lands were commonly called at that time, as an example of a society that had offered its people freedom of religion. Yet he held up Locke's writings as offering a path toward religious freedom in the West. Three pages after his comment on the Tartars, he lavished praise on the idea of tolerance in Locke's constitution. "Cast your eyes over the other hemisphere. Behold Carolina! Whose laws were framed by the wise Locke."[2]

✵

In the seventeenth century, nearly five hundred years after Genghis Khan founded the Mongol Empire, an unexpected voice emerged to reclaim his vision. The author of the first European book in centuries to be written about Genghis Khan was as unusual as her message. Anne de La Roche-Guilhem, who described Genghis Khan as "a lover of Virtue," was a French Protestant. Contrary to the barbaric images painted by his enemies, she wrote that the people of his time were "full of Respect and Esteem for his Virtue, which had rendered his name so famous in Asia."[3] At a time when few details about the life of Genghis Khan were known in the West, her book was a romantic fantasy with only a tenuous connection to the outlines of the khan's life. Nevertheless, for a reading public almost exclusively familiar with Christian tradition and stories from the classical civilizations of Rome and Greece, her book opened another world and presented a new heroic figure.

The author knew no Asian language and had spent her life primarily in France, the Netherlands, and England, but she knew religious persecution and found in her own suffering the inspiration to write *Zingis: A Tartarian History*. As a Huguenot, she had been forced to flee from her native France when Louis XIV had revoked the laws of tolerance instituted under Henry IV and outlawed her faith in 1685.[4] Suddenly, worshipping in the way she had been taught by her family became a crime punishable by death. She saw in Genghis Khan a model of the kind of visionary leader she felt to be so lacking in Europe, a striking contrast to the French king under whom she was born and whose language and culture she shared. When she wrote, "They look upon us still as Scythians; that is to say, People without Laws, without Gods, and without Religion," she could have been writing about her own country as well as the Mongols.[5]

In words close to those of Chaucer, she described Genghis Khan as "Chaste, Just, and Temperate; an excellent Husband, Father, Friend and Master, and a great General" who "was famous in Asia" for his inability to endure injustice, and "guilty of no Crime, but that of having too much merit." *Zingis* reintroduced Genghis Khan to a new generation, not as a wanton pillager of cities, but as a wise and virtuous lawmaker.

Anne de La Roche-Guilhem reclaimed the image of Genghis Khan and made him more famous than he had ever been in Europe. At a time when trade between Asia and Europe was becoming increasingly important, interest in Asian culture and history grew and she provided a focus for that budding interest. Her influence was to endure for a whole century as one literary, musical, and historic work after another focused on the mysterious Mongol khan. The subject of Genghis Khan, or Zingis, became a new fad, and thus de La Roche-Guilhem's book found its way into George Washington's library at Mount Vernon.

Her work inspired popular interest within a Europe just awakening to the outside world. In 1710 the French translator and scholar François Pétis de la Croix, using research done by his father, produced the first authoritative biography of Genghis Khan, *History of Genghizcan the Great, First Emperor of the Ancient Moguls and Tartars.* Drawing from original sources in Persian, Arabic, Turkish, and Hebrew, Pétis de la Croix carefully examined the life and laws of the Mongol khan using newly emerging historical techniques of objective scholarship. He considered in detail the laws of Genghis Khan and suggested to his readers that it was his laws that set him apart from other conquerors. His version of the Mongol laws began with the statement that "by the First Law it is ordained to believe that there is but one God the Creator of Heaven and Earth, who alone gives Life and Death, Riches and Poverty, who grants and denies whatsoever he pleases, and who has over all things an absolute Power."[6]

Among the educated classes, the predominant language of intellectual discourse and publishing was French, but Pétis's book was so interesting that it was translated into numerous languages. The writer Penelope Aubin translated it into English and published it in 1722, but English scholars often dismissed this French enthusiasm for Eastern ideas. One mocked de la Croix's biography, describing it as "one of the cabbage gardens to which manufacturers of histories have recourse for padding."[7] The Americans, largely immune to this condescension, believed that there were parallels and possibly even genetic ties between the Mongols and the native tribes of North America, who also embraced personal freedom and a spiritual openness that contrasted with the constricted heritage of European Christianity.[8]

卐

At the same time that Pétis de la Croix's book was being published in Paris, Genghis Khan reappeared, or at least a reincarnation of him appeared as the Mongol king of Tibet. Lhazang, the leader of the western Mongol tribe of Khoshud, claimed to be Genghis Khan reborn and tried to continue his work both as a conqueror and as a patron of all religions. With the backing of the Qing emperor, a succession of three khans descended from Genghis Khan's brother Khasar controlled a large swath of Inner Asia, from the border of Russian Siberia in the north to the borders of India and Bhutan in the south, including western Mongolia, the Uighur and Muslim regions of western China, and central Tibet. To emphasize their connection to the original Mongol Empire of Genghis Khan, the new khans revived old imperial titles such as "Dalai Khan, Ruler of All Within the

Sea," which had last been used by Genghis Khan's son Ogodei and grandson Guyuk. When the new Dalai Khan of the Khoshud died in 1701, his son Lhazang claimed his office with the title Genghis Khan.

To restore order in Tibet, Genghis Khan Lhazang led one army on Lhasa while his powerful wife Jerinrasi commanded the other.[9] Both were strong supporters of the Yellow Hat sect of the Dalai Lama. In an era when some monks led openly degenerate and worldly lives, the Yellow Hats preached a return to the most basic values of Tibetan Buddhism, with a strong emphasis on correct behavior, including celibacy for monks. Yet in the years prior to the invasion, the Yellow Hats, too, had become worldly and corrupt. In order to keep power in his own hands, the Tibetan regent had recently installed a teenage boy, Tsangyang Gyatso, or Ocean of Pure Melody, as the sixth Dalai Lama, assuming that because of his age he would be pliable and easily managed. It was a terrible choice. A sensual, handsome, and rebellious teenager, he loved sports, songs, and sex, accompanied by liberal amounts of alcohol, and had no interest in becoming a monk and giving up his carousing nights in Lhasa. He refused to become a lama and to have his beautiful long hair shaved.

After the Mongol victory, Queen Jerinrasi's army captured the Tibetan regent, who had been the real power in the country. She summoned him before her and, despite the pleas and lamentations of the lamas, had him executed on September 6, 1705.[10] The khan and his queen then purged other prominent lamas and officials, sending some into exile and executing others, while lavishing gifts on their supporters such as the Panchen Lama. The queen lived only a few more years, until her death in 1708. Lhazang was left as sole ruler of Tibet under sponsorship of the Manchu Qing emperor.

Although he showed no inclination to repeat the conquests of Genghis Khan, Lhazang wanted to revive the spirit of his namesake's cosmopolitan empire. He built his new capital in Lhasa and immediately revived the policies of free trade and free religion instituted by the original Genghis Khan. Under the rule of Genghis Khan Lhazang, Lhasa became one of the most open, cosmopolitan, and international centers in Asia. "The city of Lhasa," wrote a Christian priest living there at that time, "is densely populated by people born in this country and also by a great multitude of foreigners from various nations who engage in business there: Tartars, Chinese, Muscovites, Armenians, Kashmiris, Hindustanis, and Nepalis."[11]

Following the example of the original khan, Genghis Khan Lhazang opened his court and Tibet to people of various faiths: Christians, Muslims, and Hindus as well as the traditional Tibetan religion called Bon. He encouraged the foreigners to study and teach in the Buddhist schools and invited European priests of different Christian orders to live in Lhasa. The Mongols addressed all of these religious leaders by the title *Lama*. Europeans arrived from Italy, Portugal, Germany, and other countries to work and study. He allowed them to live and conduct daily Mass at Sera Monastery, where the Christians quickly learned the Tibetan language.

Enjoying protection and patronage from the Mongol ruler, the Christians in Tibet praised him profusely. "His own valor made Genghis Khan feared and respected by all, his own subjects as well as foreigners," wrote one. "In his character he was very good-humored and affable, acting friendly to all, readily granting audience and giving comfort, and of a very liberal temperament. He showed an unusual love for foreigners; the more distant their countries the greater was his kindness toward them, and the great kindness that I experienced from him moved me to admiration. His intelligence was sharp and quick."[12]

Despite the displays of affection by fawning foreigners, the Tibetans hated Lhazang. Just as his wife had killed their regent, he, in turn, killed the Dalai Lama. Genghis Khan Lhazang arrested the twenty-three-year-old sixth Dalai Lama and took him away, with the stated intention of turning him over to the Qing authorities in Beijing or perhaps letting him be reinstalled in a safer place in Mongolia. But neither of these things happened, and the young Dalai Lama mysteriously died, or disappeared from public, en route to his unknown destination. "The Grand Lama of Tibet until about 1707 was a very dissolute and wild young man," wrote an Italian member of the Jesuit order, Ippolito Desideri, from Lhasa. "His vices were all the more harmful to the people in that they were exhibited by the highest dignitary so greatly reverenced by the Tibetans. Since Genghis Khan was unable to remedy the evil caused to his kingdom by the licentiousness of its chief lama and pastor either through admonition or threats, he decided to resolve the situation with the lama's death. After first informing the Chinese emperor, he used the pretext of sending the lama to China with a large escort of the king's own Tartars and had the lama beheaded en route."[13]

Thus passed the sixth Dalai Lama, the Ocean of Melody, a martyr to life, love, and poetry.

Not everyone accepted the Christian priest's account of the lama's end. Some Mongols believed that he had escaped to the safety of Mongolia, where he lived a long life, founded a new monastery, and has been successfully reincarnated since then. Tibetans claimed that his soul had escaped back to Tibet, where he was secretly reborn. Lhazang chose a new seventh Dalai Lama, who some believed was actually his own son, and with the backing of the Qing emperor he decreed that anyone who refused to recognize the new Dalai Lama would be put to death.[14] With central Tibet subdued and order maintained, he pushed into the surrounding areas, but his Mongol-Tibetan army was defeated by strong resistance from the soldiers defending Bhutan in 1714. Convinced that his territory had reached its maximum extent, he concentrated on developing Tibet.

The Christians were very active in Tibet under Lhazang. Francesco Orazio Olivieri della Penna, a Capuchin missionary from central Italy, compiled a Tibetan dictionary and translated Tibetan works into Latin while Lama Giovacchino practiced Western medicine in the community. The most productive of the Christian scholars in eighteenth-century Tibet was Ippolito Desideri, who presented the Mongol ruler with a book he wrote as a set of dialogues, like those of Plato, but in Tibetan under the title *Daybreak: The Sign of the Dawn That Dispels Darkness*.[15] His purpose was to promote Christianity by undermining Genghis Khan Lhazang's claim that each religion, in its purest form, leads people toward the goal of goodness. Desideri plainly stated his intention "to demonstrate the falsity of the maxim current among the unbelievers that everyone can be saved through his own religious law and to establish this more important truth, that there is only one law that leads to Heaven and eternal salvation."[16]

"By the end of December 1716, I finished the book with God's help, had a copy made in a good hand and put into order, with its dedication to the king," wrote Desideri. He presented the book on a symbolically important day, January 6, 1717—the day Catholics celebrated the Feast of the Epiphany, when the three Magi of Asia arrived bearing gifts to the infant Jesus in Bethlehem. The Mongols had often been associated in Western belief with descendants of one of the three wise men. Because the three Magi had accepted Christianity, Desideri hoped that on this occasion Genghis Khan Lhazang might also.

Genghis Khan Lhazang accepted the book from the Christian lama in the presence of a large congregation of Buddhist lamas and began reading it aloud to them in Tibetan. He found the Christian's writing in the Tibetan language to be awkward and difficult to follow, so he handed the book to an assistant to continue reading aloud.[17] "Having listened attentively for some time, the king took back the book and said to me that there were several principles in it that were contrary to those of their sect but that nevertheless appeared to him to be most just and worthy of serious and thorough discussion. . . . As he had a quick and penetrating intellect, he advanced various difficulties and objections against . . . these points," explained Desideri. "He continued on in this way for quite a while without a single digression until noon, when, very happy and satisfied, he turned to the entire audience and praised me more profusely. Then, turning all of his attention toward me, he said that he was very pleased with the gift of the book I had offered him that day, which he valued and highly esteemed. He added that he had not been able to finish reading it now, but when he had more leisure he would give it careful consideration, that he also wanted some of the more eminent and intelligent lamas to read and examine it, and after thus hearing their opinions, he would let me know at his convenience the outcome and which religion he judged the more efficacious." In other words, Genghis Khan Lhazang did not like the book in the least.

After careful examination of the text, the khan "decided to hold a debate, with myself on the one side and the lamas and doctors of religion of that country and its universities on the other. He understood the gravity of this matter quite well and did not want me to be caught off guard without knowing what weapons my adversaries might use against me. Therefore he did not wish me to go into battle immediately but to do what I could in the meantime to educate myself thoroughly in the principles and books of that sect, to read their most exemplary authors, and to familiarize myself with their methods of dialectic and argumentation. . . . [H]e wanted me to spend some time in certain of their universities attending the lectures and debates that were frequently held there. To that end he ordered that I be given free access to enter and stay at any monastery or university in the country."[18]

Before he completed his studies and the debates could be organized, the Dzungar, a rival group of Western Mongols, invaded Tibet. Most Tibetans sided with the invaders because of their animosity toward Genghis Khan Lhazang and their horror at his treatment of the Dalai Lama. "These were the first sparks that, after years of drawn-out and hidden plots, ignited the blaze that took the king's life and his kingdom,"[19] wrote Desideri. "The king was cruelly murdered, his family and most of his faithful ministers killed, and Lhasa, the capital, sacked, stunned, and in mourning."[20]

To restore order the Qing officials began to close off Tibet. After the fall of Genghis Khan Lhazang, foreigners began to leave, but they took with them new information on this hitherto little-known land. Their writings introduced the wonders of Tibetan civilization to the outside world, including the concept of Shambala, the mystical land of the far north, which became better known as Shangri-la in the West.

"The native tongue is Tibetan, but the people also speak Tartar and Chinese; they are of an elevated intellect," wrote Francesco Orazio della Penna, sometimes known as the "white haired lama."[21] Although the Christian priests spoke Tibetan and not Mongolian, in their writing they used the more familiar Mongolian names when describing the country. "The name of *Thibet* is foreign in the country itself. It is employed only by the Mongols and Mahomedan tribes of Asia; it appears to be of Turkish origin."[22] They identified the head of the Yellow Hat sect using his Mongolian title of *Dalai*, rather than his Tibetan name Gyatso, and thereafter this line of monks became known internationally as the Dalai Lamas of Tibet.

᠌

In the 1700s, a majority of people in Europe and America were illiterate, but this did not prevent a growing fascination with Genghis Khan and other Eastern potentates. Playwrights brought his conquests to the stage in a number of works. In Italy the opera *Genghis Khan, Emperor of the Mongol Tartars* debuted in 1741,[23] and three years later an English ship was christened the *Zingis Cham*.[24]

The theater proved a perfect medium in which to portray the life of Genghis Khan. Under Mongol rule in China, drama had reached an unprecedented pinnacle. Educated Chinese scholars scorned such common entertainments, but the people enjoyed plays and patronized them as an art. One important work from that era was *The Great Revenge of the Orphan of Zhao* by Ji Junxiang, a dramatic play with music and song. In 1735, Jesuit missionary Joseph Henri de Prémare translated the play into French; *L'Orphelin de la Maison de Tchao* was the first Chinese play published in a European language. Voltaire appropriated it, substituted a love story for the theme of revenge, changed the main character into Genghis Khan, and published it as *L'Orphelin de la Chine* in 1753. His version appeared onstage in the summer of 1755 at the Théâtre Français in Paris.[25]

Unlike the laudatory works of Pétis de la Croix and Anne de La Roche-Guilhem, who praised Genghis Khan, Voltaire described him as a "cruel tyrant King of Kings" who turned Asia into a vast sepulchre. He piled insults and abuse upon Genghis Khan, saying that he "comes in blood, the world at his command." Voltaire's words derided the religion of Genghis Khan as nothing more than the worship of the barbarian god of nature, "untaught and unimproved" by education or civilization.

Voltaire portrayed an aging Genghis Khan as deeply disappointed by his conquests, convinced they had produced little moral benefit for him or his subjects. "Are these my promised joys? Is this the fruit of all my labors? Where's the liberty, the rest I hoped for? I but feel the weight without the joys of power. . . . I am distracted with a thousand cares, dangers, and plots, and foes on every side; intruding rivals, and a wayward people, oppress me; when I was a poor unknown I was more happy."[26] Voltaire dramatized Genghis Khan's practical approach to the value of religion. "At length, my friends," he has Genghis Khan tell his circle of intimates, "it is time to sheathe the sword, and let the vanquished breathe; I've spread destruction and terror through the land, but I will give the nation peace. . . . Henceforth we will not raze their boasted works, their monuments of art, their sacred laws; for sacred they esteem the musty rolls, which superstition taught their ancestors to worship." Religion in this account serves an important but largely unrecognized role in that it "employs the people, and may make them more obedient."[27]

The play caused such a sensation that in addition to performances, public readings were held. One famous painting shows such a reading by the actor known as Lekain in the salon of Marie Thérèse Rodet Geoffrin. The painting, *Lecture de la tragédie de "l'orphelin de la Chine" de Voltaire dans le salon de madame Geoffrin*, represents more than fifty of the greatest intellectuals and luminaries of the era, including Jean-Jacques Rousseau, Denis Diderot, the Baron de Montesquieu, Étienne, Bonnot de Condillac, Claude-Adrien Helvétius, and the Comte de Buffon, Georges-Louis Leclerc, listening attentively to the story about Genghis Khan.[28]

The play was a spectacular critical and commercial success in Paris, and it immediately inspired several imitations in England. Various English versions were made, the most successful of which was by the Irish playwright Arthur Murphy, who produced his own adaptation of *The Orphan of China,* closer to the original Yuan drama. With strong backing from Robert Walpole, the first prime minister of Great Britain, the play opened at London's Drury Lane Theatre in April 1759. The occasion was important enough for the British poet laureate, William Whitehead, to compose a poem as a prelude to be delivered before each performance. The play was presented as an attempt to widen its audience's cultural scope beyond tired classical themes. As Whitehead declared in the opening lines of his prelude:

> Enough of Greece and Rome! The exhausted store
> Of either nation now can charm no more.[29]

Recognizing the high position of women in Mongol society, Murphy restored their importance in his play, unlike Voltaire, who reduced his Mongol princesses and queens to emotionally fickle characters longing for love.[30] Murphy substituted action for emotion. He criticized Genghis Khan's barbarous laws and his unwillingness or inability to embrace Confucian thought.

Writing in the *Critical Review* a month after the play opened, Oliver Goldsmith, one of the most respected literary figures of the era, observed: "The first night the whole house seemed pleased, highly and justly pleased."[31] In June 1759, only two months after the play opened, a critic for *The Monthly Review* wrote: "Every one has, by this time, seen or read" *The Orphan of China,* "and most have applauded it."[32] The following year the play opened in two theaters simultaneously in Dublin.

Other, more positive dramas about Genghis Khan quickly appeared. The most successful of these debuted on the London stage in the winter of 1768–69, written by Scottish playwright Alexander Dow, who had served as a British army officer in India and learned about the Mongols from Persian and Moghul sources. An advertisement for the play declared that it was intended for "those who are not conversant in the history of the Asiatic nations." For many people whose worldview was limited, discovering the Mongol leader and his history was eye-opening. "Zingis Chan, whether we regard him as conqueror or legislator, was, perhaps, the greatest prince that ever appeared in history," declared an explanatory note. "He not only secured the empire of all Asia to his posterity for some ages, but even to this day, two thirds of that immense continent remains in the possession of princes of the blood. . . . The Emperor of China, the Mogul of India, the great Chan of Tartary, and the princes of Krim Tatars, derive their blood from Zingis; and it is remarkable, that at one period, there were five hundred crowned heads of his race in Asia."[33] Another reviewer writing in the *London Chronicle* on January 7, 1769, echoed this praise: "The character of Zingis is entirely new and magnificent; inflexible and determined in his resolutions, through policy, but at the same time generous and noble."

Not everyone embraced Genghis Khan as a virtuous lawgiver; many continued to portray him as a ruthless barbarian tyrant. In an ironic epilogue, the narrator at the end of the play objected to the chosen subject matter of an Asian conqueror over the classical European heroes. "Will you, ye Criticks, give up Rome and Greece?" he asked. "I hate the Tartars,—hate their vile religion," because "they have no souls." He gave a resounding declaration, "Greeks and Romans for me!"[34]

Largely the audience delighted in the play, but not everyone shared this enthusiasm. One reviewer found the subject matter dreary and boring. "Some speeches in this tragedy are very well written, and the play on the whole cannot fairly be called a bad one," he wrote. He then complained that the play's author was "peculiarly unfortunate in his choice of the subject—one feels no interest in the transactions of the Tartars, and one is disgusted at the introduction of so many barbarous names."[35]

Around 1783, Italian poet and playwright Giovanni Battista Casti wrote *Gengis Cano* or *Il Poema Tartaro*, an epic of 408 stanzas that made the Mongols appear superior to the European rulers. His work seemed to be sympathetic to the recent revolutions in America and France.[36] Casti submitted his poem to the Holy Roman Emperor Josef II in Vienna for permission to be published, but angered by the liberal sentiments attributed to Genghis Khan, the emperor publicly rebuked the author soon thereafter and suggested that he leave the country.[37] He took the hint and left.

A few years later Antonio Salieri, an Italian composer and rival of Wolfgang Amadeus Mozart at the Hapsburg court in Vienna, collaborated with Casti to produce an opera of similar sentiments, shifting the hero from Genghis Khan to his grandson Khubilai Khan. Salieri completed the music for *Cublai gran kan de' Tatari* on the eve of the French Revolution, which soon gave way to tyranny and terror. The opera portrayed the corruption at the Russian court, which mirrored the Hapsburg court, and was thus considered too dangerous to stage. Two hundred and twenty years later in 1998, the liberal opera finally debuted at the Mainfranken Theater in Würzburg, Germany.

Some of those newly interested in Genghis Khan were practicing Christians, but his popularity was greatest among those, like Voltaire and Alexander Dow, who considered themselves adherents of no particular religion. Many enlightened scholars appreciated the spiritual values of Christianity and other religions while rejecting the authority of the church. They valued reason over ritual, thought over belief. This type of spirituality without a church became known as Deism. Although new in the West, it was recognized by some as akin to Eastern thought, and specifically to the belief system of shamans or steppe nomads. As Charles Mills, a nineteenth-century English historian and follower of Edward Gibbon, put it, "the religion of Zingis was the purest deism, yet the Christians, the Jews, the Muhammedans, and the Idolaters, preached and prayed in undisturbed security; and exemption from taxes and war distinguished the Rabbi, the Imam, and the priest."[38] Genghis Khan became a counterpoint role model to the Christian rulers of Europe, and was embraced by some of the newer religious sects who rejected the many rules of established religions and stressed the importance of humanity in the quest for justice and harmony.

Although the revival of interest in Genghis Khan in the West began with seventeenth-century French scholars, his legacy had its greatest impact in eighteenth-century North America, as colonial leaders chafed under the authority of a distant king. In their struggle to achieve independence, American rebels sought historic models outside the confines of European experience. During the eighteenth century, colonial merchants from Charleston to Boston sold books on the Mongol leader. Benjamin Franklin, a connoisseur of French culture and a freethinking Deist, did much to popularize Pétis de la Croix's biography by printing advertisements for it in his newspaper and selling it by mail order from Philadelphia for delivery throughout the colonies.

Eighteenth-century American scholars, without a true intellectual history of their own, searched eagerly for models of moral government and justice beyond the pool of Western European experience. In the quest for alternate concepts, they read widely about the history of Asian leaders. Benjamin Franklin was in London during the debut of Murphy's play, and he not only acquired a copy for his library but also bought copies of the vituperative "celebrity feud" correspondence between Murphy and Voltaire over who deserved credit for the play.[39]

In March 1764, *The Orphan of China* opened in America at the

New Theatre on Queen Street in Charleston, South Carolina,[40] followed by openings at the Southwark Theater in Philadelphia in 1767 and in New York at the John Street Theater the following year.[41] In 1779, the play was revived using British soldiers as actors during their occupation of New York at the height of the American Revolution. It was performed in 1789 in the newly selected capital of Philadelphia and continued to be popular for another fifty years.[42]

Thomas Jefferson was one of many intellectuals to embrace the new popular interest in Chinese subjects. In a letter dated August 3, 1771, to his brother-in-law Robert Skipwith, he skipped over both the Murphy and Voltaire plays about Genghis Khan and recommended that he read the original Yuan dynasty version, then available only in a French translation.[43] Jefferson was deeply influenced by Pétis de la Croix's biography of Genghis Khan. He too perceived some good in all religions but not enough in any one of them. Earlier, he had bought several copies of the Genghis Khan biography in the original French language; he kept some for himself and offered others as gifts, including one to his daughter.[44] One of these copies joined the first books to enter the United States Library of Congress. After the British burned the new capital city of Washington in the War of 1812 and destroyed the three thousand volumes of the congressional library, Jefferson offered his library for sale to form a new Library of Congress. Some congressmen sought to prevent the acquisition of his collection of "irreligious and immoral books, works of the French philosophers, promoting infidel philosophy" written "in languages which many cannot read, and most ought not."[45] When Jefferson refused to remove any of the books from the collection, one member of the congressional library committee proposed that the offending books be identified and suggested "these books should be burnt by the committee."

Thomas Jefferson supported the idea of religious freedom and tolerance long before he encountered the laws of Genghis Khan. The idea of tolerance was embraced at the time by various circles of political and philosophical thought. What all of these thinkers lacked, however, was a simple, concrete example of how to implement religious freedom. As inevitable as the American principle of religious freedom seems to us now, it was the fruit of a long intellectual and moral and political struggle. The philosophers agreed it was a laudable goal, but had any society ever succeeded in making this idea into a reality? Genghis Khan's law provided the model for an age searching to find just such an example.

Pétis de la Croix's biography highlighted Genghis Khan's religious tolerance. "Far from ordaining any punishment or persecution against those who were not his sect," he wrote, he had clearly forbidden anyone "to disturb or molest any person on account of religion, and desired that everyone should be left at liberty to profess that which pleased him best."[46] The elegance and simplicity of this statement attracted Jefferson's attention.

Jefferson began writing his law of religious freedom in 1777, but it took nearly a decade to find the right wording before the Virginia General Assembly enacted it on January 16, 1786. His proposal was hotly debated, edited, and amended, but the final key words were close to those first attributed to Genghis Khan's edict. Jefferson's new law prescribed "That no man shall . . . suffer on account of his religious opinions or belief; but that all men shall be free to profess . . . their opinions in matters of religion."[47] These words had made their way from Central Asia to the United States, translated from Mongolian into Persian, then Turkish, French, and finally English. Though they may not have been Genghis Khan's original words, they perfectly embodied the spirit of his inclusive and expansive quest for God.

In an undated memo preserved in the Library of Congress, Jefferson requested that only three of his achievements be engraved on his tombstone. These are the things, he wrote, for which "I wish most to be remembered." He listed them as "Author of the Declaration of American Independence, of the Statute of Virginia for religious freedom & Father of the University of Virginia."

As first enacted in Virginia, Jefferson's law applied only to that state, but it was later incorporated into the United States Constitution as the First Amendment. Over the years, it has made its way into the constitutions and laws of most countries. From Genghis Khan through Juvaini, Rashid al-Din, Bar Hebraeus, Chaucer, La Roche-Guilhem, Pétis de la Croix, to Thomas Jefferson and the world, the concept of religious freedom as a fundamental national principle has survived.[48] Whether citizens today, in an increasingly globalized world marked by a rise in both religious pluralism and religious fundamentalism, can uphold and honor the spirit of this law is the next chapter in our history, one that we all continue to write.

Epilogue: The Thunderbolt of God

After writing their history, we have recorded some-
thing of what is found in their books regarding their
beliefs and religion; which we offer as a matter of
astonishment and not as truth and certainty.

~*Ata-Malik Juvaini,* The History of the World-Conqueror,
Baghdad, thirteenth century

Myths can be more inspiring than truth, particularly during times of crisis. When old systems of thought prove to be inadequate, some people will embrace ideas that in more stable times would appear totally irrational. The more improbable a story, the easier it suddenly is to believe. Amid the warring ideologies and violent religious movements of the twentieth century, Genghis Khan offered a unique appeal to some who favored peace, as well as to others who did not.

In 1921, thirty-five-year-old Roman Nikolai Maximilian von Ungern-Sternberg, commonly known as the Mad Baron, arrived in Mongolia from Siberia with an anti-Bolshevik cavalry of 1,500 Cossacks, Russians, Tibetans, Mongols, and a few Japanese and Chinese riding under the banner of a yellow swastika. A self-proclaimed

Buddhist descendant of Attila the Hun and reincarnation of Genghis Khan, he had supported the restoration of Czar Nicholas II to the Russian throne and, when the czar and his family had been executed, he had imagined that he could bring about a new golden age from Mongolia, in which the emperor of Japan would be the new world ruler and the Panchen Lama of Tibet the new spiritual leader. Dressed in a red silk jacket and blue pants and filled with an inexhaustible nervous energy, he dashed around the capital of Urga in his chauffeured Fiat, chain-smoking cigarettes, handing out death sentences, ordering people to pick up trash, and shooting any dog found eating a human corpse. He ruled Mongolia for one hundred days, until the Red Army seized him and executed him by firing squad.

The horrors of Mongolia titillated and repulsed people in equal measure, and excited the imagination of some who were eager to enter this bizarre world of living gods, mad revolutionaries, and hills littered with dragon bones, as dinosaur fossils were called. The 1920s witnessed two major expeditions sponsored from New York to the Gobi Desert. The American Museum of Natural History, with financial backing from J. P. Morgan and John D. Rockefeller, among others, sponsored Roy Chapman Andrews on his search for fossils of the first humans, which he figured must have evolved in Mongolia, the "Scientific Garden of Eden." Andrews did not find the origins of humanity, but he did unearth an unrivaled collection of dinosaur fossils and their previously unknown eggs.

Ten years later, a British writer, James Hilton, introduced the world to a mythical land named Shambala, or Shangri-la, through his bestselling novel *Lost Horizon*. Inspired by Hilton's novel, some mystics began to see Mongolia as the spiritual center of the universe and suggested that Shangri-la would soon emerge from under the ground somewhere in its hills. No one seemed certain exactly where in Mongolia this mythic land would be found, but the search for Shangri-la found some unexpected adherents.

At the height of the global economic depression between the two world wars, the United States surreptitiously embarked on a quest to find the secrets of Genghis Khan. American officials funded the search to locate the sacred Chandman jewels of Buddhism, one of which was said to have been in the hand of Genghis Khan at his birth, and to discover the entrance to the underground world of Shambala or Shangri-la.

Between 1934 and 1936, President Franklin D. Roosevelt's secretary of agriculture Henry Wallace quietly provided government money for his controversial guru, the Russian artist Nicholas Roerich, who claimed to be a reincarnation of the fifth Dalai Lama. With Wallace's backing, Roerich planned to find Shambala and to unearth the wish-granting jewel that Genghis Khan had, according to Buddhist chronicles, clutched at birth. The two men called their project "The Sacred Union of the East." Aware that their quest might seem quixotic and be resented by taxpayers at a time of debilitating national poverty, they code-named the project "Kansas," a nod to a popular American story about a girl from Kansas who set off in search of the mysterious Wizard of Oz.[1] Under the official guise of seeking drought-resistant grasses to transplant in the Dust Bowl of the American Midwest, Roerich went to search for the stone and Shambala as part of his goal to initiate the new World Order of Peace by 1936.

Equipped for the expedition by Abercrombie & Fitch and accompanied by a ragtag militia of White Russians with weapons supplied by the U.S. Department of War, Roerich set out across Inner Asia in a camel caravan. Despite reputed links to Japanese imperial spies, the group traveled beneath the Stars and Stripes "fastened to a Mongolian spear," which they called the Spear of Salvation.[2] Roerich hoped that by finding the stone he would miraculously solve all the world's woes, create peace and cooperation with the Soviets in Russia, the imperialists of Japan, the Nazis in Germany, Buddhists in Tibet, Communists in Mongolia, the capitalists in America, and everyone else at war over ideas, ideology, or religion. He believed that through this work he could persuade "the summits of Asia and the heights of America to clasp hands."

Some mysterious power seemed to be working in Wallace's favor as

Franklin Roosevelt chose him as his vice president in the election of 1940. With the authority of his new office, Vice President Wallace, who labeled himself "a *practical* mystic,"[3] became the first high-ranking American official to visit Mongolia and look for the shrine of Genghis Khan. As World War II was still being fought in the summer of 1944, Wallace flew secretly from Alaska to Siberia and then made a series of airplane hops to Lanzhou, deep inside Nationalist China.

With the help of a Chinese warlord, monks from a Buddhist monastery seized the shrine of Genghis Khan and temporarily incorporated it into their worship while protecting it from the Japanese army.[4] Wallace made a long trek to the monastery to visit the shrine.

Mongols believed that anyone who sought divine power needed to go to the shrine of Genghis Khan and pray for it. Over time, many Mongol khans and queens had come to the shrine seeking the blessing of Genghis Khan. Some had their wishes granted by the unseen spirit of the shrine, but many came away with nothing. A few were actually mysteriously killed at the shrine or soon after visiting it.

Wallace visited the shrine shortly before the Democratic convention of 1944. He came away with nothing. In fact, shortly after his visit fate turned against him. His critics in the Republican Party had obtained access to some of the more than 250 so-called Guru Letters he had been writing to Roerich and other members of the secret quest. A scandal erupted as papers charged that he had wasted money on his mystic projects. In the ensuing outrage, President Roosevelt was forced to drop Wallace as vice president and substitute the lesser-known Harry Truman. Wallace never became president, and he never found the magic stone, the holy chalice, the sacred spear, world peace, or the entrance to Shambala. Instead, Truman became the first American president to drop a nuclear bomb.

Genghis Khan continued throughout the twentieth century to be a potent symbol in Asia, inspiring groups struggling to break free of European colonization. The movements he inspired were diverse and unexpected, from imperialists in Japan to Jawaharlal Nehru in India. Leaders of opposite political persuasions found inspiration in his deeds. In the midst of World War II, Mao Zedong wrote an epigraph for Genghis Khan's tomb, describing him as "that proud son of Heaven."[5] Later, the fourteenth Dalai Lama wrote that "what Genghis Khan achieved, he did through a determined exercise of courage and physical strength." Therefore, he concluded, "it is fitting to remember with pride what he accomplished for Mongolian independence, unity, and freedom."[6]

While Mao Zedong and Wallace paid their respects, in his homeland of Mongolia, Genghis Khan otherwise largely faded into history. As long as Mongolia remained under control of the Soviets, his name and image were banned. Anyone suspected of a kinship connection to him or openly exhibiting interest in him was subject to persecution. On dark nights, *Nogoon Malgai*, the Green Hats of the secret police, came wearing black coats and carrying bright flashlights to haul away such antirevolutionaries. Any attempt to glorify Genghis Khan, or even to mention his name, was condemned with a mixture of nasty labels: reactionary feudalism, right-wing nationalism, Japanese imperialism, Chinese hegemony, or Western capitalism. The paranoia of the Russians was only intensified by Chinese praise for Genghis Khan, the Japanese effort to build a new monument celebrating Genghis Khan as the father of pan-Asianism, and the visit of the American vice president to his shrine. In the mid-twentieth century, mere possession of a written family genealogy connecting one back to Genghis Khan was sufficient reason to be sentenced to death in Mongolia. Every identifiable descendant of Genghis Khan was executed, along with lamas, shamans, and other innocent civilians accused of being feudalists, antirevolutionaries, or Japanese spies.

The Mongols could no longer worship the founder of their nation, but they learned to honor him secretly without saying his name, to call on him without seeming to do so. The dashing revolutionary poet Dashdorjiin Natsagdorj, who had studied in Russia, France, and Germany, showed his nation the secret way. Following his interest in embedding secret messages in literature, Natsagdorj translated Edgar

Allan Poe's "The Gold Bug," a somewhat bizarre tale about the sophisticated coded letters in a treasure hunt. This inspired him to follow
the example of Genghis Khan, who had compelled his soldiers to use
poetry, song, and elliptical phrases as the primary means of military
communication. Natsagdorj now turned to poetry again as a means
to resist political repression.

He was imprisoned for his suspect loyalties, and emerged from
prison at the end of 1932 with a poem that was to become a virtual
scripture in the religious wasteland of socialist Mongolia. *Minii
Nutag* (*My Homeland*) contains no drama and virtually no action.
To outsiders who read it, the poem seems static, a boring recitation
of locations in Mongolia in the new style of socialist realism. The
phrases are trite, like stale travel advertisements: the rivers are crystal
or blue, the grass green, the desert is like an ocean, the steppe covered
in grass, the animals well fed. The poem ends by praising the red flag
of socialism flying over a new era in Mongolia's history.

Like Dante, who used coded words to deceive ecclesiastical watchdogs, Natsagdorj had concealed a code completely obscure to Stalin's
censors. He packed the essentials of Mongolian history into the stanzas
of this one poem. The first word was the name *Khentii*, the district
around Burkhan Khaldun where Genghis Khan was born, and the second
was *Khangai*, the sacred forested zone on the mountains from whence the
Huns, Turks, and Uighurs originated. Every word contained a hidden
story, marking out the geographic territory of Mongolia and the life of
the nation's founder. Natsagdorj's poem was the opening verse of modern
Mongolian literature, and other writers followed his example after his
tragic and mysterious death at age thirty-one in 1937, supposedly after
falling into an alcohol coma. They took old poems and songs about
Genghis Khan and substituted features of the landscape for his name.
Their poems preserved their history and the true faith of the Mongolian
people, the worship of their nation. During the long totalitarian winter
of the twentieth centuries, the poets kept the spirit of Genghis Khan alive.

In December 1989, as the Soviet Union crumbled, a new generation of inspired Mongols gathered on the plaza in front of the Lenin

Museum in the capital of Ulaanbaatar to demand their freedom from Soviet occupation and Communist repression. In the blistering cold, their individual breaths mingled with the rising breath of others to form a foggy mist as their voices united in a call for democracy. For seven decades the memory of Genghis Khan had been repressed, but they still called on his name to lead them and turned to him for inspiration. The Mongols found their voice once again, and with it they sang the praises of their founder. One breath, one voice, one soul.

For some faithful believers, the history of "the Holy Lord Genghis of us Mongols"[7] has not finished. In the nineteenth century, guardians at the Shrine of Genghis Khan in the Ordos predicted that he would return to the land of his birth after eight to ten centuries.[8] This is now the ninth century since he created his empire.

For some of those who await his return, Genghis Khan's Mongol Empire was merely one phase in the eternal spiritual journey of the universe. In the thirteenth century, the world could not accept an empire in which rival religions cooperated in pursuit of the good of all, and still today, the world is not ready for such a dream.

True believers hold that in the blinding light of the sunrise over Mount Burkhan Khaldun, Genghis Khan will emerge from the sacred city of the Holy Lord Khormusta to complete the Mongol conquest of the world. In his next manifestation, he will appear as the Thunderbolt of God, mounted on a stone horse with wings of wind, clutching the sacred spear of salvation, and leading a million holy warriors out from the gates of Shambala, crossing the crystal Tengis Ocean of precious jewels to liberate our world of darkness from corruption, sin, and evil.[9]

With the strong cord of his lasso and the power of his golden whip, he will return all religions to the rightful path and hitch them to the Golden Star of the North. After his army has punished the wicked and united the honorable, the long-awaited God of the Future will emerge from the mists to vanquish the past, abolish history, erase knowledge of evil, and reign over the Pure Land of Goodness and Light.[10]

Boltugui, boltugui, as the Mongols say. May it be so!

A Note on Sources
and Further Reading

The *Secret History* is available in several translations today. In English, the most authoritative study of the text is by Igor de Rachewiltz, running more than 1,500 pages in two large volumes and one smaller appendix. The most easily read is a shorter translation by Urgunge Onon, a Daur Mongol from Inner Mongolia, and his ethnic background provides invaluable insights into the culture and meaning behind the text. The worst translation was made by Francis Woodman Cleaves and published by Harvard University Press. Cleaves attempted to be overly literal while at the same time writing in a Shakespearean-biblical tone. The result is an insult to the Bible and Shakespeare as well as to the Mongolian language. It is still worth reading a little of it if for no other reason than to see how a translation should not be done. Fortunately, Paul Kahn revised and abridged this text into the most literary of the English translations, and his poetic rendition is a good starting point for an initial reading of the *Secret History*.

Muslim accounts fell into rival pro- and anti-Mongol factions, and almost all drew their information from two chroniclers with similar names but totally opposed views. The highly sophisticated Persian Ata-Malik Juvaini, like his father and many male relatives, served the Mongols faithfully. He was born in 1226, just before the death of Genghis Khan, and he lived in the Mongol capital at Kara-korum for part of his youth and eventually became the Mongol governor of Baghdad. Juvaini gave the most intimate account of the Mongol court and sought to justify Genghis Khan's actions and those of his descendants in terms of Quranic teaching. His authoritative book was titled *Tarīkh-i Jahān-gushā*, or *History of the World Conqueror*, and it is still the best work on Genghis Khan, not only for its wealth of information but also for the rich beauty of his Persian language. His excessive use of imaginative metaphors might disturb some more picky literati, but I love it and tried to borrow as many of them as I could.

His scholarly rival, Minhaj al-Siraj Juzjani, fought against the Mongols and hated them with a passion. He thought of them as the vilest and most ungodly creatures on Earth. Born in 1193 in what is now Afghanistan, he was a contemporary of Genghis Khan, but never met him. Instead he fled the Mongol invasions and took eventual refuge in Delhi, where he vehemently warned the Muslim world that the Mongols were the greatest threat in the history of their religion. He attributed nearly superhuman strength to the Mongols and offered incredible statistics of millions slain in cities that never had more than a hundred thousand inhabitants.

Gregory Bar Hebraeus, born to a Jewish family in 1226, the same year as Juvaini's birth in what is now Turkey, became a priest, a bishop, and eventually a saint in the Syriac Orthodox church. He wrote many theological and historical texts, including a work titled *Chorography*, meaning world history, and he consistently praised the Mongols as messengers from God sent to rescue Christians from Muslims.

Of all the chroniclers, the most extensive and probably the fairest was the Persian Rashid al-Din, who wrote a history of the world known as *Jami al-Tawarikh*. Fate dealt him the severest of blows. His lifetime, from 1247 to 1318, spanned almost the entirety of Mongol rule in what is now Iran and Iraq, and he became one the richest and most powerful men in the Mongol government. As a Jewish convert to Islam working for the Mongols, he acquired many opponents who mistrusted the Jews and hated the Mongols. When his patron Oljeitu Khan of the Ilkhanate died in 1316, Rashid al-Din's enemies seized their chance to move against him, accused him of poisoning the khan, and executed him in 1318. Although he was initially buried as a Muslim, religious radicals eventually desecrated his grave and in the early fifteenth century shifted his bones to the Jewish cemetery. They probably would have destroyed his manuscripts if the Mongols, whose history he had written, had not rescued them and lavishly illustrated them with some of the most beautiful miniature paintings of all time.

Much of the work of Rashid al-Din was lost or has not yet been translated, but *The Successors of Genghis Khan* contains some valuable information. Although his prose fails to match that of Juvaini, the illustrated editions of his works contain some of the most magnificent and frequently reproduced of the Persian miniature paintings.

Almost all of the early information on Mongols in the West initially came from two envoys, both Catholic priests, who visited Mongolia soon after the death of Genghis Khan, while many who knew him were still alive. Giovanni of Plano Carpini, one of the early disciples of Saint Francis, was sent by Pope Innocent IV as an envoy and spy in 1245. Although fat and old at more than sixty, he managed to make it back and offered up a brief but valuable account of his trip and of the Mongols whom he encountered. Supplemented by comments from Stephen of Bohemia, who accompanied him, his report gives some interesting information, but favored criticism and condemnation over description and analysis.

The second Catholic envoy, William of Rubruck, was sent by the French king Louis IX in 1253, and he left an even more detailed account. Younger and much better educated than Carpini, William enjoyed better access to the Mongol imperial court and the capital at Karakorum, and he wrote in a more vivid style. He relished describing

Mongol religious ideas and those of the other faiths so that he could demonstrate, usually unconvincingly, their errors and his superior logic.

Each account is heavily biased in some ways, usually against the Mongols, but some are fiercely defensive of them. This combination of works in Mongolian, Chinese, Latin, Persian, Armenian, Arabic, and Russian offers a rich and multifaceted view of the life of Genghis Khan and the culture of the Mongols from differing perspectives: Taoist, Muslim, Confucian, Christian, and Buddhist. Each offers unique insights.

Chinese works, particularly the reports of the first Southern Sung envoys, Chao Hung, P'eng Ta-ya, and Hsü T'ing, remain the earliest eyewitness descriptions of the Mongols at the moment of their rise and therefore offer some of the most reliable information, albeit in the form of brief and dry bureaucratic reports to the royal court. Facing the terrifying threat of Mongol invasion, the envoys stressed military information above all else. In 1370, after the fall of the Yuan dynasty, its Ming successors produced the Yuan Shi, the official authoritative encyclopedia of the Mongols from the time of Genghis Khan. Despite the constraints of being written in a short time, having to balance contradicting claims, and find a way to transliterate difficult Mongol names, it remains the more authoritative work on the Mongol Empire. Only a little of it is available in English.

Beginning in the seventeenth century with the conversion of the Mongols to Buddhism, several scholars produced fascinating histories of the Mongols. Later Mongol chronicles supplied very little information about traditional Mongol religious practice because they were written by Buddhist monks and scholars who sought to make the early history conform to their own theological teachings. These secondary chronicles, sometimes transcribed into multiple editions with slight but important differences, bear similar names, most referring to precious metals or gems—*The Golden Chronicle, The Jeweled Chronicle, The Pearl Rosary, The Jewel Translucent*. Some can be found in English, but the translations are stiff and render the most exciting stories opaque and boring.

In the nineteenth century, when much of Asia suffered under the oppression of European colonization, scholars and activists began to look to Genghis Khan as the first pan-Asian ruler. Kencho Suyematsu, a Japanese student studying at Cambridge University, wrote his history thesis on Genghis Khan, published in London in 1879 as *The Identity of the Great Conqueror Genghis Khan with the Japanese Hero Yoshitsune* and later translated into Japanese. Suyematsu claimed that Genghis Khan was actually a twelfth-century Japanese samurai hero, Minamoto Yoshitsune, who had faked his death, fled to Hokkaido, and then traveled on to Mongolia, where he had raised an army and begun to conquer the world.[1] This outlandish claim coincided with the rise of industrial Japan. Having been closed to the world for so much of its history, Japan was now ready to claim its place. Suddenly the idea of Genghis Khan as Japanese elevated the country's role in world history. Other writers expanded on this idea, connecting Japan to Mongolia and finding in the link to Genghis Khan the historical precedent for a new Asian empire.

One exceptional writer stands out from the rest: a nineteenth-century descendant of Genghis Khan by the name of Injannasi, living in Inner Mongolia. Like a modern Yelu Chucai, he was trained as a Chinese scholar and was at once fiercely loyal to and highly critical of his Mongol people. His father had left behind an unfinished novel on Genghis Khan and Injannasi developed it into one of the most profound works of Mongolian philosophy and identity. Known as *The Blue Chronicle*, it stands in marked contrast to the Buddhist texts, as it was a philosophical work set in a novel. *The Blue Chronicle* was one of the most important contributions to Mongol literature since the writing of the *Secret History* seven centuries earlier.[2]

One of the most interesting parts of *The Blue Chronicle* is its long introduction, which outlines Injannasi's ideas about philosophy and religion. Living in the final century of the Qing dynasty, he saw corruption and defeat all around him. Although he had been born rich, he had lost much of his property due to a failed coal mine investment and a peasant uprising on his estates. Amid the chaos of his devastating circumstances, he found inspiration in Genghis Khan's more liberal and orderly vision of society. His example demonstrated that Asians did not need to look to the West for ideas about freedom, democracy, and social justice; they could find precedents close to home in the great Asian leaders such as Confucius, Buddha, Lao Tzu, and Genghis Khan. Without attacking the Qing officials directly, he invoked their teachings to offer scathing critiques of his fellow Chinese citizens, whom he saw as weak, hypocritical, and vain. Asia had once been a driving force in history, he argued, and by following the actions and ideals of these earlier leaders, it could once again become the philosophical and political center of the world.

In the spirit of Injannasi, a new generation of Mongolian scholars is today at work on the history of their own nation. It is my hope and expectation that their analyses will surpass these earlier works, certainly including my own, to give a fuller picture of Genghis Khan so that his unique insights might help us navigate through the future storms.

NOTES

Preface: Genghis Khan, Thomas Jefferson, and God

1. Edward Gibbon, *The History of the Decline and Fall of the Roman Empire*, vol. III, chap. XXXV.
2. Ibid., vol. VI, chap. LXIV. The correct modern spelling of Genghis Khan's title in Mongolian is Chinggis Khaan, but outside of Mongolia, his name has been spelled in many different ways: *Chingiz* in Arabic and Persian, *Chingischam Imperator* in the first Latin references in Europe, *Cambyuskan* in the earliest English writings of Geoffrey Chaucer. There are several systems of Romanization for the Mongolian language and a variety of spellings are used in this book according to what seems easiest for the reader to pronounce or easiest to use for further research. Similarly, Chinese and Arabic names and words are usually presented according to the spelling of the English-language sources, without forcing all of them into one system. Alternative spellings and forms of Romanization are presented in notes as deemed helpful to the reader.
3. A facsimile reproduction of the manuscript has been published as *The Fundamental Constitutions of Carolina dated July 21, 1669 drafted under the supervision of John Locke*, foreword by Justice Sandra Day O'Connor, (Charleston: Charleston Library Society, 2012).
4. Books in the Mount Vernon library: http://librarycatalog.mountvernon.org/cgi-bin/koha/opac-detail.pl?biblionumber=4983&shelfbrowse_itemnumber=5995#shelfbrowser. *Zingis, historie tartarie* appeared simultaneously in two English translations issued by separate London printers as *Taxila or Love prefer'd before Duty* and *Zingis a Tartarian History*. For more information on the author's life, see Alexander Calame, *Anne de La Roche-Guilhen: Romancière huguenote (1644–1707)* (Geneva: Librairie Droz, 1972).
5. Jefferson inscribed his French copy of *Genghizcan* to his granddaughter Cornelia Jefferson Randolph (1799–1871) for her seventeenth birthday (July 1816). This copy later was given to the University of Virginia. Kevin J. Hayes, *The Road to Monticello: The Life and Mind of Thomas Jefferson* (New York: Oxford University Press, 2008), 426, 689.
6. Thomas Jefferson, 1783 Catalog of Books (circa 1775–1812), 32, *Thomas Jefferson Papers*, electronic ed. (Boston: Massachusetts Historical Society, 2003). www.thomasjeffersonpapers.org; http://catdir.loc.gov/catdir/toc/becites/main/jefferson/88607928.toc.html. As late as May 26, 1795: *The Papers of Thomas Jefferson*, vol. 28, *1 January 1794–29 February 1796*, ed. John Catanzariti (Princeton, NJ: Princeton University Press, 2000), 357–59.
7. Pétis de la Croix, *Histoire du grand Genghizcan: premier empereur des anciens mogols et Tartares*, published in 1710, 78–90. Jefferson bought several copies in French.

Introduction: The Anger of the Gods

1. Minhāj Sirāj Jūzjānī, *Ṭabakāt-i-Nāṣirī: A General History of the Muhammadan Dynasties of Asia*, vol. 2, trans. H. G. Raverty (London: Gilbert & Rivington, 1881), 1078–79.
2. *Kirakoz Gandzaket'i's History of the Armenians*, trans. Robert Bedrosian (New York: Sources of the Armenian tradition, 1986), 234.

3. Peter Olbricht and Elisabeth Pinks, 69.
4. Injannasi, 59.
5. Hend Gilli-Elewy, 353–71.
6. "They put to death the Caliph, and sacked Bagdad, just as they sacked the cities of Russia and Hungary," wrote President Theodore Roosevelt at the start of the American imperial century. "They destroyed the Turkish tribes which ventured to resist them with the thoroughness which they showed in dealing with any resistance in Europe. . . . They conquered China and set on the throne a Mongol dynasty. India also their descendants conquered, and there likewise erected a great Mongol empire. Persia in the same way fell into their hands. . . . They struck down Russians at a blow and trampled the land into blood mire beneath their horses' feet. They crushed the Magyars in a single battle and drew a broad red furrow straight across Hungary, driving the Hungarian King in panic flight from his realm. They overran Poland and destroyed the banded knighthood of North Germany in Silesia." Theodore Roosevelt, "Foreword," in Jeremiah Curtin, *The Mongols* (Boston: Little, Brown and Company, 1908).
7. Eric Voegelin, "Mongol Orders of Submission to European Powers," *Byzantion* 15, 1940–1941. In *The Collected Works of Eric Voegelin, vol. 5; Published Essays: 1940–1952* (Columbia, MO: University of Missouri Press, 2000), 133.
8. Ibid., 96–98.
9. "Sweet and venerable" seems to refer to the Manichaean notion that Jesus was sweet, which can be found in one of the Manichaean Psalms. "Taste and Know that the Lord is sweet. Christ is the word of Truth; he that hears it shall live. I tasted a sweet taste, I found nothing sweeter than the word of Truth. Taste and Know that the Lord is sweet." The Gnostic Society Library: *Manichaean Writings*; http://www.gnosis.org/library/manis.htm.
10. Voegelin, "Mongol Orders of Submission to European Powers," 95–96.
11. Juvaini, 105.
12. Pétis de la Croix, 214.
13. Bar Hebraeus, 355.

Chapter 1: The Teeth That Eat Men

1. The oldest known copy of the *Secret History* consisted of 281 numbered sections; most translations into most languages use this same system, making it easier to use the § (section) rather than page number. Editions by Arthur Waley and Paul Kahn are easier to read and are also listed in the bibliography.
2. *The Pearl Rosary (Subud Erike)*, trans. Johan Elverskog (Bloomington, IN: The Mongolia Society, 2007), 36–37, 43–45.
3. "Olqonud kemekü ulus-un ciletü mergen-ü gergei öelüng ekener-i buliyan abuɣad qatun bolɣabai . . . ɣurban sar-a-tai daɣaburi kuu arban sar-a güicejü. . . . törögsen temüjin." Quoted from manuscript, "History of Four Parts" (Dörben jüil-ün teüke 15/96: 10, 1094/96: 10). Explained in Kápolinás Olivér, "The Identity of Chinggis Khan's Father According to Written Mongolian Accounts," *Mongolica*, vol. XIV, St. Petersburg, Russia, 2015, 62–66.
4. "Nidürmegchi mergen Jarchigudai," Injannasi quote from Walther Heissig, *Geschichte der Mongolischen Literatur*, 285.
5. Het'um the Historian's *History of the Tartars: The Flower of Histories of the East*, trans. Robert Bedrosian (Long Branch, NJ: Sources of the Armenian Tradition, 2004), bk. 3, § 16. Author was also known as Hetum and as Hayton of Corycus. https://archive.org/stream/HetumTheHistoriansFlowerOfHistoriesOfTheEast/Hetum_djvu.txt.
6. *Secret History*, § 149.
7. Ibid., § 66.
8. Ibid., § 71.
9. Igor de Rachewiltz, *Secret History*, § 72.
10. Lubsang-Danzin, § 23.

11. *Secret History*, § 72.
12. Igor de Rachewiltz, *Secret History*, § 101.
13. Š. Čojmaa, "Die Persönlichkeitsmerkmale Čingis Chaans," in *Čingis Chaan und Sein Erbe,* ed. U. B. Barkmann (Ulaanbaatar: National University of Mongolia, 2007), 216–32, 229. Мах идэх шvд аманд аюу (баймуй). Хvн идэх шvд сэтгэлд аюу. "Чингис Хааны бие хvний онцлог," Ш. Чоймаа, in *Чингис Хаан хийдээг Тvvий Өв,* 27.
14. Burgi: Bürgi.
15. *Secret History*, § 97. Some translations identify the item as bellows for iron-working rather than a drum. For an explanation of the meaning, see T. D. Skyrnnikova, "Sülde—The Basic Idea of the Chinggis-Khan Cult," *Acta Orientalia Academiae Scientiarum Hungaricae*, vol. XLVI, 1992/93, 54.
16. Old woman: Qo'aqchin or Qo'aγchin, *Secret History*, § 103.
17. Volker Rybatzki, "Die Personnennamen und Titel der Mittelmongolischen Dokumente," 10, 317, 716. The name is related to Modern Mongolian words such as *zasag*, the principle of government administration; *zasakh*, to improve; and *zarchimlakh*, to establish or follow a principle.
18. Universal Mother: G. Mend-Oyo, *Altan Ovoo*, trans. Simon Wickham-Smith (Ulaanbaatar: Mongolian Academy of Culture and Poetry, 2012), 173–76.
19. "The Orkhon Inscriptions: Being a Translation of Professor Vilhelm Thomsen's Final Danish Rendering," *Bulletin of the School of Oriental Studies*, University of London, vol. 5, 1930, 864. For more information, see Talât Tekin, *A Grammar of Orkhon Turkic*, Indiana University Uralic and Altaic Series, vol. 69 (Bloomington, IN: Mouton, 1968).
20. Rashid al-Din quoted in John Andrew Boyle, "Turkish and Mongol Shamanism in the Middle Ages," *Folklore*, vol. 83 (1972): 177–93, 182.
21. "It was from a naked prophet, who could ascend to heaven on a white horse, that he accepted the title of Zingis, the Most Great, and a divine right to the conquest and dominion of the earth." Edward Gibbon, vol. III, chap. XXXVI.
22. Nora K. Chadwick, "The Spiritual Ideas and Experiences of the Tatars of Central Asia," *The Journal of the Royal Anthropological Institute of Great Britain and Ireland*, vol. 66 (1936): 291–329.
23. Earth also known as Mother Umay.
24. Juvaini, 56.
25. *Secret History*, § 254.
26. Ibid., § 204.
27. Ibid., § 149.
28. A person's power, strength, and humanity were symbolized by the belt or sash they wore. To remove one's belt was to stand powerless before another person or a sacred spirit. Ibid., § 103.

Chapter 2: The Golden Whip of Heaven

1. *Secret History*, § 79.
2. Ibid., § 80.
3. Ibid., §§ 79–81.
4. *Sulde:* сvлд sülde.
5. Hend Gilli-Elewy, 364.
6. Knowledge learned while growing up becomes like the morning sun: Өсөхөд сурсан эрдэм Өглөөний нар мэт. Janice Raymond, *Mongolian Proverbs* (San Diego: Alethinos Books, 2010), 214.
7. Injannasi, 41–42.
8. *Secret History*, § 103.
9. Ibid., § 104.
10. *Abui Babui: The Secret History of the Mongols,* § 174; also see Igor de Rachewiltz, 630.
11. *Secret History*, § 104.

12. Jūzjānī, trans. Raverty, 1078–79, quoted in George Lane, *Genghis Khan and Mongol Rule* (Westport, CT: Greenwood Press, 2004), 37.
13. Juvaini, 38–39.
14. Igor de Rachewiltz, *Secret History*, § 97.
15. *Secret History*, § 110.
16. Ibid., § 112.
17. Igor de Rachewiltz, *Secret History*, § 113.

Chapter 3: Wisdom of the Steppe

1. "Mao-tun's title *'T'ang-li ku-t'u Shan Yü'* means, literally translated, *Shan Yü* with the charismsa (*kut*) of the Heaven"—Later "during the reign of Lao-shan, the Hsiung-Nu sovereign was called 'the Great Hsiung-Nu Emperor installed Heaven and Earth and born of the Sun and Moon.'" Elçin Kürsat-Ahlers, "The Role and Contents of Ideology in the Early Nomadic Empires of the Eurasian Steppes," *Ideology and the Formation of Early States,* ed. Henri J. M. Claessen and Jarich G. Oosten (Leiden, Netherlands: E. J. Brill, 1966), 141.
2. Sophia-Karin Psarras, "Han and Xiongnu: A Reexamination of Cultural and Political Relations (II)," *Monumenta Serica*, vol. 52 (2004): 56.
3. Kürsat-Ahlers, "The Role and Contents of Ideology," 141.
4. Sima Qian, "The Account of the Xiongnu," *The History of Mongolia*, ed. David Sneath and Christopher Kaplonski (Folkestone, Kent, UK: Global Oriental, 2010), 48.
5. Joseph P. Yap, *Wars with the Xiongnu: A Translation from Zizhi tongjian* (Bloomington, IN: AuthorHouse, 2009), 170.
6. Ammianus Marcellinus, *The Roman History of Ammianus Marcellinus*, trans. C. D. Yonge (London: George Bell & Sons, 1894), 572–82.
7. Seers: μάντεις read omens and predicted the future; shamans, referred to as 'ερεις or priests. Names of high-ranking officials such as Ataqam, Ἀταχάμ meaning Father of Shamans, or Eskam, Ἐσχάμ who was the father of one of Attila's favorite wives, further indicates the importance of shamans in Hun culture. Otto Maenchen-Helfen, *The World of the Huns: Studies in Their History and Culture* (Berkeley: University of California Press, 1973), 268–69.
8. Powerful women: They were not old women stirring a pot in a *ger*; they were active in the centers of power and seem to have been younger and more beautiful women. In the early sixth century the Rouran (Нирун in Mongolian; also known as Juan-Juan) leader Chounu Khan fell in love with a beautiful female shaman, but his affair so disrupted the plans of his mother that she had him killed in the year 520 and replaced by another of her sons. Denis Sinor, *Studies in Medieval Inner Asia* (Brookfield, VT: Ashgate Publishing, 1997), I-294.
9. Attila: Ἀττίλας, Atala, Atalum, possibly meant Father Ocean.
10. According to Jordanes's *Getica*, a summary of the otherwise lost work of Cassiodorus on the Goths. *Hunnorum omnium dominus et paene totius Schthiae gentium solus in mundo regnator.* Latin quote from Theodor Mommsen, ed., *Jordanes (Jordanis Romana et Getica)* (Berlin, 1882), 178, also quoted in Omeljan Pritsak, "The Hunnic Language of the Attila Clan," *Harvard Ukrainian Studies*, vol. 6 (1982): 444. Also Maenchen-Helfen, *The World of the Huns*, 277.
11. The name Tengis is variously transcribed by Greek and Romans as *Dengizich, Denzig,* and *Tengizich,* Δεγγίχ, Δεζίχιρος, Δεζίριχος, Δεγιρζίγ. Pritsak, "The Hunnic Language of the Attila Clan," 446.
12. Kharbalgas in Mongolian, but also known as Karabalghasun, Mubalik, the Bad City, and Ordu-Baliq, City of the Court or Capital City.
13. For the most extensive collection of these Turkic inscriptions transcribed, transliterated, and translated, see this Kyrgyz Web site: http://bitig.org/?lang=e.
14. *Nwm snk*: inscribed on the Bugut Stele, Volker Rybatzki, "Titles of Türk and Uigur Rulers in the Old Turkic Inscriptions," *Central Asiatic Journal*, vol. 44 (2000). Some scholars incorrectly translated *snk* as Sanskrit *samgha*, referring to

the Buddhist religion, but its meaning has been clarified by two Japanese researchers, T. Moriyasu and Y. Yoshida, "A Preliminary Report on the Recent Survey of Archaeological Sites and Inscriptions from the Turkic and Uighur Period in Mongolia," *Studies of the Inner Asian Languages*, vol. 13 (1998): 129–70.

15. Jonathan Karam Skaff, *Sui-Tang China and Its Turko-Mongol Neighbors: Culture, Power, and Connections, 580–880* (New York: Oxford University Press, 2012), 120. Also see Huis Tolgoy Memorial Complex inscription: http://irq.kaznpu.kz/?lang=e&mod=1&tid=1&oid=3.

16. "The Orkhon Inscriptions: Being a Translation of Professor Vilhelm Thomsen's Final Danish Rendering," *Bulletin of the School of Oriental Studies*, University of London, vol. 5 (1930): 862, 867. Also see Peter B. Golden, "The Türk Imperial Tradition in the Pre-Chinggisid Era," *The History of Mongolia*, ed. David Sneath and Christopher Kaplonski (Folkestone, Kent, UK: Global Oriental, 2010), 79, note 67, 87. Talât Tekin, *A Grammar of Orkhon Turkic* (Bloomington: Indiana University Publications, Uralic and Altaic Series, vol. 69, 1968), 261–73.

17. Öze Kök : Teŋiri : asïra : yaɣïz : Jer : qïlïntaquda : ekin ara : kisi : oɣulï : qïlïnmïs : kisi : oɣulïnta : öze : ečüm apam : Bumïn qaɣan : Estemi qaɣan : olurmïš : olurupan : Türük : buduniŷ : Elin : törüsün : tuta : bermis : iti : bermis : http://irq.kaznpu.kz/?lang=e&mod=1&tid=1&oid=15&m=1.

18. Juvaini, 54–55.

19. Sinor, *Studies in Medieval Inner Asia*, I-306.

20. Ibid., I-312–15.

21. Tekin, *A Grammar of Orkhon Turkic*, 283–90.

22. "When the sword gets rusty the warrior's condition suffers, when a Turk assumes the morals of a Persian his flesh begins to stink." Robert Dankoff, "Inner Asian Wisdom Traditions in the Pre-Mongol Period," *Journal of the American Oriental Society*, vol. 101 (1981): 87–95, 90–91.

23. From Kashgari's *Diwan Lugat at-Turk* (c. 1075), quoted in Robert Dankoff, "Kāšġarī on the Beliefs and Superstitions of the Turks," *Journal of the American Oriental Society*, vol. 95 (1975): 70. Spelled *Tängri* in original.

24. *Tenger* in Modern Mongolian, *Tenggeri* in Classical Mongolian.

25. E. Denison Ross and Vilhelm Thomsen, "Being a Translation of Professor Vilhelm Thomsen's Final Danish Rendering," *Bulletin of the School of Oriental Studies*, vol. 6 (1930): 37–43.

26. "The Orkhon Inscriptions: Being a Translation of Professor Vilhelm Thomsen's Final Danish Rendering," *Bulletin of the School of Oriental Studies*, vol. 5 (1930): 870.

Chapter 4: Conflicting Selves

1. *Secret History*, § 116.
2. *Sülde, Secret History*, § 201.
3. Ibid., § 118.
4. Ibid.
5. Ibid., § 123.
6. Thomas T. Allsen, "Mongolian Princes and Their Merchant Partners, 1200–1260," *Asia Major*, vol. 2 (1989): 86.
7. *Secret History*, § 123–25.
8. Ibid., § 126.
9. Ibid., § 127.
10. Ibid., § 129.
11. Ibid.
12. Ibid., § 204.
13. Leland Liu Rogers, 75
14. Peter Olbricht and Elisabeth Pinks, 12, 60.
15. Jautau: For the etymology and meaning of this term see *Secret History*, § 134.

16. *Secret History,* § 53.
17. Igor de Rachewiltz, *Secret History,* 302. Also see Denis C. Twitchett, Herbert Franke, and John King Fairbank, *The Cambridge History of China: Vol. 6, Alien Regimes and Border States,* 332.
18. J. Kroll, "The Term *yi-piao* and 'Associative' Thinking," *Journal of the American Oriental Society,* vol. 93 (1973): 359.
19. Ibid., 46.
20. Arga: *apɜa, Secret History,* § 166.
21. Pétis de la Croix, 44.
22. *Secret History,* § 150.
23. Bar Hebraeus, 352.
24. Lev Gumilev, *Searches for an Imaginary Kingdom: The Legend of the Kingdom of Prester John,* trans. R. E. F. Smith (Cambridge, UK: Cambridge University Press, 2009).
25. Igor de Rachewiltz, *Secret History,* § 189.
26. *Secret History,* § 195.
27. Ibid., § 242.
28. Rashid al-Din clearly states that Genghis Khan executed his uncle. The *Secret History* also states clearly that Genghis Khan condemned him to death, but then adds that before the sentence could be carried out, he relented and spared the uncle. In either case, whether dead or alive, the uncle disappeared from history at that moment, and no further mention of him was made. For the conflicting accounts, see *Secret History,* § 255, and Igor de Rachewiltz's discussion of the issue in *Secret History,* 652.

Chapter 5: Messenger of Light

1. Michael R. Drompp, *Tang China and the Collapse of the Uighur Empire* (Leiden, Netherlands: Brill, 2005), 226.
2. The Greek words coming into Turkic and Mongolian were mostly (κοινή) Hellenistic words. Volker Rybatzki, 2006, 633.
3. *Kutadgu Bilig,* quoted in İsenbike Togan, *Flexibility and Limitation in Steppe Formations: The Kerait Khanate and Chinggis Khan* (Leiden, Netherlands: Brill, 1998), 53.
4. T'ang hui-yao quote from "Shiruku rōdo to songudojin" ("Silk Road and the Sogdians," *Tōyō gakujutsu kenkyū* 18, 1979, 30, quoted in Mariko Namba Walter, "Sogdians and Buddhism," *Sino-Platonic Papers,* vol. 174 (2006): 11.
5. Togan, *Flexibility and Limitation in Steppe Formations,* 53.
6. Heuser and Klimkeit, *Studies in Manichaean Literature and Art,* 158.
7. Cyril Glassé, *The New Encyclopedia of Islam* (Lanham, MD: Rowman & Littlefield, 2008), 63.
8. Quoted in Sinor, *Studies in Medieval Inner Asia,* V-10.
9. *Manichaean Texts from the Roman Empire,* ed. Iain Gardner and Samuel N. C. Lieu (Cambridge, UK: Cambridge University Press, 2004), 118.
10. Samuel N. C. Lieu, *Manichaeism in the Later Roman Empire and Medieval China* (Tübingen, Germany: J. C. B. Mohr; 2nd ed., rev. and expanded edition, 1992), 282.
11. Colin Mackerras, "The Uighurs," in *The Cambridge History of Early Inner Asia,* ed. Denis Sinor (Cambridge, UK: Cambridge University Press, 1990), 335.
12. Hans-J. Klimkeit, "Buddhism in Turkish Central Asia," *Numen,* vol. 37, Fasc. 1 (1990): 57.
13. Tsui Chi, "Mo Ni Chiao Hsia Pu Tsan, 'The Lower (Second?) Section of the Manichæan Hymns,'" *Bulletin of the School of Oriental and African Studies,* University of London, vol. 11 (1943): 174–219, verse 238.
14. Hans-Joachim Klimkeit, in *Gnosis on the Silk Road: Gnostic Texts from Central Asia* (San Francisco: HarperCollins, 1993), 216.

15. Johann Jako, Philip Herzon, Albert Schaff, et al., *The New Schaff-Herzog Encyclopedia of Religious Knowledge* (New York: Funk and Wagnalls, 1910), 153–62.
16. Klimkeit, in *Gnosis on the Silk Road*, 178–81.
17. Manfred Heuser and Hans-Joachim Klimkeit, *Studies in Manichaean Literature and Art* (Leiden, Netherlands: Brill, 1998), 193.
18. Richard Foltz, *Religions of the Silk Road*, 2nd ed. (New York: Palgrave Macmillan, 2010), 78.
19. Cologne Manichaean Codex; http://essenes.net/index.php?option=com_content &task=view&id=649&Itemid=926.
20. *Secret History*, § 217.
21. Tasaka Kōdō, "Kaikotsu ni okeru Manikyōhankugai undō," *Tōhō gakuhō*, vol. 11, no. 1 (1940): 223–32. Quoted in *The Uighur Empire: According to the Tang Dynastic Histories*, ed. and trans. Colin Makerras (Columbia, SC: University of South Carolina Press, 1972), 9, 152.
22. Hans-Joachim Klimkeit, "Manichaean Kingship," *Numen*, vol. 29 (1982): 17–32, 23.
23. Wen Jian Lu quoted in A. G. Maliavkin, *Materialy po istorii Uigurov v IX–XII vv: Materials on the History of the Uighurs IX–XII Centuries* (Novosibirsk: Izdatel'stvo "Nauka" Sibirskoe Otdelenie, 1974), 92.
24. Anatoly M. Khazanov, *Nomads and the Outside World*, 258.
25. Quoted in Resat Baris Unlu, "The Genealogy of a World-Empire: The Ottomans in World History," Ph.D. diss. (Department of Sociology, State University of New York, Binghamton, 2008), 65.
26. Peter Olbricht and Elisabeth Pinks, 16.
27. Tatar Tonga also spelled as Tatar-Tong'a, Tatatungga.
28. Juvaini, 7.
29. Mongolian words: Болор, сахар, чихэр архи, болд, титим, чинжал, саван, анар, тоть, шатар, алмааз, маргад, инжир эрдэнэ. Борчууд in Modern Mongolian. Bells (*tsan* from Persian *chang*), notebook (*depter* from Persian *defter* from Greek δίπτυχα—related to English *diptych*). Similarly the Uighur word for sweat began to be used for wages. The Mongols also eventually used their word for sweat *хөлс* similarly to signify pay, wages, hire, and concepts that had not previously existed.
30. Mongol division of people into good and bad: People were either *el*, peaceful allies and subjects who kept their eyes, or they were *bulqa* (Modern Mongolian *булга*) or *dayijiju* (*dayijiju qarchu odu'at*, those who have gone out or departed); Igor de Rachewiltz, *Secret History*, § 188.
31. Klimkeit, "Manichaean Kingship," 26.
32. Mary Boyce, *The Manichaean Hymn-Cycles in Parthian* (London: Oxford University Press, 1954), 101. See also Mary Boyce, *A Reader in Manichaean Middle Persian and Parthian* (Leiden, Netherlands: Acta Iranica 9, 1975), 165. Other translation in Klimkeit, "Manichaean Kingship," 17.
33. *Secret History*, § 21. In another Manichaean influence on the *Secret History* and the tale of Alan Goa, a Parthian fable attributed to Mani described a man on his deathbed who called his sons together and told them the tale of the bundle of sticks. Available in German translation: "Der Apostel erzählte dem Turan-Schach ein Gleichnis: Es war ein Mann, und es waren sieben Söhne. Als die Stunde des Todes gekommen war, rief er seine Söhne. Sieben—uranfängliche—und—Treibstock—gebunden. Er sprach: '[Alle] zugleich zerbrecht!' Keiner war dazu [imst]ande. Darauf öffnete er [das Band—]." In turn this Manichaean story possibly was taken from (or shared a common source with) the Greek tales of Aesop. R. Merkelbach, "Eine Fabel Manis," *Zeitschrift für Papyrologie und Epigraphik*, vol. 75 (1988): 93–94.
34. Mongols incorporated many of the stories about Alexander the Great into the history of Genghis Khan. In 1246, at the time of the visit of the first European

envoy to the Mongols, Friar Giovanni di Plano Carpini heard stories from the *Romance of Alexander*, but the stories had been adapted to Mongolia and were associated with Mongol khans. He reported that in a battle against India, the leader of the Indian forces had dummy warriors made of brass propelled by a fire inside. When they approached the steppe warriors, the brass dummies shot out fire that burned the horses and routed the invaders. The *Romance of Alexander* reported precisely the same story regarding Alexander's attempt to invade India. Behind the dramatic, and mostly fictitious, folk tales and myths about Alexander was a sophisticated ideology with a complex view of the relationship between politics and religion. It was at heart a version of Greek philosophy, principally that of Alexander's teacher Aristotle, but filtered through the lens of Mani's teachings.

35. Plato, *The Republic*, trans. Benjamin Jowett (New York: Anchor Books, 1973), 211.
36. Ibid., 42–50.
37. Klimkeit, in *Gnosis on the Silk Road*, 356–62.
38. Ibid., 356. For further explanation of *ichtin nom, tashtin il*, the religion within and the state without: Heuser and Klimkeit, *Studies in Manichaean Literature and Art*, 286.
39. Ibid., 225.
40. Klimkeit, in *Gnosis on the Silk Road*, 22, 274.
41. One of Mani's scriptures, known as the *Book of the Two Principles*, remained largely unknown in the West. It may not have been translated into a European language, but it was translated from Syriac into Chinese and Turkic to become the most influential of Mani's scriptures in the East. The doctrine of two principles became so popular in Asia that the Taoists included it as one of their sacred scriptures for more than a century, from 1016 until the doctrine was banned by Sung authorities as foreign and false. *Book of Two Principles*: ibid., 372–73. Original title: *Sâbuhragân* (*Sutra of the Two Principles*), the book of advice for his patron Shāpūr I. Chinese version (*Erh-tsung ching*), Turkic version (*Iki yiltiz nom*) translated into *Il-tirgügk* of the Qarluq Turks, one of the Uighur subordinate tribes. Samuel N. C. Lieu, Manichaeism in Central Asia and China (Leiden, Netherlands: Brill, 1998), 148.
42. *Nomos*: Sogdians adopted the word from Manichaeism, and Sogdian Buddhists used it as a translation for the Sanskrit *dharma*. Volker Rybatzki, 633.
43. King of the whole law: *Nom qutï kadilmiš* and *qamaɣ nom iligi*, refers to all law, religious and secular. Klimkeit, "Manichaean Kingship," 17–32, 26.
44. Tsui Chi, "Mo Ni Chiao Hsia Pu Tsan, 'The Lower (Second?) Section of the Manichæan Hymns,'" *Bulletin of the School of Oriental and African Studies, University of London*, vol. 11 (1943): 174–219, verses 76, 84.
45. Klimkeit, "Manichaean Kingship," 17–32, 29.
46. Golden cord: *altan argamj, Secret History*, § 254.
47. "The term *Sog* was an abbreviated ethnonym for Sogdians (*Sog dag*) during the imperial period and became an ethnonym for Mongols (*Sog po*) after their rise to power in the thirteenth century. *Hor*, or *Hor pa*, a Tibetan ethnonym originally associated with the Uighurs during the imperial period, was later used to identify Mongols in general beginning from the thirteenth century. Later still the term was used to designate specific Mongol tribes that underwent varying degrees of Tibetanization and settled in the regions east and northeast of central Tibet" (Rolf Alfred Stein, *Tibetan Civilization,* Stanford: Stanford University Press, 1972, 34). Also see "Representations of Efficacy: The Ritual Expulsion of Mongol Armies in the Consolidation and Expansion of the Tsang (Gstang) Dynasty" by James Gentry, in *Tibetan Ritual*, José Ignacio Cabezón, ed. (Oxford: Oxford University Press, 2010), 158.
48. Dīn al-Majūsīya, referring to the fire-worshipping Magi of Persia. Dīn al-Nijashīya, religion of the auditors. Walter J. Fischel, "Ibn Khaldūn's Sources for Jenghiz Khān," *Journal of the American Oriental Society,* vol. 76 (1956): 99.
49. For examples of the use of *Magi* by Christians as the term for Auditors, see Johann Lorenz von Mosheim, Robert Studley Vidal, and James Murdock, *Historical*

Commentaries on the State of Christianity during the First Three Hundred and Twenty-Five Years from the Christian Era (New York: S. Converse, 1853), 400.
50. *An Etymological Dictionary of Pre-Thirteenth Century Turkish* (Oxford, UK: Oxford University Press, 1972), 324. Also, Volker Rybatzki, "Die Personnennamen und Titel der Mittelmongolischen Dokumente," 234.
51. Bar Hebraeus, 355.
52. Charles R. Bawden, *Mongolian Literature Anthology* (New York: Columbia University Press, 2003), 318.
53. Bayan Khan Mani's tale is collected in Ordos but relates to a hunting trip of Temujin near the Bogd Khan Mountain on the Tuul River. Marie-Dominique Even, *Chants de chamanes Mongols* (Paris: Société d'ethnologie, Université de Paris, 1992), 307, 434.

Chapter 6: Jesus of the Steppe
1. *Secret History*, § 186.
2. Peter Olbricht and Elisabeth Pinks, 1980, 3, 31.
3. In my book *The Secret History of the Mongol Queens*, I attempted to recreate this lost history of the daughters of Genghis Khan, primarily through accounts of the marriages made for them. More detailed information can also be found in George Qingzhi Zhao, 2008.
4. Christian wife reported by Vincent of Beauvais in *Speculum Historiale* and Simon of Saint-Quentin. Quoted in Gregory G. Guzman, "Simon of Saint-Quentin," *Speculum*, vol. 46 (1971): 233.
5. *Book of the Tower*, Mārī b. Sulaimāb, "The Karaits of Eastern Asia," D. M. Dunlop, *Bulletin of the School of Oriental and African Studies*, University of London, vol. 11 (1944): 276–89.
6. Nicholaus of Cusa, "On the Peace of Faith (De Pace Fidei)," trans. William F. Wertz, *Toward a New Council of Florence* (Schiller Institute, 1993), § XVI.
7. Gumilev, *Searches for an Imaginary Kingdom,* 368.
8. *Secret History,* § 143.
9. Ibid., § 181.
10. Bar Hebraeus, 353.
11. *Secret History,* § 208.
12. Comment made in reference to Guyuk Khan's court. Juvaini, 259.
13. Thomas T. Allsen, *Commodity and Exchange in the Mongol Empire: A Cultural History of Islamic Textiles* (Cambridge, UK: Cambridge University Press, 1997), 35.
14. Bar Hebraeus, 354. After the shattering of their illusion that the Mongols were the fabled Christian army of Prester John who would liberate the world from the Muslims, European observers decided that the Mongols were Jews. The generally well-informed chronicler Matthew Paris and many other intellectuals of the thirteenth century thought that the Mongols were one of the lost tribes of Israel. Part of the evidence rested on the fact that they wrote in what a Hungarian bishop reported as being the Hebrew script, *literas Judaeorum.* (Sophia Menache, "Tartars, Jews, Saracens and the Jewish–Mongol 'Plot' of 1241," *History*, vol. 81, 1996: 333.) The Jews fared well under Mongol rule. According to Bar Hebraeus this was because "with the Mongols" there is "neither believer nor pagan; neither Christian nor Jew; but they regard all men as belonging to one and the same stock." (Bar Hebraeus, 490.) Muslims and Jews both had nomadic roots, unlike the Chinese, whose civilization depended on agriculture. Genghis Khan found people of pastoral heritage much easier to understand. Some chroniclers referred to his law as the Torah, using the same word as for the Jewish law, recognizing that in addition to being a conqueror he was an important lawgiver, an act that they associated with prophets and saints. For Muslims, Muhammad was the last and final prophet, after whom there would be no more, but the Arab chronicler Ibn Wasil wrote in 1260 that the Mongols also considered Genghis Khan a prophet. ("Ibn Wāṣil war der Ansicht daß Dschingis Khan bei den Mongolen den Rang eines

Propheten habe. Abstammung war unter den Mongolen wesentliches and si-
chtbares Zeichen einer von Gott legitimierten Herrschaft." Stefan Heide-
mann, *Das Aleppiner Kalifat AD 1261*, Leiden, Netherlands: E. J. Brill, 1994,
165.) Some Muslim writers referred to his teachings as *The Torah of Genghis
Khan*, and the *Torah-i-Chingizi* is a body of law that continued to have philosophical and legal importance in Moghul India for centuries. The belief in a
reputed Jewish connection was shared by many European Jews of the time,
based on the evidence of the Mongols' Semitic alphabet (their script was in fact
derived from ancient Syriac). A letter written by a Jew in Sicily reported that
the Mongols carried documents "written in Hebrew characters and . . . signed
up and down with twelve golden seals." The net result was that "the King of
Spain, and the King of Germany, and the King of Hungary, and the King of
France are in fear and shaking." (Sophia Menache, Ibid., 334.) According to
the Jewish calendar, the year 5000 was approaching (1240 in the Christian
calendar), and many thought that the Mongols had been sent to defeat the
forces of evil in preparation for the arrival of the long-awaited Messiah. Genghis Khan's leniency toward Jews in his conquest of Khwarizm and the service
of Jews in the Mongol army and government further strengthened this belief.
The identification of Mongols with Jews grew stronger as the Mongols approached Jerusalem leading up to the Battle of Ayn Jalut in 1260. Jewish poet
and scholar Meshullam da Piera was certain that they had come to restore the
temple of Solomon. (Maurice Kriegel, "The Reckonings of Nahmanides and
Arnold of Villanova: On the Early Contacts Between Christian Millenarian-
ism and Jewish Messianism," *Jewish History*, vol. 26, 2012, 25.)
15. Taken with slight edits from William of Rubruck, 52.
16. Ibid., 38.
17. Ibid., 56.
18. *Secret History*, § 208.
19. Considered a type of wild horse by the Mongols, the onager is classified by
    westerners as a wild ass, *Equus hemionus*.
20. Leland Liu Rogers 88; Lubsang-Danzin, § 28.
21. Lubsang-Danzin, §§ 30–32.

Chapter 7: The Making of the Mongol Nation
1. Évariste Régis Huc, *Christianity in China, Tartary and Thibet*, vol. 1 (London: Longman et al., 1857), 123.
2. *Meng-Ta Pei-Lu und Hei-Ta Shih-Lüeh*, 12.
3. The khan's complete epithet consists of nineteen words—*Kün Ay Tängritä Kut
   Bolmish Ulug Kut Omanmish Alpin Ärdämin El Tutmish Alp Arslan Kutlug Köl
   Bilgä Tängri Xan*—Who Has Obtained Charisma from the Sun and the Moon
   God, Who Is Imbued with Great Charisma, Who Has Maintained the Realm with
   Toughness and Manly Virtue, Courageous Lion, Blessed Ocean of Wisdom, Divine Khan. Zsuzsanna Gulácsi, *Mediaeval Manichaean Book Art: A Codicologi-
   cal Study of Iranian and Turkic Illuminated Book Fragments from the 8th–11th
   Century East Central Asia* (Leiden, Netherlands: Koninklijke Brill, 2005), 55.
4. *Secret History*, § 74.
5. *Grigor of Akner's History of the Nation of Archers*, trans. Robert Bedrosian
   (Long Branch, NJ: Sources of the Armenian Tradition, 2003), § 1; https://archive
   .org/details/GrigorAknertsisHistoryOfTheNationOfArchersmongols.
6. *Het'um the Historian's History of the Tartars: The Flower of Histories of the
   East*, trans. Robert Bedrosian (Long Branch, NJ: Sources of the Armenian
   Tradition, 2004), bk. 3, § 16; https://archive.org/stream/HetumTheHistorians
   FlowerOfHistoriesOfTheEast/Hetum_djvu.txt.
7. Alice Sárközi, "Mandate of Heaven: Heavenly Support of the Mongol Ruler,"
   Altaica Berolinensia: The Concept of Sovereignty in the Altaic World, ed. Barbara Kellner-Heinkele (Wiesbaden, Germany: Otto Harrassowitz, 1993), 220.
8. Juvaini, 39.

9. Kirakos Ganjaketsi's History of the Armenian, § 32.
10. *Secret History*, § 202.
11. Unity creates success: *Evlevel butne.*
12. Sechen Jagchid and Paul Hyer, *Mongolia's Culture and Society*, Boulder, CO: Westview Press, 1979), 255.
13. *Secret History*, § 63. The story of Dei-Sechen's dream may well have been inserted into the *Secret History* at some later date in order to appease or flatter members of his clan who became very powerful through the many queens produced by his descendants. It seemed more symbolic than factual.
14. Maria Magdolna Tatar, "New Data About the Cult of Chinggis Qan's Standard," *Altaica Osloensia*, ed. Brent Brendemoen (Oslo: Universitetsforlaget, 1990), 336.
15. *Secret History*, § 121. The Chinese summaries of the *Secret History* glossed *törö* as *tao-li*, which de Rachewiltz explains as "fundamental matters concerning governance," 451. For the complicated explanation for the unusual term *Nendü Khutukh* see Igor de Rachewiltz, 784–85.
16. Juvaini, 38–39.
17. Put them into the right: *shidurkhutkhaju*, *Secret History*, § 202.
18. Ibid., § 234.
19. Ibid., § 154.
20. Hans-Joachim Klimkeit, "Manichaean Kingship," *Numen*, vol. 29 (1982): 21.
21. *Secret History*, § 203.
22. Ibid., § 203.
23. P. Ratchnevsky, "Šigi Qutuqu," in *In the Service of the Khan: Eminent Personalities of the Early Mongol-Yüan Period*, ed. Igor de Rachewiltz, Hok-lam Chan, Hsiao Ch'i-ch'ing, and Peter W. Geier (Wiesbaden, Germany: Otto Harrassowitz, 1993), 75–94.
24. Kokochu: Kököchü.
25. *Secret History*, § 204.
26. Caroline Humphrey with Urgunge Onon, *Shamans and Elders* (Oxford, UK: Oxford University Press, 1996), 324.
27. The worst of men *become* shamans: Хунийг муу бөө болох.
28. бөө (бөөдийн), to vomit (бөөлжих), to castrate (бөөрлөх), an opportunistic person without scruples (бөөрөний хун), and the basic term for lice, fleas, and bedbugs (бөөс). Хулгийг муу жоро болох. *A Modern Mongolian-English Dictionary*, ed. Denis Sinor (Indiana University, Uralic and Altaic Series, vol. 150, 1997), 69.
29. Nine-tongued people: *Yisün kelten iren*, *Secret History*, § 245.
30. Minhāj Sirāj Jūzjānī, *Ṭabakāt-i-Nāṣirī: A General History of the Muhammadan Dynasties of Asia*, vol. 2, trans. H. G. Raverty (London: Gilbert & Rivington, 1881), 949.
31. Lubsang-Danzin, § 21.
32. Leland Liu Rogers, 75, 105.
33. Dragon snake: *gürölgü manqus*, *Secret History*, § 195.
34. Ibid., § 244.
35. Ibid., § 245.
36. Jūzjānī, *Ṭabakāt-i-Nāṣirī*, 949.
37. *Secret History*, § 246.
38. Ibid., § 216.
39. Ibid., § 217.
40. Original in vol. 27 of the encyclopedia of Shihab al-Din Ahmad b. 'Abd al-Wahhab al-Nuwayri (died 733/1333): Nihdyat al-arab ftlfuniin al-adab ("The Highest Aspiration in the Varieties of Cultures"), quoted in Reuven Amitai, "Did Chinggis Khan Have a Jewish Teacher? An Examination of an Early Fourteenth-Century Arabic Text," *Journal of the American Oriental Society*, vol. 124 (2004): 693. Also see Lyall Armstrong, "The Making of a Sufi: Al-Nuwayri's Account of the Origin of Genghis Khan," *Mamluk Studies Review*, vol. 10 (2006): 154–60.
41. Qur'an, 3:49, and Qur'an, 5:110.

42. *Toriin Sulde: Töriin Sülde.*
43. Christopher Atwood, *Encyclopedia of Mongolia and the Mongol Empire*, 10–11.
44. *Secret History,* § 208, *minu uruq bidan-u oro sa'uju ene metu tusa kiksen toro setkiju.* See Igor de Rachewiltz, *Index to the Secret History of the Mongols* (Bloomington: Indiana University Publications, vol. 121, 1972), 119–20.

Chapter 8: Guardians of the Flame

1. *Secret History,* § 230.
2. Ibid., § 147.
3. Ibid., § 124.
4. Ibid., § 209.
5. Ibid., § 125.
6. Leland Liu Rogers, 70–74.
7. *Secret History,* § 125.
8. Igor de Rachewiltz, *Secret History,* § 211. Similarly, Borte was called *qutuqtu* and *sutai,* § 111. Also used in the name of Shigi-Khutukhu, § 239.
9. *Secret History,* §§ 230–31.
10. The word *ordu* became known in the West as *horde,* referring to the large and seemingly wild spirit of the Mongol army, but in India the same word became *Urdu,* the name of the courtly language and in modern times the official language of Pakistan.
11. "Die Personnennamen und Titel der Mittelmongolischen Dokumente," 575.
12. Aldo Ricci and Luigi F. Benedetto, *Travels of Marco Polo* (Delhi: Asian Education Services, 1994), 129.
13. Peter Olbricht and Elisabeth Pinks, 141, 161.
14. *Secret History,* § 177.
15. Lubsang-Danzin, § 22.
16. Peter Olbricht and Elisabeth Pinks, 53.
17. Yusuf Khass Hajib, *Wisdom of Royal Glory (Kutadgu Bilig): A Turko-Islamic Mirror for Princes,* trans. Robert Dankoff (Chicago: University of Chicago Press, 1983), § 2091; § 2098, "Wine is an enemy."
18. *Secret History,* § 195.
19. C. Ž. Žamcarano, *Mongol Chronicles of the Seventeenth Century,* trans. Rudolf Loewenthal (Wiesbaden, Germany: Otto Harrassowitz, 1955), 84.
20. If something bad happens, you can find a way out: Элдэв муу юм болсон бол аргалж болон! Alena Oberfalzerovám, *Metaphors and Nomads* (Prague: Triton, 2006), 32.
21. *Secret History,* § 208. Also see L. N. Gumilev, *Searches for an Imaginary Kingdom,* trans. R. E. F. Smith (Cambridge, UK: Cambridge University Press, 1987), 206.
22. Plato, *The Republic,* trans. Benjamin Jowett (New York: Anchor Books, 1973), 234.
23. Ibid., 104.
24. Ibid., 59.
25. Ibid., 140.
26. Plato, *The Republic* (San Diego: ICON Classics, 2005), 93.
27. *Secret History,* § 195.
28. Plato, *The Republic,* trans. Jowett, 113.
29. Ibid., 85–88.
30. Ibid., 91.
31. "The Travels of John de Plano Carpini and other friars, sent about the year 1246, as ambassadors from Pope Innocent IV to the great Khan of the Moguls or Tartars," *A General History and Collection of Voyages and Travels,* vol. 1, ed. Robert Kerr, 148.
32. Ibid., 132.
33. Kirakos Ganjakets'i's *History of the Armenian,* § 32.

34. Friar Giovanni DiPlano Carpini, *The Story of the Mongols Whom We Call the Tartars*, trans. Erik Hildinger (Boston: Branden Publishing, 1996), 45.
35. Bar Hebraeus, 455.
36. Al-Nuwayrī quoted in Amitai, "Did Chinggis Khan Have a Jewish Teacher?," 693.
37. "Histoire Genealogique des Tartares," vol. I, 51, cited in Évariste Régis Huc, *Christianity in China, Tartary and Thibet*, vol. 1 (London: Longman et. al., 1857), 157.
38. Injannasi, 59. Injannasi was an eighth-generation descendant of Altan Khan and his son Senggedügüreng Khan.
39. Juvaini, 23–24.
40. Ibid., 25.
41. Ibid., 24.
42. Ibid., 23.
43. H. Desmond Martin, "The Mongol Army," *Journal of the Royal Asiatic Society of Great Britain and Ireland*, no. 1 (1943): 60.
44. Injannasi, 44.
45. Virlana Tkacz, Sayan Zhambalov, Buryat Mongolians, and Wanda Phipps, "We Play on the Rays of the Sun," *Agni*, no. 51 (2000): 160.
46. *Secret History*, § 100. Quoted from expanded edition of Paul Kahn (Boston: Cheng & Tsui, 1998), 35.

Chapter 9: Two Wings of One Bird

1. Igor de Rachewiltz, "Personnel and Personalities in North China in the Early Mongol Period," *Journal of the Economic and Social History of the Orient*, vol. 9 (1966): 98.
2. Quoted from a stone stele, Tao-Chung Yao, "Ch'iu Ch'u-chi and Chinggis Khan," *Harvard Journal of Asiatic Studies*, vol. 46 (1986): 203.
3. René Grousset, *The Empire of the Steppes: A History of Central Asia*, trans. Naomi Walford (New Brunswick, NJ: Rutgers University Press, 1970), 225.
4. Thomas Allsen, *The Royal Hunt in Eurasian History* (Philadelphia: University of Pennsylvania Press, 2006), 26.
5. Peter Olbricht and Elisabeth Pinks, 61.
6. Minhāj Sirāj Jūzjānī, *Tabakāt-i-Nāṣirī: A General History of the Muhammadan Dynasties of Asia*, vol. 2, trans. H. G. Raverty (London: Gilbert & Rivington, 1881), 954.
7. Peter Olbricht and Elisabeth Pinks, 60.
8. Marco Polo and Rustichello, *The Travels of Marco Polo: The Complete Yule-Cordier Edition in Two Volumes* (New York: Dover Publications, 1993), vol. 1, 238.
9. Voltaire, *The Orphan of China*, trans. William F. Fleming (Start Publishing, 2012), act 1, scene 3.
10. *Secret History*, § 272.
11. *Autumn of the Palace Han: Han Koong Tsu*.
12. Igor de Rachewiltz, 36–37.
13. He supposedly sent messengers to the provinces of Tibet with a decree, reading: "Now, so that I, the Khan, can complete the great deeds of the state, I need to support and spread the Buddha's religion by inviting lamas and [their] disciples to our Mongol lands." *The Pearl Rosary* (*Subud Erike*), trans. Johan Elverskog (Bloomington, IN: The Mongolia Society, 2007), 43–45.
14. The good custom of the Chinese *nom: Kitad-unb-nom-un sayin yosun-u sudur nigen-i jalaju abubai*. Ibid., 14r5, 110.
15. When he had assembled . . . to protect and support living beings: *Chasutu agula-yin engger-tür uchiragulju tör-yi tedkükü baruqu. Amitan-i asaraqu tedkükü yosun-i asagauju sayisisyan magtagad*. Francis Woodman Cleaves, "Teb Tenggeri," *Ural-Altaische Jahrbücher*, vol. 37 (Wiesbaden, Germany:

Harrassowitz, 1967), 248–60, 254–55. Original Mongolian quotes appear in *Altan Kürdün minggan kedesütü bichig* 1739, II 4v6–10, and *Chinggis ejen-ü altan urug-un teüke Gangga-yin urusqal neretü bichig orosiba* (*The Book Entitled the Glowing of the Gangaa [Ganges], a History of the Golden Lineage of Lord Chinggis*), 54b10–11.

16. *Secret History,* § 263.
17. E. A. Wallis Budge, *The Monks of Kublai Khan Emperor of China, or the History of the Life and Travels of Rabban Sawma* (London: The Religious Tract Society, 1928), 124–35.
18. E. Bretschneider, *Mediaeval Researches from Eastern Asiatic Sources* (London: Kegan Paul, Trench, Trubner & Co., 1910), 37–39.
19. Y. H. Jan, "Hai-yün," *In the Service of the Khan: Eminent Personalities of the Early Mongol-Yüan Period,* Igor de Rachewiltz, Hok-lam Chan, Hsiao Ch'i-ch'ing, and Peter W. Geier, eds. (Wiesbaden, Germany: Otto Harrassowitz, 1993), 226.
20. Li Chih-Ch'ang, *The Travels of an Alchemist—The Journey of the Taoist Ch'ang-Ch'un from China to the Hindukush at the Summons of Chingiz Khan,* trans. Arthur Waley (London: Broadway Travellers, 1931), 7.
21. Speakers to heaven: This phrase was recorded in the Chinese version. Maybe, тэнгэрийн итгэглч in Modern Mongolian—which would not be so much a speaker to heaven as *of* or *from* heaven. One who clarifies or elucidates—илтгэгч. Similar, but different word, *itgel*. In speaking to Muhali just before he died, Genghis Khan used the phrase "*itegelten in'ut,*" translated by de Rachewiltz in *The Secret History* as "trusted friends" (*ina'ut* being the plural of *inaq*) (page 972), "Now you two, Borc'orču and Muqali, are my trusted friends." *Secret History,* § 266.
22. Arthur Waley, 8.
23. Y. H. Jan, "Hai-yün," *In the Service of the Khan: Eminent Personalities of the Early Mongol-Yüan Period,* Igor de Rachewiltz, Hok-lam Chan, Hsiao Ch'i-ch'ing, and Peter W. Geier, eds. (Wiesbaden, Germany: Otto Harrassowitz, 1993), 227. Despite claims in Buddhist chronicles such as the *Rosary of White Lotuses* that Genghis Khan met with him and with various lamas from Tibet, Genghis Khan was not in the area at that time.
24. Haiyun served Mongke Khan and Khubilai Khan as an adviser.
25. Thomas Allsen, *Culture and Conquest in Mongol Eurasia* (Cambridge, UK: Cambridge University Press, 2001), 83.
26. *Nom: Nâwm* (Sogdian transcription), Bar Hebraeus, 355–56.

Chapter 10: God's Omnipotence

1. Mirza Muhammad Haidar Dughlát, *The Tarikh-i-Rashidi: A History of the Moghuls of Central Asia,* trans. E. Denison Ross, ed. N. Elias (New York: Cosimo Classic, 2008, reprint of 1895 edition), 293.
2. Juvaini, 64.
3. Ibid., 65.
4. Mirza Muhammad Haidar Dughlát, *Tarikh-i-Rashidi: A History of the Moghuls of Central Asia,* trans. E. Denison Ross, ed. N. Elias (London: Curzon Press, 1898), 253–55.
5. Juvaini, 66.
6. Juvaini, 67.
7. Ibid.
8. Oration in Honor of Julian, *Selected Orations, Volume I: Julianic Orations,* Libanius, ed. and trans. A. F. Norman (Cambridge, MA: Harvard University Press; Loeb Library edition, 1969). The reign of Julian is discussed in considerable detail by Edward Gibbon in Volume II of *The History of the Decline and Fall of the Roman Empire.*
9. Klaus Lech, *Das Mongolische Weltreich,* German translation of *Masālik al-abṣār fī mamālik al-amṣār* (Wiesbaden: Otto Harrassowitz, 1968), 95, 193.
10. Penalty for killing a person (*man tarqaraba bi-li-aṣnān*): ibid., 113.

11. Juvaini, 26.
12. Igor de Rachewiltz, 1962, 25, 37.
13. Juvaini, 68.
14. Minhāj Sirāj Jūzjānī, *Ṭabakāt-i-Nāṣirī: A General History of the Muhammadan Dynasties of Asia,* vol. 2, trans. H. G. Raverty (London: Gilbert & Rivington, 1881), 974–75.
15. Juvaini, 78.
16. Ibid.
17. Ibid.
18. Ratchnevsky, 120.
19. Juvaini, 79.
20. Henry Hoyle Howorth, *History of the Mongols,* 74.
21. Juvaini, 79.
22. *Secret History,* § 253.
23. V. V. Barthold, *Four Studies on the History of Central Asia* (Leiden, Netherlands: E. J. Brill, 1956), 36.
24. Juvaini, 19–20.
25. Ibid., 80.
26. Golden Cord: *altan argamj, Secret History,* § 254.
27. *Secret History,* § 265.
28. Kolgen: Kölgen.
29. Igor de Rachewiltz et al., *In the Service of the Khan,* 47.
30. Igor de Rachewiltz, 1962, 19.
31. Igor de Rachewiltz et al., *In the Service of the Khan,* 48.
32. Igor de Rachewiltz, 1962, 19.
33. Ibid., 24.
34. Ibid., 46.
35. Ibid., 19.
36. E. Bretschneider, "Si Yu Lu (Ye-lu Ch'u Ts'ai)," *Mediaeval Researches from Eastern Asiatic Sources* (London: Kegan Paul, Trench, Trubner & Co., 1910), 17–21.
37. Igor de Rachewiltz, 1962, 58.
38. Juvaini, 84.
39. *Shahnama*: also known as *Shahnameh,* quoted by Juvaini, 86.
40. Juvaini, 99.
41. Ibid., 92.
42. Ibid., 396.
43. Ibid., 397.
44. Ibid., 398.
45. Ibid., 123.
46. Ibid., 124.
47. Ibid., 125–26.
48. *A History of the Moghuls (Tarikh-i-Rashidi)*; http://persian.packhum.org/persian/main.
49. Muhammad b. Ali Shabankarah'i, *Majma' al-ansab,* 1986, 227. Quoted in Michal Biran, *Chinggis Khan* (Oxford, UK: Oneworld Publications, 2007), 119.
50. Ghiyas al-din Muhammad Khwand Amir, *Habīb al-siyār,* vol. 1, trans. W. M. Thackston (Cambridge, MA: Department of Near Eastern Languages and Civilizations, 1994), 14. Cited in Richard Foltz, *Religions of the Silk Road* (New York: Palgrave Macmillan, 2010), 106.
51. Jalālu-d-Dīn Ḥassan III, 1187–1221, imam from 1210 to 1221. Meeting between envoys: Juvaini, 703. Juvaini refers to the imam by the first part of his name, Jalal-al-Din, but he is not the same person as the shah with the same name.
52. *Het'um the Historian's History of the Tartars: The Flower of Histories of the East,* trans. Robert Bedrosian (Long Branch, NJ: Sources of the Armenian Tradition, 2004), bk. 3, § 24; https://archive.org/stream/HetumTheHistorians FlowerOfHistoriesOfTheEast/Hetum_djvu.txt. In addition to myths about the Nizari in Marco Polo, one of the most influential modern works on them was the novel *Alamut.* It was written by the Slovenian writer Vladimir Bartol (trans.

Michael Biggins [Berkeley, California: North Atlantic Books, 2007]) as an allegory against the Fascist ideology of Benito Mussolini in 1930s Italy, and later used as a similar critique against subsequent dictators and totalitarian systems around the world. The novel was made into a dramatic opera by Slovenian composer Matjaž Jarc (Križnar, Franc, "On 'Alamut,' and Opera in Three Acts," Fontes Artis Musicae 55.2 [2008]: 377–88). Bartol's novel introduced the phrase, "nothing is absolute reality, all is permitted," later made more famous by William Burroughs as "nothing is true, everything is permitted," as a theme in his novel *Naked Lunch* (New York: Penguin, 2015).

53. Marshall G. S. Hodgson, *The Order of Assassins: The Struggle of the Early Nizari Isma'ilis Against the Islamic World* (The Hague: Mouton, 1955), 87–88.
54. Juvaini, 725.
55. Juvaini, 703.
56. Timothy May, "A Mongol-Ismâ'îlî Alliance?: Thoughts on the Mongols and Assassins," *Journal of the Royal Asiatic Society*, 3rd series, vol. 14 (2004): 231–39.
57. Ibid., 235.
58. Ibid., 239.
59. Devin DeWeese, "Stuck in the Throat of Chingīz Khān: Envisioning the Mongol Conquests in Some Sufi Accounts from the 14th to the 17th Centuries," *History and Historiography of Post-Mongol Central Asia and the Middle East,* ed. Judith Pfeiffer and Sholeh Alysia Quinn (Wiesbaden, Germany: Harrassowitz, 2006), 39.
60. Ibid., 43.
61. Rashid al-Din, *Jami' al'Tavarikh,* ed. Mohammad Roushan and Mustafah Musavi (Tehran: Nashr Albaraz, 1994), 516. Cited in George Lane, *Daily Life in the Mongol Empire* (Westport, CT: Greenwood Press, 2006), 182.
62. DeWeese, "Stuck in the Throat of Chingīz Khān," 36.
63. Juvaini, 105.
64. Ibid., 104.
65. C. Ž. Žamcarano, *Mongol Chronicles of the Seventeenth Century,* trans. Rudolf Loewenthal (Wiesbaden, Germany: Otto Harrassowitz, 1955), 84.
66. Pétis de la Croix, 341–43.
67. L. N. Gumilev, *Searches for an Imaginary Kingdom,* trans. R. E. F. Smith (Cambridge, UK: Cambridge University Press, 1987), 40.
68. DeWeese, "Stuck in the Throat of Chingīz Khān," 29.
69. Lyall Armstrong, "The Making of a Sufi: Al-Nuwayrī's Account of the Origin of Genghis Khan," *Mamluk Studies Review* X-2 (2006): 154; Reuven Amitai, "Did Chinggis Khan Have a Jewish Teacher? An Examination of an Early Fourteenth-Century Arabic Text," *Journal of the American Oriental Society*, vol. 124, 693.
70. *The Travels of Ibn Battuta A.D. 1325–1354,* vol. 3, trans. H. A. R. Gibb (Cambridge, UK: Cambridge University Press, 1971), 583. Quoted in DeWeese, "Stuck in the Throat of Chingīz Khān," 31.
71. *The Chronicle of Novgorod, 1016–1471,* Camden Third Series, trans. Robert Micheli and Nevili Forbes (London: Camden Society, vol. XXV, 1914), 66. Similar sentiments were expressed throughout Europe: "The Influence of the Mongols on the Religious Consciousness of Thirteenth Century Europe," Devin DeWeese, Mongolian Studies, vol. 5, 1978 and 1979, 41–78.

Chapter 11: The Thumb of Fate

1. *Secret History,* § 33.
2. Ibid., § 255.
3. Ibid.
4. *Kirakoz Gandzaket'i's History of the Armenians,* trans. Robert Bedrosian (New York: Sources of the Armenian Tradition, 1986), 195.

5. C. Ž. Žamcarano, *Mongol Chronicles of the Seventeenth Century*, trans. Rudolf Loewenthal (Wiesbaden, Germany: Otto Harrassowitz, 1955), 84.
6. *Olan ulus-barisu*
        Beye inu quriyatala
        Sedkil-in inu quriyagtunedkil-I quriyabasu
        Beye inu qamig-a oduqu
    Lubsang-Danzin, 28. See also Shagdaryn Bira, *Mongolian Historical Writing from 1200 to 1700*, trans. John R. Krueger, 2nd ed. (Bellingham, WA: Center for East Asian Studies, Western Washington University, 2002), 182. Bira/Krueger's translation: "Strong in body, one conquers units; strong in soul one conquers a multitude." The quote appears in different Mongolian chronicles and is attributed alternately to Genghis Khan and to Khubilai Khan (who may have been quoting his grandfather).
        Ta uru ut minu mona qoyina
        Ulus irgen-i quriyabasu gesü
        Beyeyi anu quriyatala
        Setgili anu quriyabasu setgili anu
        Guriyaca beyas anu qa-a e'ütqun.
    Entry 93, 123, Najm'al-Ajāib. Also quoted in L. Ligeti, "Monuments en ecriture 'Phags-pa," *Monumenta Linguae Mongolicae Collecta*, vol. 3 (Budapest, 1972), 123. And in Sh. Bira, "Qubilai Qa'an and 'Phags-pa bLa-ma," *The Mongol Empire and Its Legacy*, ed. Reuven Amitai-Preiss and David Morgan (Leiden, Netherlands: Brill, 2001), 242.
7. Rashid al-Din, 137–38.
8. Ibid., 138.
9. Description of a Mongol hero adapted from G. Mend-Oyo, *Altan Ovoo*, trans. Simon Wickham-Smith (Ulaanbaatar: Mongolian Academy of Culture and Poetry, 2012), 58.
10. Mongolian proverb, Энэ морь өмнөгүүрээ тоос гаргаж үзээгүй.
11. Minhāj Sirāj Jūzjānī, *Ṭabakāt-i-Nāṣirī: A General History of the Muhammadan Dynasties of Asia*, vol. 2, trans. H. G. Raverty (London: Gilbert & Rivington, 1881), 1039–42.
12. Ibn Battuta, *Travels in Asia and Africa, 1325–1354* (London: Routledge, 2004), 179.
13. Juvaini, 405.
14. P. Ratchnevsky, "Šigi Qutuqu," *In the Service of the Khan: Eminent Personalities of the Early Mongol-Yüan Period*, ed. Igor de Rachewiltz, Hok-lam Chan, Hsiao Ch'i-ch'ing, and Peter W. Geier (Wiesbaden, Germany: Otto Harrassowitz, 1993), 75–94.
15. Juvaini, 407.
16. Ratchnevsky, 75–94.
17. Jonathan L. Lee, *The Ancient Supremacy: Bukhara, Afghanistan and the Battle for Balkh, 1731–1901* (Leiden, Netherlands: E. J. Brill, 1996), 15.
18. Annemarie Schimmel, *Rumi's World: The Life and Work of the Great Sufi Poet* (Boston: Shambhala Publications, 1992), 158.
19. Juvaini, 132.
20. Pétis de la Croix, 310.
21. Voltaire, *The Orphan of China*, trans. William F. Fleming (Jersey City, NJ: Start Publishing, 2012), act 3, scene 2.
22. Juvaini, 151–52.
23. Ibid., 133. *Matykan* (Juvaini), *Mwatwkan* or *Mö'etüken* (Rashid al-Din); also written as *Metiken* and *Mutukan*. He is not included in the *Secret History*, probably because of the lingering prohibition by Genghis Khan against mentioning his death.
24. *Kirakoz Gandzaket'i's History of the Armenians*, trans. Robert Bedrosian (New York: Sources of the Armenian tradition, 1986), 221.
25. Injannasi, xx.

26. Juvaini, 408.
27. Ibid., 409.
28. Ibid., 410.
29. Ibid.
30. Ibid.

Chapter 12: Wild Man from the Mountain

1. Arthur Waley, 111.
2. Igor de Rachewiltz, 48.
3. Paul D. Buell, "Yeh-lü A-hai (ca. 1151–1223), Yeh-lü T'u-hua (d. 1231)," *In the Service of the Khan,* ed. Igor de Rachewiltz, Hok-lam Chan, Hsiao Ch'i-ch'ing, and Peter W. Geier (Wiesbaden, Germany: Otto Harrassowitz, 1993), 112–21.
4. Qiu Chuji: also known as *Ch'ang-Ch'un.*
5. E. Bretschneider, *Mediaeval Researches from Eastern Asiatic Sources* (London: Kegan Paul, Trench, Trubner & Co., 1910), 37.
6. Arthur Waley, 23.
7. Ibid., 129.
8. Igor de Rachewiltz, *Secret History,* note to § 121, 451. Mongolian: *apea.*
9. *Kirakoz Gandzaket'i's History of the Armenians,* trans. Robert Bedrosian (New York: Sources of the Armenian Tradition, 1986), 234.
10. *Xuanfeng qinghui lu. Changchun zhenren xiyou ji.* Qiu Chuji's companion Li Zhichang described the encounter in detail and published it as *Accounts of Felicitous Meetings with the Mysterious School.*
11. Travels to the West, *Xiyou ji,* 長春真人西遊記.
12. *Changchun zhenren xiyou ji,* published in 1228. Igor de Rachewiltz, 1962, 1–128.
13. Igor de Rachewiltz, Hok-lam Chan, Hsiao Ch'i-ch'ing, and Peter W. Geier, 145.
14. Arthur Waley, 80.
15. Tao-Chung Yao, "Ch'iu Ch'u-chi and Chinggis Khan," *Harvard Journal of Asiatic Studies,* vol. 46, no. 1 (June 1986): 204–5. The claim that Genghis Khan wanted a magical potion to guarantee immortality seemed to be a revision of the ancient Chinese myth that China's first emperor, the founder of the Qin dynasty (221–209 BC), sought such an elixir in order to rule the world until the end of time. Almost the same story can be found in the *Romance of Alexander* about the Greek conqueror ("An Early Version of the Alexander Romance," *Harvard Journal of Asiatic Studies,* vol. 22, 1959, English on p. 60; Mongolian on p. 44).
16. Tao-Chung Yao, "Ch'iu Ch'u-chi and Chinggis Khan," 209.
17. *Čingis Boɣda olan öber-e yosutan-i erke-degen quiryaɣsan,* Francis Woodman Cleaves, "Teb Tenggeri," *Ural-Altaische Jahrbücher,* vol. 39 (Wiesbaden, Germany: Harrassowitz, 1967), 254–55.
18. Arthur Waley, 1931, 111–12.
19. *Tengri Mongke Ken*: or *Tenggeri Möngke kümün,* ibid., 101.
20. Ibid., 102.
21. Ibid., 116.
22. Igor de Rachewiltz, 1962, 28.
23. Arthur Waley, 115.
24. *Hsüan-feng Ch'ing Hui Lu,* Wieger's catalog of Taoist writings, No. 1410. Arthur Waley, 21.
25. Arthur Waley, 22.
26. Ibid., 25.
27. Ibid., 118.
28. *Hsüan-feng,* quoted in Tao-Chung Yao, "Ch'iu Ch'u-chi and Chinggis Khan," 214.

29. Arthur Waley, 126. *Li* is a measure equal to about half a kilometer or one third of a mile.
30. In chapter three of *Pien-wei-lu*, quoted in Joseph Thiel, 18.
31. Igor de Rachewiltz, 1962, 25–30.
32. Ibid., 26.
33. Ibid., 29.
34. Atwood, 433.
35. Joseph Thiel, 20.
36. Arthur Waley, 112.
37. Minhāj Sirāj Jūzjānī, *Ṭabakāt-i-Nāṣirī: A General History of the Muham-madan Dynasties of Asia*, vol. 2, trans. H. G. Raverty (London: Gilbert & Rivington, 1881), 1078–79.
38. Arthur Waley, 152.
39. Ibid., 126.
40. Ibid., 130–31.
41. Joseph Thiel, 22.
42. Arthur Waley, 148.

Chapter 13: The Confucian and the Unicorn

1. Anna Contadini, "A Bestiary Tale: Text and Image of the Unicorn in the Kitāb nāt al-hayawān (British Library, or. 2784)," *Muqarnas*, vol. 20 (2003): 17–33.
2. *The Romance of Alexander the Great by Pseudo-Callisthenes*, trans. Albert Mugrdich Wolohojian (New York: Columbia University Press, 1969), 126–27.
3. *The Travels of Marco Polo: The Complete Yule-Cordier Edition*, vol. I, chap. XXIX. *The Romance of Alexander* spread, and elements of Alexander's life and fictional stories were adapted into various local oral traditions. In the *Epic of King Gesar*, the stories of Alexander and Genghis Khan blend. Combined with other real and mythical figures, the hero was sometimes identified as Gesar Genghis ("The Tuvan Legend of Genghis Khan," by Sarangerel, *Senri Ethnological Studies* 86, 215–221).
4. Alice Sárközi, "Mandate of Heaven," *Altaica Berolinensia: The Concept of Sovereignty in the Altaic World*, ed. Barbara Kellner-Heinkele (Wiesbaden: Harrassowitz, 1993), 216.
5. Lee Dian Rainey, *Confucius and Confucianism* (West Sussex, UK: John Wiley & Sons, 2010), 12–16.
6. *Yellow History, Shira Tuguji*, quoted in Shagdaryn Bira, *Mongolian Historical Writing from 1200 to 1700*, trans. John R. Krueger, 2nd ed. (Bellingham, WA: Center for East Asian Studies, Western Washington University, 2002), 188–89.
7. "An Early Version of the Alexander Romance," English on p. 60; *"dalai ötö-gen-i yeke tenggis-i tenggisün irug[ar-i] tu[gulju] irebe bi Sumur tag-un orai deger-e garba naran singgekü -in jug qaranggu-yi dagaba qoyar od yabuju gutugar on,"* Mongolian on p. 44.
8. Ibid., 44–45.
9. Francis Woodman Cleaves, "An Early Mongolian Version of The Alexander Romance," *Harvard Journal of Asiatic Studies*, vol. 22 (1959): 1–99.
10. "An Early Version of the Alexander Romance," English on p. 61, *"qan bolju aba ane ale gajar deger-e m[in]u metü jirgagsan qan es-e törejü bülege namayi ükübesü dalai-yi nigete bitügülüdkün angqa urida mingan narid ökidi ming-yan kü,"* p. 45.
11. Walther Heissig, *A Lost Civilization: The Mongols Rediscovered*, trans. D.J.S. Thomson (New York: Basic Books, 1996), 236–37.
12. Igor de Rachewiltz, Hok-lam Chan, Hsiao Ch'i-ch'ing, and Peter W. Geier, 164–65.
13. Igor de Rachewiltz, 1962, 46.
14. *The Cambridge History of Chinese Literature*, vol. 1, ed. Kang-i Sun Chang and Stephen Owen (Cambridge, UK: Cambridge University Press, 2010), 594.

15. Igor de Rachewiltz, 1962, 17.
16. Ibid., 40.
17. Ibid., 41, 84.
18. Ibid., 28.
19. Yunag-Kang Wang, *Harmony and War: Confucian Culture and Chinese Power Politics* (New York: Columbia University Press, 2011).
20. Peter Olbricht and Elisabeth Pinks, 210.
21. Illuminati: Also called a "steppe intelligentsia"; Paul D. Buell, "Činqai," *In the Service of the Khan: Eminent Personalities of the Early Mongol-Yüan Period*, ed. Igor de Rachewiltz, Hok-lam Chan, Hsiao Ch'i-ch'ing, and Peter W. Geier, 95.
22. N. S. Trubetzkoy, *The Legacy of Genghis Khan* (Ann Arbor: Michigan Slavic Publications, 1991), 169.
23. Juvaini, 204.
24. Igor de Rachewiltz, 1962, 36.
25. Ibid., 37.
26. Ibid., 38.
27. Jan Yün-hua, "Chinese Buddhism in Ta-tu," *Yüan Thought: Chinese Thought and Religion Under the Mongols*, ed. Hok-lam Chan and Wm. Theodore de Bary (New York: Columbia University Press, 1982), 384.
28. Igor de Rachewiltz, 1962, 35.
29. Jan Yün-hua, "Chinese Buddhism in Ta-tu," 388.
30. Igor de Rachewiltz, 1962, 36.
31. Ma Juan, "The Conflict Between Islam and Confucianism," *Eurasian Influences on Yuan China*, ed. Morris Rossabi (Singapore: ISEAS Publishing, 2013), 63.
32. Thomas T. Allsen, "Ögedei and Alcohol," *Mongolian Studies*, vol. 29 (2007): 5.
33. Igor de Rachewiltz, 1962, 36–37.
34. http:://www.linguamongolia.com/Muhammad%20al-Samarqandi.pdf. For contrasting views of the poems, see these two articles: T. Gandjei, "Was Muhammad al-Samarqandi a Polyglot Poet?," *Istanbul Üniversitesi Edebiyat Fakulteei Turk Dili ve Edebiyatî Dergisi* (TDED), vol. XVIII (1970): 63–66; Igor de Rachewiltz, "The Mongolian Poem of Muhammad al Samarqandī," *Central Asiatic Journal*, vol. 12 (1969): 280–85.

Chapter 14: The Last Campaign

1. Larry V. Clark, "From the Legendary Cycle of Činggis-qaγan: The Story of an Encounter with 300 Tayičiγud from the Altan Tobči (1655)," *Mongolian Studies*, vol. 5 (1978 and 1979), 25.
2. Yesüngge.
3. Injannasi, 84.
4. The right way: *arqacha sayin anu*.
5. Igor de Rachewiltz, *Secret History*, 780.
6. Ibid., § 205.
7. Nikolai Sergeevich Trubetzkoy, *The Legacy of Genghis Khan*, trans. Kenneth Brostrom (Ann Arbor: Michigan Slavic Publications, 1991), 173–74.
8. Pétis de la Croix, 364.
9. *Secret History*, § 265.
10. Reddish-gray horse: *josotu boro*.
11. Leland Liu Rogers, 108.
12. King of Heaven: Ssanang Ssetsen (Chungtaidischi), *Erdeni-yin Tobci, Geschichte der Ost-Mongololen und ihres Fürstenhaues*, trans. Isaac Jacob Schmidt (St. Petersburg: N. Gretsch, 1829), 101. Also see the *Erdeni-yin Tobci* adaptation, Paul Kahn (1998), 182–85.
13. Leland Liu Rogers, 104. See also Ssanang Ssetsen (Chungtaidischi), 97.

14. Evgenij I. Kychanov, "The State and the Buddhist Sangha: Xixia State (982–1227)," *Journal of Oriental Studies*, vol. 10 (2000): 119–28.
15. Weirong Shen, "A Preliminary Investigation into the Tangut Background of the Mongol Adoption of the Tibetan Tantric Buddhism," *Contributions to Tibetan Buddhist Literature*, ed. Orna Almogi (Halle, Germany: International Institute for Tibetan and Buddhist Studies, 2008), 326–27.
16. Ibid., 315–44.
17. *Secret History*, § 267.
18. Ruth W. Dunnel, *The Great State of White and High: Buddhism and State Formation in Eleventh-Century Xia* (Honolulu: University of Hawai'i Press, 1996), 124.
19. *Secret History*, § 268.
20. Lubsang-Danzin, §§ 44–45.
21. Ibid., §§ 47–48.
22. Ibid., 59–60, translation quoted in Shagdaryn Bira, *Mongolian Historical Writing from 1200 to 1700*, trans. John R. Krueger, 2nd ed. (Bellingham, WA: Center for East Asian Studies, Western Washington University, 2002), 180–83.
23. *Erdeni tunumal neretü*, trans. from Mongolian to German by Karénina Kollmar-Paulenz (Wiesbaden, Germany: Harrassowitz Verlag, 2001), § 2. Also translated into English as Johan Elverskog, *The Jewel Translucent Sūtra* (Leiden, Netherlands: Brill, 2003), 63.
24. Letter of Genghis Khan to Ch'ang-ch'un, Arthur Waley, 1931, 158. Genghis Khan wrote to the Taoist sage in the eleventh lunar month of 1223.

Chapter 15: War, Inside and Out

1. Juvaini, 189.
2. Ibid., 188.
3. Ibid., 184–85.
4. "A Mongol-Ismâ'îlî Alliance?: Thoughts on the Mongols and Assassins," Timothy May, *Journal of the Royal Asiatic Society*, 3rd series, vol. 14, 2004, 237.
5. Juvaini, 181, 256.
6. *Eagle's Nest: Ismaili Castles in Iran and Syria*, Peter Willey (London: Tauris, 2005), 76–77.
7. Igor de Rachewiltz, 1962, 35.
8. Klaus Sagaster, "The History of Buddhism Among the Mongols," *The Spread of Buddhism*, ed. Ann Heirman and Stephan Peter Humbacher (Keude, Netherlands: Koninklijke Brill, 2007), 379–432, 389.
9. Igor de Rachewiltz, 1962, 25.
10. *Secret History*, § 276.
11. Ibid., § 272.
12. Death of Subodei: "*A la mort d'Ogodaï, il y eut une grande assemblée de tous les princes de la famille de Tchingkis. Batou ne voulait pas s'y rendre; mais Souboutaï lui représenta qu'étant l'aîné de tous ces princes, il lui était impossible de s'en dispenser. Batou partit donc pour l'assemblée qui se tint sur le bord de la rivière Yetchili. Après l'assemblée, Souboutaï revint à son campement sur le Tho-na (Danube), et il y mourut à l'âge de soixante-treize ans. Conformément à l'usage des Chinois, on lui donna un titre qui rappelait ses plus belles actions: ce fut le titre de roi du Ho-nan, à cause de la conquête de cette province qu'il avait enlevée aux Kin. L'épithète honorifique qui fut jointe à son nom fut celle de* fidèle *et invariable. Il laissa un fils nommé Ouriyangkhataï, qui, disent les Chinois, après avoir soumis toutes les tribus des Russes, des Polonais et des Allemands, fut envoyé pour conquérir le royaume d'Awa et le Tonquin.*" Jean-Pierre Abel-Remusat, *Nouveaus Mélanges Asiatiques*, vol. II (Paris: Schubart et Heideloff, 1829), 96–97.
13. Rashid al-Din, *The Successors of Genghis Khan*, 187.

14. Juvaini, 258.
15. Carpini, Friar Giovanni DiPlano, *The Story of the Mongols Whom We Call the Tartars,* trans. Erik Hildinger (Boston: Branding Publishing, 1996), 109.
16. Ibid., 112–113.
17. Ibid., 116.
18. It took Carpini another year to return to Rome. Although Matthew Paris noted in his entry for 1247 that the pope's envoy had returned, he did not mention Carpini by name. Instead he sniffed at the Khan's claim of superior power when he reported the pope "received a mandate from the king of the Tartars ordering him to become his subject. This king, in daring and profane words, asserted in his letter that he was immortal." Paris gives the impression that the Khan was quoting the Bible by claiming "he and his followers were those of whom it was written, 'the Lord gave the earth to the children of men'" [Psalms 115:16]. In the confusion, and not knowing anything of the Mongol's history, Paris and many others assumed that they were Jewish, one of the Lost Tribes of Israel. *Chronicles of Matthew Paris: Monastic Life in the Thirteenth Century,* ed. and trans. Richard Vaughan (New York: St. Martin's Press, 1984), 94. After such a long and unprecedented trip, Carpini received an appointment as the archbishop of Antivari on the Dalmatian coast of modern Montenegro. He wrote up his observations about the Mongols and his recommendations for how to deal with them diplomatically as well as militarily in his *Historia Mongalorum quos nos Tartaros Appellamus (The History of the Mongols Whom We Call the Tartars).* The book provided an important ethnographic sketch of the Mongols and a short history, including an account of the life of Genghis Khan and his role in founding the Mongol people. Vatican librarians lost it amid their troves, and like many of the Mongol letters and documents sent to the Vatican, it was not to be seen or read again for several centuries.
19. *Matthew Paris's English History from the Year 1235 to 1273,* trans. J. A. Giles (London: Henry G. Bohn; reproduced ed., New York: AMS Press, 1968), vol. I, 155.
20. *Angel-faced* is translated as *peri-faced* based on a Persian word for angel. Ibid., 188.
21. Official was Kuo Pao-yü: Igor de Rachewiltz, "Personnel and Personalities in North China in the Early Mongol Period," *Journal of the Economic and Social History of the Orient,* vol. 9 (1966), 126.
22. Minhaj al-Din Juzjani, *Tabaqāt-i nāsirī,* vol. 2, trans. H. G. Raverty (Osnabrück, Germany: Biblio Verlag, 1991; 1881 reprint), 1157–58. Cited in Richard Foltz, *Religions of the Silk Road* (London: Palgrave Macmillan, 2010), 111.
23. Eric Voegelin, "Mongol Orders of Submission to European Powers," *Byzantium,* vol. 15 (1940–41), in *The Collected Works of Eric Voegelin, vol. 5, Published Essays: 1940–1952* (Columbia, MO: University of Missouri Press, 2000), 133.
24. Juvaini, 265.
25. Ibid., 266.
26. Voegelin, *Published Essays: 1940–1952,* 79, 96.
27. Juvaini, 565.
28. Juvaini, 569.
29. Juvaini, 595.
30. Rashid al-Din, *The Successors of Genghis Khan,* 215.
31. William of Rubruck, 221–22.
32. Ibid., 222.
33. *Secret History,* § 203. For a discussion of Shigi-Khutkhu during this time, see commentary in Peter Olbricht and Elisabeth Pinks, 149.
34. Igor de Rachewiltz, *Secret History,* 832–834.
35. Rashid al-Din, *The Successors of Genghis Khan,* 186.
36. Ironically, six centuries later the Russian writer Alexander Puskhin described the Mongols as "Arabs without Aristotle or Algebra."

37. Rashid al-Din, *The Successors of Genghis Khan*, 210.
38. Ibid., 211.
39. Juvaini, 51.
40. Rashid al-Din, *The Successors of Genghis Khan*, 210–13.
41. Ibid., 213.
42. Ibid.
43. Juvaini, 246.
44. Ibid., 247.

Chapter 16: Burning the Books

1. Elizabeth Endicott-West, "Notes on Shamans, Fortune-tellers and *Yin-Yang* Practitioners and Civil Administration in Yüan China," *The Mongol Empire and Its Legacy*, ed. Reuven Amitai-Preiss and David Morgan (Leiden, Netherlands: Brill, 1999), 224–39.
2. William of Rubruck, 108.
3. Comments on shamans made on William of Rubruck's final audience with Mongke Khan, May 31, 1254.
4. William of Rubruck, 239.
5. William E. Henthorn, *Korea: The Mongol Invasions* (Leiden, Netherlands: Brill, 1963), 75, 96.
6. Meir Shahar, *The Shaolin Monastery* (Honolulu: University of Hawai'i Press, 2008), 36.
7. Arthur Waley, "Introduction," 30.
8. Joseph Thiel, 34.
9. Ibid.
10. Igor de Rachewiltz, "The Hsi-Yu Lu 西 遊 錄 by Yeh-Lü Ch'u -Ts'Ai 耶 律 楚 材," *Monumenta Serica*, vol. 21 (1962): 81.
11. Juvaini, 607.
12. William of Rubruck, 228–30.
13. John Andrew Boyle, "Turkish and Mongol Shamanism in the Middle Ages," *Folklore*, vol. 83 (1972): 177–93, 178.
14. Eric Voegelin, "Mongol Orders of Submission to European Powers" (Letter of Aldijigiddai to Saint Louis), *The Collected Works of Eric Voegelin, vol. 10, Published Essays: 1940–1952* (Columbia, MO: University of Missouri, 2000), 93–94.
15. William Woodville Rockhill, *The Journey of William of Rubruck to the Eastern Parts of the World, 1253–55* (London: Hakluyt Society, 1900), chap. XVI.
16. Arthur Waley, 20–33.
17. Joseph Thiel, 35.
18. *Pien wei lou*, chap. III, 68 r°, col. 12. Ed. Chavannes, "Inscriptions et pièces de chancellerie chinoises de l'époque mongole," in *T'oung Pao*, vol. V (1904), 375.
19. Joseph Thiel, 37.
20. Arthur Waley, 30. Chinese sources identified Namo as a native of Kashmir, but he practiced Tibetan Buddhism. He recognized early the coming importance of the Mongols, or the "imperial feeling in the air towards the Northeast," and that "his own country was about to collapse in the general upheaval which was overwhelming the world."
21. *Zizhi Tongjian Gangmu: Tong Kien Kang Mu* or *Kangmu*, quoted from Sir Henry Hoyle Howorth, *History of the Mongols*, 504–5.
22. Ed. Chavannes, "Inscriptions et pièces de chancellerie chinoises de l'époque mongole," 381.
23. Ibid., 374.
24. Juvaini, 666.
25. Farhad Daftary, *The Isma'ilis: Their History and Doctrines* (Cambridge, UK: Cambridge University Press, 1990), 427.

26. Ibid., 682.
27. Ibid., 719.
28. Ibid., 725.
29. Minhāj Sirāj Jūzjānī, *Tabakāt-i-Nāṣirī: A General History of the Muhammadan Dynasties of Asia*, vol. 2, trans. H. G. Raverty (London: Gilbert & Rivington, 1881), 1245.
30. John Andrew Boyle, *The Mongol World Empire 1206–1370* (London: Variorum, 1977), 158.
31. Hend Gilli-Elewy, 361–62.
32. Ibid., 366. "Hulegu seized the treasures of Baghdad, the enumeration of, and amount of which wealth, the pen of description could neither record, nor the human understanding contain, and conveyed the whole—money, jewels, gold, and gem-studded vases, and elegant furniture—to his camp." Minhāj Sirāj Jūzjānī, *Tabakāt-i-Nāṣirī: A General History of the Muhammadan Dynasties of Asia*, 1255–56.
33. Bar Hebraeus, 430.
34. L. J. Ward, "The Zafar-Nmah of HamdAllāh Mustaufī and the Il-Khān Dynasty of Iran," Ph.D. diss. (University of Manchester Faculty of Arts, October 1983), 76.
35. Hend Gilli-Elewy, 368.
36. Joseph Thiel, 1–81.
37. Li Zhichang died in 1256 despite other claims that he died two years or twenty years later.
38. Joseph Thiel, 40.
39. Ibid., 7.
40. Ibid., 41.
41. Ibid., 43.
42. Pseudo Ibn Fowati quoted in George Lane, "Whose Secret Intent?," in *Eurasian Influences on Yuan China*, ed. Morris Rossabi (Singapore: Institute of Southeast Asian Studies Publishing, 2013), 12.
43. "The old Mongol tradition," wrote Russian scholar Nicholay Gumilev, "had been poured out too widely to remain of a piece and the streams formed from this source could not, and did not wish to, flow along one course." (*Searches for an Imaginary Kingdom*, by L. N. Gumilev, trans. R.E.F. Smith [Cambridge, UK: Cambridge University Press, 1987], 203). Nineteenth-century Mongolian writer Injannasi reached the same conclusion. "The decline of our Mongols was the result of too much easy living," he wrote. Yet, "when one tries to explain this fact, he is accused of being an infidel or heretic before he is heard"(*Köke Sudur* [*The Blue Chronicle*], trans. John Gombojab Hangin [Wiesbaden, Germany: Otto Harrassowitz], 1973, 51).

Chapter 17: Life After Death

1. *The De Monarchia of Dante Alighieri*, trans. Aurelia Henry (Chesterland, OH: General Bookbinding Co., 1896), book III, chapter VIII, 2, 26.
2. Ibid., book I, chapter XV, 4, 196.
3. "*Questi non ciberà terra né peltro, / ma sapïenza, amore e virtute, / e sua nazion sarà tra feltro e feltro.*" *The Divine Comedy of Dante Alighieri: Inferno*, trans. Allen Mandelbaum (New York: Bantam Classics, 1982), canto I, lines 103–5, 6. Many Renaissance scholars have rejected this supposed Mongol symbolism and insisted instead that the symbols derived from classical Greek and Roman sources. The connections to Genghis Khan via Marco Polo are explained in Cesare Emiliani, "The *Veltro* and the *Cinquecento diece e cinque*," *Dante Studies*, vol. 111 (1993): 149–51. Other background information is available in Leonardo Olschki, *The Myth of Felt* (Berkeley: University of California Press, 1949). Gran Cano also bears similarity to the nickname *Cangrande*, given to one of Dante's patrons, Francesco della Scala.

4. *As of the secte of which that he was born*
    He kept his lay, to which that he was sworn;
    And therto he was hardy, wys, and riche,
    And pitous and just, alwey yliche. . . .
Geoffrey Chaucer, *The Squire's Tale* (Norman, OK: University of Oklahoma Press, 1990), 131.

5. *The Pearl Rosary*, trans. Johan Elverskog (Bloomington, IN: The Mongolia Society, 2007), 15.

6. For centuries, Guards kept foreigners away from the shrines, and only a few Mongols could enter. Not until centuries later did the first foreigners, two Belgians, manage to see the shrines and describe them. According to their report, the tents "contained various precious objects, such as a gold saddle, dishes, drinking-cups, a tripod, a kettle, and many other utensils, all in solid silver." *Missions Catholiques*, No. 315, June 18, 1875, 293, quoted in *The Book of Ser Marco Polo*, trans. Henry Yule, chap. X (London: John Murray, 1903), 249. Another visitor described the shrine as "two large white felt tents, placed side by side, similar to the tents of the modern Mongols." Because of the secrecy surrounding the shrines, many people erroneously assumed that they contained the remains of Genghis Khan. One such report claimed that "a red curtain, when drawn, discloses the large and low silver coffin, which contains the ashes of the Emperor, placed on the ground of the second tent." He had been buried at Burkhan Khaldun, and although the portable shrines had moved around with the items that had belonged to him, he never again left his beloved mountain. M.C.E. Bonin, *Revue de Paris*, February 15, 1898, quoted in ibid., 250.

7. N. Hurcha, "Attempts to Buddhicise the Cult of Chinggis Khan," *Inner Asia*, vol. 1 (1999).

8. Ibid., 49.

9. In the Hellenistic kingdoms that arose in Afghanistan after Alexander the Great, Heracles became the protector of the Buddha known as Vajrapani. Heracles was frequently depicted in art and on coins as the perfect embodiment of manhood, and according to Greek mythology, he usually carried a large club with which he had slain a lion as his first heroic act. In the Greco-Buddhist synthesis of art and religion, Heracles and his club represented the Bodhisattva Vajrapani and his thunderbolt, with which he protected the Buddha. His name meant "holder of the thunderbolt," from the Sanskrit *vajra*, meaning both thunderbolt and diamond.

10. *White History*: This document was supposedly written in the time of Khubilai Khan in the late thirteenth century and miraculously rediscovered in the late sixteenth century. Most likely it was written in the sixteenth century but possibly with some original portions from the thirteenth. Shagdaryn Bira, *Mongolian Historical Writing from 1200 to 1700*, trans. John R. Krueger (Bellingham, WA: Center for East Asian Studies, Western Washington University, 2002), 64. Also on Vajrapani, see Michael Jerryson, "Buddhist Tradition and Violence," *The Oxford Handbook of Religion and Violence*, ed. Mark Juergensmeyer, Margo Kitts, and Michael Jerryson (Oxford, UK: Oxford University Press, 2013), 56.

11. Ibid., 53.

12. Walther Heissig, *A Lost Civilization: The Mongols Rediscovered*, trans. D.J.S. Thomson (New York: Basic Books, 1996), 86.

13. Karl Sagaster, *Die Weise Geschichte* (Wiesbaden, Germany: Harrassowitz, 1976), 315.

14. Larry Moses and Stephen A. Halkovic, Jr., *Introduction to Mongolian History and Culture*, Indiana University Uralic and Altaic Series, vol. 49 (Bloomington, IN: Research Institute for Inner Asian Studies, 1985), 211.

Chapter 18: The Unfulfilled Law

1. John Locke, *The Fundamental Constitutions of Carolina*, 1669, §§ 95–110.

2. Tobias George Smollett, Thomas Francklin, et al., *The Works of M. de Voltaire: A Treatise on Toleration*, vol. 24 (London: Newberry et al., 1764), 46.
3. Anne de La Roche-Guilhem, trans., 9. The book also appeared simultaneously from a different printer with a different title: *Taxila or Love prefer'd before Duty*. For information on her life, see Alexander Calame, *Anne de La Roche-Guilhem: Romancière huguenote (1644–1707)* (Geneva: Librairie Droz, 1972), 44.
4. On October 18, 1685, Louis XIV issued the Édit de Fontainebleau, which revoked the Édit de Nantes of Henry IV in 1598 giving rights to Huguenots.
5. Anne de La Roche-Guilhem, 3–9, 88.
6. Pétis de la Croix, 78–90.
7. Minhāj Sirāj Jūzjānī, *Ṭabakāt-i-Nāṣirī: A General History of the Muhammadan Dynasties of Asia*, vol. 2, trans. H. G. Raverty (London: Gilbert & Rivington, 1881), 1010.
8. Adams in a letter to Jefferson on June 28, 1813, compares the war techniques of Zingis to those of American Indians and the Mongol hunting battue to those used in Scotland. *The Writings of Thomas Jefferson*, vol. 5, ed. H. A. Washington (Washington, DC: Taylor & Maury, 1854), 148. Newspapers of the time contained articles linking Indians and Tartars and the army of Zingis Khan: "From the American Magazine," *The Connecticut Journal*, November 12, 1788, 2; *Salem Mercury*, November 18, 1788, 1; *Worcester Gazette*, November 20, 1788, 1; *Newport Herald*, December 4, 1788, 1; *Albany Gazette*, December 26, 1788.
9. Luciano Petech, "Notes on Tibetan History of the 18th Century," *T'oung Pao*, 2nd series, vol. 52, livr. 4/5 (1966): 272.
10. Luciano Petech, "The Dalai-Lamas and Regents of Tibet: A Chronological Study," ibid., vol. 47, livr. 3/5 (1959): 368–94.
11. Ippolito Desideri, 229.
12. Ibid., 244.
13. "The sorrowful news of his death and the manner in which he had died spread throughout Tibet, and the universal grief it excited is beyond description, as was the bitter hatred aroused toward the new king among all classes of people, especially those who make a show of being churchmen and religious. It was even more disastrous for the new Grand Lama who had been chosen as the replacement by the king himself. The king had forced his discontented people to accept the new Grand Lama under the threat of violence and with the aid of a foreign power, the emperor of China, who had allied himself with his royal relative and supported his decision in this manner. The emperor and the king issued a joint edict ordering a mandatory death sentence for anyone unwilling to recognize the new Dalai Lama." Ibid., 244–45.
14. Ibid., 245.
15. Tibetan title: *Tho rangs mun sel nyi ma shar ba'i brda*. Trent Pomplun, "Natural Reason and Buddhist Philosophy: The Tibetan Studies of Ippolito Desideri, SJ (1684–1733)," *History of Religions*, vol. 50 (2011), 388.
16. Ippolito Desideri, 185.
17. Ibid., 187.
18. Ibid., 187–88.
19. *Mission to Tibet: The Extraordinary Eighteenth-Century Account of Father Ippolito Desideri, S. J.*, trans. Michael Sweet (Somerville, MA: Wisdom Publications, 2010), 245.
20. Ippolito Desideri, 192.
21. M. Klaproth, "Account of Tibet, by Fra Francesco Orazio Della Penna de Billi, 1730," *Monthly Register for British and Foreign India, China, and Australia*, vol. XV (1834): 296.
22. Ibid., 298.

23. *Genghiscano Imperador de' Tartari Mongoli.*
24. *London Daily Post,* December 19, 1744.
25. Liu Wu-Chi, "The Original Orphan of China," *Comparative Literature,* vol. 5 (1953): 193–212.
26. Voltaire, *The Orphan of China,* trans. William F. Fleming (Jersey City, NJ: Start Publishing, 2012), act 4, scene 1.
27. Ibid., act 2, scene 6.
28. Portrait of a salon reading of the work: www.histoire-image.org/etudes/salons-xviiie-siecle?i=1258, *Lecture de la tragédie de "l'orphelin de la Chine" de Voltaire dans le salon de madame Geoffrin.* The picture shows a gathering of distinguished guests in the drawing room of French hostess Marie-Thérèse Rodet Geoffrin (1699–1777), who is seated on the right.
29. Arthur Murphy, *The Orphan of China, a Tragedy,* 3rd ed. (London: P. Valliant, 1772; original publication, 1759), 1.
30. Hsin-yun Ou, "Gender, Consumption, and Ideological Ambiguity in David Garrick's Production of *The Orphan of China* (1759)," *Theatre Journal,* vol. 60 (2008): 383–407.
31. Liu Wu-Chi, "The Original Orphan of China," 211.
32. "Review of The Orphan of China, a Tragedy," *The Monthly Review* 20 (June 1759): 575, art. 24. Quoted in Hsin-yun Ou, 383.
33. Alexander Dow, *Zingis a Tragedy, as it is performed at the Theatre Royal in Drury Lane* (London: T. Becket & P. A. De Hondt, 1769), 1. Review in *The Gentleman's Magazine,* vol. 39 (1769): 40–43.
34. Alexander Dow, 85.
35. *Some Account of the English Stage,* vol. 5 (Bath, England: H. E. Carrington, 1832), 220.
36. Gio Batista Casti, *Gengis Cano* or *Il Poema Tartaro* (Brusselles, Belgio: Presso H. Tarlier, 1829).
37. Lorenzo da Ponte, *Memoirs,* trans. Elisabeth Abbott (New York: The New York Review of Books, 2000), 142.
38. Charles Mills, *History of Muhammedanism* (London: Black, Parbury, and Allen, 1817), 216.
39. I. Pottinger, *A Letter from Mons. De Voltaire to the Author of the orphan of China* (London, 1759). *The Library of Benjamin Franklin,* ed. Edwin Wolf and Kevin J. Hayes (Philadelphia: American Philosophical Society, 2006), 815, entry 3535.
40. Article from *South Carolina Gazette,* March 17, 1764, published in "Historical Notes," *The South Carolina Historical and Genealogical Magazine,* vol. 14 (1913): 171–72. Liu Wu-Chi, "The Original Orphan of China," 211.
41. *Pennsylvania Gazette,* January 15, 1767.
42. Harold Lawton Bruce, "Voltaire on the English Stage," *University of California Publications in Modern Philology,* vol. 8 (1918): 142–43.
43. John Kuo Wei Tchen, "George Washington: Porcelain, Tea, and Revolution," *Racially Writing the Republic: Racists, Race Rebels, and Transformations of American Identity,* ed. Bruce Baum and Duchess Harris (Durham, NC: Duke University Press, 2009), 36. Also see John Kuo Wei Tchen, *New York Before Chinatown: Orientalism and the Shaping of American Culture* (Baltimore and London: Johns Hopkins University Press, 1999), 19–22; A. Owen Aldridge, *The Dragon and the Eagle: The Presence of China in the American Enlightenment* (Detroit, MI: Wayne State University Press, 1993), 95; Philip Vallenti, "The Orphan of Zhao—A Chinese Inspiration for the American Revolution?," seminar sponsored by the New York Chinese Opera Society, New York, 2015.
44. Thomas Jefferson, "1783 Catalog of Books [circa 1775–1812], 32 [electronic edition]. Thomas Jefferson Papers: An Electronic Archive (Boston: Massachusetts Historical Society, 2003), www.thomasjeffersonpapers.org.

45. Cyrus King of Massachusetts quoted in Charles Jared Ingersoll, *History of the Second War Between the United States of America and Great Britain*, vol. II (Philadelphia: Lippincott, Grambo & Co., 1852), 273.
46. Pétis de la Croix, 78.
47. "A Bill for Establishing Religious Freedom, 18 June, 1779": Well aware that the opinions and belief of men depend not on their own will, but follow involuntarily the evidence proposed to their minds; that Almighty God hath created the mind free, and manifested his supreme will that free it shall remain by making it altogether insusceptible of restraint; that all attempts to influence it by temporal punishments, or burthens, or by civil incapacitations, tend only to beget habits of hypocrisy and meanness, and are a departure from the plan of the holy author of our religion, who being lord both of body and mind, yet chose not to propagate it by coercions on either, as was in his Almighty power to do, but to extend it by its influence on reason alone; that the impious presumption of legislators and rulers, civil as well as ecclesiastical, who, being themselves but fallible and uninspired men, have assumed dominion over the faith of others, setting up their own opinions and modes of thinking as the only true and infallible, and as such endeavoring to impose them on others, hath established and maintained false religions over the greatest part of the world and through all time: That to compel a man to furnish contributions of money for the propagation of opinions which he disbelieves and abhors, is sinful and tyrannical; that even the forcing him to support this or that teacher of his own religious persuasion, is depriving him of the comfortable liberty of giving his contributions to the particular pastor whose morals he would make his pattern, and whose powers he feels most persuasive to righteousness; and is withdrawing from the ministry those temporary rewards, which proceeding from an approbation of their personal conduct, are an additional incitement to earnest and unremitting labours for the instruction of mankind; that our civil rights have no dependence on our religious opinions, any more than our opinions in physics or geometry; that therefore the proscribing any citizen as unworthy the public confidence by laying upon him an incapacity of being called to offices of trust and emolument, unless he profess or renounce this or that religious opinion, is depriving him injuriously of those privileges and advantages to which, in common with his fellow citizens, he has a natural right; that it tends also to corrupt the principles of that very religion it is meant to encourage, by bribing, with a monopoly of worldly honours and emoluments, those who will externally profess and conform to it; that though indeed these are criminal who do not withstand such temptation, yet neither are those innocent who lay the bait in their way; that the opinions of men are not the object of civil government, nor under its jurisdiction; that to suffer the civil magistrate to intrude his powers into the field of opinion and to restrain the profession or propagation of principles on supposition of their ill tendency is a dangerous fallacy, which at once destroys all religious liberty, because he being of course judge of that tendency will make his opinions the rule of judgment, and approve or condemn the sentiments of others only as they shall square with or differ from his own; that it is time enough for the rightful purposes of civil government for its officers to interfere when principles break out into overt acts against peace and good order; and finally, that truth is great and will prevail if left to herself; that she is the proper and sufficient antagonist to error, and has nothing to fear from the conflict unless by human interposition disarmed of her natural weapons, free argument and debate; errors ceasing to be dangerous when it is permitted freely to contradict them. *We the General Assembly of Virginia do enact* that no man shall be compelled to frequent or support any religious worship, place, or ministry whatsoever, nor shall be enforced, restrained, molested, or burthened in his body or goods, nor

shall otherwise suffer, on account of his religious opinions or belief; but that all men shall be free to profess, and by argument to maintain, their opinions in matters of religion, and that the same shall in no wise diminish, enlarge, or affect their civil capacities. And though we well know that this Assembly, elected by the people for the ordinary purposes of legislation only, have no power to restrain the acts of succeeding Assemblies, constituted with powers equal to our own, and that therefore to declare this act irrevocable would be of no effect in law; yet we are free to declare, and do declare, that the rights hereby asserted are of the natural rights of mankind, and that if any act shall be hereafter passed to repeal the present or to narrow its operation, such act will be an infringement of natural right. http://founders.archives.gov/documents/Jefferson/01-02-02-0132-0004-0082.

48. John Adams, one of the Founding Fathers and the second president of the United States, remained critical of the excessive praise heaped on Genghis Khan. Because of his diplomatic problems dealing with Napoleon, Adams had a strong dislike for conquerors in general. In a letter to Thomas Jefferson, who was the sometimes rival and sometimes ally of Adams, on July 16, 1814, Adams criticized Napoleon as a "military fanatic" comparable to Alexander, Caesar, Muhammad and Genghis Khan. In another letter to Jefferson on March 10, 1823, Adams criticizes Napoleon's campaigns because conquest is always bad. He wrote that Genghis Khan destroyed "many millions of lives, and thought he had a right to the whole globe, if he could subdue it" (*The Writings of Thomas Jefferson*, ed. H. A. Washington [New York: H. W. Derby, 1861]).

Epilogue: The Thunderbolt of God

1. John McCannon, "By the Shores of White Waters: The Altai and Its Place in the Spiritual Geopolitics of Nicholas Roerich," *Sibirica,* vol. 2 (2002): 183.
2. Roerich, *Heart of Asia,* 3, 119.
3. Theodore A. Wilson, "Parsifal in Politics: Henry Agard Wallace, Mysticism and the New Deal," *Irish Journal of American Studies,* vol. 5 (December 1996): 10.
4. Nasan Bayar, "On Chinggis Khan and Being Like a Buddha," *The Mongolia-Tibet Interface: Opening New Research Terrains in Inner Asia,* ed. Uradyn E. Bulag and Hildegard G. M. Diemberger (Leiden, Netherlands: Brill, 2007), 197–221, 211. Photographs of the buildings and surroundings are in the Wallace Collection at the University of Iowa; http://digital.lib.uiowa.edu.
5. "Snow," 1945, Mao Zedong, *Poems* (Beijing, 1959); Michal Biran, *Chinggis Khan* (Oxford, UK: Oneworld Publications, 2007), 137.
6. Message of Dalai Lama XIV to the Mongolian Nation, dated August 31, 2006: *Их Монго Улс Great Mongolian State,* ed. Do, Chuluunbaatar, et al. (Ulaanbaatar: Master, 2007), 290.
7. Quote from poem in chapter 68 of Book XXIII in *Köke Sudur Nova (Injannasi's Manuscript of the Expanded Version of His Blue Chronicle)*, Part I, ed. Gombojab Hangin (Weisbaden, Germany: Harrassowitz, 1978), xix.
8. Prjevalsky (Mongolia and Tangut; story of Khatun Gol) in *The Travels of Marco Polo,* trans. Henry Yule, 917.
9. *Shambala,* as it is known in Mongolian, comes from the Sanskrit term *Sambhala,* also known from Tibetan sources by spellings *Xembala* (used in the seventeenth-century Portuguese explorers' reports), *Shambhala* (often used by English-speaking followers of Tibetan Buddhism), and *Shamballa* (used by some mystics). It gave rise to the English concept *Shangri-la* as an earthly paradise.
10. One legend predicts that Genghis Khan will return and rule again in a place of precious stones with a holy lake. "A legend about Chings Khan's ruling in

the future," by Kápolinás Olivér, paper delivered at Summer School of Young Mongolists, Ulaanbaatar, 2011.

A Note on Sources and Further Reading
1. Junko Miyawaki-Okada, "The Japanese Origin of the Chinggis Khan Legends," *Inner Asia*, vol. 8 (2006) 123–34.
2. Injannasi, 59.

BIBLIOGRAPHY

Amitai-Preiss, Reuven, and David O. Morgan, eds. *The Mongol Empire and Its Legacy*. Leiden, Netherlands: Brill, 1999.

Atwood, Christopher P. *Encyclopedia of Mongolia and the Mongol Empire*. New York: Facts on File, 2004.

Baabar, Bat-Erdeniin. *History of Mongolia from World Power to Soviet Satellite*. Edited by Christopher Kaplonski. London: White Horse Press, 1999.

Baljinnyam, B. *Mongolchuudin Buren Tuukhiin Tovchooh*. Ulaanbaatar: Admon Publishing, 2006.

Barfield, Thomas J. *The Perilous Frontier*. Cambridge, MA: Blackwell, 1992.

———. *The Nomadic Alternative*. Englewood Cliffs, NJ: Prentice Hall, 1993.

Bar Hebraeus. *The Chronography of Gregory Abû'l-Faraj 1225–1286. The Son of Aaron, the Hebrew Physician Commonly Known as Bar Hebraeus*, vol. I. Translated from the Syriac by Ernest A. Wallis Budge. First published in 1932. Amsterdam: Philo Press, 1976.

Bawden, Charles R. *The Mongol Chronicle Altan Tobchi*. Wiesbaden, Germany: Göttinger Asiatische Forschungen, 1955.

Bazargür, D., and D. Enkhbayar. *Chinggis Khaan Historic-Geographic Atlas*. Ulaanbaatar: TTS, 1997.

Bira, Shagdaryn. "The Mongols and Their State in the Twelfth to the Thirteenth Century." In *History of Civilizations of Central Asia*, vol. IV, part 1, edited by M. S. Asimov and C. E. Bosworth. Paris: UNESCO Publishing, 1998.

———. *Mongolian Historical Writing from 1200 to 1700*, 2nd ed. Translated by John R. Krueger. Bellingham, WA: Center for East Asian Studies, Western Washington University, 2002.

Biran, Michal. *Qaidu and the Rise of the Independent Mongol State in Central Asia*. Richmond, UK: Curzon, 1997.

———. *The Empire of the Qara Khitai in Eurasian History: Between China and the Islamic World*. Cambridge, UK: Cambridge University Press, 2005.

———. *Chinggis Khan*. Oxford, UK: Oneworld Publications, 2007.

Blake, Robert P., and Richard N. Frye. "History of the Nation of the Archers (The Mongols) by Grigory of Akanc." *Harvard Journal of Asiatic Studies*, vol. 12 (December 1949).

Boinheshig. *Mongolian Folk Design*. Beijing: Inner Mongolian Cultural Publishing House, 1991.

Bold, Bat-Ochir. *Mongolian Nomadic Society*. New York: St. Martin's Press, 2001.

Boldbaatar, J. *Chinggis Khaan*. Ulaanbaatar: Khaadin san, 1999.

Bretschneider, E. *Mediæval Researches from Eastern Asiatic Sources*, vol. I. New York: Barnes and Noble, 1967.

Buell, Paul D. *Historical Dictionary of the Mongol World Empire*. Lanham, MD: Scarecrow Press, 2003.

Bulag, Uradyn E. *The Mongols at China's Edge*. Lanham, MD: Rowman & Littlefield, 2002.

Carpini, Friar Giovanni DiPlano. *The Story of the Mongols Whom We Call the Tartars*. Translated by Erik Hildinger. Boston: Branding Publishing, 1996.

Chambers, James. *Genghis Khan*. London: Sutton Publishing, 1999.

Chan, Hok-Lam. *China and the Mongols*. Aldershot, UK: Ashgate, 1999.

——, and William Theodore de Bary, eds. *Yüan Thought: Chinese Thought and Religion Under the Mongols*. New York: Columbia University Press, 1982.

Cleaves, Francis Woodman. *The Secret History of the Mongols*. Cambridge, MA: Harvard University Press, 1982.

Conermann, Stephan, and Jan Kusber. *Die Mongolen in Asien und Europa*. Frankfurt: Peter Land GmbH, 1997.

Dawson, Christopher, ed. *The Mongol Mission: Narratives and Letters of the Franciscan Missionaries in Mongolia and China in the Thirteenth and Fourteenth Centuries*. New York: Sheed and Ward, 1955.

Desideri, Ippolito. *Mission to Tibet: The Extraordinary Eighteenth-Century Account of Father Ippolito Desideri, S. J.* Translated by Michael Sweet. Somerville, MA: Wisdom Publications, 2010.

Elias, N., and E. Denison Ross. *A History of the Moghuls of Central Asia: Being the Tarikhi-I-Rashidi of Mirza Muhammad Haidar, Dughlát*. London: Curzon Press, 1895.

Fitzhugh, William W., Morris Rossabi, and William Honeychurch. *Genghis Khan and the Mongol Empire*. Hong Kong: Odyssey Books, 2013.

Ge Menghe. *Genghis Khan's Philosophy*. Translated by Zhang Fuyong. Lanham, MD: American Academic Press, 2015.

Gilli-Elewy, Hend. "Al-Ḥawādit al-ğāmi'a, A Contemporary Account of the Mongol Conquest of Baghdad, 656/1258." *Arabica*, vol. 58 (2011): 353–71.

Grousset, René. *The Empire of the Steppes*. Translated by Naomi Walford. New Brunswick, NJ: Rutgers University Press, 1970.

——. *Conqueror of the World*. Translated by Marian McKellar and Denis Sinor. New York: The Orion Press, 1966.

Gumilev, Lev N. *Searches for an Imaginary Kingdom: The Legend of the Kingdom of Prester John*. Translated by R. E. F. Smith. Cambridge, UK: Cambridge University Press, 2009.

Haenisch, Erich. *Die Kulturpolitik des Mongolischen Weltreichs*. Berlin: Preussische Akademie der Wissenschaften, Heft 17, 1943.

Heissig, Walther. *A Lost Civilization*. Translated by D. J. S. Thompson. London: Thames and Hudson, 1966.

——, ed. *Die Geheime Geschichte der Mongolen*. Düsseldorf: Eugen Diederichs Verlag, 1981.

Howorth, Sir Henry Hoyle. *History of the Mongols*. London: Longmans, Green, 1876.

Humphrey, Caroline. *Shamans and Elders*. New York: Oxford University Press, 1996.

——, and Hurelbaatar Ujeed. *A Monastery in Time: The Making of Mongolian Buddhism*. Chicago: University of Chicago Press, 2013.

Injannasi, Vanchinbalyn. *Köke Sudur (The Blue Chronicle)*. Translated by John Gombojab Hangin. Wiesbaden, Germany: Otto Harrassowitz, 1973.

Juvaini, Ata-Malik. *Genghis Khan: The History of the World-Conqueror.* Translated by J. A. Boyle. Seattle: University of Washington Press, 1997.

Kahn, Paul. *The Secret History of the Mongols: The Origins of Chingis Khan.* Boston: Cheng & Tsui, 1998.

Kaplonski, Christopher. "The Role of the Mongols in Eurasian History: A Reassessment." In *The Role of Migration in the History of the Eurasian Steppe*, edited by Andrew Bell. New York: St. Martin's Press, 2000.

Khan, Almaz. "Chinggis Khan: From Imperial Ancestor to Ethnic Hero." In *Cultural Encounters on China's Ethnic Frontiers*, edited by Stevan Harrell. Seattle: University of Washington Press, 1995.

Khazanov, Anatoly M. *Nomads and the Outside World.* Madison: University of Wisconsin Press, 1994.

Klopprogge, Axel. *Ursprung und Ausprägung des abendländischen Mongolenbildes im 13. Jahrhundert.* Wiesbaden, Germany: Otto Harrassowitz Verlag, 1993.

Lamb, Harold. *Genghis Khan.* New York: Garden City Publishing Company, 1927.

Langolis, John D. Jr., ed. *China Under Mongol Rule.* Princeton, NJ: Princeton University Press, 1981.

Lattimore, Owen. *Studies in Frontier History.* New York: Oxford University Press, 1962.

——. "Chingis Khan and the Mongol Conquests." *Scientific American*, vol. 209, no. 2 (August 1963).

Lhagvasuren, Ch. *Ancient Karakorum.* Ulaanbaatar: Han Bayan Co., 1995.

——. *Bilge Khaan.* Ulaanbaatar: Khaadin san, 2000.

Lubsang-Danzin. *The Mongol Chronicle Altan Tobchi.* Translated by Charles R. Bawden. Wiesbaden, Germany: Göttinger Asiatische Forschungen, 1955.

Man, John. *Genghis Khan: Life, Death, and Resurrection.* London: St. Martin's Griffin, 2007.

May, Timothy. *The Mongol Art of War: Chinggis Khan and the Mongol Military System.* Yardley, PA: Westholme Publishing, 2007.

Olbricht, Peter, and Elisabeth Pinks. *Meng-Ta Pei-Lu und Hei-Ta Shih-Lüeh: Chinesische Gesandtenberichte über die frühen Mongolen 1221 und 1237.* Wiesbaden, Germany: Otto Harrassowitz, 1980.

Olschki, Leonardo. *Marco Polo's Precursors.* Baltimore: The Johns Hopkins University Press, 1943.

Onon, Urgunge, translator. *The History and the Life of Chinggis Khan (The Secret History of the Mongols).* Leiden, Netherlands: Brill, 1990.

——. *The Secret History of the Mongols: The Life and Times of Chinggis Khan.* Richmond, Surrey, UK: Curzon Press, 2001.

Pétis de la Croix, François. *The History of Genghizcan the Great: First Emperor of the Ancient Moguls and Tartars.* London: Printed for J. Darby etc., 1722.

Polo, Marco. *The Travels of Marco Polo.* Translated by Ronald Latham. London: Penguin Books, 1958.

——. *The Travels of Marco Polo: The Complete Yule-Cordier Edition.* New York: Dover Publications, 1993.

Rabban Sauma. *Monks of Kublai Khan, Emperor of China: Medieval Travels from China Through Central Asia to Persia and Beyond.* Translated by Earnest Alfred Wallis Budge. London: I. B. Tauris, 2013.

Rachewiltz, Igor de. "The Hsi-Yu Lu 西遊錄 by Yeh-Lü Ch'u -Ts'Ai 耶律楚材." *Monumenta Serica*, vol. 21 (1962): 1–128.

——. *The Secret History of the Mongols: A Mongolian Epic Chronicle of the Thirteenth Century*, 3 vols. Leiden, Netherlands: Brill, 2003–2013.

——, Hok-lam Chan, Hsiao Ch'i-ch'ing, and Peter W. Geier, eds. *In the Service of the Khan: Eminent Personalities of the Early Mongol-Yüan Period.* Wiesbaden, Germany: Otto Harrassowitz, 1993.

Rashid al-Din. *The Successors of Genghis Khan.* Translated by John Andrew Boyle. New York: Columbia University Press, 1971.

Ratchnevsky, Paul. *Genghis Khan.* Translated by Thomas Nivison Haining. Oxford, UK: Blackwell, 1991.

Raymond, Janice. Өсөхөд сурсан эрдэм Өглөөний нар мэт. *Mongolian Proverbs.* San Diego: Alethinos Books, 2010.

Roche-Guilhem, Anne de La. *Zingis: A Tartarian History.* Translated by J. M. London, 1692.

Rockhill, William Woodville. *William of Rubruck's Account of the Mongols,* edited by Rana Saad. Maryland: lulu.com, 2005.

Rogers, Leland Liu, translator. *The Golden Summary of Činggis Qayan: Činggis Qayan-u Altan Tobči.* Wiesbaden, Germany: Harrassowitz Verlag, 2009.

Rossabi, Morris. *Khubilai Khan: His Life and Times.* Berkeley: University of California Press, 1988.

——. "The Reign of Khubilai Khan." In Herbert Franke and Denis Twitchett, eds. *The Cambridge History of China, Volume 6: Alien Regimes and Border States, 907–1368.* Cambridge, UK: Cambridge University Press, 1994.

——. *The Mongols and Global History.* New York: W. W. Norton, 2010.

——. *Eurasian Influences on Yuan China.* Singapore: ISEAS Publishing, 2013.

Rybatzki, Volker. "*Die Personennamen und Titel der Mittelmongolischen Dokumente: Eine lexikalische Untersuchung.*" Doctoral dissertation, University of Helsinki, Faculty of Arts, Institute for Asian and African Studies, 2006.

Sinor, Denis, ed. *The Cambridge History of Early Inner Asia.* Cambridge, UK: Cambridge University Press, 1990.

——. *Studies in Medieval Inner Asia.* Brookfield, VT: Ashfield Publishing Co., 1997.

Skelton, R. A., Thomas E. Marston, and George D. Painter. *The Vinland Map and the Tartar Relation.* New Haven, CT: Yale University Press, 1965.

Sneath, David. *The Headless State: Aristocratic Orders, Kinship Society, and Misrepresentations of Nomadic Inner Asia.* New York: Columbia University Press, 2007.

——, and Christopher Kaplonski, eds. *The History of Mongolia,* 3 vols. Folkestone, Kent, UK: Global Oriental, 2010.

Ssanang Ssetsen (Chungtaidschi). *Erdeni-yin Tobci, Geschichte der Ost-Mongololen und ihres Fürstenhaues.* Translated by Isaac Jacob Schmidt. St. Petersburg: N. Gretsch, 1829.

Tekin, Talât. *A Grammar of Orkhon Turkic.* Indiana University Uralic and Altaic Series, vol. 69. Bloomington, IN: Mouton, 1968.

Thiel, Joseph. "Der Streit der Buddhisten und Taoisten zur Mongolenzeit." *Monumenta Serica,* vol. 20 (1961).

Thomsen, Vilhelm, and E. Denison Ross. "The Orkhon Inscriptions: Being a Translation of Professor Vilhelm Thomsen's Final Danish Rendering." *Bulletin of the School of Oriental Studies,* University of London, vol. 5 (1930): 861–76.

Trubetzkoy, Nikolai S. *The Legacy of Genghis Khan*. Translated by Anatoly Liberman. Ann Arbor: Michigan Slavic Publications, 1991.

Vladimirtsov, Boris Y. *The Life of Chingis-Khan*. Translated by Prince D. S. Mirsky. New York: Benjamin Blom, 1930.

Voegelin, Eric. "Mongol Orders of Submission to European Powers." In *The Collected Works of Eric Voegelin, volume 5* and *volume 10, Published Essays: 1940–1952*. Columbia, MO: University of Missouri, 2000.

Voltaire. *The Orphan of China*. In *The Works of Voltaire*, vol. XV. Translated by William F. Fleming. Paris: E. R. DuMont, 1901.

Waley, Arthur, translator. *The Travels of an Alchemist—The Journey of the Taoist from China to the Hindukush at the Summons of Chingiz Khan*, by Li Chih-Ch'ang. London: Broadway Travellers, 1931.

———. *The Secret History of the Mongols and Other Pieces*. New York: Barnes & Noble, 1963.

Zhao, George Qingzhi. *Marriage as Political Strategy and Cultural Expression: Mongolian Royal Marriages from World Empire to Yuan Dynasty*. New York: Peter Lang, 2008.

INDEX